D0598446

Self-Examination

**Recent Titles in the
Beta Phi Mu Monograph Series**

"An Active Instrument for Propaganda": The American Library During World War I
Wayne A. Wiegand

Libraries and Scholarly Communication in the United States: The Historical Dimension
Phyllis Dain and John Y. Cole, editors

Carnegie Denied: Communities Rejecting Carnegie Library Construction Grants, 1898-1925
Robert Sidney Martin, editor

Publishing and Readership in Revolutionary France and America: A Symposium at the Library of Congress, Sponsored by the Center for the Book and the European Division
Carol Armbruster, editor

Daring to Find Our Names: The Search for Lesbigay Library History
James V. Carmichael, Jr., editor

American Libraries before 1876
Haynes McMullen

Defining Print Culture for Youth: The Cultural Work of Children's Literature
Anne Lundin and Wayne A. Wiegand, editors

Self-Examination

The Present and Future of Librarianship

JOHN M. BUDD

Beta Phi Mu Monograph Series
Art Young, Series Editor

A Member of the Greenwood Publishing Group

Westport, Connecticut • London

Library of Congress Cataloging-in-Publication Data

Budd, John, 1953-
  Self-examination : the present and future of librarianship /
John M. Budd.
        p.   cm. — (Beta Phi Mu monograph series, ISSN 1041-2751)
  Includes bibliographical references and index.
  ISBN-13: 978-1-59158-591-6 (alk. paper)
  1. Library science—Philosophy.   2. Libraries and society.
3. Libraries—Aims and objectives.   4. Librarians—Professional ethics.
5. Libraries—Sociological aspects.   I. Title.
  Z665.B92 2008
  020.1—dc22   2007019948

British Library Cataloguing in Publication Data is available.

Copyright © 2008 by Libraries Unlimited

All rights reserved. No portion of this book may be
reproduced, by any process or technique, without the
express written consent of the publisher.

Library of Congress Catalog Card Number: 2007019948
ISBN-13: 978-1-59158-591-6
ISSN: 1041-2751

First published in 2008

Libraries Unlimited, 88 Post Road West, Westport, CT 06881
A Member of the Greenwood Publishing Group, Inc.
www.lu.com

Printed in the United States of America

The paper used in this book complies with the
Permanent Paper Standard issued by the National
Information Standards Organization (Z39.48-1984).

10   9   8   7   6   5   4   3   2   1

Contents

Introduction

A STATEMENT BY PIERCE BUTLER of the Graduate Library School at the University of Chicago may be the most frequently quoted in librarianship, but people turn to it because it seems always to apply. More than seventy years ago he (1961 [1933]) wrote, "The librarian apparently stands alone in the simplicity of his pragmatism: a rationalization of each immediate technical process by itself seems to satisfy his intellectual interest" (pp. xi-xii). Given that his words are still invoked, all of us in the profession should ask why he said this and why it's repeated. Many say librarians are specialists at organizing and providing access to information; others counter that what librarians do is organize and provide access to documents (in the broadest sense). Still others might say that librarians are experts on books and reading, or on organization of information, or on any number of other things. Of course these could also be perceived far too narrowly. There can be a tendency to see organization as a mechanical operation, placing a work in its proper "place." There can be a tendency to see providing access as a pointing (used figuratively) function. I am by no means claiming that these tendencies prevail, or even that they are extensive; I am simply saying that they exist and that they are formidable. The counterpoint is a realization that librarianship embodies a richness of history and of intellectual, political, and ethical potential. If there is a shortcoming such as the one Butler observed, it might be described as absence—the absence of reflection. The purpose of this book is to provide opportunities and suggestions for reflection. Within these pages there will be observations, statements by others, opinions, and some serious examination (and certainly not just by me) of librarianship—what it is and what it can be.

Reflection and self-examination are not unique to the present book. Following Butler, many have shared the fruits of their introspections. For example, Jesse Shera examined libraries and librarianship repeatedly and deeply. Most recently Michael Gorman has turned inward as a way to articulate not just who he is but also who we (all librarians) are. Some may dismiss the work of these three individuals plus many more in our profession as mere ruminations or reminiscences. Many librarians, however, appreciate (in two senses of the word) the outcomes of the reflections. The appreciation stems from meaning; readers find their contemplations meaningful to themselves, personally and professionally. Butler (1961 [1933]) also wrote, "A professional philosophy would give to librarianship that directness of action which can spring only from a complete consciousness of purpose" (p. 103).

Shera (1976) added to Butler's call for a philosophy: "It is the mastery of the library resources that is the apotheosis of librarianship, the glory that is revealed in us as truly professional librarians" (p. 199). Gorman (1998) has said, "We are right to love books not, in most cases, as objects but as the best medium for an activity that is at the heart of culture and society—reading" (p. 29). The pages that follow represent an attempt to offer some professional self-examination; in many ways this book is a quest for meaning in the profession. At all times, though, it will be a critical self-examination of librarianship; that is, the examination includes possibilities that have been insufficiently explored. The phrase "consciousness of purpose" is one that should be ever on our minds and should be the basis for our reflection.

Among the numerous concerns related to librarianship is the goal of informing people, of providing shape and form to their thoughts and questions. The first element of this concern is how we inform ourselves. Perhaps the very definition of "information" is, in operation anyway, taken for granted. A working definition appears to assume that information is the content included in packages or objects (physical or virtual). Moreover, it is that content that people seek. "Content" is a problematic word. Of course it refers to the words, sounds, and images that are transmitted, but the customary usage of the word tends to go no further. The words, sounds, and images are intentionally produced and people try to infer meaning from them. The content might be better conceived as communicative actions, signs, or potential truth-bearing utterances. People want to see, to read, to comprehend, to answer. With that information—and people's quest for it—as a beginning, the profession aims at giving people something they value. Some variations of the objective have people seeking meaning or seeking to alleviate their anomalous states of knowledge. Those ideas are not without their skeptics; both sides (the advocacy and the skepticism) need exploration. Relevance is a concept we keep returning to—for good reason. It would be rather foolish to think that people want *ir*relevant information. The challenge for us is to understand relevance, not simply as a concept. People make psychological, cognitive, and practical decisions about what is relevant and what is not.

There is ample evidence that becoming informed is a social, and not solely an individual, phenomenon. Individuals' ideas are affected by the ideas of others in at least two very important ways: (1) we listen to and read what others say as a way to frame questions and to address them, and (2) we want to be informed because others want us to be informed (teachers make assignments, employers and co-workers want problems solved, etc.). We also cannot ignore that some people want to *know* things; they want a broader and deeper understanding of things. Librarianship can ask what role information plays in knowledge growth, what it contributes to both what people know and how they know. Is information the same as knowledge (are we really in a knowledge industry; do we organize knowledge)? Is it a step on a path to knowledge? Is knowledge a process, an object, a state? These are some of the most challenging questions we face, and part of librarianship's responsibility is to take them seriously and not merely accept answers that have been suggested elsewhere.

In the first act of self-examination a delving into the past is presented, solely as a means to bring us up to the present. The locus of work—the library—has a substantial history, even though that history is hardly a continuous or linear path. The varying and variable history of libraries signals an uneven history for librarians—just as it signals an uneven history for communication—and this is explored in the first chapter. The different conceptions of the locus and its purposes had to come from somewhere. Librarians (if we may call what historically have been keepers of books, scholars, and collectors by that name) were always integral to shaping the locus in all its elements. Over time, growth in the numbers, kinds, and functions of social institutions formed junctions, spatial connections, and sometimes integration with libraries (and vice versa). Ways of perceiving the world changed, made huge leaps, doubled back upon themselves, created surety, and generated confusion. At each moment the manners by which people have envisioned and described the world and themselves in it have transformed. At times the manners of transformation have involved rejection of old ideas and ways of expressing them; at times they have been efforts to recapture lost time. At times the manners of transformation have been meldings of traditional purposes and emerging means.

Librarianship not only followed the above patterns, in many ways it has embraced them. Modes of organizing and describing works have also been tied to evolving social institutions. Part of librarianship's ongoing challenge is comprehending fully the institutional influences on organization and schemes and practices, along with developing a clearer understanding of people's consciousnesses and the ways *they* categorize their worlds. As creations of human intellect and will, libraries have, across time, represented the desire and need of people to encompass, to bracket, what is said and what is known. One question upon which we might reflect is: Do libraries still represent people's will and intellect, or do they represent cabalistic enclaves of an old guard? Another way of asking this is: Are libraries mere collections, or are they participants in learning, exploration, and discovery?

The institutional influences include both grand societal and cultural forces and the more mundane demands of the institutions with which libraries and librarians are affiliated. The latter will have a greater impact on day-to-day work in librarianship. Such institutions define, for the most part, the communities of libraries. Communities, of course, differ in size and in kind. Chapter 2 shows how the last century and a quarter has seen enormous growth in libraries and in the profession for a number of reasons—the growth of cities and towns (and philanthropy that spurred the building of libraries), an accompanying growth in public education and its accessibility, an increase in the numbers and sizes of colleges and universities, and a need for resources and librarians in governmental, business, and professional endeavors. At the time many professional and learned societies were being founded, librarians also congregated around what was perceived as professional commonality. Before long, however, the perceived commonality fractured, and multiple associations and divisions proliferated. Efforts centered on some specific goals—and, eventually, around technology—have made some dialogue among professionals more feasible. Along with the growth, change, and division, education for the profession has evolved and transformed as well. The present condition in education is tense; a future that fosters a reflective profession should be one that resolves some of the sources of tension (without creating a Prozac Profession). Some degree of agonism will always be with us; we have to ensure that it does not become antagonistic.

Chapter 3 inquires into the matter of how librarians are influencing, at least to some degree, their own identity. There are additional influences, though. For example, what we say influences who we are. In fact, some of what we say addresses directly visions of who we are. It might be said that some of our professional discourse is aimed at our identity, our collective "self." The discourse may not tackle this head on, but in many ways it is an exploration of authenticity and authority. That is, it seeks to find and to state what makes librarianship what it is, what identifies our purpose, our *telos*. Librarianship, in part through the vehicles of professional associations, articulates purpose and the nature of our work. It may do so positively—by stating what we do, and for whom—or negatively—by stating what is not included in the profession. The professional discourse also expresses how we define communities, again by inclusion and exclusion. Our discourse frequently addresses the questions that are deemed essential to praxis. The questions deal with organization and management, technology and its uses, how to work effectively, and why and how to conduct research. The importance of our professional discourse has been recognized by some among our number, but its importance may not be fully appreciated; its character as an internal practice may not be fully apprehended. Also, the foregoing is in no way intended to imply that there is anything like complete agreement within our discourse. The diversity in what we say is not merely interesting, it is an identifying characteristic of *us*. For that reason it deserves close attention. Not surprisingly, reflection must include education for librarianship. This is hotly contested ground at the present time, and reflection on essential knowledge and skills, as well as how to imbue beginning professionals with them, is inadequate.

All of the issues mentioned so far have an accompanying question that will be the basis of Chapter 4. Is there a *right* way to conduct ourselves as professionals? The profession of librarianship has answered this question in the affirmative through the mechanisms of a code of ethics, statements on intellectual freedom, expressions of core values, and other ways. Even with these formal articulations, there are some concerns regarding the ethical practice of librarianship. Our relationship with patrons and communities receives much attention, but there may be more to say about our relationships with one another (professional to professional). The professional relationship extends beyond the library to include trustees, school administrators, academic provosts, and others who have governance, and possibly even fiduciary, relationships with librarians. Governance relationships are complicated ones, and can lead to strains in difficult fiscal times; nonetheless, these relationships should also have political and ethical grounding. Our profession also depends on others, for the most part, to create and produce the documents and media we provide access to. Changes in media ownership, the aggregation of resources, possible limitations on available content, affect what can be found by readers and information seekers. If librarianship is not merely a passive vessel or conduit, ethical responsibility is manifest in our connections between content and community. Perhaps the most discussed, as well as the most complex, locus of ethical action is that of intellectual freedom. To an extent, law and government policies enter the picture to guide some decisions and, at times, to proscribe some action. As is the case in other walks of life, there may be some antagonism between rights and freedom. In some ways, the antagonism is expressed in librarianship as the tension between, for example, intellectual freedom and social responsibility. In almost every instance we will have to favor one over the other, but we cannot do so without weighing both elements. Serious examination can help us recognize the times when choices must be made and also what reasoning can help us make the choices.

Following the ethical requirements of librarianship (openly or tacitly) is the location of our profession within a democracy. This, too, is spoken of in our professional statements, and will be the focus of Chapter 5. Not all libraries, however, are public. The corporate world, private schools, and private colleges and universities are also home to librarians. These locations are most definitely not completely separate and apart from democracy, but they do operate in ways that differ substantively from public sector settings. For those libraries that do exist in the public sphere there is the thorny question: What is democracy? The word tends to be mentioned without a hint of definition; there are actually several ways to conceive "democracy?" Should all librarians agree upon one conception of democracy and then act according to that definition? More specifically, should libraries agree to one idea of public good, and shape the profession accordingly? It may be difficult to imagine unanimous agreement among the many tens of thousand of librarians (who are likely to reflect the diverse opinions of the citizenry in general). It is not common, though, for the various possible conceptions of democracy to be discussed in our literature or at our conferences. The actual working of democracy entails dirtying one's hands with the messy business of negotiation, compromise, and dissent. We may speak in terms of ideals, but we also have to accept that ideals may bump up against what some might see as a realpolitik of librarianship. In the realms of the ideal and of the pragmatic there are likely to be opposing ideologies (with the word "ideology" used here simply to mean the ideas and beliefs that a group may share). The conflict may manifest itself as a discussion of differing beliefs, but it can also lead to clashing efforts at domination. Technology, perhaps presumed to be purely objective, is also part of the democratic dialectic. We do, and we must, employ technology in librarianship, but we also cannot blind ourselves to the human origins of economics, distribution, use, and other factors related to technology.

Beyond the public good that the profession serves is a multifaceted and unequal world. The word "globalization" is bandied about, but it tends to be used, much more often than not, to describe economic initiatives. That said, the world of information is disjointed, unbalanced, and anything but free. In short, there is no such thing as *the* Information Society. As is the case with democracy, there are multiple definitions and multiple operationalizations of Information Society. "Information Society" may be thought of as a theoretical construct that has many elements, all of which are contested. There are numerous writings, mostly outside of librarianship, about the Information Society, and there are disparate claims regarding what it means and what it should be. It may seem self-evident, but librarianship cannot be absent from the discussions of meaning (what people perceive as meaningful). The theoretical constructs are intended to be put into action—through policy at many levels and through practice on many fronts. When the practical aspect becomes clear, we see that there are ethical implications of information, as well as implications for democracy. The distinctions (sometimes becoming battles) between individual and collective good influence the day-to-day praxis in libraries. Services, collections, and access are all designed and carried out within some framework (that may be explicitly stated, but implicitly based on some conception of an Information Society). The contest that is inevitably part of any idea of something like an Information Society also influences perceptions of what a library is. The word "library" may be appropriated for purposes that can be non-, or even anti-democratic. Decisions about libraries as places are influenced by the far-reaching shibboleth of "Information Society." The very idea of professional purpose is ineluctably connected to the grand notion of Information Society. Chapter 6 delves into the complicated world of an Information Society, and will include a suggestion for a revised taxonomy to define the components.

The last chapter will provide a culmination of all of the aforementioned concerns. Rather than recapitulate the points made and the questions asked in the first six chapters, the last will be an attempt to consolidate the discussion around a few key points, one of which is the existence, perhaps the predominance, of a very specific kind of dualism in librarianship. The dualism can be (inadequately) summed up here as the contest between library as end and library as means. Examples will be used in Chapter 7 to clarify the dualism. Another point is the idea of the library as place. While we may want to reduce the notion to comfort, amenities, and the like, "place" connotes purpose—individual, collective, and professional. The place of the library, then, is a rich, dynamic, and complex sphere in which people seek, explore, learn, investigate, and attempt to re-create themselves. There is no easy way to simplify this complexity. As a suggestion toward resolution of the challenges librarianship faces, a method will be offered—dialectical phenomenology. The task of resolving contradictions and conflicts can't be avoided if librarianship aspires to be a reflective profession. The ultimate message of the chapter and the book is optimism. Problems, while substantial and looming, are not insurmountable; that said, they also can't be ignored.

As professionals we associate formally with one another. These associations create essential forums where we not only can but must engage in open conversation. Professional meetings can all too easily become places where orthodoxy is confirmed, where universal authority is expressed through the reduction of communication to monologue. Such a state effectively stifles not only growth but *Being* itself. If, as librarians, we are to be authentic individuals and professionals, we can only become so through dialogue. This may sound prescriptive, but it is prescriptive only insofar as it strongly suggests a means to an end. Professionals will disagree with one another on matters conceptual and practical; *stifled* dialogue seldom allows the voicing of disagreement, much less debate and compromise. A dominant orthodoxy not only stymies professional growth, it also renders problematic the profession's engagement with governing bodies, policy makers, other fields, and communities. Both the present and the future are threatened by an imposed orthodoxy and, conversely, both are enlivened by an accommodating dialogue. The education of future professionals depends on genuine dialogue that explicitly recognizes the voice of the Other and embraces a discourse ethics. Evolution happens, but the evolution of librarianship should be intentional, guided by professionals who are cognizant of and sensitive to the world in which librarianship exists . . . and will exist. The aim of this book is the initiation of self-examination—in expression and in process—that will be joined by others.

CHAPTER 1

Genealogy of the Profession

LET'S BEGIN THIS SELF-EXAMINATION with a truism: in order to understand where we are now, we have to examine how we got here. We've all heard this before, frequently as we begin courses at colleges and universities. While there may be the temptation to think of the statement as a cliché, in this instance it is vital for us to delve into the past in order to understand most fully the genuine foundations of our profession and its environment (educational institutions at all levels, municipalities, corporations, and the politics and economics that affect them all). This exploration means traveling through the past to get a grasp of how libraries came to be, what purposes they have served, what's been in them, who librarians are, what they do, and where they are going. What follows is a brief excursion through the past so that at least a historical consciousness can be created. Creating such a consciousness is a shockingly difficult thing to do—not because of our faculties, but because of the nature of history itself. Friedrich Nietzsche writes about punishment in *The Genealogy of Morals* (1967 [1887]), that

> As for the other element of punishment, the fluid element, its "meaning," in a very late condition of culture . . . the concept "punishment" possesses in fact not *one* meaning but a whole synthesis of "meaning": the previous history of punishment in general, the history of its employment for the most various purposes, finally crystallizes into a kind of unity that is hard to disentangle, hard to analyze and, as must be emphasized especially, totally *indefinable.* . . . Only that which has no history is definable. (pp. 79–80)

So libraries and librarianship are like punishment, not in any semantic way, but inasmuch as both do have a history. I wouldn't go so far as Nietzsche and say that this makes our profession indefinable, but it does, as Nietzsche suggests, give the illusion of a kind of unity today. At an opposite extreme from Nietzsche is historicism, usually defined as the search for covering laws that explain history and can be used to prepare us for the future. This extreme has been refuted; the path from past to present isn't so easily governed by material regularities. The challenge of history's complexity makes necessary, at the outset, something of a genealogical approach (drawing from Michel Foucault, but not entirely). Foucault (1971) writes, "The genealogical aspect concerns the effective formation of discourse, whether within the limits of control, or outside of them, or as is most frequent, on both sides of the delimitation" (p. 233). The borrowing from Foucault means that the means of examination here is not just what is said about the past, but in what context, according to what rules of interpretation, with what dissension. Reflection is made difficult by the complexities of history, but definitely not impossible, and definitely not unnecessary.

The entirety of this book is aimed at all professional librarians; in order to fulfill our professional responsibilities we need to step back and examine our *telos* (our purpose), our ethos, and our world. To that end, we should remember that some consistency runs, not only through this excursion into the past, but throughout the entirety of this book. From the earliest days of proto-libraries to libraries as we have come to know them, these institutions have been created and built by people for people. There have always been human purposes to libraries, even to those that have been hidden from most eyes. A warning needs to accompany this realization: while there have always been human intentions behind libraries, human intention has changed over time. The beliefs and actions of people in antiquity, for example, were not the beliefs and actions of people today. If we are genuinely to comprehend libraries and librarianship we have to guard against the fallacy of imparting motives to those who lived before us based on our own motivations. The following glimpse into the past is a start along the road to understanding. The "genealogy" referred to in the chapter title is an explicit homage to Michel Foucault, who uses the word to signify a particular kind of study of human discourse and human institutions. Foucault's project is a kind of history, but not in the mold of traditional intellectual history. As he (1977) puts it,

> Genealogy does not resemble the evolution of a species and does not map the destiny of a people. On the contrary, to follow the complex course of descent is to maintain passing events in their proper dispersion; it is to identify the accidents, the minute deviations—or conversely, the complete reversals—the errors, the false appraisals, and the faulty calculations that gave birth to those things that continue to exist and have value for us. (p. 146)

Genealogy, as applied here, is much like family histories. Concrete factors, as well as subjectivism and sometimes willfully contrarian elements, combine in myriad ways. They are interesting and important for their own sakes and they are connected in ways for newness and difference, usually manifest through discourse.

ANTIQUITY

A genealogy such as the one undertaken in the chapter relies on a record. For much of recorded human history libraries have served needs that transcend themselves, that is, haven't been created simply as repositories for stuff.

There wouldn't be libraries of any sort if there weren't something to put in them and especially some communicative purpose for their existence. In other words, early on libraries became institutions—human organizations that serve human purposes. In order for there to be communication there has to be language; do we know what the first language was, how it came to be, who spoke it? Perhaps as far back as 50,000 BCE humans were making regular, communicative, markings in stones (Martin, 1994, p. 3). Maybe this indicates that there was some rudimentary language that was shared, at least within an immediate community. Since the evidence is rare, and is open only to speculation, we have to look for some firmer evidence, which is in the form of writing. As far as we know, writing dates back around 6,000 years; there was probably some kind of pictographic writing in Mesopotamia around 4,000 BCE. By around 3,600 BCE the Sumerians were developing cuneiform (which means wedge-shaped). The symbols are combinations of wedges, written in vertical columns from top right to bottom left. The medium that has survived is the rectangular clay tablet, which was used when moist and impressed with a wooden, bone, or other kind of stylus. The clay could be kept moist to be re-used, or dried to create a permanent record. Dried tablets, when kept, were placed in baskets or on shelves. The drying of tablets, to speculate further, suggests that some records were of sufficient importance that they were kept intact, that they were preserved. Preservation of records indicates the beginning of a sophisticated communication process—not merely wanting to speak, but wanting to be heard.

There have been substantial numbers of tablets found at a few locations: Nearly 30,000 tablets were found at Tello, near Lagash, at the confluence of the Tigris and Euphrates Rivers not too far from the Persian Gulf (c. 2350 BCE). Thousands were also found at Nippur, south of Baghdad (c. 2000 BCE) (Harris, 1984, p. 15). There have been other finds at various temples or places of business. The early tablets that have been found were mainly records of transactions; little about the cultures is evident from the information on the tablets. Then about the time of Hammurabi (after 2000 BCE) there was an effort at gathering a history of Mesopotamia and preserving it. Given that there is almost no cultural record up to that point, we might surmise that the history that was written down during Hammurabi's time was the history of memory, orally transmitted for generations. Historical records signify a particular human action, the transmission, intended for those to come, of meaning through stories. A genealogy in the Foucauldian sense could begin at about the time of Hammurabi, that is, with the recording of history came the beginnings of discourse. Hammurabi is known especially for the code attributed to him. In a rather succinct form (a stele inscribed on all sides), the code's purpose was to communicate a civil law that fits into the customs of the place and time, and the authority of the ruler (Martin, 1994, p. 77). The power and force of writing and of making the writing public had never been more evident, and the social and cultural importance of communication had never before been so integrated into life.

Meanwhile, in Egypt there were also a number of collections of records, the earliest dating back to 3200 BCE. Early writing in Egypt was hieroglyphic, which means sacred stone-writing. The pictographs (hieroglyphics) were carved on stone at first, but then they were written on papyrus and other sur-faces. Hieroglyphics were quite elaborate and were best suited for ceremonial writing. For more mundane tasks, hieroglyphics evolved into hieratic script, and then into demotic script; each was a simplification of the earlier. Again, the forms suggest social significance attached to acts of communicating. People were aware that they were writing for a reason and were writing *for* others. It seems that around 2000 BCE the literacy level began to rise, since there are more findings of records kept for a variety of purposes and in private hands. Scribes were not only important to the transmission of written records; they were, almost by virtue of their positions, active in the politics of the day (Jackson, 1974, p. 2).

Communication having political import is therefore an ancient deve-lopment. As we'll see in later chapters, institutions of preservation and communication—as *social* institutions—include inherent political implica-tions. Much of surviving writing is religious in nature, which tells us more about the people than having only business transactions (although that's helpful, too). Beginning about the seventh century BCE the Egyptians were ruled by outsiders, and writing reflected the outside influences—Assyrians, Persians, Greeks in succession. Writing began to change from Egyptian to Greek, then later to Latin, then Arabic, with changes in how things would and could be expressed (accompanying changes in *why* people expressed things). The language shifts were not merely material in form; they reflect more sweeping changes.

After Greek ascendance, the greatest Hellenic library wasn't in Greece, but was at Alexandria (named for Alexander the Great). Alexandria was a major trading port and political and cultural center; it may be that some of the trade was in "books." It is probable that when ships came into harbor, the writings they had were appropriated so that copies could be made; some-times the copies were then returned and the originals retained in the collec-tion. The copying operation, given its scope and its organization, points to a clear purpose for the Alexandrian Library. The impetus to have everything written may stem in part from a desire to know other peoples (for reasons of commerce, defense, or other strategic purposes) and, perhaps, to provide foundations upon which new knowledge may be built. If this supposition is at all accurate, the construction, growth, and maintenance of the library were an incredibly ambitious venture. Humans have always learned from direct experience; when we see, hear, or touch something we gain some understand-ing of a phenomenon. The Alexandrian Library, perhaps to a greater degree than any institution up to that point in human history, was a remarkable monument to indirect learning and its value as an endeavor. The preservation function was undoubtedly essential; no less important, though, was the use function of the library. The effort to obtain everything was an intentional one, and one that would enable readers to examine, compare, contrast, and learn from all extant texts. This, of course, is an inference; records don't allow extensive inquiry into motives. The collection of the library, though, and its substantial use, indicate that the library was foundational in a specific way. It was to provide the basis for further scholarship and literary creation.

The work of the library wasn't left to chance; Pharaoh selected the heads of the library, and a series of remarkable scholars held the position. An early head of the library, Callimachus, devised an organizational scheme for the contents, and began what we might call a classified list of the materials. This is another advance that can't be overestimated. Storage and preservation for their own sakes don't necessarily require organization; finding specific items does. By all accounts the Alexandrian Library was a place of exploration, learning, and knowledge growth. A later Director (if we can use the title), Eratosthenes, served in the position from about 245 to 205 BCE (Casson, 2001, p. 41). Eratosthenes was something of a polymath, although his specialty was geography. His abilities in so many areas of study earned him some criticism for being rather a jack of all trades, but that breadth of knowledge enabled him to oversee growth in the numbers of works on science stored in the library. Eratosthenes apparently held the title librarian (Canfora, 1990, p. 186), which meant that he did have some supervisory responsibilities. One task for workers in the library was to translate works into Greek (which was, more or less, the lingua franca of the time). While records of the library's workings are scarce, what exists points to an organized operation of acquisition, organization, translation, and use. Nothing indicates a parochial attitude; the collection was apparently broad and deep.

As an important center of commerce and exercises of power, Alexandria was subject to the hazards of political control and the wresting of control by others. The library thrived until the reign of Ptolemy VIII (c. 90 BCE); Ptolemy was forced from Alexandria and in the battle when he tried to return the library was partly burned. When Julius Caesar invaded in 47 BCE it seems that the fires from burning ships set off more fires on land and damaged, but did not completely destroy, the library. Centuries later, during the Arab occupation of Alexandria, Caliph Omar issued a decree about the disposition of the library,

> As for the books you mention, here is my reply. If their content is in accordance with the book of Allah, we may do without them, for in that case the book of Allah more than suffices. If, on the other hand, they contain matter not in accordance with the book of Allah, there can be no need to preserve them. Proceed, then, and destroy them. (Canfora, 1990, p. 98)

The books and scrolls were then moved to the public baths, where they were fed into the ovens that warmed the waters. The statement by Caliph Omar implies that the works in the library meant nothing, since they were either unnecessary to Islam or they were contrary to the Koran. The books' destruction, however, hints at some deep and dangerous meaning in the works that could be threatening to beliefs and to a position of dominance. Could it be that Caliph Omar recognized the dangerous side of Francis Bacon's dictum, knowledge is power? The development of the library served a purpose; its destruction served a very different purpose. We shouldn't lose sight of the fact that both actions were outcomes of purpose and choice.

The Alexandrian Library, and the one established at Pergamum, was possible because of writing. This is not to say that there was no oral culture at the time and place of the emergence of these libraries, but writing of all sorts and forms had a profound effect on communication and also on memory. In an oral culture, one must be in the presence of a speaker in order to have an opportunity to commit words to memory. With writing, the physical connection is not as necessary. Further, memory is affected through visual means with writing, rather than the aural means of hearing and listening. A library such as the one at Alexandria offered the possibility committing words, even entire texts, to memory by means of a particular cognitive process. As Mary Carruthers (1990) says, "a written word has a visual shape (its *painture*) and calls to mind sound (its *parole*)" (p. 224). A reader "sees" words and the sight can be translated into sound. Memory, then, is transformed from a function of hearing to a function of seeing. The transformation was begun in ancient times, but centuries would pass before it would be widespread. It's one thing for writing to make a cognitive shift possible; without reading the shift cannot have impact on large populations. Literacy, on such a large scale, would be a phenomenon of a later time.

EMPIRE AND AFTER

The balance of power in Western Europe shifted from Greece to Rome in the early centuries of the common era (CE). The heyday of the Roman Empire wasn't inconsequential when it came to libraries, but there is little that distinguishes the period and the place for the purposes of this genealogy (that is, there's little that contradicts, contravenes, or otherwise detours what had gone before in a substantial way). There is a question, though, that's appropriate: What marked the decline of the Empire and, so, its libraries? As is usually the case with the fall of empires, there wasn't a simple cause and the fall was not marked by a single event. The decline was gradual and many factors contributed to it. In the year 212 CE the Emperor Caracalla decreed that anyone doing business in the Empire must be a Roman citizen; one reason for this was to increase the tax rolls. As tax revenues increased so did the burden of administering the management of tax collection in an increasingly far-flung empire. The territory that constituted the business of Rome was immense, and many of the new "citizens" were not especially pleased with either their status or their taxes. A rift between people and government was thus created. It became increasingly difficult to enforce the rules of tax and commerce throughout the Empire; natives of other lands were commissioned to enforce them. The natives of, say, Gaul had more sympathy for their countrymen, though, and enforcement began to break down. Lands became less willing to obey Roman rule and ignored it or reclaimed their land, or were invaded. One result of the breakup of the Empire was the isolation of many parts of Europe. It was a dangerous time; travel was hazardous and, not infrequently, fatal. When one's life is uncertain, food and shelter take precedence over reading and learning. Small wonder we hear little about libraries and keepers of books during the first few centuries CE.

Along with the Empire's growth in territory came the growth and expansion of Christianity (this growth continued after the dissolution of the Empire). The Eastern Empire (Byzantium) flourished a bit longer than the Western Empire, but it was religiously different from the West. There were rifts between the Eastern and Western Churches, which further led to isolation. For a variety of reasons, including the need to establish contemplative communities, the desire to prepare preachers who could move among the people, and the wish to reproduce sacred texts, monasteries were founded across Europe. From about the fourth century CE monastic life in the West began to grow, slowly at first, but then quite rapidly. As the Empire dissolved more monastic orders were founded, in part as efforts to preserve the faith and authorized Scripture. After the Ostrogoths invaded Rome the Empire was sliced into smaller fragments, each looking mainly to its own survival. Communication and travel were increasingly difficult; it wasn't safe to venture very far from home. Reliance on writing at the time signaled an example of the isolation. Just as it was difficult for goods to be traded over any considerable distance, so too were the limitations on the exchange of texts. Literacy levels fell, and libraries were few and far apart. Statistics aren't readily available on literacy levels, but Cassiodorus (see below) remarked on the decline of both Greek and Latin literacy (Colish, 1997, p. 50).

Even in the midst of difficulties, there were some efforts at preserving learning and writing by monastic orders. In 529 Benedict of Nursia established a monastery at Monte Cassino, ninety miles southeast of Rome. In the Benedictine order meditation and reading were inseparable, and copying was done locally so that the monks had scripture to read. In 589 the monks had to leave Monte Cassino; it was destroyed by Lombard invaders. They moved to Rome, to the relative safety of the city; there they turned more to learning and the preservation of reading and texts. These activities were more easily accomplished in the city. Benedict established a set of rules for monastic life that were, in essence, adopted by most of the monastic orders founded after his. He envisioned the purpose of the monastery to be a self-contained community, dependent on outside society for nothing. While perhaps unstated, this attitude further limited communication and, so, learning and the sharing of knowledge. Not long after his death, however, the Benedictine order, along with other orders, became central to society in general. The primary reason for monastic influence was the strict order and efficiency of the community, which was something that the rest of society felt they required. The monastic influence affected not only the pious life, but education, politics, law, and many other aspects of medieval life (Cantor, 1993, pp. 149–52).

Also in the sixth century Cassiodorus founded a monastery (the Vivarium) near the Mediterranean. The brothers there preserved secular, as well as religious writing. Copying was facilitated by a relatively new (third-century) development—the codex volume. At first, wood blocks were tied together; naturally this resulted in a heavy and cumbersome volume. Then, scrolls were cut to uniform size and bound together. This was easier to copy from, and pages of vellum or parchment were easier to copy onto, since they could be kept flat. This medium was also easier to store and use. Cassiodorus wanted to ensure a learned brotherhood, so he adopted the structure of the seven liberal arts (proposed by Martianus Capella in the fifth century, taking a cue from the biblical Book of Wisdom, which spoke of the seven pillars of wisdom). These liberal arts were divided into the trivium (grammar, dialectic, and rhetoric) and the quadrivium (geometry, arithmetic, astronomy, and music). Cassiodorus's codification of this basis of knowledge as part of the order's educational system spread to other monastic orders, and eventually to universities in later centuries, and became what was effectively the curriculum of monastic schools (Cantor, 1993, pp. 82–83).

From about 500 until the late 1100s the vast majority of the copying took place in monasteries. Different orders had different rules and customs, but the process of copying was fairly consistent. In many instances the copying was literally just that; a monk sat at a desk in a scriptorium and made copies of the manuscript before him. The monk may not even be able to read the text he was copying. Some errors could easily be introduced if the copyist's attention flagged, if lighting was less than optimal, or if there were any interruptions. In larger monasteries there might also be "correctors" who would read the copied text in comparison with the original and note errors for correction. Illumination would usually be undertaken by specially trained and gifted monks, who were usually literate in Latin. The Lindisfarne Gospels and the Book of Kells (dating back to the eighth and ninth centuries, respectively) are excellent examples of the illuminator's art. Illuminations sometimes incorporated satire and commentary on the texts that were copied. A despised bishop might be portrayed as a weasel, for example. Even with literate monks changes in texts might, at times, be made deliberately. The most complete examination of such occurrences may be Bart Ehrman's (2005) recent study of the transmission of the New Testament, *Misquoting Jesus*.

At most monasteries, though (especially in Southern Europe), the copying and reading done was solely of scripture and maybe some (approved) religious commentary. Some of the pagan (especially Roman, since Greek was scarcely used and studied in the Middle Ages) literature was bawdy and deemed inappropriate for the monasteries or churches and was only sporadically preserved. For example, records from the Alexandrian Library indicate that Sophocles wrote 132 plays, but only 7 survive today. However, by the sixth and seventh centuries, monasteries were quite common through the remains of the Empire. The monastic schools, coupled with Benedict's rules, exerted a substantial influence over life in general. The ubiquity of monasteries, and their penchant for copying and preserving texts, prompt Marcia Colish (1997, pp. 42–55) to refer to monasteries and their founders as "transmitters." Benedict, for example, set out in his monastic rules that the priests, brothers, and nuns of the order read sacred texts in private as part of their contemplative life. Naturally, this means that, to be members of the monastic community, these individuals had to be literate. Benedict, and, by extension of the adoption of his rules by other orders, many monastic communities had to provide education for their members. The influence of the rules extended the requirement of literacy, at least within the cloisters, for several centuries.

The problem of localized isolation (the relative insecurity of small areas) was greater in the southern parts of Europe because of the frequency of invasions and the general instability of the area. The north was relatively secure, largely due to the larger-scale isolation of, for example, Britain and Ireland. Out of the reach of both secular and religious rule (insofar as the two can be separated at this time), in some places there was greater sensitivity to breadth of literature. This was particularly true of Ireland; Patrick got the ball rolling by creating an atmosphere conducive to the formation of monasteries that were open to secular, as well as religious writing. There was substantial sharing of manuscripts for copying; some monks sailed to Scotland, Wales, and the north of England to found monasteries there. One notable one was formed by St. Columba in the sixth century at Iona, an island off the coast of Scotland that became a copying center. Some clergy, such as the Venerable Bede, undertook programs aimed at the secular learning of the public. Among other things, some texts in Greek were preserved through copying at Irish and Irish-founded monasteries. Monastic rules in Ireland were considerably different from those in most of Europe. Until the latter part of the seventh century the Church in Ireland and in parts of Britain was more tolerant of Druidic and other pagan traditions and, in some ways, less parochial than the Church of Rome. "Book learning," while not common in Ireland, was at least possible.

There was a bit of export from the north to Central Europe, particularly during the reign of Charlemagne in the eighth century; he recruited scholars from England to help build libraries and foster learning, notably Alcuin of York, who commissioned copies of works in the monastery at York to be sent south to add to cathedral libraries. He commissioned secular writings also, such as works on rhetoric. Alcuin exerted substantial influence over Charlemagne when it came to books, learning, and copying. Monasteries and copying in England continued with little or no interruption until the ninth century, when Danish invasions began; some monasteries were destroyed and education and existing culture suffered greatly due to the encompassing disruptions of the invasions and the establishment of the invaders on the island. Copying of all kinds of works continued in Ireland, though, which is why Thomas Cahill (1996) credits Ireland with the salvation of civilization. The copied manuscripts were so numerous and of such diversity that many libraries, from Britain southward through Gaul, had been able to obtain them. The destruction of some libraries at monasteries was not sufficient to snuff out the light that these texts could provide. Words like "many" and "numerous" have to be read as relative terms, since the extent of sharing copies, Ireland included, was not great.

We have to be careful of Western bias in looking at early medieval times. One thing we have to be aware of is that the Eastern Empire of Byzantium enjoyed a substantially longer period of prosperity and security than did the Roman Empire. A basis of trade and the production of goods enabled many citizens to thrive. A related benefit of the prosperity was the health of libraries that housed many ancient Greek works, as well as works of science and mathematics that were extremely rare in the West. Further to the east there was a flourishing educational structure and the preservation of many works in the Moslem and Jewish world. As early as the sixth century what is now Syria was at the heart of preservation of Greek culture and learning. Especially from 750 to about 1050 learning grew under the Abbasid rulers, or the Caliphate; many libraries were built and grew. There was even some east-west exchange on a very limited basis until about 1000. Works on astronomy, optics, physics, and other subjects were written by Arab scholars who used very sophisticated mathematics and logic to arrive at novel conclusions. However, Europe at the end of the first millennium was ill-equipped to make use of, and learn from, those scholars. The tradition that was beginning to be created in the west at the time was a sleepy and suspicious one; short-sightedness and self-satisfaction were common.

Moslem scholarship and culture wasn't limited to the east; centers at Cordoba, Seville, and elsewhere on the Iberian peninsula were larger and more active than almost all in the West. What is today called the region of Andalusia was home to the Umayyads, who had been in conflict with the Abbasids. They called their home al-Andalus. Cordoba of the mid-eighth century was an about-to-be-burgeoning home of Muslims, Jews, and Christians who, for almost seven centuries (the last couple uneasy) would live side by side and would learn from one another. It's estimated that, in its heyday, the library at Cordoba had 600,000 volumes. María Rosa Menocal (2002) has studied this flourishing time period in detail. She writes that

> There were books that would have astonished any Christian visitor, with his necessarily vague knowledge of the classical world. The Andalusians, thanks to their regular intercourse with Baghdad, which had made translations of the Greeks a prized project, also housed the libraries of crucial traditions long lost to those in the rest of the Latin West, and unknown to them still, in the tenth century. (p. 34)

By the beginning of the millennium politics, religion, and communication were in chaotic states just about everywhere in Europe (save for the paradise of Andalusia). Upheaval began the period of cooperation, building, and growth, and upheaval ended it. At each stage there were costs, but the highest cost was the destruction of a collaborative environment of learning and many of the representations of learning. The West was certain that its version of knowledge was superior. In 1492 the Moors, as well as the Jews, living in Spain were expelled and their libraries ruined. The politics, including the nationalism, religious intolerance, and racism of the day, affected all aspects of life. As was the case in earlier days (and as would soon be the case) societies and cultures suffered.

There was one feature of the time between 500 to 1000 that would eventually work in favor of expanded learning and libraries—increasing urbanization. It was deemed to be a bit safer in large cities that could defend themselves better than more remote or smaller locations. As cities grew some particular needs arose; since land was built on, food and other goods had to be brought in. The major result was the beginnings of a system of commerce that would grow by leaps and bounds when Europe became safer and more stable, and in many ways utterly transformed.

THE LATE MIDDLE AGES AND THE RENAISSANCE

By the later Middle Ages even things like reading were transformed. Across most of Europe in the tenth century books did not look exactly the way they eventually would. Texts were not separated into discrete words. The primary reason for this structure was that Scripture and religious works were intended to be read aloud. If one could transport back to a monastery of the year 900 a likely scene might be monks in their chambers, each reading in low tones, but audibly. Speaking the words was itself a part of the devotion. With the appearance of some (though not large numbers) of secular texts, such as technical or scientific works, the devotional aspect of reading did not apply.

For quite a while, though, the simultaneity of orality and writing was common practice. In time books began to be copied with spaces between words, which could facilitate silent reading. Just as writing initiated changing cognitive processes in humans, so too did silent reading. Paul Saenger provides the most complete analysis of this underappreciated milestone in human history in his book, *Space Between Words: The Origins of Silent Reading* (1997). As he states throughout the book, a major difference between the ancient and the modern worlds is the latter's appreciation and valuing of an ability to read texts quickly (such as for reference purposes) and to read texts closely, especially highly technical or esoteric works. The latter reading was applied to texts that were not meant for repetition or memorization. In the transition from the early to late Middle Ages there was also the transformation in physical texts that enabled a different kind of reading, plus reading by people who previously had no access to texts. John Hale (1994) applauds the fifteenth- and sixteenth-century people for raising literacy levels and making works by ancient authors available once again. His may be too simple praise; physical, economic, technological, and other changes contributed to a society that no longer resembled what had gone before.

By the Renaissance what had begun centuries earlier was about to culminate in an earth-shattering new technology. This technology accelerated what was an ongoing phenomenon—the change from an oral- to a writing-based culture in the West. Walter Ong (1982) examines this transformation very closely. As was noted earlier, writing necessitates a cognitive shift within us; we think in large part through the sense of sight. There are other shifts that writing brings about as well, and these shifts are still with us. As Ong (1982) says, "There is no way directly to refute a text. After absolutely total and devastating refutation, it says exactly the same thing as before. This is one reason why 'the book says' is popularly tantamount to 'it is true'. It is also why books have been burnt. A text stating what the world knows is false will state the falsehood forever, so long as the text exists" (p. 79). The immutable character of a book is a boon to learning, discussion, growth, but it also presents challenges that we see constantly in today's libraries. Some in libraries' communities may be tempted to believe that, because something is printed and bound in a book, it is true. Others may presume that, since some of what is printed is false, print itself is not trustworthy. Our dilemma is, in part, that we want our community members to be open-minded (if not skeptical) readers, and we also want the falsehoods preserved so that they can be studied and refuted. Here is a blessing and a curse of the book, and an ongoing challenge for us.

But how did printing come about? There are numerous works that address the events of the mid-fifteenth century—too many to review here, and the primary thrust of their messages is that printing marked a revolutionary change that affected many aspects of life. Leaving that to one side for now, we're still left with the question of where printing came from (as if we could fully answer such a question). Let's reflect on complex events of the mid-fourteenth century as part of our self-examination. At that time a darkness fell across much of the world. Over just a few years the Black Death affected most of the sea-trading north. The pandemic has attracted artists, writers, theologians, and others since that time who have tried to capture the horror of the plague. Conservative estimates hold that one-third of the population of Europe fell prey to the plague. Historians have frequently drawn from Thomas Malthus's 1798 treatise, *Essay on the Principles of Population*, to explain, in population dynamics terms, the sudden and drastic reduction in the numbers of people in an over-taxed production economy. Early in the fourteenth century there were strains on abilities to provide food, clothing, and other goods to the European population that had reached relatively large numbers. Periods of famine came and went, but, as David Herlihy (1997) points out, the total population of Europe had remained stable for at least fifty (and possibly as much as one hundred) years prior to the Black Death. Herlihy offers a divergent examination of data and records to suggest a very different analysis of the plague years and the subsequent century.

According to Herlihy, the years following the Black Death of 1348 and 1349 (in much of Europe) were not merely a time of recovery, where the old pre-plague life was retrieved. The devastation, and the alterations to the social fabric it wrought, brought about a change in kind. For one thing, the European population was slow to recover; the numbers were essentially static until the early fifteenth century. The changes to European society and its economy were extraordinarily complex; we can deal with only a brief summary here. The plague years took their toll across Europe; parish priests died as they initially attempted to tend to the sick and then fell victim themselves. Labor in general became scarce, both on farms and in cities and towns. In post-plague years urban jobs were filled, to an extent, with people who moved to cities from the country, and wages escalated dramatically. In the post-plague years people also had to respond to the disruption in society that the Black Death brought. Throughout the twelfth, thirteenth, and early fourteenth centuries universities were founded throughout the continent. Skilled scribes had been required to provide for the needs of the students and masters. The Black Death itself depleted the student bodies and the faculties of the universities. Herlihy remarks that "the enrolled students at Oxford declined in the late fourteenth century from a pre-plague high of some 60,000 to 30,000" (1997, p. 69). By the fifteenth century there was a shortage of clergy (many of whom studied at the universities). In the years of recovery, even allowing for a stable population, there was expansion of universities. Both Oxford and Cambridge added new colleges.

Also during this time guilds of artisans were recruiting into their numbers people who would previously have been excluded from work in skilled crafts. The numbers of people in guilds remained more or less constant, even in the face of a severely depleted populace. This implies that a substantially large portion of the population was engaged in the crafts regulated by guilds. So we come to the printing revolution, which, it appears, was a bit less revolutionary than it was responsive to an altered European society. In the person of Gutenberg we have a culmination of the transformations that the continent had experienced over the century between the Black Death and printing from movable type. He was an educated man; he had training as an engraver; he had worked a printing press in Strasbourg; he was experienced in accounting (see Man, 2002). There were other experimenters who were trying to make printing a more financially viable enterprise (suggesting that there was some urgency attended to developing a working print shop). Add to this mix the fact that Mainz and environs were experiencing just about the highest rate of population growth in Europe. The business model—gain expertise with block printing first, apply existing metalworking knowledge to the production of type, select a marketable product, and acquire the capital to undertake the project—that failed Gutenberg (for many complicated reasons, not the least of which was his need to go deeply into debt) succeeded for Johan Fust and Peter Schoeffer, and later for hundreds of printers by the year 1500. In the time it took for a scribe produce a couple of Bibles, a print shop could produce 1,000. John Man (2002) notes a 1499 tribute to Gutenberg recorded by a cousin of Gutenberg's (Adam Gelthus):

IN MEMORY OF THE INVENTOR OF THE ART OF PRINTING

> D.O.M.S. [*Deo Optimo Maximo Sacrum*: Sacred to God in the Highest]
> To Johann Gensfleisch
> Inventor of the art of printing
> Deserver of the best from all nations and tongues
> To the immortal memory of his name
> Adam Gelthus place [this memorial].
> His remains rest peacefully
> In the church of St. Francis, Mainz. (p. 214)

Herlihy maintains, then, that the Black Death precipitated changes sufficient in magnitude and in kind to contribute to a new world of communication. If we look at Herlihy's hypothesis in light of other technological advances that have had a transforming impact on society, it's a reasonable explanation into which printing fits well. By the mid-fourteenth century some universities were more than 100 years old and more were founded in later years. By 1450 there were about 5,000 students enrolled in Italian universities (Grendler, 2002). These data indicate that by the mid-fifteenth century there was a need for books earmarked for the mundane uses of education. So the European population was reduced by a third by the Black Death; an outcome of the population reduction was a labor shortage which led to higher wages, especially in jobs where skill was required. People were seeking creative ways to make the best uses of available labor. John Kelly (2005) sums up the connections succinctly:

> During the thirteenth and fourteenth centuries, the demand for books increased steadily, propelled by a growing class of merchants, university-trained professionals, and craftsmen. But making a book in the Middle Ages was a very labor-intensive project; it required several copyists, each of whom would write out a section of the book, called a quire. In the pre-plague era of low wages, this method could still produce an affordable product, but not in the high-wage postplague era. Enter Johann Gutenberg, an ambitious young engraver from Mainz, Germany. In 1453, at the near-centenary of the mortality, Gutenberg introduced the printing press to the world. (p. 288)

The rise of printing was no mere moment in time. It was part of its time, inextricably linked to the totality of life (and death) of late medieval/early Renaissance Europe.

The primary impact of printing was to establish, for the first time, a mass medium. David McKitterick (2003), in his masterful work on printing, says, "From the 1450s onwards, printed books were international objects of merchandise, and therefore of reading" (p. 5). One of the outcomes of the medium was to accelerate the spread of recorded knowledge in a variety of subject areas, including law, medicine, and science. As a medium, printing assisted education in both formal and informal senses. It also facilitated the development of national languages through enabling accessibility to the languages. Printing helped to energize (but did not cause) the High Renaissance. Printing, by spreading recorded knowledge through a mass medium, made it possible to make intellectual connections between and among ideas that have gone before, to make new combinations of existing ideas. Printing also helped to standardize texts; some errors could be more easily corrected. With the uniformity of texts scholars could communicate with one another and call attention to specific passages. With printing, preservation takes on new meaning. Manuscripts were relatively rare, only a few copies might exist. The printed book is more fragile than the manuscript codex, but the content is more robust since there are so many more copies that increase the probably of the content surviving over time. And works could much more readily be reprinted. If a manuscript is destroyed, the only copy of a work might be lost. If a printed book is destroyed, hundreds more copies may survive.

Printing also facilitated religious change. It is said that on October 31, 1517, Martin Luther nailed a piece of paper to a church door in Wittenberg, containing ninety-five theses, challenging the existing practices of the Church. (His nailing the ninety-five points of debate may be another myth, but there is no doubt that he did compose the theses and, eventually, they were made public.) Before printing the debate begun by Luther would likely have spread much more slowly, but by December 1517 his theses had been printed in three different cities. It's difficult to imagine that the spread was this rapid without the knowledge and at least the tacit approval of Luther. It didn't take long before Protestants and Catholics were separated along lines of doctrine and practice, and also culture and lifestyle. Once again, indulgences feature prominently; Luther was appalled at the practice of selling indulgences, especially when the proceeds were used to feather the beds of the Pope, Cardinals, bishops, and clergy. By 1520 Luther was excommunicated and copies of his books were being burned. He, in turn, burned some Church-approved books (ostensibly because he had given up any hope of his enemies learning the errors of their ways). A genealogical approach to Luther's influence, as evidenced by the work of Ulinka Rublack (2005), illustrates the pieces that can come together. She writes, "Wittenberg was marginal, a dot on the map. Even so, and because of its smallness, an intellectual and prophetic community developed. It disseminated its new truth so efficiently that many existing attempts to reform church and society were catalysed" (p. 61).

Censorship, which wasn't new (in Europe and elsewhere), also got a boost from printing; there was more to censor, more to fear. Both state and Church got involved with censorship; in 1535 the King of France prohibited printing in the kingdom. The religious and other disputes were seen by him as a potential threat to his reign. School materials were also censored; in 1546 an announcement was made in Brussels regarding what would be considered proper reading matter. A similar communication came from the rector of Louvain University in 1550. Copyright was used in the sixteenth century to limit the numbers of printers and thus to regulate them more effectively; the limitations could be interpreted as an effort at a kind of de facto censorship. The business of printing was constrained (in England, for example), but the portability of printing enhanced printers' ability to produce works that would meet with disfavor from Church and state. In 1559 the first edition of the Church-sponsored *Index Librorum Prohibitorum* came out. The *Index* was, in some ways, internally inconsistent; it even included some works by one of the most prominent late-Renaissance scholars and theologians, Erasmus (while Erasmus did favor some reform in the Church he was opposed to the extreme measures advocated by Luther). One problem that plagued everyone, censors and readers alike, was the lack of bibliographic control over the mounting numbers of printed works (between 1500 and 1600 about 150–200 million books were printed). At mid-century Conrad Gesner tried to compile a list of all printed works in his *Biblioteca Universalis* to provide an accurate record. His efforts landed him in the *Index*.

Despite (because of?) what may seem like complete suppression of ideas, the sixteenth century in particular marked a time of debate, disputation, rebellion, and reaction. To say that printing alone was responsible for the new era would be an overstatement, but printing contributed a structure of mass communication that the world had never before seen. Many copies of consistently printed texts could be disseminated across Europe remarkably quickly. Learned people could read identical texts, and could discuss those texts with one another. A new print culture was born. As individuals were able to read works for themselves, they were able to evaluate those works, and to respond to them. As Elizabeth Eisenstein (1983) says, "The transmission of received opinion could not proceed smoothly once Arabists were set against Galenists or Aristotelians against Ptolemaists. Not only was confidence in old theories weakened, but an enriched reading matter also encouraged the development of new intellectual combinations and permutations" (p. 44). Naturally much more could be said about this fascinating period in our history. Eisenstein's superb short version of her work (1983) is perhaps the best place to turn to learn more.

BEYOND THE RENAISSANCE

By the end of the sixteenth century there was an increasing impact by printing on education at all levels. Even cathedral schools and other (what we would know as) primary schools could have some textbooks to supplement instruction. The impact was more keenly felt in higher education, though. A university needed to have a more substantial library than it had a century before. Teaching and learning were becoming more mature and were transcending simple lecture and recitation, at least at many universities. This is not to say that lecture and recitation had disappeared, but some additions were made to the curriculum and to the expectations of students and scholars. The case of Oxford is particularly instructive. As the year 1600 approached, the library at Oxford was not much to speak of; it had an inadequate building and small and haphazardly collected amalgamation of books. One person, Thomas Bodley, undertook the revival of the library. He was sufficiently wealthy to be able to make an impact, so Oxford accepted his help. He had a vision for the library that exceeded its past capacity and content. To realize his vision, he enlisted John Bill's help to buy books on the continent; he assured Bill that there would be money to buy what was needed. In addition to his own money, he solicited donations from friends, acquaintances, and those who had some vested interest in the success of the university. Unofficial, philanthropic support from individuals and groups has augmented library collections and budgets for centuries, fusing private and public politics for libraries.

In addition to helping to enhance the collection, he oversaw the rebuilding of the library, which opened in 1602. A librarian, Thomas James, was hired at nine shillings per week (top carpenters at that time made about seven shillings a week). James set to work fulfilling the enormous expectations that Bodley had for Oxford's library. In 1605 he produced a printed catalog of the library's collection; it listed 5,611 main entries for both printed books and manuscripts and was in shelf list order. The building was eventually named for its benefactor and is still known as the Bodleian. In 1610 the Bodleian benefited by an agreement signed with the Stationer's Company that designated the library as a depository site (along with universities at Cambridge, Dublin, and Edinburgh). This marked another development in copyright history. In addition to the registration of works for protection and establishment of authorship and production, copies of registered works were deposited at the four libraries so that a physical record would accompany the record of registration.

In the seventeenth century censorship in England was a matter of official policy and was operational at the front end of the process. We have to keep in mind that "censorship" did not have all of the negative and pejorative connotations we attach to it today. Regulation of what was printed and published was seen to be a necessary duty of state and Church (or churches), for the good of the people. In England, the process of registration was regulated by an official state body. In 1637 the Court of Star Chamber conferred authority to determine what could be registered (and, effectively, printed) on the two archbishops, the Bishop of London, and the Chancellors of Oxford and Cambridge. Archbishop Laud also happened to be Chancellor of Oxford, so he was very powerful (in effect he had two votes). The activities of this group prompted John Milton (1957) to protest the lack of freedom in his essay, "Areopagitica" (from Areopagus, the supreme tribunal of Athens) written "in order to deliver the press from the restraints with which it is encumbered" (Milton, 1957, p. 831). The essay was intended to be an address to Parliament (though he never intended to deliver the address) and was first published in 1644. The essay is without doubt a product of its time (freedom was certainly not deemed absolute), but in some ways it is still the most eloquent argument in favor of an open system of communication. (It's a challenge to locate a present-day analogue to Milton's open system. Recent developments relating to open access, inasmuch as they're designed to eliminate obstacles to communication, may be the closest example.) Milton wrote at that time, "I deny not that it is of greatest concernment in the church and commonwealth to have a vigilant eye how books demean themselves as well men; and thereafter to confine, imprison, and do sharpest justice on them as malefactors. . . . But a good book is the precious lifeblood of a master spirit, embalmed and treasured up on purpose to a life beyond life" (Milton, 1957, p. 720). Milton's essay has continued to be influential; as we'll see in Chapters 4 and 5, John Stuart Mill's ideas on liberty hearken back to Milton. Milton's Puritan sympathies alienated him from Archbishop Laud, so Milton lost the battle, and Parliament was not persuaded to limit the powers of those in authority. A few years later, though, when Oliver Cromwell had usurped power, Archbishop Laud was executed. Even after Cromwell (and in part in reaction to his takeover), at the time of Restoration the state's hold on censoring was strengthened by the Licensing Act of 1662. What, then, did "knowledge" mean in England during this time? Whose will held sway?

Elsewhere in Europe there were some developments in the world of libraries. For instance, in France a young scholar, Gabriel Naudé, turned his attention to libraries and wrote *Advice on Establishing a Library* in 1627. This represented an early treatise on the goals and practice of collection development and also on a library's organization. He had an opportunity to use his own advice; he greatly influenced the content of the libraries of Cardinals Richelieu and Mazarin. He also influenced Louis Jacob, who began the compilation of the national bibliography of France. For the most part, though, and for some time to come, the position of librarian was marginal. Naudé was a writer who spent only some of his time and attention on libraries. It was common, in the seventeenth to the nineteenth centuries, for librarians to be part-timers who frequently were looking for other means of employment. Part-time or not, Naudé was doubtless aware of Francis Bacon's admonitions regarding scientific method, urging order to inquiry. Naudé's ordering of the library also was succeeded by Descartes's *Discourse on Method* and Hobbes's *Leviathan*. Naudé was undeniably creative; he was also undeniably a seventeenth-century man.

Later in the seventeenth century a burgeoning interest in science was leading to practical scholarship on a scale and of a type that had never been seen before. This scholarship was proceeding at a rapid enough pace that a new medium had to be created—the journal. The first was the *Journal des scavans*, which appeared on January 5, 1665. A few months later the *Philosophical Transactions of the Royal Society* began publication. They mostly contained abstracts of books and letters presenting updates on inquiry. Soon the astronomical discoveries of Edmund Halley, Robert Hooke's work on respiration, and Isaac Newton's optics were being communicated in the pages of journals. If the scientific revolution had its beginnings with Copernicus, it was in its heyday in the late seventeenth and early eighteenth centuries. As was the case with religious foment, scientific progress was facilitated by mass communication through printing. It was also regulated by relatively new organizations, like the Royal Society. Lisa Jardine (1999) has reported, "From the very start, scientific 'intelligence' (the latest information in scientific matters) was not freely available to all the members of the Royal Society equally, let alone to all and sundry" (p. 323). Discursive power tends to be institutionalized, as well as exercised by individuals. The Royal Society was a controlled environment; some people were admitted, some weren't. The members could also reject some ideas posited by their colleagues. The social dynamic of the Society certainly valued reason and rigor as validation of ideas, but other, less rational, factors also entered in.

By 1700 the growth in the trade of books and the growth of authorship reached a point at which some legal issues had to be addressed. On April 10,

1710, the Statute of Anne took effect in Britain; it dealt principally with property rights. From 1710 living authors had the right, or assigned the right, to print work for twenty-one years. Eventually that was changed to a period of fourteen years, renewable for an additional fourteen. The Statute of Anne formed the basis for most subsequent copyright law, including the law of the United States, enacted in 1790. The codification of rights was a clear signal that businesses of printing, publishing, and writing were maturing. In some ways the Statute signaled application of the liberalism of John Locke and his emphasis on the private ownership of property. The people responsible for the creation of the products were able to reap the material gain. While copyright does date back to the eighteenth century, these rights were limited to the author's home country. There was no effective international copyright, so the piracy of foreigners' works was common in just about every country (including the United States). One indicator that the establishment of some formal copyright provides is a growing attention to authority. Who says what and the fidelity of what is said begins to have meaning.

Another major eighteenth-century event was the founding of the British Museum. It opened in 1759, but got its start as an idea in 1707. Major funding came from a lottery in 1753, which netted £95,000. Parliament purchased the private library of Sir Hans Sloane, a physician who amassed an impressed collection in the course of his life, for £20,000. These initial funds were spent primarily for the establishment of the library (which was part of the Museum), including the purchase of Montagu House, which would be the first home of the library. Little continuing funding was available for the library during the first fifty years of its existence, so the collection grew mainly through donations from individuals and the transference of some royal collections to the Museum, continuing the private and public politics of support. The British Museum was also soon designated a depository, in addition to the four university libraries mentioned above. The library began to grow in collections and in stature in the nineteenth century under the leadership of Antonio Panizzi. Panizzi had immigrated to England from Italy for political reasons. One indication of the success of the library is the fact that, by the end of the nineteenth century it housed about 2 million volumes. In 1970 the British Library was officially separated from the Museum.

Technically, the British Museum laid the groundwork for modern national libraries, but there had been royal, imperial, or in some senses nationalistic libraries for some time. Most notable was what became the Bibliothèque Nationale in France. It had its beginnings in the fourteenth century when Charles V moved his personal library into the Louvre. This was still, however, a personal library. About a century later, in the reign of Louis XI, a more consistently collected body of materials was akin to a national library. France was also ahead of England in establishing a deposit program. Francois I decreed in 1537 that all printers and booksellers were required to deposit in the royal library a copy of every book offered for sale in the kingdom. The royal library continued to grow until the Revolution. In revolutionary time, in the late eighteenth century, the royal library was appropriated and was renamed the national library (Bibliothèque Nationale). Collections of nobility, churches, and others were confiscated and added to the national library. The Bibliothèque Nationale today is one of the world's great libraries.

It may strike a reader that one thing is missing in this history. There has been no mention of public libraries so far (although some of the libraries discussed were open at least to some people not directly affiliated with the organization). Much of Europe (until the twentieth century) didn't have what we would call public libraries—libraries funded by the people and open to all. In the mid-nineteenth century Great Britain made provisions for public libraries through the Public Libraries Act of 1850. While this Act did provide a formal basis for taxation and the opening of libraries, new libraries didn't arise in substantial numbers until the 1880s, when Andrew Carnegie began to provide funds. Later legislation allowed for more flexible taxation levels, and stimulated growth in numbers and in complexity. More recently British public libraries have been eligible for national grants. For more on British Public libraries, see Kelly (1977). The growth of public libraries, particularly in the United States (as we'll soon see), is related to a changing idea of "public."

COLONIAL LIBRARIES

As might be expected of a new settlement, the American colonies had to first address the survival of the people. Whether the purpose of migrating west was religious freedom or agrarian prosperity, the first order of business was to carve out a living and to build forts, villages, etc. Granted, Harvard College was founded in 1636 to educate new generations of clergy, but it was a very small institution for many years. That said, it should be noted (to put things into perspective) that the founding of Harvard preceded the English Civil War. This isn't a trivial fact; the beginning of the Civil War in 1642 stemmed the flow of immigrations to Massachusetts and severely curtailed the influx of cash. The English Civil War's beginnings were more complicated than simply religious differences (although that was one of the several causes), but the movement to the New World, specifically the Bay Colony, was largely grounded in Puritans seeking to free themselves from what they saw as an Anglican Church gone wrong. As the colony began to recover after the Restoration in 1660 (albeit in the face of attacks by natives of the land, including King Philip's War in the 1670s), the College continued, but could hardly be said to thrive as an open intellectual environment. Some of Harvard's seventeenth-century leaders were indeed learned and fostered learning, but others, such as Leonard Hoar, seemed to enjoy exercising a kind of lordship over the students. As Andrew Schlesinger (2005) reports, Hoar's tenure was disastrous: "no bachelor's degrees were awarded in 1672, four in 1673, two in 1674, three in 1676" (p. 12). The state of affairs at the time was, in large part, aimed at maintenance and preservation of the Puritan faith.

The Harvard library has as meager a beginning as did the College itself. The College early on was aided by a bequest of £779 17s. 2d. (more than $70,000 in purchasing power), and 300 books from John Harvard, for whom the college was then named. The importance of Harvard's gift cannot be overestimated. Louis Shores (1966) quotes Charles Franklin Thwing as saying, "It is not improbable that the gift of John Harvard made in the exigency in which it was made, saved, or at least helped to save, the infant College from premature death" (p. 11). Harvard's history can serve as an indication of the growth patterns and challenges that all of the colonial college libraries faced. One thing that was typical of these early libraries is their limited size and quarters. Shores (1966) uses some primary documents to indicate the state of Harvard's early library: "The Edifice is very faire and comely within and without, having in it a spacious Hall; (where they daily meet at Commons, Lectures, Exercises;) and a large Library with some Bookes to it; the Gifts of diverse of our Friends" (p. 12). "Large," of course, would have to be a relative term; the collection, such as it was, was really ancillary to instruction at the College. What is depicted here with the case of Harvard is an example of a phenomenon that we today have to be cognizant of. Until relatively recently libraries in the United States have been small, not carefully developed or maintained, open to users only a few hours a week, and not frequented by many people. Even with such a realization, the growth and development of libraries had to begin somewhere, and the early college libraries provide indications of the birth of libraries in this nation.

The record of a librarian (or, more properly, a keeper of the books) being employed at Harvard dates back to 1667, when Solomon Stoddard, who had only recently graduated from the College, was appointed. It's likely that he served just a few years, but under his watch a set of library regulations were formulated and adopted. A few of these regulations provide an indication of the limitations of the library:

1. No person not resident in the Colledge, except an Overseer shall borrow a book out of the Library, . . .
3. No one under master of Art (unless it be a fellow) shall borrow a Book without the allowance of the Praesident, . . .
13. The ordinary time for borrowing & returning books shall be between ye Hours of eleven in the forenoon & one in the afternoone. (Shores, 1966, pp. 181–83)

It was a matter of custom for some time, at Harvard and elsewhere, for the hours of opening to be extremely limited and for there to be little or no reading space in libraries. One reason for the limited hours of operation was the scarcity of what we would today call a librarian—someone whose sole duty was to the library and to the services it can provide. In colleges, and well into the nineteenth century, it was common for the keeper of the books to be a recent graduate who assumed the duties for a limited time and who also taught or tutored. Since a major purpose of the colonial colleges was the preparation of young men for religious ministry, those who performed the job of keeper of the books did so while awaiting a position in a church. A reason for the lack of reading space was the inadequacy of light and the reluctance to allow candles because of the fire hazard. There were some in the early days who didn't approve of reading, since there was the possibility of the corruption of young minds. Arthur Hamlin (1981) reported, "Naturally, such reading interests did not meet with universal approval. Cotton Mather disapproved of them because youths who entered college as pious young men graduated as skeptics or even heretics. He claimed that students filled their rooms 'with books which may be truly called Satan's library'" (p. 11). When considering knowledge coming to the New World we have to be aware of what would be deemed "knowledge" at the time. Mather's opinion illustrates that to some, texts had the power to corrupt and obscure genuine knowledge. Books were subject to the validation of some authority.

Some additional colonial colleges (that still exist today) were established; their support, and the support of their libraries, followed Harvard's lead. By 1764 Harvard's library had about 5,000 volumes, and it was the biggest by a substantial margin. The educational method and structure of the time at these colleges did not demand that they have extensive library collections. Instruction was almost entirely comprised of lecture and recitation, much as it had been for 500 years. Also, the student bodies were small in number and the course of study was quite limited. Lee Shiflett (1981) correctly observed that

> The place of the library in such a scheme of education was a minor one. Libraries were small, inadequately funded, and opened only a few hours a week. The books represented rather a memorial collection of donation than any well-planned utility of the college. . . . The library was an ornament to the college. . . . Consequently, the librarian provided no vital service to the college in his capacity as caretaker of the books comparable to the service of the faculty and his status in the collegiate family derived from other duties he performed. (p. 48)

Shiflett used the masculine pronoun advisedly; eventually in the nineteenth century women could avail themselves of higher education.

Many colonial libraries were influenced by religion, as was the formation of the colonies themselves. We have to remember that public libraries as we know them did not exist in colonial times. The concept would have to wait until the nineteenth century to be realized in the United States. This is not to say that the colonies were without libraries, books, and reading. A very important figure in the early days of libraries in the United States was Thomas Bray. In fact, Bray was probably the most influential single individual regarding the founding of colonial libraries. He was a British clergyman, educated at Oxford, earning a bachelor's degree from All Soul's College and a doctor of divinity degree from Magdalen College. His religious interest was catechetical (teaching) and he saw the best way to do this was as a missionary; where better than the benighted colonies? He established a voluntary group to help with his missionary plans, the Society for the Promotion of Christian Knowledge. In 1700 he sailed for America, specifically to Maryland, to help with educating youth. His experiences illustrate the problematic state of religion in the colonies. In the year he arrived an Act of Establishment was introduced in the British Parliament. The Act was designed to provide financial support for Anglican clergy in the colonies. It was defeated that year, primarily because of organized resistance by Quakers, who left England in dissent over the power of the Church of England. The Act did pass in 1701, and Maryland both had a Church of England congregation maintained by the mandated financial support *and* toleration for dissenters, including Quakers.

Later in the eighteenth century there were some efforts to make libraries accessible to some of the public (although there were still no public libraries as we know them). One kind of library that existed was called the subscription library (or circulating library). One particular library illustrates how they worked. In 1731 Benjamin Franklin, with some help, started the Library Company of Philadelphia by getting fifty people to pay £2 (approximately $500 in today's currency) up front and pledge 10s. (or about $250) per year for fifty years. The Library Company was an outgrowth of the pooled collections of the members of a debating society Franklin had helped found a few years earlier (Shera, 1949, pp. 31–32). With James Logan he put together a list of books and the Company committed £45 (nearly half its assets) to buy books in England through Peter Collinson. The first purchases leaned to the practical and scientific (not surprising, given Franklin's own interests), and they arrived in October 1732. In November the Company hired a librarian, Louis Timothée, who later became a printer in South Carolina. The Library Company was open from 2 to 3 Wednesdays and 10 to 4 Saturdays to "any civil gentleman"; loan was only to subscribers (one book at a time). Borrowers signed promissory notes equal to the value of the book they were taking. The Library Company was successful enough to generate competition; in 1746 and in 1757 other subscription libraries opened in Philadelphia. Eventually the idea spread to other places; some incorporated as businesses. Those in smaller towns charged less, but their expenses were less (and people were poorer). Franklin (1964) said of the purpose of the Library Company and other subscription libraries that followed it, "These libraries have improv'd the general Conversation of the Americans, made the common Tradesmen and Farmers as intelligent as most Gentlemen from other Countries, and perhaps have contributed in some degree to the Stand so generally made throughout the Colonies in Defense of their Privileges" (pp. 130–31).

The kind of library that Franklin had a hand in developing (which Shera called "social libraries") grew in popularity throughout New England in the eighteenth century. There tended to be two basic types of circulating or subscription library—a high-priced version that catered to an exclusive and wealthy clientele, and a more moderately priced organization that was open to the middle class. Shera (1949) provided a description of the circulating library:

> Generically and reduced to its simplest constituent elements, the social library was nothing more than a voluntary association of individuals who had contributed money toward a common fund to be used for the purchase of books. Though every member had the right to use the books of the organization, title to all was retained by the group. Book acquisition might proceed by large purchases or through gradual accumulation and could therefore be financed either by a considerable investment or by moderate annual fees received from the members. Social libraries could be either informal or legal. (pp. 57–58)

As the social library movement matured, it became evident that formal incorporation was necessary for the library to ensure its preservation and for the volunteers to protect their investment.

By 1800 the events that had shaken Europe, most notably the French Revolution, were not having widespread impact in the new United States (save upon a few of the more intellectually and politically inclined citizens). The focus here tended to be on nationalism, creating a governmental structure, and setting forth a body of laws to govern the country. These were, of course, necessary concerns. Also, expansion was a major activity. In the eighteenth century migration was to Ohio and Kentucky, and settlements began to be permanent and stable. In 1803 the Louisiana Purchase greatly expanded the new nation's territory and, in relatively short order, became the new frontier. The libraries that existed in 1800 weren't, in general, impressive in size or scope, although a few subscription libraries had reached the size of 10,000 (their contents tended to reflect the popular taste, "popular" defined as the educated upper middle class). In 1807 the Boston Athenaeum was chartered as a business. Sidney Jackson (1974) quotes a source indicating that the new institution was intended to be similar to

> Athenaeum and Lyceum of Liverpool; combining the advantages of a public library, containing the great works of learning and science in all languages, particularly such rare and expensive publications as are not generally to be obtained in this country; with a reading or news room, furnished with all the celebrated political, literary, and commercial journals of the day, foreign

and domestic. And no book, pamphlet, or newspaper is ever to be permitted to be taken from the rooms by subscribers; so that the patrons of the institution may be certain at all times of finding any publications, which they may have occasion to read or refer to. (p. 292)

It offered lectures as well, and women were permitted to attend some of them. The social impact of the Athenaeum was considerable, if one ignores that a small portion of the population could be admitted to it. If the Athenaeum was intended to be a locus for sharing knowledge, the sharing took place within a rather constrained social group. These early American libraries were indeed centers for learning, but the subjects of learning (in terms both of the topics of works included and the people seeking to learn more) were limited. The will to knowledge, and the exercise of control of it, that Foucault speaks of was evident at the beginning of this nation. Key to the will to knowledge is how it is institutionalization and controlled, how knowledge is defined and applied in a society, and how it is vetted and transmitted. The will likely was influenced by some peculiarities of the new nation that Alexis de Tocqueville (1945 [1835]) observes:

> America has hitherto produced very few writers of distinction; it possesses no great historians and not a single preeminent poet. The inhabitants of that country look upon literature properly so called with a kind of disapprobation; and there are towns of second-rate importance in Europe in which more literary works are annually published than in the twenty-four states of the Union put together. (p. 326)

In reality, colonial printing at the time was also a very small enterprise. This is not to say that colonists did not take books seriously, but much of what individuals owned and libraries held came from Europe. There is evidence in the above sections of the contents of libraries. In keeping with what has been said so far in this chapter, quite a considerable amount of the printing that was done before 1700 was religious in content. Puritans and Anglicans sought to spread the word through the printed page, so Bibles, commentary, sermons, and the like were printed and distributed. At times the writings of clerics and preachers raised quite a stir. In 1739 George Whitefield sailed from England to the colonies and used the printed word to his advantage as he traveled and preached. Julie Hedgepeth Williams (1999) tells us,

> The Great Awakening which followed Whitefield's arrival was born of his preaching and nurtured by the press. Whitefield himself was energetic and spiritually vivacious. His conviction commanded attention. He created in his listeners a vigorous desire to seek salvation. The combination was irresistible for the press, which became the unwitting publicity agent for Whitefield. (p. 87)

The religious example brings together the confluence of what were probably the two most significant forces in the printed word—religion and newspapers.

In eighteenth-century Europe newspapers (and pamphlets) were extremely popular and cities would have several published locally. These were usually of varying political stripes and were read by those who tended to agree with their positions. The popularity traveled across the Atlantic. The first newspaper in the colonies (very short-lived; only one edition appeared before it was suppressed by the rulers of Massachusetts, who had not authorized its publication) was the *Publick Occurrences both Forreign and Domestick* in Boston. *The Boston News-Letter* began publication in 1704 and continued until 1776 (Wroth, 1964, p. 19). By the end of the first quarter of the eighteenth century governing powers stopped the practice of prior restraint, and newspapers were freer to print what they chose. Newspapers of that time did mark a formal means of communication, but didn't immediately affect the lives of citizens, who were well connected with clergy and politicians. Richard D. Brown (1989) draws from Samuel Sewell's life which demonstrates the importance of such connections, and mentions, "the introduction of the newspaper . . . was not the momentous event that it may seem in retrospect. Instead it embodied only a marginal improvement in convenience for merchants and officials" (p. 36). Newspapers were, however, valuable as records of events, speeches, and the like, and were sent to those who lived outside the cities. The role of newspapers at that time indicates a phenomenon that we must return to later. Tocqueville (1945 [1835]) suggests,

> The more equal the conditions of men become and the less strong mean individually are, the more easily they give way to the current of the multitude and the more difficult it is for them to adhere by themselves to an opinion which the multitude discard. A newspaper represents an association; it may be said to address each of its readers in the name of all the others and to exert its influence over them in proportion to their weakness. (p. 122)

Religious works and newspapers didn't comprise the entirety of the printed word in colonial America. A variety of other types of works were represented, although in small numbers. John Tebbel (1987) has reported,

> Most of the categories of modern publishing were in existence by [1700], and the colonies' growing population guaranteed that even more variety would soon be demanded. Bookmaking technology had advanced scarcely at all during the century, and the products of the press were not distinguished by their craftsmanship or intrinsic beauty. Publishing was still a century away from its modern foundations. But the groundwork had been done, and what was needed primarily was freedom from restrictions of every kind so that books could become the free forum in an open society that they were destined to be. In the eighteenth century, the means to make that ultimate end were possible. (p. 7)

While the means were in place, printing didn't experience what we could call a boom until the latter part of the eighteenth century. Mark Lause (1991) presents an analysis of printed items in America and observes, "Coinciding with the pre-Revolutionary political crisis was a boom in printing, evident in an almost 75 percent increase for items in the 1770s over the total for the previous decade. In 1790 the American craft had a history of over a century and a half, but well over a quarter of the total number of published items had been printed in the previous ten years" (p. 6). Also, throughout the eighteenth century Boston's preeminence as the center of printing declined as Philadelphia and New York rose in importance.

THE NINETEENTH CENTURY: LIBRARIES AND LEARNING

These hundred years saw dramatic changes in the new nation. Many social, cultural, political, and educational elements converged to have equally dramatic impact on libraries, publishing, and related areas of life. In some ways the transformation was rooted in the Enlightenment ideals that influenced many of the founders of the nation. The numbers tell part of the story, but more personal accounts also illustrate the scope of change and growth. Brown (1989) relates the story of William Bentley, a polymath clergyman who built one of the most impressive personal libraries (second in size only to Jefferson's) of his time. His library was comprised of about 4,000 volumes, but only about 20 percent of the titles were U.S. imprints. Bentley shared his extensive learning over twenty-five years via a bi-weekly newspaper column covering all topics. As Brown notes, Bentley embodied the belief in an informed citizenry and in Jeffersonian democracy. Brown (1989) writes, "What was awesome erudition in Bentley would be viewed as dilettantism a generation or two later" (p. 198), and "Probably Bentley was more learned and better informed than anyone anywhere had been a century before he lived, however in the century after his death his ambition came to be viewed as romantic, futile, and perhaps pointless" (p. 217). Bentley's life crossed the eighteenth and nineteenth centuries, not only in time, but in spirit.

The first half of the nineteenth century saw a continuation of establishment of subscription libraries, but a different way of conceiving of book availability was finding its way into the relatively new nation. The first acknowledged library fully supported by public funds was in the town library of Peterborough, New Hampshire, in 1833. It was so successful by the 1850s that it absorbed the social library. Peterborough (and some other early public libraries) were significant, but on a small scale. More significant was the founding of the public library in Boston (which was the fourth largest city in the United States in 1840). Jesse Shera (1949) points out that by 1840 Boston was developing mechanisms for dealing with public health, public education, fire protection, etc. While Shera's observation does indicate that Boston was maturing as a city, there are some differences between these public services

and the public library. The public library got its start financially through philanthropy, then a tax base was established. Shera maintained that the founding and development of Boston Public Library was the result of a larger social
change and of group effort that involved the growing middle class. Sidney
Ditzion (1947) advocates the view that the beginning of the public library
movement, as exemplified by Boston Public Library, was a sign of the strength
of democracy. He writes that

> The very nature of nineteenth-century America, characterized as it was
> by a swing of the political pendulum toward greater participation by the
> whole people in decision making, by an expansion of the limits of knowl-
> edge which offered unprecedented challenge to a formerly supreme su-
> pernaturalism, added tremendous impetus to the demand for materials
> of learning. Scientific knowledge and reason were supplanting faith. The
> attainment of such knowledge meant increasing the individual's ability to
> control more adequately his own destiny. . . . With a naturalistic conception
> of life gaining ascendancy, and with knowledge being rapidly added to the
> supply of weapons for progress, no wonder then that men came generally
> to believe in the indefinite perfectibility of individuals as well as of society
> itself. (p. 192)

Michael Harris disagrees with Ditzion and says that the Boston Public
Library was hardly a democratic organization. Regardless of which, one of
the observers may believe it's true that George Ticknor played a major role in
Boston Public Library's founding, as did certain others of the upper class in
Boston (the Brahmins). Ticknor had spoken to friends about the founding
of a library for some years before Boston Public Library. The argument surrounding Boston Public Library's founding hinges on intent—on one side is
the view that it symbolizes genuine democracy by being a library *of the people*;
on the other side is the view that the assertion that Boston Public Library was
of the people was a charade to gain public support in the form of financing
with public funds. The latter view, articulated by Harris, states that Boston
Public Library was an elitist institution. Harris (1984) writes,

> The rather naïve belief in the library's potential as "conservator of order"
> in an ever more chaotic world partially explains the care with which the
> upper classes in American society have retained control of its development.
> The selection of men for the boards of American public libraries was rarely
> an exercise in democracy. The trustee was generally male, "past his prime,"
> white, Protestant, well educated, wealthy, a member of the social elite, and
> usually a member of a profession or a business executive. (p. 2511)

Which argument is the more persuasive? Now, an important question is
whether Boston Public Library is typical of metropolitan public libraries.
Phyllis Dain makes a rather persuasive case that sweeping generalizations
aren't possible, particularly if the development of New York Public Library is
examined. The reality is that what is called the public library movement is

consistent primarily on the basis of the development of public support mechanisms. Some public libraries were truly open to the public; others were less accessible and open. Whatever the purpose or procedure of public libraries, they grew in number in the third quarter of the nineteenth century. In 1876 the U.S. Bureau of Education published a massive report, *Public Libraries in the USA*. This report included data on *publicly supported* libraries (including some in public schools and higher education) having collections of at least 500 volumes. The report has data on about 3,000 libraries, the vast majority opened between 1850 and 1875 (not surprising, given the rate of westward migration and the establishment of new towns). One result of the analysis shows that the vast majority of libraries were very small: 2,441 held fewer than 5,000 volumes; only 99 had more than 20,000. In reading Ditzion, Harris, and Dain we have to take care to recognize when the authors are imposing a latter-day democratic sensibility and character upon a previous age. The documents of the Boston Public Library indicate that the founders espoused a view of democracy. A report written by George Ticknor and Edward Everett states, "Reading ought to be furnished to all, as a matter of policy and duty, on the same principle that we furnish free education. . . . It is of paramount importance that the means of general information should be so diffused that the largest possible number of persons should be induced to read and understand questions going down to the very foundations of social order" (quoted in Harris, 1984, p. 226).

Academic libraries in the first half of the nineteenth century, like public libraries, tended to be small and poorly funded, but neither were they unimportant. Colleges had few students and many were in a rather fragile state. With westward movement came the establishment of a number of colleges. Some were founded by religious sects and had small enrollments and very little financial support. The funding of higher education was such that the libraries received little or no support, and the contents of the libraries were largely the result of donations. Some of the best-supported colleges did put some funds into their libraries, but these were in the distinct minority. The lack of support was most frequently evident in the absence of a librarian (other than a recent graduate who would try to maintain order and keep the room clean) and the hours of operation. In the middle of the nineteenth century the following was typical: the library at the University of Virginia was open nine hours a week; at Columbia University their library was open four hours a week; Bowdoin College's library was open only three hours a week. Up until mid-century, students on some campuses took it upon themselves to pay for books and to build their own collections to match their thirst for knowledge. These efforts were customarily tied to literary societies, to which many of the students belonged. The Dialectic and Philanthropic Society at the University of North Carolina was a rather extreme example; in 1849 the Society had 8,800 books, while the University library had 3,500. Higher education, along with the rest of society at the time, had its own ideas and customs of learning that, by mid-century, were coming to be recognized by students as inadequate.

In the latter half of the nineteenth century there were a few monumental events that had major effects on libraries. Of course the most dramatic event was the Civil War. The War was of such scope and breadth, and affected so many people, that the nation, in many ways, ground to a halt. Trade became all but impossible in some parts of the country; the vast majority of young men joined the armies; life was disrupted by battles and invasions. As might be expected, books, reading, and education weren't the highest priorities. Public and academic library buildings, with a few exceptions, survived the war, but the economic and social devastation, and the deaths of so many people, had a devastating impact on the normal course of life. It would be a number of years before there could be sufficient recovery that schools, public libraries, colleges, and universities would begin to grow again. Even during the war, though, some events would pave the way for growth. The first Morrill Act (that established land-grant academic institutions) was passed in 1862; that and the second Morrill Act (1890) would provide support for public higher education, especially agricultural education. The practical bent (a political propensity with far-reaching effects) of many American people extended to learning at all levels.

The U.S. Bureau of Education's 1876 survey, mentioned above, alerted people to the state of libraries at that time. The survey also indicated a new impetus for the growth of publicly supported libraries in schools, communities, and colleges and universities. The founding of the American Library Association in that same year can also be seen as a development in the perceived importance of libraries and in the profession. One other event in 1876 had an effect on academic libraries. The Johns Hopkins University was founded that year. It was established as a research university, which signaled a somewhat different way of thinking about and operating an institution. It also signaled a need to have the resources essential for research and soon had established its own press. With the growth in research and greater accessibility to colleges and universities, library collections began to grow as a well. Hamlin (1981) provides data on the sizes of academic libraries at the turn of the century. By 1900 Johns Hopkins had 194,000 volumes (up from 5,000 in 1876), the University of Michigan had 160,000, the University of Chicago had 303,000, Columbia University had 345,000, and Harvard had 976,000 volumes. However, the growth was not universal; in 1900 the University of Virginia's library had 50,000 volumes, Ohio State University's 45,000 volumes, the University of North Carolina's 43,000, Michigan State University's 23,000, the University of Tennessee's 16,000, and the University of Maryland's only 3,000 (Hamlin 1981, pp. 232–37).

The state of reading in America, especially before 1860, was an uneasy mix of recreation and edification. As women were gaining greater (though certainly not equal) access to schooling, including higher learning, there was an increasing literacy rate. Some "light" reading was deemed acceptable for women, so fiction was finding something of an expanding market. The nineteenth century was a time for religious reform, and a number of movements found some success. The movements tended to enforce an idea of the work ethic, which had an impact on reading. Autodidacticism found favor in the reform movements, since reading could improve a person's mind and morals. On the other hand, the reform movements valued action over study. The nation faced economic tribulations, substantial poverty, and a gap between rich and poor. Reading and study were not eliminated from the set of tools that could be used for self-improvement (Scripture and newspapers were read), but they were not at the top of the list. Further, industriousness was valued so highly that recreational reading was condemned as a waste of time and a distraction from work. That said, the practical concerns of people regarding literacy translated into more than 122 million McGuffey readers being sold by 1900 (Clement, 2003, p. 44). The tension between reading and work was not simple to resolve, in part, as Isabelle Lehuu's (2000) research has shown, because reading was not institutionalized in the same ways that other aspects of life had been. It was essentially a private act (although it could occasionally be made public through readings in social settings). In the latter part of the century, as cheap novels came to be readily available, leisure reading of fiction could be engaged in by people from almost all walks of life.

The latter part of the nineteenth and early part of the twentieth centuries also saw greater interest in science and research. The beginnings of modern science in the seventeenth century and of the Industrial Revolution in the eighteenth century were maturing by the nineteenth century. Science (and scholarship in many fields) was becoming institutionalized by that time, both in colleges and universities and in professional and learned organizations. The disciplines of chemistry, physics, engineering, psychology, economics, etc. were founding societies that would provide events (conferences) at which the professionals could gather, and journals to publish the results of their work. Bernard Houghton (1975) reports that while, in 1800, there were only about 750 scientific journals, the number increased to 5,100 by 1885 and to 8,600 by 1895 (p. 102). These numbers are dwarfed by today's numbers of journals, but the growth rate was dramatic for the time.

Part of the late nineteenth century was also referred to as the Progressive Era, which was, in part, a populist movement. Education was an important component of this movement. There was an expansion of schools, especially outside urban areas. There was also some development of libraries in the schools. With Progressivism came not only a belief in people and what could be achieved, but also development in people's opportunity to achieve. This particular political philosophy would contribute to changes, but it also signaled a problematic version of liberalism that will be explored in a later chapter. More people had ready access to elementary and secondary schools.

More people also had access to higher learning (there were some internal changes in higher education at that time). During the late nineteenth century Harvard introduced an elective-based curriculum, replacing a highly structured set of courses that almost every student had to follow. While that move may seem trivial, it was at the same time progress toward an expansion of learning and teaching and exemplary of the national striving for what might be new. With greater freedom in education at all levels came some changes in information production and dissemination. All libraries had greater choice than they had before (although we should not apply the information landscape of today to that time). Steps were taken that would accelerate, albeit with bumps and curves, in the twentieth century.

LIBRARIES IN THE TWENTIETH CENTURY

This section will provide a very brief lead-in to discussion of the present. Following chapters will include more in-depth explorations of the state of libraries and our profession today. There was an expansion of libraries of all types, beginning in the late nineteenth century and extending into the twentieth century. The rise in the number of public libraries was largely due to the philanthropy of Andrew Carnegie, who provided funds for communities without public libraries with both the money for construction and the design support (in the form of plans for the buildings). In his biography of Carnegie, Peter Krass (2002) writes,

> Through 1898, Carnegie had provided for just 9 libraries. Over the next two years, he added 38 to the list. Now the pace leaped to such a jarring speed the newspapers couldn't keep track; the *Tribune* noted just over 50 libraries for 1901 in the paper's index, while, in fact, he gave 131. In addition to New York, other notable donations included $1 million for St. Louis, $500,000 for Glasgow—in gratitude, Glasgow University conferred on Carnegie the degree of LL.D.—and $100,000 for San Juan, Puerto Rico. (p. 419)

Eventually 2,811 Carnegie libraries were built (1,679 in the United States); some still serve as libraries. Carnegie was criticized quite widely for providing funds only for the library building; communities had to pay for books and staff. The imposition of spending requirements was resisted in some towns, but Carnegie's contention was that each community should select the books that would best fit its needs. (Parallels between Carnegie's and Bill and Melinda Gates's philanthropy have been observed; see Janes, 2004.)

It would be difficult to overstate the impact of Carnegie's philanthropy on library development in this country. These libraries were, in many ways, a bridge across two ages of the United States. The idea put into practice of free libraries in communities fit perfectly with the Progressive ideal of universal learning for all. At the same time, the libraries operated according to a more

Victorian etiquette, where children were welcome, as long as they behaved themselves. The most complete study of Carnegie libraries is Abby Van Slyck's book, *Free to All* (1995). Her examination includes the architecture itself—how it fit into the communities, how it organized activity as well as materials, and how it leant a sameness that was comforting and off-putting. She concludes:

> No matter what their class or cultural background, the young generation of library patrons who came of age in the era of Carnegie were unusually well placed to understand the complex meaning of the simple phrase, "free to all." For the children of the many working-class families that could ill afford the cost of an annual subscription, a library that leant books free of charge was a clear and undeniable boon. Even the offspring of more comfortable families welcomed a cultural institution built to support more liberal policies of book retrieval and use. (pp. 215–16)

The twentieth century began with a continuance of the growth and expansion of the late nineteenth. Of course the Depression had adverse effects on both publishing and libraries. However, the adverse impact on libraries was mixed. As would be expected, libraries of all types experienced fiscal distress that accompanied the economic hard times. Library use, on the other hand, tended to be active. People who were out of work turned to the library in order to read newspapers, to study, to escape in popular literature. Public libraries saw the highest use levels, but public college and university libraries were also used heavily. Reading was active during the Depression, so there was some publishing activity. Both recreational and uplifting/improving works were read. Some wanted to escape the dire economic straits of the time; others sought to learn more so as to have some potential for employment. World War II created employment in a number of areas, including manufacturing and the development of technologies. The technological development was directed toward military advantage, but in the years following the war the development proved to have broader application, including for information storage and retrieval. Immediately following the war there was official government attention to the further development of scientific and technical knowledge and products. Also, with the passage of the G.I. Bill, more people were able to attend college and universities. The economic stability and growth of the late 1940s and the 1950s led to the beginnings of development of schools, higher education, and public libraries on a widespread and coordinated basis.

In more recent years there have been some legislative acts that have had major impacts on libraries in many settings. In 1956 the Library Services Act was passed as a means to assist with the development of public libraries. In the aftermath of Sputnik (1957) there was concern about the educational readiness of the population and the recognition that something official had to be done. The primary response was to ensure more financial support for education—so, the Higher Education Act and the Elementary and Secondary Education Act were passed, and libraries in both environments benefited from the money. The Library Services Act was soon changed to the Library Services and Construction Act (LSCA), so the building of new public libraries (some in communities that didn't libraries prior to the passage of the Act) accelerated. LSCA initially was used by some communities to replace their Carnegie libraries. In the 1960s a lot of money was put into libraries. In the 1970s the economy took a downturn and libraries took a bit of a hit.

More recently some areas have been hit hard, especially California, where some libraries closed and most suffered severe cuts (including public, school, higher education). There is better news today, but only somewhat better. Beginning in the 1970s the price of information began to climb precipitously; this has continued nonstop. Also beginning in the 1970s, technological possibilities were becoming realities. While these developments helped libraries and information agencies, there is a price tag that goes with them.

It is time to end this look at the past, incomplete as it is. As any genealogy indicates, the present state is an uneasy mix of many things that have gone before—some of those things live on, some have been transformed, some have been reflected, and some have been lost or forgotten. The remaining chapters offer an assessment of the present and a gaze into the future. As has been this genealogical beginning, they will be selective; that is, they will be one person's conception of what we should take to heart.

The genealogy suggests that complex factors have always influenced human communication and media. Social, economic, political, religious, cultural, and environmental challenges have been part of the phenomena of human communication and human action in general. The genealogy helps remind us that the societies we live in have had origins and some non-linear pathways to the present. This kind of historical journey illustrates some of what has changed and some of what hasn't. The intention here has been to set a tome for self-examination in our profession (individual and collective). While the remainder of the book will address some of the essential and fundamental matters that underlie who we are and what we do (and why), it will not tackle many specific operations, functions, and choices. Attention to the fundamental matters will, I hope, provide us with a lens through which we may perceive the largest epistemological challenges and the most particular daily activities. The next chapter will address the library itself, as well the fundamentals of our profession in the United States (including education for librarianship).

CHAPTER 2

Place and Identity

OF MAKING MANY BOOKS

S. R. Ranganathan (1952), Indian pioneer in our field, propounded these five laws more than half a century ago:

Books are for use.
Every reader his book.
Every book its reader.
Save the time of the reader.
A library is a growing organism.

With some minor changes they have application today, and will have for the foreseeable future. Ranganathan's laws don't capture all of the existing and potential functions of libraries and our profession, but they are a positive beginning. The genealogy that was sketched in the first chapter illustrates, to an extent, the efficacy of the laws. They provide us with a continuation of the genealogy, examples of continuity and disruption. Organization (cataloging, classifying, describing), as we will see later, is intended not only to save the time of the reader, but also to help the reader accomplish all that he or she wants, and more. The other laws were relatively new when Ranganathan articulated them. This is not to say that libraries in the United States were not built for use or for reading, but one idea that carried weight in American librarianship for some time was provision of the "best" reading for people. The second law was eschewed as policies and actions were designed for edification and moral improvement. The theme of the 1895 ALA Annual Conference dealt with identifying and excluding improper books. That heritage prompts us to ask whether simply having books makes something a library. Addressing this question requires that we explore the purpose of libraries and librarianship today, especially in light of questions regarding virtual versus physical space and the profession of librarianship.

The question also necessitates taking books, in particular, seriously. As the author of *Ecclesiastes* writes, "of making many books there is no end." We should remember that the verse continues, "and much study is a weariness of the flesh." The passage is definitely not praising books or study; it explicitly connects the two as dangers to be avoided. Obviously for many centuries it has been clear that books are indeed physical objects, but they carry much more import than that. The study of books entails the study of communication, the transmission of thoughts, ideas, emotions, etc. This examination includes the technological, political, economic, cultural, social, religious, and other aspects of communication. It is in no way a Luddite endeavor; it seeks to understand the people in the social, cultural, intellectual, and all other milieus. Robert Darnton (1990) offers a diagram of a print-centric communication circuit. At the center of his circuit are elements of intellectual influences, economics and social influences, and political and legal sanctions. Around that center there is a flow that includes all of the players in the communication process. The circuit does not adequately describe communication outside the world of print, but it could be modified to do so. The heart of the model, especially, depicts fundamental human elements of formal communication. Regardless of medium or technology, that human element is undeniably essential. Of course the media and technology affect communication; McLuhan demonstrates that they do. Of primary emphasis here, though, is that human communication can be formative (can influence the development of technologies and their use) and reactive (taking advantage of technologies in ways that may or may not be anticipated at the time of development).

GROWING: APART AND TOGETHER

Libraries of all types have grown enormously over the last century and a quarter, both in number and in size. The first chapter chronicled something of this growth in public and academic libraries. It should be noted that education became much more important during this time period. Schooling, while variable in quality and support, is ubiquitous in the United States. Higher education is also widely accessible, although there are serious challenges to the accessibility (that are beyond the scope of the discussion here). The growth over this time has led to a seemingly odd psychological state for many of us—people today cannot, are completely unable to, conceive of a world without libraries. (Such a perceptual state had its beginnings in the genealogy and can certainly have its challenges. Later in this chapter we will explore the ideas of libraries, books, reading, and other phenomena in more detail.) This is likely to be a peculiarly Anglo-American phenomenon; much of the world does not "know" libraries because of some powerful differences in communication (partly cognitive, partly cultural, partly economic). In our lives, though, it is likely that the presence of "library" is taken for granted, perhaps (or especially, since "library" might be considered a community landmark) even by people who do not set foot in the buildings. The public library is something that a community has and is part and parcel of the civic reality. The school has something called a library (perhaps excellent, perhaps poor) and it is presumed to be part of what a school is. The college or university has its library that is deemed to be essential, in its existence if not in its vitality.

This state of being taken for granted is usually tacit; many people probably expect a library to be in those above settings and they would be most fully conscious of the library if it were to disappear. The psychological state has two paradoxical implications. On the one hand, support for libraries tends to be taken as just another civic obligation; taxes or institutional funds are earmarked for libraries. We could almost say that the support is invisibly visible; it's there but we don't pay much attention to it. On the other hand, the tacit aspect of support for libraries tends to work against anything more than incremental increases in support (at best). The ubiquity and persistence of libraries' (and indeed of education's) existence militates against a sudden and dramatic change in the collective public attitude toward funding. Dramatic events may lead to dramatic responses; war and disasters, for example, offer stark visual evidence of a need to act. The status quo, or even gradual decline, generally cannot elicit such a response. In the absence of a universal public sentiment on the order of "We absolutely have to increase library support dramatically or our entire population and way of life will be threatened," funding changes little. The times of enormous growth may be behind us, since communities, school, and colleges and universities *have* libraries now. (Of course the existence and the idea of libraries continue to evolve.) It must happen first in our profession, but people must become conscious of what they have come to be unconscious of. Any change in the state of growth (and, in some places, existence) of libraries requires serious and informed reflection, which is something that should be a tangible part of our professional lives.

Growth, of course, can be defined in a number of ways. As an example, let's take the serials collection of a medium-sized academic library. Twenty years ago this library may have been able to afford subscriptions to about 2,000 titles in various disciplines, and still maintain resources to purchase a substantial number of books. About ten years ago this library may have been able to afford about 1,500 subscriptions. Moreover, even with the reduction in the number of subscriptions, the library was purchasing fewer books than it was a decade earlier. The accelerated prices of journals, especially (but not exclusively, see Budd and Christensen, 2003) in scientific and technical fields, had a decidedly deleterious effect at the time on this library's collection and on its ability to meet the community's needs. The rate of growth of information available to the university community was reduced to a point where the work of faculty and students was rendered more difficult. More recently, though, this library joined a statewide consortium of college and university libraries.

The negotiating power of such a consortium enables every institution to get more for its money. Instead of the individual library subscribing to some journals and perhaps licensing access to a limited number of databases and services, it now has expanded access to serial literature. In fact, it may be able to provide the community access to three or four times the number of journals as it could twenty years ago. Planning, cooperation, and foresight can help libraries realize growth in tough times. Phenomena such as consortia don't arise without considerable reflection and planning that can lead to efficiency *and* effectiveness.

Without a doubt, cooperation is one of the most essential elements of the success of libraries at present and into the future. We can, however, look at the past of our profession and recognize a cautionary tale. This section will not delve deeply into a history of librarianship, but it provides, again, a genealogical lesson. The momentous year 1876 saw, among other things, the establishment of the American Library Association (ALA). Soon after its founding Melvil Dewey provided the Association's motto: "The best reading for the largest number at the lowest cost." As Wayne Wiegand (1986) says, ALA was able to unite around "the best reading" as *the* focus for its conferences and in setting a direction for the profession.

> The 1876 conference set the tone and direction of the American Library Association for the next 15 years. The establishment of the association symbolized a break with an era when librarians were expected to acquire and preserve socially beneficial and culturally substantive knowledge. The new breed of librarians, represented by such notables as [Justin] Winsor and [William Frederick] Poole, looked to create a missionary spirit among fellow professionals that would encourage and facilitate use of the sources of knowledge they acquired. These librarians believed that public exposure to good literature would inevitably lead to a better informed, more orderly society. (Wiegand, 1986, pp. 11–12)

The effort to develop intelligent and aesthetically aware readership culminated in 1893, when ALA exhibited its Model Library at the Chicago World's Fair. This collection was intended to be the essential works that any public library should own. As Wiegand (1994) warns, though, the collection "also reflected the conservative dominant canons of late-nineteenth-century America that Dewey found so comfortable and familiar" (p. 249).

As Wiegand further says, it was disputes over the largest number and the lowest cost that fomented some dissention. By the turn of the twentieth century ALA had many more sections and committees, and more diverse membership, than it did in 1876. Attendance at the annual conference leaped from 103 in 1876 to 1,018 in 1902 (Wiegand, 1986, pp. 246–48). The growth was evidence of greater diversification and specialization among ALA members and conference attendees. Even with that growth, the leadership of the association was reluctant to provide services and conference sessions of a specialized nature. Although library education was young, there was some dissatisfaction voiced about its perceived narrowness and about the enormous influence exerted by Melvil Dewey and his school in Albany. For those of us who may think the tension between practice and education is new, the history of ALA can provide some comfort (or distress). Also (of possible comfort to some and probable distress to many more), ALA members in the early years were unable to rally around any specific recommendations or prescriptions for education. The subject of education for librarianship will be treated more extensively later in this chapter.

A bit of good news is that, over the past several years and continuing today, a number of cooperative efforts include multiple kinds of environments. Public and school libraries cooperate in some locales; academic and public libraries may cooperate in others. By way of example, in the state of Missouri the consortium MOBIUS began as a way to bring all of the state's college and university libraries together. Its recent expansion has brought the Missouri State Library and some public libraries into the mix. In this instance, and other similar settings, there are some fairly deeply ingrained ways of thinking to be overcome. The attitudes can include assumptions about purpose, collections, access, users, policies, services, etc. Another potential obstacle to cooperation, even among libraries of the same type (academic, public, special), is the existence of weak inter-organizational ties. Librarians in one organization try to meet the challenges of that library and the needs of that community first; only later are they likely to turn to the needs of other organizations. The mutual benefit of cooperation could be clouded by the immediate operations of the library. As we'll see in Chapter 5, the tendency towards weak inter-organizational ties may well be a component of a larger and more complex political dynamic. The self examination of reflection must admit to the extensive scope of our profession.

To an extent the varying institutional assumptions may be confirmed (or at least given continued life) by the separation of affiliations (work environments and membership in organizations). That is, a public librarian who is an active member of the Public Library Association (PLA) is usually not also a member of the Association of College and Research Libraries (ACRL). There are some divisions of ALA that are intended to bring together people who share common functional or service concerns. The Reference and User Services Association (RUSA) and the Association for Library Collections and Technical Services (ALCTS) are two examples. There are some areas of overlap in such divisions, such as collection development in the cases of RUSA and ALCTS. Each of these two ALA divisions has a section that focuses on collection development. Further, each section has several committees. One question we may ask relates to the memberships of these committees; what the relative numbers of academic librarians, public librarians, and others might be. ALCTS is the home of the Collection Management and Development Section (CMDS). Its committees address a number of issues, including electronic media, education, policy, and quantitative measures. RUSA includes the Collection Development and Evaluation Section (CODES), which has committees dealing with evaluation techniques, liaison with users, reviewing, policy, and education. CMDS committee membership is comprised predominantly of academic librarians, according the *ALA Handbook of Organization 2005–2006*; 87.6 percent of committee members in 2005–2006 worked in academic libraries, and only 4.4 percent worked in public libraries. The majority of CODES committee members were also academic librarians, but the majority is slightly smaller than it is in CMDS. A total of 78.6 percent were academic librarians and 16.2 percent were public librarians. Academic librarians may be more likely to have more funding for travel and participation. Since ALA conferences can be expensive, institutional support can make a big difference in individuals' decision to join committees. That said, membership in ALA is substantial and has been growing over the years. Also, membership in state library associations appears to be very healthy. For example, the Texas Library Association reported having about 6,400 members in 2001; by 2006 the membership figure is 7,200.

Unfortunately, the potential cooperative ventures that could cross environmental lines are hampered, sometimes by structural obstacles and sometimes in less obvious ways. One example of the structural barrier is the fact that in several states the school library media specialists have their own association, separate from that of the rest of the librarians in the state. Further, in some cases, the two associations do not meet in conjunction and have few formal consultative or communicative mechanisms in place. There are issues that do distinguish environments, but there are also many issues that all libraries share interest in. Where there are closer structural ties among librarians in a state there may be enhanced communication, greater collaboration in addressing problems and concerns that are commonly held, and an increased likelihood of cooperative relationships (especially geographical proximity). Another potential benefit to cooperation within a state is more efficient use of financial resources. A common or united annual conference could reduce some administrative costs and attract more, and more diverse, vendors. Also (and primarily), the range of programming and sessions might be increased, resulting in both learning opportunities for attendees and informal sharing of experiences across types of libraries. The foregoing is not a recommendation for the merger of state associations; it is presented only as an argument for cooperation and collaboration.

These examples suggest that we have some progress still to make on cooperation. Perhaps the greatest need for cooperation is internationally. If a global priority is a narrowing of the digital divide, libraries can assist substantively in the effort. The first step toward progress entails understanding, not merely of libraries, but of people. A library, as we have seen, is a social construction; it is not something that simply occurs in nature. The library is both a functional and practical organization that is aimed at helping people accomplish certain things *and* an ideal that transcends function and strikes at our human essences. We humans are, of course, *Homo sapiens*, but there are other ways to describe us—*Homo faber* (makers of things), *Homo symbolicus* (communicators through symbols), *Homo economicus* (self-interested creatures), and *Homo religious* (religious beings), etc. The library is created by, and responds to, all these aspects of our selves. It is a product of our thought, our creative constructions, and our exchanges. At times the various aspects of our being may be in conflict. The conflict can manifest itself within each of us and also among us at particular times. If in a given instance I'm prone to an emotional response to the situation while another person is offering a rational response, there could be disagreement. That said, the library includes works by fellow human beings, but it also is, in itself, a work of human ingenuity. It is constructed (in several senses of the word) and it is a source of communication; it, in fact, communicates itself. This description of the human element of libraries is a preamble to an argument that libraries, while exhibiting environmental distinctions and embodying some different ideas regarding social construction (differing emphases on the varying aspects of our selves, for instance), do actually share some common features that may overcome the conflicts that can exist. Perhaps most importantly, librarians of all stripes share some common goals and concerns.

VALUES

ALA, especially in recent years, has sought to articulate what it is what values are shared by professionals. The most ambitious of these efforts have attempted to state core values. In 1999 a task force was formed as part of the recommendations of the first Congress on Professional Education (CPE). That Congress in general aimed to steer discussion and outcomes toward the future; that is, the objective was not so much to describe what is, but to envision what could be. Programs targeting normative goals frequently come under fire from some quarters, and this one was no exception. The most common criticism is that norms would be constraining and confining and would, in fact, violate some of our professional principles. Taken in the abstract, the criticism could be construed as correct; it is possible that some norms may limit professionals' judgment and discretion. Not all norms, however, so constrain and hamstring professionals. Law and medicine have normative regulations that guide the actions of the practitioners in the interest of the public good. Transcending the abstract to the concrete, a requirement to have no norms of practice would, itself, be a norm. Moving beyond the above criticisms, there remains the very difficult task of agreeing upon precisely what goals, norms, and values librarians will adopt (and by what process).

The values identified by the first Task Force were:

Connection of people to ideas
Assurance of free and open access to recorded knowledge, information, and creative works
Commitment to literacy and learning
Respect for the individuality and the diversity of all people
Freedom for all people to form, to hold, and express their own beliefs
Preservation of the human record
Excellence in professional service to our communities
Formation of partnerships to advance these ideas

Some members of that Task Force wrote about both the process behind and the rationale for the statement of those values. After the first Task Force reported, Don Sager (2001) said, "I do not believe the profession can afford to place this issue on the shelf.... A set of core values would allow the profession to better articulate to our public and users the important role that libraries and librarians play in society" (p. 149). The draft of the first Task Force was not accepted by ALA Council, though, and a second Task Force was charged with developing a set of core values. ALA Councilors complained that the draft lacked passion and inadequately articulated the value of intellectual freedom. A motion was passed at the 2000 ALA Annual Conference to establish a process by which the need for, and content of, a statement of values could be discussed. Donald Sager, who chaired the first Task Force, requested that the Task Force be discharged. The first thing that has to be recognized about the process that guided the first Task Force is that it was imposed; it followed from the first CPE. A recommendation that came out of the CPE was

> to clarify the core values (credo) of the profession. Although the Association has issued a number of documents that imply values for the profession (e.g., the Code of Ethics, statements on intellectual freedom, and Libraries: An American Value), there is no clear explication to which members can refer and through which decisions can be assessed. (ALA , 1999)

Inherent in the charge is an expectation that a simple (or at least simply stated) set of values can be effectively articulated. We will explore momentarily whether such a goal is feasible, much less desirable.

The criticisms of the first Task Force were fairly numerous and sometimes quite severe. John Berry (2000), who devoted a *Library Journal* editorial to the draft, concluded, "Let's then agree that the codification of values is better left to God, Jefferson, and Ranganathan. Let us agree to disagree, because our best bet is to encourage every librarian to continue to debate those values, in ALA, in libraries, wherever library workers talk to each other" (p. 6). Perhaps the most instructive point of Berry's editorial is that he points to two undeniably great thinkers—Jefferson and Ranganathan—who are also brilliant at expressing their thoughts. He tells us that the complexity of meaningful values probably cannot be expressed simply. Sager (2001) summarized some of the other objections that librarians expressed regarding the draft prepared by the first Task Force. Some indicated that there was inadequate connection to existing policies and statements (even though the charge to the Task Force was to create something different from those documents); some said the values statement was too brief to capture the needs of the profession; some doubted that a short statement could embrace the diversity of the profession (pp. 151–52). In short, the kinds of criticisms just described amount to skepticism. There were some specific parts of the set of values suggested by the first Task Force that were objects of dispute, but the most substantive questioning centered on the expression of any values. Before going any further on the matter of general skepticism, we can turn to the results of the second Task Force.

In 2004 the ALA Council approved the report of the second Task Force. That report's summary of values was:

Access
Confidentiality/Privacy
Democracy
Education and Lifelong Learning
Intellectual Freedom
Preservation
The Public Good
Professionalism
Service
Social Responsibility

This list is accompanied by brief elaborations on each value. While the second version does connect explicitly to the ALA policies, it would be a stretch to say that it is a more complete, more articulate, or less problematic expression than the report of the first Task Force. The first report included "Assurance of free and open access to recorded knowledge;" the second only "Intellectual Freedom." The first report attempted specificity, expressing what access may entail, and adding "Freedom of all people to form, to hold, and to express their own beliefs." Further, the value of "The Public Good" says simply that libraries *are* public goods (presumably by virtue of their existence), but no effort is made to define what might constitute public good. That is, the report does not indicate explicit goods for the public, except that libraries serve democracy (again, not defined).

In later chapters "public good," a very important and complicated idea, will be explored in detail. On its own, "public good" is unclear as a value. We might value libraries existing in, and libraries acting in, the public interest. The meaning of the term also depends on the definition of public. Is it to be taken as the users of the library, the population in the library's service area, or something else? If it is defined as the first, then non-users may be ignored or even further isolated. If that interpretation is not the one intended by the Task Force, a preferred interpretation should be offered. Likewise, "good" must be defined. Does it mean the items, materials, and bits of information requested or demanded by people? Is it connected to other values, such as preservation? The literature of political science contains numerous works on the concept of public good, including opposing definitions and applications. It is, however, through that discourse that people can grasp the idea of public good and what it means in our daily lives. The past, present, and future of libraries requires that we take "public good" very seriously, and that is likely to occur only through extended deliberation in formal venues (as Berry urges). The discussion to come later in this book will include democracy, intellectual freedom, social responsibility, and other matters.

Within the association's efforts aimed at the derivation of values, and the writings of librarians about values, are some peculiarities that the profession as a whole must address. As reflective practitioners we are *obliged* to examine the assumptions, stated and unstated, that underlie values in general and the values of professionals in particular. This is a necessity, not a luxury. Moreover, the examination of values in one profession must be intentional in a specific sense: we hold a set of beliefs and we engage in a process of reasoning based on those beliefs, leading to an intention to take particular actions (Searle, 2001, p. 44). This kind of intentionality depends on the set of beliefs (what it is that we hold to be worthy of guiding our actions) and rationality. "Being subject to rational criteria of assessment is internal to and constitutive of intentional phenomena, in a way that winning and losing are constitutive of football games" (Searle, 2001, p. 109). What Searle is saying is that intentionality can only exist if there is some assessment based in reason and reasoning; values, as intentional phenomena, are thus subject, by their being intentional, to reason. Accepting such conditions (and I am arguing that we must accept them if values are to make sense to us) necessitates a process of examination that is not always evident in our professional discourse. Self-examination is fundamental to professional progress and growth.

The very nature of value and valuing can be the starting point for our reflection. While it's accurate to say that the value of something (belief, idea, etc.) is the worth of the thing, that doesn't really help us along the road to understanding values. Douglas Magendanz (2003) elaborates on worth in a way that we can use as instructive: "When we value something, we interpret it, but in doing so we also insert a normative arrow into our explanation, as it were, reflecting a judgment as to the worth of the thing, along with an attachment to it" (p. 444). In other words (perhaps stating the obvious), value means much more than price or cost. Value is rooted in meaning, not simply that a value (say, democracy) can be comprehended, but that it *provides* meaning for decisions we make and for things we do. A value is interpreted (we seek to understand what it is), but it is also interpretive in that it guides the formation and interpretation of our actions. It is a very important point to remember that if a person holds some belief to have value, then that person is likely to act according to the precepts of that belief. This can serve as a beginning to reflection on any statement of what a profession *does* or *should* value.

A next step in the examination of the nature of values is the recognition that they can be presumed to be one of two fundamental types. David Alm (2004) identifies the two kinds as atomistic or holistic. He says, "Stated intuitively, atomism is the view that the 'contribution' that at least some feature make to the value of an object is always the same, independently of context. Call such a feature invariant. Holists, by contrast, deny that any feature's contribution is ever independent of context" (p. 312). Jonas Olson (2004), adopting similar definitional distinctions, calls the two kinds intrinsic and conditional. Olson, employing technical philosophical languages, states,

> To start with, assume that the final value of F is dependent on its context C. First, it is not the case that the value of F here is merely contributive, since, *ex hypothesi*, it is finally valuable and not the whole, C, in which F appears (C may be devoid of value, or C may be valuable, not for its own sake, but for the sake of F appearing in it). Second, to say that the final value of F depends on its context C is not to say that the value of F is derived. The dependence relation that holds between the final value of F and F's appearing in C is not a relation of derivation, but of supervenience. Supervenience and derivation are different kinds of dependence relations. (p. 35)

More simply put, something (intellectual freedom, for example) has intrinsic value because of what it is, and retains that value in all circumstances. The countering view would be that intellectual freedom is a guide to action in *particular* circumstances. Intellectual freedom, according to the latter dictate, *can* be a value, but is not, in and of itself, a value. ALA's statements on intellectual freedom appear to reflect an intrinsic quality. The report of the second Core Values Task Force reads, "We uphold the principles of intellectual freedom and resist all efforts to censor library resources." In the words of Alm (2004), intellectual freedom is a value by virtue of "invariant morally fundamental simple features (not necessarily features of that object)" (p. 316). Alm argues in favor of atomism; he asserts and tries to defend a set of theses:

1. Any object with moral value has this value ultimately in virtue of, and only of, morally fundamental features (not necessarily features of that object).
2. If a feature is morally fundamental (in some context or other), then it is invariant.

3. Morally fundamental features are simple.
4. Hence, the moral value of any object ultimately in virtue of, and only of, invariant morally fundamental simple features (not necessarily features of that object)—i.e., atomism. (pp. 319–20)

Olson (2004) disagrees with Alm and argues in favor of conditionalism. He states his position thusly: "The former view [intrinsicalism] . . . holds that the final value of any F supervenes solely on features intrinsic to F, while the latter view [conditionalism] thus allows the final value of F may supervene on features non-intrinsic to F. Conditionalism thus allows the final value of F to vary according to the context in which F appears" (p. 31). Let's use an example to illustrate Olson's point. A community member comes into a public library and expresses concern regarding one particular book in the collection. The value of intellectual freedom applies in the context of the library's response to the challenge. Following the Core Values, all censorship is to be opposed because intellectual freedom is an intrinsic value, so the book is not to be removed (actually removal is not to be considered). If intellectual freedom, on the other hand, is a conditional value, the library's response depends upon the context of the challenge; the decision about the book is not pre-ordained by any invariant nature of intellectual freedom. Let's complicate matters slightly. The Core Value of Democracy implies a deontological position regarding people, drawing from Immanuel Kant. That is, people have intrinsic dignity and are always to be treated as ends in themselves and never as means to something else. The primary question that arises in this example is: Is the person who challenges a book to be respected as a person and thus her/his objection should be taken seriously, or is that person's dignity supervened because of the value of intellectual freedom as a first principle? If there is any circumstance in which a book is removed from the library, then is intellectual freedom by definition a conditional value? Also, if intellectual freedom is a first principle, on what grounds do we make selection decisions? An atomistic approach appears to require that we accord equality to everything that's said, written, or represented in any way. This kind of atomism is not defensible in the practical action of librarians, whose judgments are very frequently conditional.

There is another facet of value that we can add to our examination. When any sort of freedom is considered by a profession such as ours, we tend not to do so in a purely metaphysical sense. That is, we don't consider every reader's or every information seeker's free will; that is beyond us. We consider freedom in a more particularly political sense and as a political value. One reason we limit our idea of freedom is that, as organizations, our libraries must take into account our responsibilities and our actions as they affect a group. The group may be a community, a portion of the community (children, for instance), a school, a college, or a business. There are social, as well as individualistic, implications for what we do. To complicate matters even further, the external conceptions of what our professional responsibilities should be are numerous and are necessarily (at any given time or situation) guided by moral, singularly interpretive, or interest-based concerns. Of course any of the foregoing *could* define external, especially political, conceptions, but they need not. Actual instances that occur in libraries, including challenges to materials or demands for certain services, can take the form of opposing ideas of what a library is and what it is for. Bernard Williams (2001) describes a "primitive freedom" that means little more than an individual's ability to do what she or he wants to do (pp. 7–9). Library visitors may be exercising primitive freedom when they say the likes of "I don't like this book; it shouldn't be in this library," or "I want information on how to make meth at home."

Williams is quick to say that primitive freedom is just that—primitive. It does not progress beyond a kind of egoism based in individual gratification. More sophisticated freedoms take into account the fact that each of us is not alone in the world, and that there are some collective standards of behavior that draws lines that we don't cross. Many of these standards are inculcated into each of us as people living in a civil society. Freedoms can conflict with one another, as can rights. That latter recognition is rather easily illustrated (at least in a narrow case); the right to free speech conflicts with the right not to be libeled or slandered. Conflicting freedoms can be more complicated and less easy to resolve. Add to the mix an altered political climate in which fear of terrorist acts has led to restrictions on individual freedoms in efforts to preserve national security, and conflict is almost inevitable. U.S. actions aside (we have a quite clear notion of the implications of such official actions as passage and renewal of the USA PATRIOT Act, among others), in Great Britain there is a reaction at the present time as a result of bombings in London in July 2005. Prime Minister Tony Blair has announced that he is prepared to restrict civil liberties in order to expedite exportation of individuals who might be suspected of having sympathetic leanings toward extreme beliefs (see news.bbc.co.uk/2/hi/uk_news/politics/4747573.stm). The restrictions in the United States and Great Britain include what some people can read and view, the basis of what might occur if some people read or view those things. The political positions of the U.S. and British governments is that it is better to place restrictions on everyone than it is to take some risks, even though the perception of risk is not based on probability. When the restrictions are placed on what citizens can learn of and reflect upon, the essence of deliberative democracy is seriously endangered (the opinions of some people to the contrary). If a professional value is the role of libraries in a democracy, then the complexity of freedom—at all times, including heightened concern for national security—has to be addressed.

As professionals we tend to respond to these kinds of actions with something more than an idea of primitive freedom. Ideally, in practice we respect the individual's objection to a specific book, but we envision freedom to be something more than placating one person or even one group. Suppose a young woman comes to the reference desk of a public library. The librarian notices that the young woman's eyes are red, she is a bit disheveled in appearance, and looks to be anxious. The young woman asks if the library has any works on methods of committing suicide. Does this person have any absolute freedom to have access to any information and to do what she pleases with the information? Should/can the librarian facilitate the freedom of the young woman and give her what she wants? The Core Value of Access as defined by the second Task Force holds, "All information resources that are provided directly or indirectly by the library, regardless of technology, format, or methods of delivery, should be readily, equally, and equitably accessible to all library users." The value is stated in deontological terms (even though mention of the human side of a request is conspicuously absent); it is an absolute that anyone seeking access to any information should be provided it. That is, it is our professional duty to provide information requested or sought in all instances. What has been missing from our professional discourse has been debate regarding the necessity, desirability, or possibility of a deontological stance. One alternative to the deontological position is the political one; each individual has definable liberty that is grounded in the polity as well as in the individual. Williams (2001) enumerates some points that illustrate the political position:

a. No one can intelligibly make a claim against others simply on the ground that the activities of those others restrict his primitive freedom, or that the extension of his primitive freedom requires action by them. At best, that is the start of a quarrel, not a claim to its solution.
b. Similarly, no sane person can expect his primitive freedom merely as such to be protected.
c. Equally, suppose that someone uses the notion of a right: no sane person can think that he has the right against others to what is demanded by his primitive freedom as such (i.e., to anything he happens to want).
d. A similar point can be made in terms of the good: no one can intelligibly think that it is good (period, as opposed to good for him) that his primitive freedom should be unlimited. (p. 12)

Another way to examine values in our profession is to determine whether or not statements have an egalitarian basis. On the face of it, this suggestion may seem to have a self-evident response. Many writers in our field have stated that it is the mission of libraries to be bastions of equality in a democracy. First, many libraries are not democratic organizations; they are affiliated with private organizations or are themselves private. We can put these libraries to one side for the moment, although they should be included in any discussion regarding core values. If we limit our attention to public libraries we can address specific issues of equality and egalitarianism. Most ALA statements adopt egalitarian language (see the mention above of Access as a core value). However, if everyone is to have free access to the information, materials, and services of a library, the objectors to, or challengers of, certain information or materials are not treated equally. Their requests for the removal of some items or the restriction of some access are not automatically honored. Common sense demands, in fact, that requests for the removal of items *not* be automatically honored. Another ALA document, *Libraries: An American Value*, includes, "We protect the rights of individuals to express their opinions about library resources and services." One challenge that this "contract" introduces is the operational definition of the right to "express." Does some expectation of action accompany this putative right? Further, the Core Value of Social Responsibility does not adopt egalitarianism as a complementary value; some causes are embraced and others are not. To use just one more example, if we adopt any epistemic values (such as processes of open inquiry) then there can also be non-egalitarianism. The kinds of complexities illustrated here are inescapable and cannot be ignored; part of our duty is to meet them openly and directly.

We can turn to some of the most difficult concerns as part of our self-examination. First, we should ask if there is a difference between values and norms. This isn't a trivial question, nor is it a trick question. What we want to know is: When we state that we value something (such as democracy or the public good), is this valuing the same as a set of directions regarding how we should act? The contested ideas of "democracy" and "public good" complicate the question. Some of the ALA statements are expressed as norms: "We protect each individual's right to privacy and confidentiality in the use of library resources and services" ("Libraries: An American Value"), or "We provide the highest level of service to all library users" ("Core Values Task Force II Report"). The core values report of the second Task Force links to documents such as the Library Bill of Rights, so there is some connection between value and norm. Jürgen Habermas, for one, sees a clear distinction between values and norms. Among other things, Habermas agrees that values can be in conflict or competition with one another. The following fairly lengthy passage from his *Between Facts and Norms* (1996) expresses the differences he perceives:

> Norms and values therefore differ, first, in their references to obligatory rule-following versus teleological [purposive] action; second, in the binary versus graduated coding of their validity claims; third, in their absolute versus relative bindingness; and fourth, in the coherence criteria that systems of norms and systems of values must respectively satisfy. The fact that norms and values differ in these logical properties yields significant

differences for their application as well. . . . From the standpoint of conceptual analysis, the terminological distinction between norms and values
loses its validity only in those theories that claim universal validity for the
highest values or goods. . . . These ontological approaches reify goods and
values into entities existing in themselves. (pp. 255–56)

Habermas's position is that without a purpose that guides both the formation and the application of values, they become real and unreal. They become
real in the sense that they are monuments preserved simply because they exist, and they are unreal in that they cease to have meaning for continuing
practice.

Let's suppose for a moment (contra Habermas) that norms are not entirely
binding, that there are some definable conditions where they should not apply. One of the tenets of the Library Bill of Rights (and of the second version
of the Core Values) is that censorship is always to be opposed. The text reads
like a norm, like something exceptionless. There are, however, some things
(documents, images, etc.) that are prohibited by law. Since child pornography, for example, is illegal, the opposition to censorship is at least slightly
conditional (albeit in a somewhat trivial sense because adherence to laws
takes precedence if some libraries are to operate as public institutions). The
safety and protection of children trumps the Library Bill of Rights in this instance. While the Library Bill of Rights may be intended to be exceptionless,
it cannot be. Of course a remedy could be a rewording of the Library Bill of
Rights to include something like, "However, some materials, images, etc. are
prohibited by law and libraries, as part of their social responsibility, are committed to compliance with laws." That addition may work *unless* some in our
profession believe that some laws are unjust and do not agree to any modifi-
cation of the Library Bill of Rights. If that is indeed the case, then our professional statements are not norms, but are values according to Habermas's definition. Values are discussed, adopted, accepted, and prioritized by particular
groups as agreed-upon guides for purposeful action.

I'll introduce something here that will be developed further in the next
chapter. The process of adoption of Core Values has rested with the ALA
Council. Drafting, as Don Sager has said, included dissemination of texts and
comments referred to the Task Forces. While there have been some events
dedicated to some consideration of values, there has been little *deliberation* on
the values. What does exist (statements and reports) is a product of rhetoric
and particular discursive practices, which tend to include not only the matter
at hand (values in this case), but also persuasion, power, and other elements
of human relationships. The rhetoric and discourse cannot be ignored; they
are integral to the social fabric of the profession. In other words, the rhetoric is part of our professional genealogy in the Foucauldian sense. There is
some institutionalization of the professional stance, and little record of deliberative discourse that questions and argues against the received view of the

institutionalized statements. Values, however, can't be imposed; for them to have practical meaning they must be accepted by professionals and put into action in libraries.

EDUCATION

To be explicit about my point of view, let me say that I am an educator. While I did spend some years as an academic librarian, it is in the world of library education that I am at home. At this point in my life and career I can no longer tell if I gravitated to education because of its importance, or I believe in its importance because I gravitated to it. One thing is certain, I enjoy—no, I love—this work for three principal reasons: students, the profession, and inquiry. Each year a new group of extremely bright and committed people show up at accredited programs eager to learn and to be challenged. That is a considerable responsibility, but it's also a source of joy. It also means that I have the continuous opportunity to learn from students. The profession is human as well; it is the people who make libraries almost infinitely more than buildings filled with books. The opportunity to talk with, learn from, and become energized by professional colleagues is vital to continued and enhanced professional action. And there are the intellectual challenges. Anyone who has read Borges, Foucault, or Eco immediately grasps that the library is not just a building. It is a space in which tangible artifacts are collected and organized, artifacts that contain the words, the pictures, the sounds, the numbers that innumerable people have pondered, connected, separated, studied. It is where ideas swim through space and among minds, where worlds await and where knowledge is created. When I was a student in a master's program the possibilities for intellectual life were striking. It was the beginning of a path of exploration, wonder, discovery—a path with branches and diversions, parallel roads, roundabouts, and fellow travelers.

I'll admit too, though, that my career choice is the source of some concern. Education in the United States and beyond has been transformed in recent years. There has been for decades a growing detachment from education as an end. I don't mean that education was or should be solely an end. It should be a means to further exploration and knowledge about who we are (individually and collectively), the world we live in, and the manifold opportunities and responsibilities of which life is made. Today a great deal of attention is paid to accountability and efficiency; it is an open question whether the attention fosters discovery and knowledge. No one would deny that educational institutions should be fiscally responsible and should avoid and eliminate wasteful spending. On the other hand, anyone who has examined education at all realizes that effectiveness in teaching, learning, and inquiry is not cheap. In a recent piece in the *Chronicle of Higher Education* Paul Trible

(2005), now president of Christopher Newport University in Virginia and former Republican U.S. Congressman and Senator, writes, "College administrators and professors must better understand what Republicans want to accomplish, and we must collaborate more closely with them. Those of us in academe must meet legislators halfway and be willing to reassess and change how we administer our institutions, perform our various roles to support our students, and contribute to the general progress of our nation" (p. B16). Part of what is to be accomplished is increase in retention and graduation rates while spending less money. If these two objectives are at odds, success is jeopardized. Where, then, is the balance between efficiency and effectiveness? Is excellence a meaningful word if accountability is of prime importance? Bill Readings (1996) some years ago published a scathing critique of what he called the University of Excellence, where excellence has become a meaningless word, a signifier without a signified. He said, "I argue that it is imperative that the University respond to the demand for accountability, while at the same time refusing to conduct the debate over the nature of responsibility solely in terms of the language of accounting (whose currency is excellence)" (p. 18). Part of the problem that the words of Trible and Readings illustrate is that of the framing of issues related to education. The problem strikes at the heart of education: If instrumental material outcomes (accounting) are preferred to understanding and knowledge (accountability), what is the *purpose* of education?

There is another aspect of purpose that I find troubling. My own institution (the University of Missouri-Columbia, or MU) is presently defining its mission largely in terms of "economic development." The newly formed Life Sciences Center touts the generation of high-paying jobs, attracting private investment, development of marketable products, and creating businesses. Official university documents now state MU's mission in terms of research, instruction, service, and economic development. If resources are to be directed toward those academic units and people who embrace the economic development mission, then what happens to those units and people who do not (by choice or by circumstance)? Perhaps members of the English Department faculty can couch their curriculum and scholarship in terms that appear to contribute to economic development. Should they? To hearken back to the discussion of values, are public good and public interest totally subsumed under the economic umbrella? If the answer is yes (and that really means that if academic administrators and state legislators answer yes), then education is instrumental; it is not good in itself, it is only good insofar as it leads to financial prosperity. The correlate to that statement is that education must lead to financial prosperity for those who are able to position themselves advantageously within this reality.

With the above brief excursus as background we can move on to library and information science (LIS) education in particular. The name—LIS education—is itself a contested point. What is the expectation for "library" education and what is the expectation for "information" education? These questions encompass much more than the two words or names of programs. First, there are several extant histories of education, so there is no need for extensive detail here. The first U.S. program was established by Melvil Dewey in 1887 at Columbia College (now Columbia University). After a few years (and not without some controversy) Dewey moved the program to Albany and renamed it the New York State Library School. His program, its curriculum, and its graduates exerted enormous influence on education for many years. The move to Albany also set a precedent for educational programs with much looser ties to colleges and universities. In the early part of the twentieth century programs were founded at the New York Public Library, the St. Louis Public Library, and the Carnegie Library in Atlanta. These programs were either moved (as was the one originally at the Armour Institute of Technology) to universities or were discontinued. A substantive assessment of education was conducted in the 1920s by Charles C. Williamson (1971). The report was critical of the state of programs and made some specific recommendations that included extending programs to two years in length and placing them at the graduate level. In 1926 the Carnegie Corporation gave $1 million to the University of Chicago to transform library education. The direction of the Graduate Library School (opened in 1928) was to be research-based, preparing graduates to inquire into libraries, reading, and other matters. The shift intended at the University of Chicago was to leave the practical administrative and technical training to other programs and to conform more to other graduate programs at the university. Eventually programs did move a bit more in the direction set by Chicago, but practical training remained a part of curricula.

With growth in higher education, K–12 education, and public libraries came growth in LIS education, especially in the 1960s. The passage of the Higher Education Act, the Elementary and Secondary Education Act, and the Library Services Act (quickly revised as the Library Services and Construction Act) provided impetus and financial support for expansion of colleges and universities, schools, and public libraries. Conversely, the global financial difficulties of the 1970s contributed to the contraction of these institutions and, in turn, LIS programs. In the 1970s and 1980s a number of programs were discontinued: Western Michigan, Oregon, Mississippi, Chicago, Brigham Young, Columbia, Denver, SUNY-Geneseo, Southern California, Emory, Peabody, Minnesota, and Northern Illinois. The reasons for the closings were both shared and individual. Both private and public institutions became concerned with enrollments; tuition revenues were becoming insufficient to warrant the continuation of some programs. Some programs' faculties were seen to be isolated from the rest of the institution. These are some of the simple issues; others were more complicated and unique to specific universities.

More recently the program at the University of California–Berkeley decided no longer to be accredited by ALA, and changed its direction to information management and systems.

The closings of programs caused considerable consternation and angst for some time, but the remaining programs appeared to learn some important lessons. Many began to revisit curricula, recruit students, and make connections on their campuses. Over the last two to three decades changes of a different nature have characterized LIS education. For one thing, the dynamics on many campuses have precipitated the merger of some units. Currently LIS programs may be situated within schools or colleges that include education, communication, computer science, or other fields. Not only is there nothing inherently wrong with these mergers, they can result in fiscally, programmatically, intellectually, and politically stronger schools. That said, there are successful and less-than-successful mergers. In order to assess the health and well-being of LIS education fully, it would be necessary to examine every program carefully. In short, there is reason to be somewhat optimistic about LIS education. The federal government has been supporting instructional initiatives through the Institute of Museum and Library Services (IMLS) over the last several years. Individual membership in the Association for Library and Information Science Education is increasing. The faculty of many programs are collaborating with colleagues across their campuses. Such developments are vital to the future of LIS education and the profession. However, not everything is beer and skittles.

One of the causes of concern is a perceived, if not an actual, disconnect between LIS programs and the profession of librarianship. As the history indicates, dissatisfaction among professionals with education is not new. A few years ago ALA and several other organizations decided to tackle the discontent; there was born the first Congress on Professional Education (CPE). The Congress, as we've seen, was ambitious and sweeping; it sought to address formal educational programs, less formal continuing professional education, and other issues. As is mentioned above the Core Values Task Forces were charged as a result of the Congress as an effort to locate common ground. The values, in the report of the first CPE, are linked to particular matters related to education. Within the same CPE recommendation that addresses clarification of core values is the call for identification of core professional competencies. The competencies may be best understood within a larger context of education for professions in general. Any field of study and practice is defined by some unifying *telos*, or purpose. This is no mere empirical, or even prescriptive, observation, especially for professions. A particular relationship should exist between professions and society—a relationship of obligation and integrity. Professions are based on expert provision of goods and/or services that enhance the well-being of people. That is, they should be.

Howard Gardner and Lee Shulman (2005) have outlined the elements that typify professions:

> In our view, six commonplaces are characteristic of all professions, properly construed: a commitment to serve in the interests of clients in particular and the welfare of society in general; a body of theory or special knowledge with its own principles of growth and reorganization; a specialized set of professional skills, practices, and performances unique to the profession; the development of capacity to render judgments with integrity under conditions of both technical and ethical uncertainty; an organized approach to learning from experience both individually and collectively and, thus, of growing new knowledge from the contexts of practice; and the development of a professional community responsible for the oversight and monitoring of quality in both practice and professional education. (p. 14)

Their outline implies a question: How do these characteristics come to be? By what means are they communicated and embodied?

As would be expected, various professions identify the six characteristics in different ways. The challenge faced is to be specific in our explication of the characteristics for the profession of librarianship. The profession itself is the ultimate arbiter in determining clienteles (or more appropriately for us, communities), the performance and actions of librarians, judgment based in integrity, and experiential learning. Education for the profession contributes to the above objectives, but it is most closely connected to developing theory and knowledge, plus imparting that knowledge to aspiring professionals. What inheres in the characteristics is a collective self-determination of goals (ends) and learning, experience, and action (means). Following Richard Bagnall (2002) I use "collective" rather than "common" because the end is a matter of aggregating the plurality of individual interests instead of a uniformly and universally shared view (p. 82). Programs of education are contributors to the self-determination, but they are not primary. Professional practice is the home of the purposes, methods, reasons, actions, and (perhaps most important) the communities that constitute being for professionals. The characteristics of a profession are tied to its locus of performance; in other words, the characteristics shape, and are shaped by, practice (the work of the profession) and praxis (the action of professionals). Moreover, the locus includes, not just the professionals and their institutions, but society.

One of the recommendations of the CPE deals directly with Standards for Accreditation, urging clarification of the programmatic aims of the Standards (that is, whether they apply specifically to librarianship or more generically to many information professions), better understanding of the accreditation process, and ensuring that accredited programs include the core competencies. Accreditation has been both a de jure and a de facto mechanism whereby some consistency of educational programs could be assured. The de jure part

applies mainly at the program level; a detailed process exists for those programs seeking accreditation or continuing accreditation. The de facto part
applies mainly at the employment level; most libraries require applicants to
have earned a master's degree from an accredited program. There is, of course,
no requirement that libraries hire applicants who have degrees from accredited programs; there is no licensure attached to education. The Standards
that are presently in place were approved by the ALA Council in 1992 and, to
some people's thinking, fall short of the goal of assurance. The Standards are
not based in quantification (e.g., minimum number of faculty, number of
students, budget, etc.). Instead there is a reliance on the programs' articulation of their goals and objectives, and requirement that programs provide
sufficient evidence, especially outcome-based evidence, that they achieve the
goals and objectives. As Margaret Stieg (1992) points out, the qualitative aspect of the Standards represent "a characteristic that inevitably opens the
possibility for interpretation. They are intended to provide guidance, but to
be indicative rather than prescriptive" (p. 159). The qualitative approach is,
as might be expected, preferred over the quantitative approach by the programs, their faculties, and their directors. The programs, under qualitative
Standards, have some latitude in setting their own direction. On the other
hand, employers may wonder if they cannot count on applicants having not
just ability to fulfill certain job requirements, but also understanding of the
environments in which they work.

Toward the goal of environmental understanding, employers may want to
know some programmatic details that extend beyond the Standards for
Accreditation. Since librarianship's concern regarding education is the preparation of future librarians, the profession should be aware of what programs
are doing towards that end. (Note: I did *not* say "preparation of people to work
in libraries"; I thank my colleague Ken Haycock for making this vital distinction. "Preparing future librarians" should be interpreted as educating individuals to combine technical competency, awareness of information package
content, and understanding of what people want and need. Absent from this
definition is a specific locus.) A large caveat has to be mentioned here, one
that all librarians are aware of: The profession, libraries, and the world are in
flux. This means that the preparation of future librarians *must* include instill-
ing understanding of, and appreciation of, change, as well as the need for
lifelong professional exploration and learning. Change, however, is not an
inherent good. So beyond understanding and appreciation, future librarians
must be prepared to shape change, to guide and direct and influence it so
that the overarching goals of enabling people to learn, read, and become informed can be achieved. In other words, a successful educational program
ensures that the horse is placed before the cart; people come before tools.

Education for librarianship, as is stated above, is locus-generic at its most
basic level. A concern that employers have, though, is putting the people of a

specific community first. This translates, not into preparation for work in academic, public, or special libraries, but preparation for academic, public, and special librarianship. Courses that would focus on buildings and processes peculiar to certain settings would likely do little to prepare those librarians. Experiences that explore the ecology of the environments would contribute to the preparation of those librarians. An ecological approach would include the community (the people who share something in common); the kinds of information and materials most wanted and needed by members of the community; the production, dissemination, access, and economics related to the information and materials; and the organizational structures that exist (or could exist) to meet these objectives (which also accounts for the organizational complexities of governance, financing, etc.). Ecological experiences can emphasize to students the interlacing human constructions in which librarians work.

CURRICULUM

As is evident from the preceding discussion, a particular arena for disagreement between education and the profession is the curriculum. As is true of almost all applied fields, questions abound regarding the need for and the content of a core curriculum in librarianship. In applied fields there are bound to be changes and shifts as new techniques are developed, new technologies are built, and new understanding flows from research (basic and applied). No applied field is static, and librarianship is no different from other fields. Medicine, for example, is constantly working on new ways to heal the sick, promote healthy habits, and understand the complex functioning of human bodies. Law, on the other hand, is still rooted in the comprehension and application of complex texts, albeit while applying the law to emergent technologies and societal dynamics. The fundamental goals of medicine and law have remained substantively unchanged. Can we say the same about librarianship? Can we say the same about LIS education? Pierce Butler (1961 [1933]) wrote not long after the founding of the Graduate Library School of the University of Chicago and not long after the establishment of graduate education in librarianship that

> A professional philosophy would give to librarianship that directness of action which can spring only from a complete consciousness of purpose. Certainly it will make a great difference for communal welfare whether this public agency is conceived as a necessary and normal social element, or as a supererogatory benefaction to fortunate individuals. By the one view the service will be rendered as an obvious duty, by the other it may easily degenerate into bureaucratic favoritism. (p. 103)

The purpose tends to define the curriculum and, conversely, the curriculum may be said to imply purpose. Michael Gorman (2004) expresses some skepticism regarding the professional applicability of LIS programs' curricula: "Many of the topics regarded as central to library education (cataloguing, reference, collection development, etc.) by would-be employers are no longer central to, or even required by, today's LIS curricula" (p. 99). Some evidence, though, points to some shifting curricular ground. Karen Markey's (2004) work purports to illustrate increasing attention to professional matters in curricula. For example, not only did the average number of required courses increase from 2000 to 2002 (5.25 to 5.68), the number of programs requiring courses in some target areas also increased during that time period. Beyond requirements, Markey concludes "that new educational trends are primarily user-centered. . . . Library educators are warned against placing too much reliance on a single niche such as users or information technology. Instead, programs should stake unclaimed or disputed areas such as the organization of information, content creation, authoritative information, and/ or collection preservation" (p. 338). Implicit in this recommendation is that previous programmatic offerings were less user-centered, which is a difficult, if not impossible, claim to validate. Of greater concern, though, is a seeming contradiction in her article relating to avoiding single niches, but then suggesting some niches that are themselves difficult to define and to actualize within programmatic goals. Organization of information and content creation are worthwhile endeavors, but staking out an area means more than offering a course or one faculty member devoting some time to the matter. The direction of any LIS program should be derived from the intersection of current resources and personnel, the likelihood of a need for what would be provided, and the possibility of garnering support to develop in new areas. Staking a claim isn't to be based merely on a perceived opportunity; most programs do not have the wherewithal to add new items to their purposes or to jettison existing core functions.

Some individual groups or bodies have formulated competencies or desired attributes for particular environments or operations. One example will suffice here to illustrate such specific viewpoints. The Association of Southeastern Research Libraries (ASERL) articulated a set of competencies ("Shaping the Future," 2001). While a few of the competency areas are particular to the place and nature of research libraries (such as an understanding of the context of higher education), others of the competency areas are more general. According the ASERL, librarians should be sensitive to institutional mission; engage in cooperation and collaboration to enhance services; have knowledge of the organization, management, dissemination, and use of resources; and adhere to the values of the profession. One might quibble whether these are, in fact, competencies, but the point here is there are some statements of professional necessities that appear to be common to librarianship.

Of less apparent concern in the professional community is an increase in the emphasis on information-related areas, perhaps at the expense of library-related areas. Again, Gorman (2004) expresses the concern that does exist: "What we used to call library schools have become hosts to information science and information studies faculty and curricula. These disciplines (if they exist at all) are, at best, peripheral to professional library work" (p. 99). John Berry (2004) echoes Gorman: "At every school I've visited in the past three years, students complain about the lack of courses and choices in traditional library areas" (p. 10). We should admit that if schools choose to take different directions, that choice is theirs; every school has not only the right, but the responsibility, to set its own direction. If, however, that direction departs from the preparation for librarianship, the schools should state as much and should rethink accreditation by ALA. Berry (2004) quotes a posting by Raymond von Dran (former Dean of the School of Information Studies at Syracuse University) to an email list: "Labeling something a crisis either is a serious misjudgment or an attempt to influence action by trying to create a crisis about a 'crisis.' Why not just say library schools are concealing Weapons of Mass Destruction and are going to harm our libraries because they hate freedom of access loving Americans" (p. 10). Obviously there is some amount of rhetorical jousting going on by both sides on this issue. What does seem to be the case is that there is not a great deal of education-profession dialogue. A thorough professional self-examination requires that we look closely at what is being referred to as an I-L split in LIS education, concluding with a discourse on the need for dialogical communication.

I AND L

The writings that do address information and librarianship (please note that I did not say information *versus* librarianship; I firmly believe that there should and can be vibrant mutual benefit for each field from the other) are not numerous. What contests do exist between the two exhibit some frequently occurring characteristics: (1) the librarianship (or L) pieces tend to bemoan a direction in LIS education that appears to exclude librarianship as a disciplinary anchor; (2) the information (or I) pieces tend to express bemusement at any distress evident on the L side; (3) at the same time the L pieces say that I-schools are indeed meeting the educational needs of librarianship; and (4) the L pieces claim that I-schools are attempting to meet librarianship's needs through adjunct instructors rather than regular faculty. Gorman and Berry have already been quoted on the L side; one more excerpt from Gorman's (2004) article helps to establish the L perspective:

> Consider a list of the faculty teaching in one of the United States' longest established and prestigious LIS schools. The list of the courses taught and

research interests of those faculty include a number of library topics—school libraries, subject access, collection management, descriptive bibliography, and so forth—but these are heavily outweighed by topics such as (chosen from many at random) user modeling, information visualization, human-computer interaction, business taxonomies, strategic intelligence, social and organizational informatics, computational linguistics, electronic commerce, and computer programming for information management. (p. 100)

ALA does accredit master's programs and for accreditation to make any sense there must be some reliability to the Standards and the review process. If Gorman, Berry, and others are correct, there are questions regarding reliability. I'll hasten to add that it is possible for a school with substantial resources to fulfill—even surpass—the ALA Standards for Accreditation *and* succeed at offering other information-related programs. In the tradition of the eighteenth-century philosopher David Hume, though, "ought" does not imply "is." That is, just because it is possible for a school to succeed at offering strong L and I programs does not necessarily mean that it does. Further, we cannot take any program's word (my own included) that it is, in fact, succeeding; a rigorous external review is needed for assurance. A program that focuses solely on librarianship may or may not do a good job preparing future librarians; such a program should definitely not be immune from scrutiny.

Upon reflection I find myself taking issue with some of what Gorman and others identify as problems (see the quote above from Gorman on course titles). Teaching students about human information behavior, visualization, and human-computer interaction can be a useful, perhaps necessary, effort to prepare people to understand more completely the ways people think about information and employ technologies to achieve their goals. LIS programs can succeed if they emphasize all four legs of the table—users, content, technology, and access. Ignoring any one of these legs jeopardizes a program's efficacy, just as it would jeopardize a table's stability. These four foci are the foundation of librarianship, especially if we remember that each of the four terms subsumes a number of more specific phenomena. For example, "access" encompasses economics, communication, management, and policy, as well as other things. For librarianship to ignore, say, cognitive aspects of people's information seeking, finding, and use would be irresponsible. Likewise, educational programs can't ignore these vital professional elements. The definition of librarianship is of a house with many mansions, capable of accommodating a large family; accommodations cannot be constrained without reason.

Now to the I side. As the foregoing suggests, I believe that there is a great deal to be learned about organizational structures, human apperception of texts, images, and sounds, and means of ensuring access to information by everyone. The language used in some of the I pieces, however, sometimes obscures common ground and dissimilates when it comes to programmatic intentions and directions. In 2002 there were the beginnings of an organizational effort aimed at bringing together I-schools, ostensibly around common curricular, research, and development issues. In 2003 a symposium was held in Chapel Hill, North Carolina, but only a select group of schools was invited. On the face of it, a closed meeting smacks of isolationism. If an inclusive impetus were driving any move toward progress, all ALA-accredited programs, and quite probably other programs as well, would have been invited. Had this been a single event it would be easy to conclude that the participating schools simply wanted to initiate a conversation that would quickly broaden. On the contrary, a formal I-School Community has been established, with limited membership (see iconference.ist.psu.edu/content/view/23/37). In 2005 this group organized a conference around the theme "Bridging Disciplines to Confront Grand Challenges." The description of the conference refers specifically to information technology as the primary discipline, raising doubt about the "bridging" objective. The conference description reads that the conference is part of "an ongoing effort to build our sense of community, purpose, partnership, and identity as well as to foster an understanding of the grand challenges we attack (and the contributions we make) as a result of our inter- and multi-disciplinary perspectives" (iconference.ist. psu.edu/content/view/26/41). In the abstract for John L. King's (former Dean, School of Information, University of Michigan) session, a question asked is, "How do those outside of the information field in the academy and in industry/government think of and interact with us?" It may be that representatives of those groups will present their views at the session (although that is not indicated in the program), otherwise it may be difficult to gauge the perceptions and possible contributions of those outside the I-field. Of course as a prelude to gauging the perceptions of those outside the field, it might be a good idea to know who is *in* the field (apart from the seventeen universities listed at the conference Web site).

A couple of names have been mentioned so far in the I context; these individuals have had founding roles in the assertion of the place of I-schools and in the formation of the I-School Community. Raymond von Dran is one of these individuals, and some of his comments are noted by John Berry. In a formal article von Dran (2004) issues something of a manifesto on information technology (IT) education, emphasizing the I. He describes the purpose of the educational initiative: "'I' schools build their programs around the four pillars of people, technology, management, and policy. Typically they offer classes in programming, distributed computing, networking, information systems, systems analysis, information-based organizations, database management systems, information analysis, and telecommunications and information policy" (p. 9). Perhaps the "people" pillar is implicit in these courses offerings. "Library"—and, more important, librarianship—is conspicuous by its absence; in part the absence can be explained by the publication of the article in *Educause*, which has a decidedly technological bent. It does seem odd, though, that (at the time of writing) the dean of a school that includes an ALA-accredited program does not allude to the successes of librarians, including Syracuse graduates, in influencing information and public policy, technological development, and (especially) connecting people and information. The omission may be an oversight, but if it isn't an oversight, what is it? It is also interesting that the disciplinary territory von Dran seeks to stake out is IT. He includes a graphic intended to illustrate the future of the information field, yet "information" is not defined.

John King (2005) has articulated what may be the most extensive vision for what he calls "the field." He uses his own school (Michigan) to offer an assessment of the current state of affairs and the preferred direction for the future. In speaking of the students in the University of Michigan program he says that the students fall into two groups; "The first is the martyrs, who know the salaries are low and the librarian's lot is to suffer, but they want to do that kind of work so they come anyway. The other class are [*sic*] students who come to SI with expectations to work in other areas of our program where salaries are higher, then they discover once in the program that they really liked the library world and are willing to accept it as it is." He then states that the situation is unfortunate, but that it's life. King's categorization of his students, especially of the first group, is insulting (whether by intention or not). It appears that he is perhaps less aware than a dean should be of the profession for which his program educates. He demonstrates equal lack of awareness of what libraries exist for: "Even if libraries were once a good example of true public goods, they aren't any more. . . . My point here is that the Public Goods model for library funding is failing politically because it is failing conceptually and practically—that dog just won't hunt any more." In short, according to King, libraries are not public goods and they shouldn't pretend that they are. These two statements of King's highlight a difficulty that permeates his paper. He isn't actually arguing a position at all; he issues dicta simply as facts that cannot possibly be challenged, rather than suggesting propositions that can be tested for both validity and truth. What is missing is not only evidence for his claims but (more important) reasoning that would indicate a process of logical and critical thought. His comments would be easy to dismiss if he weren't the dean of a school. If he speaks for more than just himself then there is indeed an L-I rift, and it is one that will not be resolved by the kind of arbitrary dismissal he indulges in.

Returning to the starting point and the characteristics of a profession identified by Gardner and Shulman, we have a basis for the development of a core curriculum. This basis does not necessarily include the courses or course content that may presently typify program requirements. The question to begin with is: What do professional librarians need to know to begin their careers?

The first step to an answer to that question is that the knowledge (the *epistēmē* and the *technē*) has to be based in a historical consciousness. The liberal-capitalist curriculum that has a decidedly laissez-faire character seeks, as Pierre Bourdieu (1998) argued, to abolish history, to relegate it to the unconsciousness (pp. 56–57). Historical unconsciousness deletes both telos and reason, so that a new purpose—one that is dismissive of the past—can be created. The new creation does not limit itself to the profession's past; it also replaces the more general social history. The necessary consciousness is certainly no mere antiquarianism or chronological erudition; it is cognizance of present being as it has been shaped over time. This last point cannot be overemphasized; "being" is historical and phenomenological. It is a totality of existence, not only of self, but of self-and-other. This definition of being captures the essential relationship between librarianship and society; the entirety of a curriculum, and a core curriculum in particular, relies on this definition.

A preliminary answer to the above question involves a binary division of education—skills and knowledge. Skills are, in some ways, the more readily identifiable components of an educational program. The profession demands that practitioners be competent users of information technology (able to make effective use of operating systems, software, databases, and other tools). Other competencies include (not exhaustively) the application of cataloging rules so as to ensure effective access to materials, the ability to account for the finances of the organization's operations, an understanding of the basics of managing an organization, and a close familiarity with collections and accessible information provided by the organization. In short, the mundane aspects of practice (although not praxis) can be translated into skills that can be taught in LIS programs. However, if education for the professions contains nothing more than these skills, LIS programs need not exist. Some apprenticeships or training experiences would suffice.

Knowledge is a different matter. If Gardner and Shulman are correct and theory, judgment, and connection with communities are important, education for the profession is not simply the design of a training program. For example, the Standards for Accreditation state that organization and description should be a component of a program's curriculum. One way to fulfill the letter of the Standard is to provide course content on cataloging rules, metadata applications, and/or assignment of classificatory identifiers (such as call numbers) to texts. Nothing at the level of practice suggests any of the characteristics of a profession. Organization and description are intellectual acts (praxis) that demand an understanding of the ontology of things (what they are, or, more important, what makes them what they are) and of the metaphysics of texts (what formal communication entails, as well as how the communication is intentionally created). Of necessity, understanding of such matters requires a facility with language and an ability to comprehend the potentiality and the limitation of language. In the former instance (ontology) the challenge is to use linguistic structures to describe things; in the latter case the challenge is to categorize language with language. Anything short of this kind of complex treatment of organization fails the profession and society. Moreover, failure to comprehend the foregoing can be seen as symptomatic of the shortcomings of education for librarianship. This may sound harsh, but fulfillment of the characteristics Gardner and Shulman spoke of requires critical apprehension, not only of the hows of practice, but of the whys of praxis.

Borrowing from Andrew Abbott's (2001) description of sociology, LIS education can be characterized by interstitiality. LIS education finds itself in between; it is both a middle ground between forces in LIS generally and the site for the tension between the forces. The chart below illustrates some of the interstices that educational programs have to deal with.

INTERSTICES OF LIS EDUCATION

Practice	Praxis
Profession	Discipline
Professional Associations	Universities and Colleges
Professionals	Educators
Subjects	Objects
Communities (real)	Community (abstract)
Organizational Being	Individual Being
Doing	Inquiring
Immanence	Transcendence

The chart begs for some explanation. Each of the pairs represents not extremes or poles, but differences. For example, practice is intended to signify the operations and functions that are central to librarianship; praxis is intended to signify the underlying purposes, ethics, and responsibilities that guide those operations and functions. The role of education is, in part, to study and teach about both of the entities and the space between them. The thorniest of the pairs is immanence-transcendence. Immanence refers to those properties of the professions that inhere in the work itself; these properties may be said to define what librarianship does. Transcendence refers to the properties that offer reason for being; these properties may be said to define what librarianship is.

I'm proposing that curricular review be grounded in the immanence-transcendence pair explicitly. To an extent this proposition represents the mix of practice and theory that many individuals and groups have called for over the years. It actually marks a shift in consciousness, though, and presents ways of accomplishing the objectives that Gardner and Shulman outline. Practice, to begin with, is much more than a set of tasks or operations; it embodies the mission of service, incorporating technical and ethical means.

The judgment that is required of a professional is not formulaic, but reflective. As Donald Schön (1983) illustrates, professionals develop a particular kind of epistemology that is executed through action. The immanence I'm speaking of includes such an epistemology, as well as autonomy for professionals to identify where judgment is necessary and how to use their judgment. Librarians, as professionals, don't merely respond passively to questions asked of them; they anticipate needs and wants through collections, access, and physical spaces. They help users discover questions they previously didn't know to ask. Immanence requires a knowledge base, a way to communicate with those served, and an ethos that defines the relationship between librarians and communities. Stemming from these requirements is the wherewithal—technical and intellectual—to translate the embodiment of immanence into daily practice.

Along with immanence is transcendence. Transcendence guides the purpose behind the particular epistemology of librarianship. There is a needed separation of the definition of professional being from the concrete requisites of practice. The reflection mentioned above can be called more specifically (again following Schön) reflection-in-action, that is, the reflective process concerns itself with what should be known and done. Transcendent reflection is different in kind; rather than targeting daily action, it is a contemplation on being. The question that immanence asks is: What should I do? The question for transcendence is: What should I be, and why? The interstice between immanence and transcendence is the space for education for librarianship to link professional action, research, and speculation. I'll hasten to add that educational programs are one vital component in the educational endeavor. A partnership between education and the profession is the only viable means by which the immanent and the transcendent can be joined. Future deliberations on education should be informed by the priority that immanence and transcendence demand; discussions should begin with the necessity of reflection as fundamental to librarianship.

So we come back to the characteristics that Gardner and Shulman identify. In fulfilling the responsibilities inherent in the characteristics—all of the characteristics—we see very clearly that education for the profession is not separate from the profession; both are parts of an integrated whole. There is an extension from the characteristics that can apply specifically to librarianship. As long as there are texts, images, and sounds there will be the need to organize these entities so that they can be used. As long as there are human beings who want and need the contents of texts, images, and sounds there will be the need to provide mediation services. As long as texts, images, and sounds are produced with the intention of communicating them there will be the need for expertise in acquiring and providing access to them. As long as communicative content is ordered and accessible there will be the need to manage the organizations that fulfill this need. As long as technologies facilitate the use of communicative content there will be the need for competence in the use of technologies. Notice that this litany does not include specific courses, but it does require clear and convincing evidence that graduates of programs accredited by ALA are able meet communities' needs. This is no different from the American Bar Association requiring that graduates of law schools know about substantive law. The culmination of the foregoing is that librarianship is clearly a profession that should embrace the six characteristics discussed here, that education for librarianship be fully integrated with the characteristics of the profession, and that a core curriculum reflect the integration. Anything less, including standing apart from the profession, is utter abdication of the responsibilities of any program to educate for librarianship.

Toward a Dialogue

What kind of communication do King and others employ? His paper, as well as other pieces, are fundamentally monologic; he admits to no divergent opinion, no other interpretation of events. What's worse, he frames the entire matter in particular terms that render disagreement very difficult. When he says that there is no feud between L- and I-schools, it is not sufficient to offer the suggestion that there is a feud. To respond to King one would have to point out that it is he who speaks of I- and L-schools; that is, he asserts that there is a separation (in fact, a dichotomy). If his aim is to contribute to shaping the future of the field, then missing is mention of communication, education, and other areas that at least linguistically, may make more sense than either L or I. After all, communication and education can be not only academic units, but ends in themselves. "Information" by itself and in the writings about "I," can be seen as (in the language of semiotics) a floating signifier (see Chandler, 2002, pp. 74–77). A signifier in semiotics is a word, sound, or image that is intended to unite with a concept or idea (signified). While there are other concepts in rhetoric that might be used for examination here, semiotics does meld both semantics and pragmatics in ways that are especially useful. A floating signifier does not necessarily connect with any object or idea; it is intentionally ambiguous so that it could be said to mean many things. As a result of the word or image not being connected to an actual or usable definition, it means very little; it isn't attached to any "thing." Mention of information as a floating signifier is not a mere linguistic conceit; it points out that in many instances information is employed purposely as a technique of obfuscation. After all, how can one disagree with a term that can mean anything?

If it appears that I'm using "I" as a punching bag, I should say that the "L" side is not blameless in sometimes employing library as a floating signifier.

If the library is variously a bastion of democracy, the heart of the college or university, a cultural storehouse, or the center of learning in schools, it may well have rhetorical, but not genuine, significance. That is, individuals may use metaphors to describe the library, but the metaphoric references may not be matched by such material matters as financial support or integration into the community. On both the L and I sides it becomes dangerously easy to say both that there is and is not a feud between the two. Who could dispute either claim; the statements are monologues.

In the monologue there are no questions, no counterpoints. There is neither reframing of the issue nor disputing the framing that has been provided by the author. In the ALISE program that describes the session in which King presented his paper there is only mention of his argument (which in fact is not an argument), not of any agreement or dissent by the responders to the paper. With both "library" and "information" we have reached a point where there is a no speaker, there is only a hearer; there is no author, there is only a reader. The stances of the two sides obliterate dialogue; we're left with only monologue. The risk of this loss of dialogue is put most eloquently by Mikhail Bakhtin (1986): "Others' words become anonymous and are assimilated (in reworked form, of course); consciousness is monologized. Primary dialogic relations to others' words are also obliterated—they are, as it were, taken in, absorbed into assimilated others' words. . . . Monologized creative consciousness frequently joins and personifies others' words, others' voices that have become anonymous, in special symbols" (p. 163). "Information" and "library" could become such self-sustaining symbols. So here's the crux of the matter; there will be only barbs thrown, only jabs exchanged, as long as monologic communication reigns. So what it the alternative?

So far there has been primarily a series of statements made about information and/or libraries in formal publications and at conferences. What has been missing is a kind of communicative action guided by principles of phenomenology. Of particular importance are the phenomenological tenets regarding being (each of us encompasses not merely ourselves as individuals but the world we contribute to and contributes to us), the relationship of self and other (every person is an "I" [as in ego, not information], a consciousness, and it is the responsibility of each of us to recognize the other as another "I") and intentionality (our actions, including communicative actions, are shaped by conscious purpose that must account for other phenomenological principles, including being and self-other relations). Bakhtin (1986) again helps us understand this difficult concept: "A human act is a potential text and can be understood (as a human act and not a physical action) only in the dialogic context of its time (as a rejoinder, as a semantic position, as a system of motives)" (p. 107). He expands on the responsibility that is connected to dialogue: "To understand an object is to understand my ought in relation to it (the attitude or position I ought to take in relation to it), that is, to understand it in relation to me myself in once-occurrent Being-as-event, and that presupposes my answerable participation, and not an abstracting from myself" (Bakhtin, 1993, p. 18).

Bakhtin sets the stage for a certain kind of communication, what Jürgen Habermas calls discourse ethics. Habermas sets his theory of discourse ethics within the context of a democracy; such a situating carries the connotation that communication is a political act with a political purpose, and that there is a specific political ideal that guides the act. If someone rejects the initial democratic ideal (explicitly or implicitly), then that person is not likely to adhere to discourse ethics. Habermas (1993) makes the democratic requirement of this communicative action very clear: "Every justified truth claim advocated by someone must be capable of being defended with reasons against the objections of possible opponents and must ultimately be able to command the rationally motivated agreement of the community of interpreters as a whole. Here an appeal to some particular community of interpreters will not suffice" (p. 53). His last sentence may be the most important; it is not sufficient to garner support from interested allies (their support may or may not have anything to do with the defense of reason). It is imperative that a claim be able to be tested on its own to earn support from those who have divergent material interests. This is a stringent and taxing requirement; it necessarily entails accepting a phenomenological recognition of being and the self-other relation. In a variety of conceptions from Husserl through Heidegger to Habermas the existence of a shared lifeworld is central. The sharing includes the purpose for beliefs and actions (outcomes that can be identified by everyone), a uniting self-clarification (communication constantly aimed at making the purpose clear—cognitively and ethically—for everyone), and comprehensibility (understanding wrought from discourse through which each individual becomes aware of the other's practices that put the purpose into action in their own lives).

What we have so far is a difficult and demanding context for open communication, open especially in the sense that individual interest is intentionally subverted both by the communication process and by the will of each participant. This requirement sets the stage for the discourse. Whereas Foucault approaches discourse descriptively through his archaeology and genealogy, Habermas approaches discourse normatively, through a democratically based ethics. So here we transcend the archaeology, the description, of Chapter 1, to a norms-directed state that aims to temper power with phenomenological ethics. Within this framework there is the potential for a genuine conversation—one in which I and L are placed to the side so that an open discussion can take place. A principal aim of the conversation is a much-enhanced understanding of the concerns of all. As Bakhtin (1986) says, "a subject as such cannot be perceived and studied as a thing, for as a subject it cannot, while remaining a subject, become voiceless, and, consequently, cognition of it can only be dialogic" (p. 161). Perhaps more to the point, the conversation should be

> concerned with the categorically different question of the norms accord-
> ing to which we want to live together and of how practical conflicts can
> be settled in the common interest of all. The peculiarly moral problematic
> detaches itself from the egocentric . . . perspective of each individual's (our
> own) way of life and demands that interpersonal conflicts be judged from
> the standpoint of what all could will in common. (Habermas, 1993, p. 24)

Purpose, place, object, method, identity. The discourse-ethical conversation needs to address all of these. If political positioning is important to some discussants, then that concern will inevitably be part of the conversation as what Habermas calls a pragmatic presupposition. The political positioning can include securing more external funding for research and development; it can include locating libraries and information services as public goods, overcoming any potential tragedy of the commons. It is essential to add those presuppositions to the mix of ethical values that shape the conversation. From that initial vantage point the conversation must proceed along lines guided by rational argumentation that invited and welcomes questioning and dissent. The obstacles to be overcome if a discourse-ethical conversation is to occur are formidable. For one thing, rationality is hard. It is cognitively, psychologically, politically, and personally demanding in that it imposes stringent procedural and communicative requirements that may be met fully only in an ideal world. The solution, then, is to hold the goal of rationality in mind as we make explicit "whys"—why we believe what we do, why we say what we do, and why we do *not* acknowledge alternatives. Another obstacle is ideology, defined here as Andrew Levine (2004) does: "a body of doctrine, more or less comprehensive, that, deliberately or not, systematically serves particular interests at the same time that it purports to represent the world as it really is or, what is often equivalent, to articulate values from a standpoint beyond particular interests" (p. 6). Again, the ideologies held must be made as explicit as possible, with honest reasons given for adhering to the ideologies. Of course, if we set realizing the ideal as our goal we are likely to fail. If we hold the ideal, however, as a guide for speaking, listening, and acting, then we just might be on to something.

The identity of librarianship as a profession is certainly an issue that can and should be discussed in many forums. Purpose should never be taken for granted; it should be reflected upon continuously. An ecological approach will, quite possibly, lead to some distinctions relating to operation, but there are common grounds that surpass environmental differences. The hallmarks of education for professions provide some tips for discovering the common ground and well as the differences. Perhaps the aspect of purpose that is least likely to be disputed is the goal of informing members of communities. This aspect strikes at the heart of a realization that libraries and librarianship have an external focus. There remains a challenge, though; what does it mean to inform someone; what does it mean to be informed? This challenge will be faced in the next chapter.

CHAPTER 3

Being Informed about Informing

"INFORMATION" IS AT ONCE a powerful and a powerless word in librarianship and in the world in general. Both in the work of librarianship and in education for the profession information is a valorized term, suggesting object and purpose. It is used in many contexts that attach it to politically and rhetorically influential ideas and practices. It is the focus of some federal legislation in the United States—sometimes with the aim of increasing people's ability to have access to it, usually through emerging technologies, and sometimes with the aim of limiting access to certain forms of it, especially by children. Information is deemed essential to commerce and strategies in the business world. It is almost in itself a currency in that fund transactions frequently entail no exchange of physical money. Information is vital to global military policy and action. "Information" also lacks power in that it is something of a transcendental concept. The word is used to mean so many things that, while it is not meaningless, it can be a source of confusion. What does it mean to be living in an information society (to be addressed in detail later)? How does an information economy function and who participates? In what ways does information technology inform? Can a genome be reduced to information? What this chapter will focus on is not so much "information" in the above uses, but the processes and acts of informing and becoming informed. Becoming informed—that is, finding meaning in (primarily) human communication—does depend on linguistic, semiotic, systemic, and epistemic structures. So "information" cannot be dismissed.

Michael Buckland (1991) distinguishes among three ways of conceiving information. He refers to:

1. Information-as-process. What someone knows is changed when he or she is informed. . . .
2. Information-as-knowledge. Information is also used to denote that which is imparted in information-as-process. . . . The notion of information as that which reduces uncertainty could be viewed as a special case of information-as-knowledge. Sometimes information increases uncertainty.
3. Information-as-thing. The term information is also used attributively for objects, such as data and documents, that are referred to as information because they are regarded as being informative. (pp. 3–4)

We can envision some specific ways, not only of thinking about but also putting into action these three views of information. We can't ignore information as object, even though it does (as the above illustrates) present some profound challenges. If we accept Marshall McLuhan's dictum that the medium is the message, then we realize that the physical or virtual object is apprehended in certain ways. Including semiotics in our study helps us to understand that if signifiers (the image and its presentation) are different, then so too may be the signifieds (the concepts or ideas). Semiotics, as was mentioned in the last chapter, focuses primarily on the pragmatic aspects of communication. The signifier is a particular physical (written) or acoustical (spoken) thing; the signified is the idea that is connected to that thing. So, we have to take the "thing" very seriously if we are to consider "process" and "knowledge." For example, in some very real ways it is a thing that is retrieved when one searches for information. We can't stop there in our investigation, though. The thing (information) represents. It is intended to convey something through some discursive action. Douglas Raber (2003) explicates this seeming dilemma:

> A potentially informative object may indeed be autonomous in the sense of physically existing apart from our perception or consciousness of its existence. On the other hand, its informative quality depends on the recognition of its informative nature. . . . Another way of describing the categorical duality of information as a theoretical object is to say that information must be a thing, but that is never all it can be. (pp. 93–94)

Technical Conceptions of Information

To digress a bit, World War II provided the context for vast amounts of energy, talent, and resources that were employed in, among other areas, communication. It is tragic that the creativity was employed in the interest of unprecedented destructive force. The bright spot (always dimmed by the constant militarist driving force) is that the initial military application of technological developments could be put to other uses after the war. Brilliant scientists, such as Norbert Wiener and John von Neuman, were engaged in developing the most efficient and effective means of troop and matériel movements, weapons guidance systems, and other purposes. These scientists were building upon the inventive thought of the likes of Charles Babbage (who first designed a programmable computer) from the nineteenth century and Alan Turing (who conceived of machines enabled with artificial intelligence) more recently. After the war their work turned to development of technological aids to all sorts of message transmission and data analysis guided to a considerable extent by Vannevar Bush in his roles as a founder of the National Defense Research Committee and director of the Office of

Scientific Research and Development. In a popular piece, Bush (1945) re-counted the work done during the war presented his idea of a device that would be able to store vast amounts of data and be accompanied by a sophisticated retrieval mechanism. His idea of the "memex," as he dubbed the device, can be taken as a kind of conceptual prototype of the computing we take for granted today. The dilemma that inspired Bush is still with us today. More than six decades ago he wrote,

> There is a growing mountain of research. But there is increased evidence that we are being bogged down today as specialization extends. The investigator is staggered by the findings and conclusions of thousands of other workers—conclusions which he cannot find time to grasp, much less to remember, as they appear. Yet specialization becomes increasingly necessary for progress, and the effort to bridge between disciplines is correspondingly superficial. (www.theatlantic.com/doc/194507/bush)

Much more could be said about the technologies we work with and even the mathematics of message transmission. Claude Shannon's name is frequently invoked when information theory is brought up, but his work has been useful primarily in engineering. Warren Weaver (1949) provided a popularized presentation of Shannon's dense mathematical equations, while still relating the conception of entropy (borrowed from the nineteenth-century physicist Ludwig Boltzmann). In clarifying the principal contribution of information theory—the difference between the technical and the semantic definitions of information—Weaver said that "in this new theory the word information relates not so much to what you *do* say, as to what you *could* say. That is, information is a measure of your freedom of choice when you select a message [emphases in original]" (p. 12). Weaver's employment of "freedom" is an attempt to distinguish information theory from thermodynamics, but an important parallel is apparent. When entropy, or freedom, is high, order is low and there is a systemic price to pay. Entropy in an engine generally means that the system ceases to operate efficiently; freedom in information theory generally means that if too many messages can be selected, efficiency in the communication system is jeopardized. Jeremy Campbell (1982), reproduces Boltzmann's equation for entropy ($S = k\log W$, where S is entropy, k is Boltzmann's constant, and W is the number of possible arrangements of a system). In relating entropy to our current concerns, Campbell says,

> Using Boltzmann's equation . . . the library's S, or entropy, is low if its W, or number of ways in which the books can be arranged on the shelves, is small. When the entropy of the library is at a minimum, with all the books in one unique, prescribed order and all the information needed to find a particular book stored in the catalogue, S has the lowest value. On the other hand, S is high if the number of ways in which the books can be arranged is large, that is to say, if W has a high value. (p. 47)

As Campbell illustrates, the idea of entropy has at least some superficial pertinence to librarianship. By this I mean that the mathematical formulation of entropy demonstrates the impact of order on the organization of information. The purpose of cataloging and indexing, recognized for some centuries, is the creation of some order out of a chaotic state. Fortunately for us, language is not entirely chaotic. Rules of vocabulary, grammar, syntax, morphology, etc. contribute an ordering of English (and most languages). Because of rules, norms, and convention, we may still be able to understand a message, even though a number of words are missing. Redundancy, or the proportion of parts of a message that can be missing and allow us to retain understanding of the message, of English is about 50 percent. This does not mean that half of a specific message could be missing and still be understood, but the 50 percent figure can be taken as a general probability measure of the redundancy of English. Understanding is based on the reality that human communication is intentionally concerned with meaning, with semantics. The order that cataloging and indexing contributes is grounded in formalized semantic structure. Use of the structure is not perfect, but it does ensure that comprehension requires shared definitional meaning. Consider Campbell's example and imagine removing "library" and inserting "Web." The concept of entropy may become clearer.

We will return to information retrieval shortly, but examples from literature may help us grasp the nature of complex messages (that are more than information-as-thing) a bit more firmly. A literary work, we would like to think, is written so that it can be comprehended. Some works test such an idea, and they do so purposely. Some authors create challenges for readers as a way to convey complexities of life, emotions, relationships, death, etc. The challenges are frequently intended to be part of the meaning of the work. James Joyce's *Finnegan's Wake*, for example, is intentionally trying on the reader in the creation of words, the mimicry of sounds, and the simulation of a kind of madness. Other works, such as Julio Cortazar's *Hopscotch*, play with space and time through a construction that insists upon multiple readings with different orders (*Hopscotch* is designed as its name implies; the author directs the reader circuitously through the book by moving the reader from, say, the end of Chapter 3 to the beginning of Chapter 12). Still other works engage us in contemplation of the library as a metaphor for our lives in a complex universe. Perhaps the most famous such literary creation is Jorge Luis Borges's story "The Library of Babel." The Library is comprised of innumerable hexagonal rooms. The books contain every possible combination of symbols, and it is supposed that there is, somewhere in the Library, a book that provides the key to all others. There is a limit to the number of books, but not to the Library. In a cyclical infinitude is found in the Order of the Library, and the hope that there is this Order heartens the author. Borges's Library is borrowed ingeniously by Umberto Eco in *The Name of the Rose*.

I mentioned earlier that the study of information involves, among other things, finding order in complex messages. Literary works present an obvious target for the finding of order. Literary scholars are, in a sense, information scientists whose task is to examine informative texts for meaning(s). Moreover, as we can see, writers sometimes employ the informational opportunity in their works. As John Johnston (1998) demonstrates, some contemporary American novelists have chosen to imbue their literary creation with the very essence of information theory. Johnston and others point to Thomas Pynchon's *The Crying of Lot 49* as a kind of prototype of the informational novel. We can readily accept that creative works of literature present us with interpretive opportunities and problems that are intentionally developed by the authors. In other words, we read, in part, to find meaning. Other texts, however, are also interpretable and offer possibilities of meaning—meaning of the work itself and transferred meaning in our lives. Scientific papers, empirical social science, newspapers, etc. present us with challenges that are similar to those of literary works. These challenges make the study of information both difficult and engaging.

Representation

The stuff of information, as we can see, is contested ground. One approach assumes that information can be described as a physical object (following one of Buckland's categories). This idea approach tends to adopt a fairly narrowly representational idea of information. The language itself—the words, the sentences, the utterances—genuinely represent the world around us *and* the ways we see the world. In this sense information is constitutive of meaning; information literally gives form and shape to the things it refers to so that information *is* the meaning. This idea is not false, but it is incomplete. If our language were not representational in some way, we wouldn't be able to communicate. If the word "tree" were not taken to represent a generic physical object, then someone saying, "There's a big tree," wouldn't be understood by others. The problem with the physicalist/objectivist stance is that it leans toward a notion of absolute representation. I say "leans toward" here because no one is likely to be a pure physicalist/objectivist. A different approach would be to hold that information is regulative (rather than constitutive) of meaning. Information provides mechanisms, normally interpretive ones, which enable us to discern meaning *and* create meaning. In this stance information is a tool we use so that we can understand the world and ourselves. This point of view is not false, but it has limitations. Complex thought, literature, creativity are all enabled by the regulative nature of information. A broader, more useful, idea of information would be to hold that it is constitutive/regulative.

This may seem a bit esoteric; let's see how we can render this idea useful. A first step is to recognize that Buckland's third concept of information (information-as-thing) is useless and counterproductive. If this notion of information defines it as an object, a document, a data set, an image, then there is no reason not to use those terms instead of "information." The history of our field illustrates that, in the past, "document" was also a problematic word. Its use was not limited solely to a physical thing. This kind of documentation was also a relative of categorization. Perhaps the foremost proponent of documentation was Paul Otlet. Bernd Frohmann (2004) succinctly sums up Otlet's conception of the work of the documentalist as realizing the "monographic principle":

> The assumptions of the monographic principle are: (1) there is such a thing as information; (2) it is recognizable in itself, and therefore extractable; (3) its criterion of identity is epistemic; (4) information is most valuable when its boundaries are sharply visible, so that it achieves presence as a unit of knowledge; and (5) information gains value through the work of documentalists, who are trained to recognize units of knowledge and extract them, even from documentary forms such as the book, which threaten to bury them under the subjective and personal padding introduced by their authors. (p. 37)

Frohmann rightly describes Otlet's affinity for a logical positivist (Budd, 2001) approach to information and knowledge, an approach that has been discredited in philosophy and science. This way of thinking about classification has been a powerful one in librarianship because it suggests that there is a discrete answer to any question of aboutness. In the logical positivist tradition of verification of knowledge, aboutness is knowable and extractable. The principal work, then, is akin to epistemological excavation; the failings of this mode of thinking about classification haven't deterred librarians and information scientists from placing great faith in it. The path that Otlet helped set us on is one of presumed value neutrality; documentation digs out meaning and describes it. Knowledge, informing, and becoming informed, however, have value and are valued in pluralistic ways (valued differently by different people and groups); this contradiction must be addressed.

Once the purely physical definition of information is abandoned, the constitutive/regulative nature can be more readily identified. The abandonment of the physicalist definition is by no means a denial of the importance of medium, but it does help us gain a more accurate comprehension of how media affect informing. To return to McLuhan, media do give literal shape to communication. Words on a page, sounds, paintings, films, online chats all give form to what is said and what is seen. Is a description of a work of art inferior to the work itself? In some respects yes, because words can't convey color, shading, depth, brush strokes, etc. in the same way a painting does.

However, the description may provide a way of looking at the painting so that the color, subject, and technique can be appreciated in ways that were not possible before. Films, the Web, all communicate in their own ways and shape communication in their own ways. Therefore, fetishizing the book, the film, or the Web would be equally foolish. A medium enables, it provides a way of communicating that is largely its own, so it can enrich (or impoverish) communicative possibilities and communicative action. At the same time, though, a medium is limited; it is unable to give the form to communication that other media can. So why would we (especially as librarians) want to forsake any medium? When we do not begin with the presumption that information containers (realizing that container is important) themselves define information, and when we focus our attention on what gives shape and form to thoughts and ideas, we may be able to use the word "information" differently.

INFORMATION AND COMMUNICATION

Information theory, information seeking, and information retrieval address communication. Claude Shannon (who, as we've just seen, was an early developer of information theory) worked to solve technical barriers to high-fidelity technical transmission of messages. Some, such as the fiction writers mentioned above, have taken the idea of information theory beyond the technical realm. If we strip the theory down to a fundamental matter, the chief concern is that a receiver of a message understands what the message's sender intended. Certainly a more highly developed technical apparatus can help achieve this goal. More than a clear channel is needed, though. What engineering strove to do was to reduce uncertainty by eliminating noise on a channel. Those who study information from the disciplines of communication, linguistics, sociology, and information science are also, in a variety of ways, concerned with reducing uncertainty. Werner Severin and James Tankard (1979), in writing about communication theories, praise information theory for awakening non-engineering fields to the need for organization and connection of messages and for giving other disciplines a heuristic model that opens more possibilities for the stuff of communication (pp. 43–50).

As one would expect, the literature on communication is voluminous. That literature will not be covered in great depth here; elsewhere I (Budd, 1992) have examined it in some detail. A few key points here will suffice at this time. Shortly after information theory began to be developed fully, Wilbur Schramm (1954) was focusing on the social elements of human communication. One of his points that is vital to a study of information is that both the sender and the receiver of a message have unique fields of experience. Each individual has a linguistic, educational, environmental, and personal past that impinges upon the creation and the reception of messages. In a conversation, for instance, the more the fields of experience of the conversants are similar, the more likely there is to be understanding. Other communication theorists have emphasized that communication (and, by extension, information) is not linear; people, drawing from their various experiences, interpret and re-interpret constantly. Human communication, then, is not merely a series of messages sent and received. Frank Dance (1967) chose the helix as the symbolic model that is most representative, since it is both grounded in the past yet is moving forward within a set of constraints. The nonlinear concept of communication is also vital to any study of information seeking, information use, and human information processing. One more example demonstrates the complexity of human communication. Mickey Smith (1988) has constructed a set of models that illustrate the influence of affective elements (feelings), memory, and cognition. Additionally, memory can be collective as well as individual, and knowledge might be shared among people. Again, the degree of sharing and overlap impinges upon communication success.

Study of communication necessarily transcends the technical aspects of information (in the narrow sense of developing a discrete, noiseless channel). That is to say, any examination of communication encompasses more than how messages are transmitted; it includes *what* is said, *how* it is said, and, perhaps just as important, what is *heard*. An essential point that must be mentioned here is emphasized by Chang (1996, p. 1999). What is said and what is heard (in any form of communication—conversation, reading, etc.) is subject to the dynamics of a specific context. Context is *always* specific; there is no such thing as "context-in-general"; such a term has no meaning, since it signifies a single context, which does not exist, even in the ideal. Any reference transaction is an example of the uniqueness of context. The distinction between the engineering perspective (which is vitally important) and the communication perspective is essential to us as we consider the study of information in our discipline and profession. For the most part, we care about interpretation, understanding, and meaning. Informing, or giving shape to, embraces such considerations. As might be expected, there is a particular challenge inherent in the communicative aspects of information. Orrin Klapp (1982) focuses on the challenge:

> Mere information that is additive, digital, analytical, accumulates easily by being counted or categorized; whereas meaning, being subjective, and referring to synthetic or holistic properties that cannot be reduced to the sum of parts, might be called a higher sort of information that does not come easily, let alone inevitably, from a growing heap of mere information. (p. 58)

As Klapp says (echoing Weaver), an overabundance of information impinges upon a person's ability to discern meaning; the amount of information itself can be a kind of inhibiting noise, even if that information is not random or senseless. So we are left with some tension between communication and meaning.

Communication, of course, is not limited to what is called the dyadic (between two) type; communications in organizations is also an opportunity for the study of information. An organization's mission, goals, and objectives can certainly be stated, for example, but are they accepted (or accepted by everyone)? Day-to-day operations rely on effective communication, but what makes such communication effective? In the private sector (although it has spread to other areas) one effort at creating a communicative environment is knowledge management. As Michael Koenig (2000) describes it, knowledge management is intended to enhance the organization's ability to innovate, create competency (individual and group), to be responsive to client need and to change, and to share both explicit and tacit knowledge among the members of the organization. Organizations may tend to build or adopt technological systems to facilitate acquiring these qualities. Such items are naturally essential to any organization's success, but a study of information and informing can tell us how to go about achieving the goals. Koenig stresses that success depends on "information" being the emphasis in information technology as applied to knowledge management; that is a challenge that might find resistance among some systems designers. This kind of knowledge management is certainly within the purview of librarianship since an objective of our profession is the creation of shared meaning (teacher-pupil, author-reader, researcher-public, or among organizational inhabitants).

Work done by Martin Tanis and Tom Postmes (2003) suggests that while social cues (of the kind that can typify life in an organization) help to individuate people—to identify them as unique individuals—computer-mediated communication (of the kind that may become part of life in an organization) tends to suppress such social cues, thus leading to assuming that individuals embody the characteristics of the group (p. 679). At times, if their suggestion holds, technology may be something of a barrier to the combining of individual and group knowledge. Some students of organizations go even further, stating that communication is necessarily intersubjective. This is to say that people engage in dialogue so as to negotiate what is taken to be meaningful within an organization. Librarianship, employing technology, can enhance dialogic communication by helping to create contexts within which conversations can occur. Anne Cunliffe (2003) writes, "'Good' knowledge is therefore not judged by whether we have built truthful theories, but by whether our statements follow the internal logic of our language community" (pp. 484-85). If this language community were to begin its deliberation with false premises, though, the outcome is likely to be a false conclusion, even if the internal logic is valid. We can see that we must examine communication, as it can have an impact on information, carefully and critically.

The study of informing and becoming informed is made more difficult because the speaker and the hearer are separated by time and space. A conversation could be said to be genuinely dialogic; the hearer can question the speaker directly and the two may be able to negotiate meaning (although imperfectly). Even in conversation, though, turns are taken in speaking, and the gaps in between are instances of interpretation. Discerning meaning, even in a real-time environment, is not definite or assured. In a classic work on communication, Colin Cherry (1978) reminds us, "The writer or speaker does not communicate his thoughts to us; he communicates a representation for carrying out this function, under the severe discipline of using the only materials he has, sound and gesture [and signs]" (p. 75). The negotiation process of the conversation is not possible in many information settings, such as the above example of you searching for relevant information in a database. As we will see later in this chapter, the task of finding "relevant" information is a real challenge. In the information world, we speak of "querying" a database. This kind of querying, while ostensibly conceived as communicating, is different from direct human communication. Patrick de Gramont (1990) offers two observations that are extremely important, both to human communication and the study of information. The first observation pertains to code systems such as language: "a language system communicates meaning based upon the requirements of a set of rules; rules which pertain to the operations of the system, not to the meaning per se" (p. 73). The second observation pertains to an intention, based in pragmatics, that is common to human communication and to information systems: "in order to communicate, we must infer what our respondent knows, in relation to what we would like her (or him) to know" (pp. 76–77).

SEMIOTICS AND LIBRARIANSHIP

For media to have informational utility, communication must be structured; for the constitutive and regulative functions to work, they must rely on the efficacy of codes. Every natural language is a code, and there are other systems of symbols that also are codes. A code is an intentional human production; it is purposely designed to communicate and/or to inform. A code might also be called a sign system. Umberto Eco (1976) says,

> A code is a system of signification, insofar as it couples present entities with absent units. When—on the basis of an underlying rule—something actually presented to the perception of the addressee *stands for* something else, there is *signification*. In this sense the addressee's actual perception and interpretive behavior are not necessary for the definition of a significant

relationship as such; it is enough that the code should foresee an established correspondence between that which *"stands for"* and its correlate, valid for every possible addressee even if no addressee exists or ever will exist. . . . *Every act of communication to or between human beings*—or any other intelligent biological or mechanical apparatus—*presupposes a signification system as its necessary condition.* (pp. 8–9; emphasis in original)

Eco explicitly approaches codes through semiotics—the study of signs and sign systems. A reader might be wondering what semiotics has to do with the study of information. In fact, there are some shared concerns and goals between the two. Certainly semiotics isn't the only framework according to which language can be studied, but it is very useful for examining formal, structured communication.

As has been pointed out, "Both semiotics and information science are concerned with the nature of relations between content and its representation, between signifier and signified, between reference and referent, and between informative objects and their meaning" (Raber and Budd, 2003, p. 507). Semiotics has been addressed in LIS by several writers. For example, as many have observed, information retrieval entails navigation through a sign system. Suppose you are looking for information on a particular topic, and you turn to some electronically available resource in an effort to find relevant information. You may begin by entering a subject term (realizing that, somehow, that subject term has been attached to some documents). The subject term, in semiotics, could be called a signifier, which is a component of a sign. The signifier is a sound, an image, or a word or term that is intended to refer to a concept or an idea (signified). In the mid-twentieth century the correspondence between signifier and signified was used by the Structuralist school. Some adherents of this school of thought sought underlying or covering laws that could be explained by structural systems. Later, semiotics was distanced from structuralism by language scholars who attempted to understand efforts to obscure as well as to communicate clearly. The connection between signifier and dignified is very seldom a one-to-one correspondence; a word does not always mean one thing, and one thing only, to everyone (Raber, 2003). "Democracy," for instance, can be attached to a variety of concepts. As a signifier, "democracy" doesn't have a single, consistently used, and agreed-upon signified. I'll emphasize here that this kind of loose coupling between signifier and signified is extremely problematic, as latter-day semioticians have pointed out. Understanding and meaning are complicated because signs can be combined in an almost infinite number of ways. The possibilities are constrained primarily by our desire to communicate effectively, to ensure that others understand what we intend.

"Information," both in our field and in general, presents the same kind of problem that "democracy" does. As a signifier, what is its signified? In information theory the signified is clear—freedom of choice, or entropy. In popular usage the signified may be the opposite of what it is in Information Theory—meaning. Buckland offers three broad signifieds. Later in the chapter we'll see even more possible signifieds for "information," each of which is the basis for research in a variety of programs in the areas of information seeking and information retrieval. Consider this question: If "information" has multiple meanings (signifieds), how do we incorporate existing research into professional challenges related to provision of services to our communities? In short, if librarianship is an information profession, what does that mean? It becomes incumbent upon us to examine very closely the particular meaning of "information" in any project; the results of the work are meaningless without definition. Further, in the absence of explicit definition we must infer an operational definition that is embedded in the research before we adopt the results. There is a term we can apply to the dilemma just described: if "information" doesn't have an agreed-upon meaning, but rather has multiple and mutable meanings (signifieds), then "information" is a "floating signifier." It is attached to nothing fixed or consistent. Instead of relating to meaning, "information" is a rhetorical device plugged into research, professional speech, or popular usage for specific persuasive purposes.

It should be noted that "sign" is not as simple a word as it may first seem. A number of different theorists have offered differing definitions of the word, as well as applications of it in their analyses of language. Eco (1984) suggests a feature of the sign that is extremely important for the study of information. He says that "the sign is also revelatory of a contact, in a way which tells us something about the shape of the imprinter" (p. 15). Eco is hinting at an application of signs that is developed further by Robert Hodge and Gunther Kress (1988). They emphasize the need for semiotics to recognize "the complex interrelations of semiotic systems in social practice, all of the factors which provide their motivation, their origins and destinations, their form and substance" (p. 1). To be taken seriously, the study of information should follow the caveat Eco states:

> A general semiotics studies the whole of the human signifying activity—languages—and languages are what constitutes human beings as such, that is, as semiotic animals. It studies and describes languages through languages. By studying the human signifying activity it influences its course. A general semiotics transforms, for the very fact of its theoretical claim, its own object. (p. 12)

In the parlance of semiotics, information study involves the examination of *langue* (language) as a means to deep investigation of *parole* (speech). In other words, we study what it is *possible* to say in order to study what *is* said. In librarianship we study what *may* be asked/needed so that we can design services, collections, and access to respond to what *is* asked/needed.

CATEGORIZING INFORMATION

We have seen that as far back as the Alexandrian library there was some classification of content. That library was intended for use, so a usable organization was devised to facilitate the work of scholars. Much later, Gabriel Naudé (who, among other things, served as Cardinal Mazarin's librarian in seventeenth-century France) endeavored to improve upon ways of categorizing books based on their contents. It shouldn't surprise us that there have been such efforts; we humans attempt to categorize everything around us, in part to enhance our functioning of the world. Efforts aimed at categorizing knowledge date back at least to Francis Bacon. Thomas Hobbes also proposed a categorization of knowledge in his *Leviathan*. The eighteenth-century French encyclopedists tried to create an exhaustive set of connections among what exists and what can be known. Auguste Comte sought to revise the hierarchy of disciplines in the nineteenth century. This is a thumbnail sketch of categorizations of the past; Francis Miksa (1998) fleshes out the background efforts to classify knowledge. A fundamental similarity among the categorizations is assuming that bits of knowledge, living creatures, and so on, can be categorized discretely; that a category contains these things, and only those things, that share a necessary and sufficient set of characteristics. So what about the platypus? In academic terms, what about biochemistry or, to pick an even more diffuse field, cultural studies? Categorization, in some important ways, stems from semiotics (even before "semiotics" was itself a signifier).

Categorization is a dicey matter. Categories don't simply include; they also exclude. Elaine Svenonius (2000), who has studied and taught cataloging and classification for a number of years, claims that "Organizing information if it means nothing else means bringing all the same information together" (p. 10). It's very difficult to dispute her proposition, but it does hinge on what "same" means. This isn't a quibble; there are practical challenges to identifying "sameness" in documents and them describing those documents in terms of *how* they are the same. This organization naturally has its up and its down side. When it comes to information it is very helpful to be able to distinguish the contents of one item (book, article, Web site, etc.) from another. For some needs the fine distinctions can save time and facilitate work. For other needs one may want to identify everything that people have said on a topic, even if they mentioned it in passing. In either case there is a problem for categorization. Is it possible to devise a *system* of classification that is not objective (in the physicalist sense used above)? Bernd Frohmann (2004) articulates (and then critiques) the received view in our field: "For information studies, the most important feature of the abstract idea of information, and the assumption underlying the hunt for the principal channel of scientific communication, is the conception of information as a particular kind of substance that can be indifferently conveyed through different channels" (p. 8). According to this model, "information" is a thing that can be represented semantically and/or semiotically. The contents of a book can be described by means of subject headings or descriptors, or by means of a code that emerges from a classification scheme.

The kinds of hierarchical categorizations that Bacon, Hobbes, Comte, and others have proposed fit the representational model that Frohmann speaks of. In the semiotic sense, a call number is a signifier and a book is the signified. To be more explicit, to "say" Q175.F76 is to "represent" Frohmann's book. On the face of it, this system is ingenious (and in fact it is a remarkable achievement that is certainly superior to no classification at all). So the system should work every time, right? That is, if one were to browse the shelves of a library one would find, conveniently co-located, all works on a topic. True, Frohmann's book is about science studies, but that's not all it's about. The first two subjects listed in the Cataloging in Publication for the book are "documentation" and "information science." Is there a good reason why the book is classified in "Q" instead of "Z?" Is there a reason it's classified in one way and not in both (apart from the need to give a physical item a physical location)? In actuality Frohmann's book is a critique of documentation and information science; can classification handle such a situation? Svenonius (2000) offers one way to indicate that professionals in our field are conscious of categorization: "Our brains are hard-wired to perceive hierarchical relationships, and, consequently, the only way to comprehend a knowledge domain is through the structure they provide" (p. 163). If she is correct, then the ideal classification scheme is achievable, since all brains operate in the same materialist way. To the extent that librarians share her perception, there may arise some questions related to categorization and cognition. Her assumption has to be addressed in any examination of informing and knowing.

The representational model, mentioned previously and demonstrated by Svenonius, usually assumes what John Searle (2001) calls a word-to-world fit. The world simply *is* and our task is to select the word (or term) that describes the world as it is. Reality (the world) exists independently of ourselves, so any aspect of reality can, effectively, be named. Extending Searle's concept, a book, for example, embodies reality, so categorization can match or fit the book's contents. Our professional challenge is to select the word or term that has an unequivocal and unambiguous link to the reality of the book. If we did not adhere to some version of realist representation, we would have no subject description or classification. I'll admit that I'm a realist, though not a realist in a strong sense. When we believe something or propose something we can then test that belief or proposition; that is, we can say it is true or false—to an extent. While we can test beliefs or propositions, though, some of them are so complex that we can't easily arrive at an assessment of their truth or falsity. Our conclusions may be provisional because our knowledge is fallible and corrigible; it is based on the best assessment available to us at the moment (for instance, in the case of scientific knowledge) and in time it can be corrected as better assessment mechanisms become available. So we categorize the contents of documents as best we can under the system's constraints of workability. In the days of the card catalog we had to limit the number of subject headings because buildings had limited physical space. The more cards, the more catalog units would be needed and the more floor space the catalog would occupy. This physical constraint no longer applies, although others do (imagine the challenge presented to an information seeker of a book with a hundred subject headings).

Theorists of categorization in librarianship, such as Paul Otlet and Henry Bliss (to follow part of our previous discussion), went along (whether by necessity or not) with what George Lakoff (1987) refers to as classical categorization: "All the entities that have given a property or collection of properties in common to form a category. Such properties are necessary and sufficient to define the category. All categories are of this kind" (p. 161). That position may be accompanied by the metaphysical stance of essentialism: "Among the properties that things have, some are essential; that is, they are those properties that make the thing what it is, and without which it would not be that kind of thing. Other properties are accidental—that is, they are properties that things happen to have, not properties that capture the essence of the thing" (Lakoff, 1987, p. 161). A strong version of classical categorization and essentialism imposes artificial order on nature, knowledge, and speech under a delusional guise that all properties are definable and immutable. For example, when the ideas that form the contents of a book are extremely diverse and almost polymathic, how would we identify the essential properties of the contents? Moreover, the strong version presumes that our minds and our language are vehicles for understanding and describing the world as it is, and not in any sense an imposition or creation of order and description. A weak version adopts a middle ground; there is a reality external to ourselves, but our minds and our language are only partially referential. That is, we have a limited capability of apprehending and naming that reality. To borrow from Hans-Georg Gadamer (1989), a document's contents are objective (they exist in a form and a place), but interpretation of the contents is a mixture of the objective and the subjective; it is open to possibilities.

There is one point that classification theorists tend not to discuss, and is the title of the previous chapter—does it matter where we are? By that I mean to ask whether the environment, kinds of information provided, and communities of users make a difference in the ways we classify and describe. Several years ago I visited a departmental library on a large university campus. The focus of the library's collection was the subject of archaeology. The subject card catalog (that may date the visit) was about thirty-six drawers; the first couple of drawers contained the very beginning of the alphabet and the last few drawers contained the majority of the alphabet. Everything else was devoted to "Archaeology." As an access mechanism this catalog was a failure, and browsing stacks was not much of an improvement, since the vast majority of the materials fell within a narrow range of the Library of Congress classification schedule. On the other hand, how fine should distinctions be in a small public library? Will divisions into "Fiction," "Biography," "History," and the like suffice? It seems evident that the environment does matter and that general systems best serve the (large) middle ground of libraries between very small and very large libraries. When there are a fair number of subject areas included and a substantial number of items, these systems are useful. For the extremes—extremely small, extremely large, extremely narrow—they are less useful. Enhancements to library catalogs, like keyword searching, tables of contents, etc., have been purposely designed to complement the strengths of classification and description systems *and* to add ways of searching and browsing that can be amenable to the extreme circumstances.

Categorization is both essential and dangerous. Classification and description of content are necessary because they are effective. They enhance access to content, and they do so because some level of representation of the content of information carriers (texts, images, sounds, etc.) is possible with reasonable fidelity. That is, the categories do, at least to some extent, describe the things categorized—not fully and completely, of course, but partially. Some may argue that description is impossible and shouldn't be undertaken; I would counter with a weak realist argument. There are things, even linguistic and intellective things, that do exist and do have definable characteristics; these can be categorized. Classification and description are, however, contingent successes. In order to be effective, they require that information seekers have some background knowledge and a foundational linguistic apparatus. As Birger Hjörland (1997) has eloquently stated, "Subjects in themselves— the objects of subject analysis—must thus be defined as the informative potentials of documents (or of other messages or information sources). . . . A potential is a rather intangible property—hence the problem with defining subjects" (p. 86). Classification and description are tools of our profession that are genuinely effective, but not absolutely effective. They should, then, be used by professionals for the purposes they suit, subject to the judgment of professionals. It is the judgment—the reflective judgment—that both sets our profession apart from others and forms the basis of our principal responsibility. It is a responsibility that carries awareness of the danger of categorization; as professionals we must understand that classifying thoughts, ideas, pictures, and so on is an undertaking that is measured by its possibilities. Not all possibilities or potentialities can be fulfilled for any number of reasons (too many possibilities in some cases, lack of awareness of all possibilities, conflicting possibilities). The flip side is that no attempt to embrace some of the possibilities, some of the potential, leads to chaos; our profession seeks the middle ground. Cataloging and classification, rather than being entirely representative of an item's content, model that content. A model is a partial representation of something complex; as such, it is useful to a point, but the entire thing (say, a book) is not represented.

The juxtaposition of information and communication is instructive in many ways, not the least of which is the illustration of the problems of meaning and understanding. It may be natural for us to want to resolve the problems once and for all, but the complexities of language stymie us. Wittgenstein's (1990 [1922]) assessment of language sums up some of the difficulties inherent in communication:

> Colloquial language is a part of the human organism and is not less complicated than it.
>
> From it it is not humanly possible to gather immediately the logic of language.
>
> Language disguises thought; so that from the external form of the clothes one cannot infer the form of the thought they clothe, because the external form of the clothes is constructed with quite another object than to let the form of the body be recognized.
>
> The silent adjustments to understand colloquial language are enormously complicated. (p. 63)

THINKING ABOUT INFORMATION

Transcending the conception of information-as-thing opens up many possibilities for study. It will be impossible to cover all of the possibilities here (it would probably be impossible to cover them all in a book), but we can touch on some important work. Beginning to think about information as process requires a substantive shift—from a physicalist point of view (information is not merely an object, manipulable in the same ways other physical objects are) to a phenomenological point of view (information depends on the intentions of message senders and the perceptions of message receivers). Information theory, as described above, is not capable of accounting for the intentional, perceptual, and interpretive phenomena of information. The most recent couple of decades have opened up the study of information to embrace the complex social, epistemic, and cognitive elements of informing. Of course such thinking dates back further, but recent work has been much more involved in aspects other than the physical. A considerable amount of the present work builds on the groundbreaking thought of Tefko Saracevic, Nicholas Belkin, Brenda Dervin, Carol Kuhlthau, and others. Their work is extremely valuable, but not without difficulties.

One effort to focus on the user rather than the object in thinking about information is what has been called the "cognitive viewpoint" in information studies. Two excellent and thorough reviews of cognitive inquiry provide a background on the cognitive viewpoint (Allen, 1991; Ingwersen and Williams, 2001). As Ingwersen points out, cognitive study of information can be divided into what amounts to two eras. Some early work in the first period by Robert Taylor (1968) addresses the negotiation process into which an information seeker enters with any information system. The negotiation is a difficult process because information need may exist at several levels with several corresponding strategies for negotiation. As might be expected from this conceptual model, there are stages of negotiation that affect the seeker's query and the means of satisfying the query. Belkin and others (1982) extended Taylor's conceptual model in the development of a target metaphor they called "Anomalous States of Knowledge" (ASK). One intention behind the employment of this metaphor was the illustration of the dynamic nature of any human information interchange. Raber (2003) helps us understand the aim of the ASK approach:

> A crucial assumption here is that truly useful information search outcomes depend on posing queries that best represent a user's problem and the needs associated with that problem. The goal is to help the user as a better question. The model of the user's anomalous state of knowledge can then be classified, essentially by a measure of the extent to which the concepts comprising it are coherently integrated and related. (p. 169)

A representational assumption does enable us, in some ways, to envision how people think about ways of becoming informed. People do engage in some representational behavior as they attempt to convert thoughts into the pragmatic language of catalogs, indexes, and databases. Raber depicts some of the most serious shortcomings of a pure, or perhaps we should say strong, representational program. The ASK model depends heavily not only on a searcher's ability to represent thought in a specific language structure, but on the initial assumption that complex thoughts equate to "states" of knowledge (even if anomalous ones). In many ways the work of Belkin and others is a valuable effort aimed at comprehending the extremely difficult process of transforming thought into a structured search. Their work, though, is limited by the cognitive viewpoint's creation of an idea of information that is not able to admit to a richer—probably more phenomenological, hermeneutic, and constructive epistemological—approach to humans' apprehension and creation of meaning. This last sentence inserts some terminology that may obfuscate rather than clarify, but it is terminology that many outside librarianship will relate to. The cognitive viewpoint begins with notions of information and searching that posit a very ordered structure for knowledge, not unlike Otlet's conception. Knowledge—and information—is material; it has form and is discrete. As such, it can be parsed into its component parts. Information is similarly structured, and can be similarly parsed; the key is to identify the proper language that should be used in a search. Wittgenstein (1958) described an alternative to the cognitive viewpoint faulty starting point: "Every sign *by itself* is dead. *What* gives it life?—In use it is *alive*. Is life breathed into it there?—Or is the *use* its life" (p. 128; emphasis in original). The use introduces interpretation (hermeneutics) and the construction of meaning. It also introduces the realization that knowledge, information, and searching are not solitary acts, but are undertaken in a communicative relationship with another creator of knowledge and information. Information seeking and retrieval is, in short, dialogic.

The second period of cognitive inquiry, according to Ingwersen and Williams (2001) is marked by recognition of the holistic melding of the totality of interactive communication and the processes of information retrieval and use that he spoke of. One feature of the second period is an expansion of the concept of representation. Rather than limit representation to topicality of the text itself, representation is both an aspect of the text and an imposition or uncovering by the reader/information seeker. The first element is problematic enough; it entails examination of the language of the text and the development of some individual definitions of terms. The second element is even more problematic; it depends upon an individual's vocabulary, disposition, and state, plus social imperatives (cultural, political, educational, economic) that influence perceived representation. Ingwersen (2002) proposed four categories of "aboutness" that influence the representation of documents:

1. Author aboutness, i.e., the contents as is;
2. Indexer aboutness, i.e., the interpretation of contents (subject matter) with a purpose;
3. Request aboutness, i.e., the user or intermediary interpretation or understanding of the information need as represented by the request;
4. Use aboutness, i.e., user interpretation of objects, e.g., as relevance feedback during interactive IR or the use of information and giving credit in the form of references. (p. 289)

There are still some inherent challenges in the more developed cognitive viewpoint, even though it must be recognized that the viewpoint *is* maturing. Ingwersen's four categories of aboutness do take into account contextual forces influencing indexing, for example, and he constructs a model that attempts to illustrate interaction among the categories, but there remains a vestige of the objectivist paradigm—objective analysis of the phenomenon. Each of the four categories of aboutness actually necessitates processes of interpretation, either a priori or a posteriori. The interpretive actions render prediction extremely difficult. Raber (2003) points out a particular element of interpretation:

> Interpretation is an act of negotiation. My need for information may be grounded in my experience, but it emerges from a negotiation I must

conduct with reality. I cannot will reality to conform to my wishes. And while my articulation of my information needs may be an outcome of an anomalous state of knowledge, the anomaly itself originates in a pre-cognitive source located in my affective responses to and my relations with the world. (p. 199)

To counter the objectivist paradigm, Birger Hjørland (1998) offers the following: "a theory about subject analysis must be very important. . . . I define the subject of a document (or of any message or sign for that matter) as the epistemological potentialities of the document" (p. 610).

Information Retrieval

Let's return to the term "information retrieval." Some place it within the context of a larger category—information behavior. Tom Wilson (1999), for example, offers a nested model in which information searching behavior (what is frequently meant by information retrieval) is a subset of information-seeking behavior, which is itself subsumed by information behavior. An information search implies that an individual has formulated not just a question, but a strategy for trying to find answers to the question. Information seeking assumes that the information may be at the stage of question identification, but no further. Information behavior is more general yet; the individual may be open to being informed but is practically and epistemically at a stage where the question cannot even be formulated with any degree of certainty yet. As Wilson says, there can be, and is likely to be, uncertainty at all stages. The uncertainty will have to be resolved to some extent for the individual to move on to another stage. If we call the entire process information retrieval here, we can examine some of the complex elements of the process and their implications for mediation services.

Examination of information retrieval, and the practice of mediation, has necessarily altered and grown over time. At one time they were fixed more in the information-as-thing stage, where, as Brenda Dervin (1977) observed, information was taken to exist independent of our perception of it, that information functions to inherently reduce uncertainty, and information naturally has an order that can be manipulated. Her own work, grounded in her background in communications, has sought alternatives to that prior state of information retrieval. She (1983) stated, "it is assumed that the individual is a sensemaker by mandate of the human condition" (p. 169). This idea of the person as the locus of intentionally regarding information is meant to counter two assumptions: "one is that information can be treated like a brick; the other is that people can be treated like empty baskets into which bricks are thrown" (p. 160). Central to a user-centered approach to information retrieval is a rejection of the reification of information that Dervin speaks of. Alfred Schutz (1967) explained how such reification comes about and what it means:

> I leave out of my awareness the intentional operations of my consciousness within which their meanings have already been constituted. At such times I have before me a world of real and ideal objects, and I can assert that this world is meaningful not only for me but for you, for us, and for every one. This is precisely because I am attending not to those acts of consciousness which once gave them meaning but because I already presuppose, as given without question, a series of highly complex meaning-contents. The meaning structure thus abstracted from its genesis is something that I can regard as having an objective meaning, as being meaningful in itself. (p. 36)

Dervin's work has had a strong influence on Carol Kuhlthau, who has focused primarily on information seeking as a way of seeking meaning. Kuhlthau (1993) admits some shortcomings in previous information retrieval work: "The traditional approach is limited to the task of locating sources of information but does not take into account the tasks of interpreting, formulating, and learning in the process of information seeking" (p. 168). In much of her work she has presented information seeking as a process involving a series of steps—initiation, selection, exploration, formulation, collection, and presentation. She has adhered to this process while introducing some new, she (1999) has explicitly acknowledged that the seeker constructs interpretive strategies and employs the strategies in ways that render the process less linear. The kinds of struggles regarding information retrieval described here are specific examples of disputes played out in a larger environment. Lewis Gaddis (2002) offers an anecdote that illustrates the objectivist bent of many social scientists, as opposed to alternative practical and epistemological actions. He had organized a conference attended by scholars from many disciplines, and asked historian William McNeil to explain the method he uses to do history. McNeill stated that he did not employ a formal method; he would explore and read, redefine the question, explore and read some more, reshape the problem, and continue that process until he would write it up and send it to a publisher. Social scientists in the audience complained that McNeil was not being methodologically sound and that he confused induction and deduction. Someone from the back of the room interjected, "That's exactly how we do physics" (Gaddis, 2002, p. 48). If the physicist is representative of his field, then natural scientists may not even accept the objectivist paradigm.

RELEVANCE

Within the study of information retrieval (perhaps central to it) is the idea of relevance. Much of the study of information boils down to grasping the complexity of relevance. In the physicalist or objectivist paradigm there is a presumption, sometimes implicit, that relevance inheres in the document itself. This presumption is at the heart of two measures that have been persistent, but are employed much less frequently now—recall and precision. Recall is defined as the number of relevant documents retrieved in a search, divided by the total number of relevant documents in the database. Suppose a searcher retrieves 100 relevant documents and there are 1,000 relevant documents in the database; the recall measure would be 10 percent. We might say that recall is an attempt to assess the *effectiveness* of the search. Precision is defined as the number of relevant documents retrieved, divided by the total number of documents retrieved. Suppose the searcher retrieves 100 documents and 50 of them are relevant; the precision measure would be 50 percent. For this measure we might say that precision is an attempt to assess the *efficiency* of a search. There is frequently a related pair of questions that go unasked in the application of these measures: What constitutes a relevant document, and who determines a document's relevance? In early experiments on information retrieval the questions were, operationally, answered by internal means; that is, relevance was deemed to be an objective attribute, so the answers could be determined without considering the searchers.

Stefan Mizzaro (1997) has exhaustively reviewed the literature on the topic of relevance, so there is little need here to delve deeply into all considerations of it. There are, however, some writings that express ideas about relevance that we do have to think about, since relevance genuinely is a foundational concept in our field. I've (Budd, 2004) previously explored relevance as addressed in our own discipline and in other fields, and will extract some of that examination here. In keeping with the objectivist paradigm, the early stage of considering relevance, as Mizzaro notes, adhered to a document- or system-centered focus. In 1971 William S. Cooper described a physicalist assessment of relevance: "A stored sentence is logically relevant to (a representation of) an information need if and only if it is a member of some minimal premises [*sic*] set of stored sentences for some component statement of that need" (p. 24). In other words, an item belongs to a category ("relevant" in this case) if it shares representational qualities with other items in the category. This assessment holds to the extent that information need (the basis for the judgment of relevance) is stable and readily definable. For example, if the need is for the average rainfall in São Paulo, Brazil, and a sentence reads, "The average annual rainfall in São Paulo is 69.4 inches," there is logical relevance. Let's take a more complicated example. Suppose you want to read some alleged refutations of the objectivist paradigm as it is employed in the social sciences. You may find a suitable refutation for your purposes that actually inheres in an intended *defense* of the paradigm. The logical relevance of the defense to your needs is not straightforward in Cooper's sense.

In our field the physicalist or objectivist has an answer for this dilemma. Abraham Bookstein (1979) acknowledged human responses to what is retrieved, but he adds a twist. He writes,

> an information retrieval system cannot predict with certainty a patron's reaction to a document, and this, we believe, is the source of many of the uses found in the literature of the term "relevance." Rather, the system transforms both the document and the request into forms it can manipulate, and on the basis of these, it assesses the relevance of the document to the user. (p. 269)

If the system transforms the request, does it, in some way, transform the requestor? Does the structure of an information system shape (inform) the possibilities that a searcher faces and may be constrained by? Bookstein identified relevance as the searcher's satisfaction with the output; satisfaction is a fairly common assessment measure in libraries as well. The reduction by Bookstein simply shifts the problem, though. How easy/possible is it to define "satisfaction" in some normative way? What about the documents retrieved leading to a searcher's satisfaction? How does the searcher himself/herself define satisfaction, and what criteria must be applied so that a satisfaction decision is reached? In short, when I try to find something meaningful, how do I know when I've found it?

Researchers into processes of informing began to recognize the limitations of a purely objectivist way of conceiving relevance some years ago. Linda Schamber, Michael Eisenberg, and Michael Nilan (1990) took a step toward a broader view and reached three conclusions about relevance:

1. Relevance is a multidimensional cognitive concept whose meaning is largely dependent on users' perceptions of information and their own information-need situations.
2. Relevance is a dynamic concept that depends on users' judgments of the quality of relationships between information and information-need at a certain point in time.
3. Relevance is a complex but systematic and measurable concept if approached conceptually and operationally from a user's perspective. (p. 774)

While their work does represent a step forward, there are still some objectivist elements. The three points seem to adhere implicitly to an assumption that relevance decisions constitute rational choices by information seekers. There is a known and defined need and documents or texts are evaluated strictly according to that need. This assumption, especially evident in the third conclusion, embodies something of an externalist view of knowledge; knowledge is grounded outside the knower's mind. Their conclusions about relevance are likewise essentially external; the user assesses the documents for the relevance inherent in them. "Something of an externalist view" should be emphasized; their position is certainly not completely externalist, but something *about* retrieved documents can be assessed by the user. While they are on the path to combining externalism and internalism (knowledge exists only within the knower's mind) effectively, their conclusions fall just short of that goal.

Schamber, Eisenberg, and Nilan paved the way for a more holistic and multidisciplinary investigation of relevance. Stephen Harter (1992) provided another building block by examining cognitive change within information seekers and the impact of such changes on relevance decisions. Let us take a look at a hypothetical scenario that is related to Bookstein's thoughts on transformation. Suppose you are looking for information about information theory. Accepting to Belkin's idea of ASK, also suppose that you are looking for information on this topic because you heard that it is important to our field and you want to find some basic explanation of information theory. You believe the search is quite straightforward, that "information theory" is a discrete term with an explicit meaning. You access a database and enter the term "information theory" as a subject heading. Your search yields fifty hits, fifty citations and abstracts of documents. You read the abstract of the first retrieved document, which speaks of entropy and borrowing from thermodynamics. This seems irrelevant to you, so you do not examine the complete document. The second abstract relates some history of the theory, focusing on Claude Shannon. This seems to be relevant to your query, so you print or copy the full text of the document. The abstract of the third item explains that Shannon was seeking a mathematical formulation of technical message transmission and that he borrowed mathematical concepts from several sources. In light of this third abstract you decide to reassess the first document. How do we account for relevance decisions in this scenario?

A key factor in relevance decisions begins to become clear now. Given our incomplete knowledge of a topic under scrutiny (after all, why else would we seek information about it), we interpret retrieved documents within the context of dynamic frameworks. In the above scenario the first document was interpreted and then reinterpreted in light of a shift in the framework (explication provided by the third document). The framework is complex; it is based in part on what we already know about a topic, what we believe about the topic and its correlates, and how we may theorize about "nonfiction" topics generally. This statement deserves, and probably requires, some elaboration. In many instances we know something about a topic; that is, we have experience (including firsthand inquiry), we have some logical reason to believe it, or we have been told about the topic, and we have grounds for justification of our experience, logical surmise, or information. Given this background, though incomplete, knowledge we delve deeper into the topic in order to extend our knowledge. The "information theory" scenario may be taken as a case in point. In other instances we may believe something about a topic; that is, we may have some experience or information that has not been justified in any strict sense. For example, we may hold a belief about the effects of tax cuts on the economy in general and on our own economic state in particular. This belief may have been formed on the basis of some anecdotal comments by a politician we trust.

Both of these types of frameworks carry implications for relevance judgments. In the case of limited knowledge, additional information that builds directly on what we know is likely to be deemed relevant, since it fits well within the framework. If, on the other hand, a retrieved document contains information that requires, to be understood, knowledge we do not have, we may well judge it as relevant. In the case of belief, an additional anecdotal statement by another trusted source would probably be taken as relevant. However, a contradictory anecdote by a political source from an opposing party might be judged not relevant. This latter framework may exist at a lower level of consciousness than the first framework. Nonetheless, it will affect relevance decisions. It will likely affect what potentially informative texts, images, sounds, etc. that a library provides access to. Things that might be considered variously as facts, research, logic, rumor, speculation, or falsehood are not formally classified as such (and, in all probability, could never be so classified). Relevance, then, is in the eye of the beholder.

The ways we theorize also constitute frameworks within which we evaluate information. Hjørland (2002) demonstrates how some epistemological schemata influence how we assess relevance. The four "schools" he focuses on are empiricism, rationalism, historicism, and pragmatism (he admits that his example is a simplified one, but it does provide an illustration of the effects of our theoretical stances on our actions and decisions). To concentrate on just one schema here for our purposes, let's take his example of empiricism (p. 117). For someone of an empiricist bent (someone who trusts sensory experience, direct observation, certain kinds of data), what is judged to be relevant is likely to fit into that schema. A retrieved document that reports findings based on extensive observations, preferably by multiple observers and displaying agreement among the observers, would probably be evaluated as relevant. Another document reporting on analyses of texts on the given subject, or on perspectives of subjects observed, might well be taken as not relevant. The other schemata rely on different assessments of relevance. Hjørland's principal point is that the schemata people use employ different discursive practices and epistemological standpoints, so representations, such as subject analysis and organization should be sensitive to the differences. The sensitivity can enhance the informative potential of documents and texts.

RELEVANCE FROM OTHER PERSPECTIVES

The multidisciplinary approach to the study of information admits that there is research in other fields that can add to our methods, frameworks,

and knowledge bases. To begin a consideration of thought related to relevance, we can look at the work of Dan Sperber and Deirdre Wilson (1986).
Their approach borrows from cognitive science and attempts to integrate
communication into the idea of relevance. Any assessment of relevance is an
assessment of some communicated utterance. Utterances are much more than
simply sentences; in fact, they are more than sentences strung together. An
utterance is an intentionally created linguistic structure meant to convey semantic representation, but also "to reveal the speaker's attitude to, or relation
to, the thought expressed; in other words, they express 'propositional attitudes',
perform 'speech-acts', or carry 'illocutionary force'" (pp. 10–11). Sperber and
Wilson are immediately including something that is missing from the objectivist idea of information and relevance—the intentionality of the utterance's
creation. A text or document stored in a database had a unique genesis; its
author meant to create something potentially meaningful. To reiterate
Dervin's warning, it is not merely a brick. Sperber and Wilson (1986) emphasize that an utterance has information intention (which comes first and embodies the desire to inform someone of something) and communicative intention (second to the first and embodying the desire to inform someone of
the informational intention) (p. 29).

Since it cannot be denied that a relevance judgment is a psychological phenomenon, an epistemological phenomenon, or both, there can be (usually
will be) some pragmatic goals related to relevance. It may be said that an information seeker wants to maximize relevance, but perhaps it is more accurate to say that an individual tries to optimize relevance (that is, to retrieve
relevant documents at as low a cost as possible). Cost, in terms of relevance,
can be defined in a few ways. Suppose you are searching for information on a
particular topic, and you come across a document that contains material
that is outside your representation of the topic. The document might, for
example, take an economic approach to an issue where you have never
thought about it in terms of economics. The cost to you to assess the document would be high; you would have to shift your thinking on the topic and
perhaps learn more about economics. Suppose further that your task is the
completion of a paper for a course and the deadline is approaching, you may
well decide that the cost of evaluating the relevance of the document is too
high (at least at this time). On the other hand, if you are writing a book on
the topic, your tolerance for cost might be considerably higher. One last possibility here: you do not see the potential gain to your knowledge base and
future work of something you retrieve. It's unlikely that you'll expend any
time or effort to read, interpret, and understand the retrieved work.

Continuing with the pragmatic aspect of Sperber and Wilson's examination of relevance, we should be aware of the foregoing effort-gain assessment
in conjunction with their equal emphasis on context. We might agree on the
basis of their suggestion that relevance is partially defined by its relationship

to a particular context. In the above example, you were asked to place yourself in a situation, and then to think about relevance within that situation. Context—or rather contexts—is generally defined by us as individuals. If you are in the market for a new car, that may signal your context at a point in time, and the context will affect relevance judgments at that time. Sperber and Wilson (1986) address context thusly:

> Relevance to an individual (comparative)
> Extant condition 1: an assumption is relevant to an individual to the extent that the contextual effects achieved when it is optimally processed are large.
> Extant condition 2: an assumption is relevant to an individual to the extent that the effort required to process it optimally is small. (p. 145)

They add a vital, and sometimes only tacitly recognized in LIS, point; context, while sometimes determined at the outset of an information search, can also be a matter of choice. Their (1986) criterion of the determinacy of the context within which relevance is assessed is extremely important to us:

> In much of the pragmatic literature, events are assumed to take place in the following order: first the context is determined, then the interpretation process takes place, then relevance is assessed. In other words, relevance is seen as a variable to be assessed as a function of a predetermined context. However, from a psychological point of view, this is a highly implausible model of comprehension. Humans are not in the business of simply assessing the relevance of new information. They try to process information as productively as possible; that is, they try to obtain form each new item of information as great a contextual effect as possible for as small as possible a processing effort. The assessment of relevance is not the goal of the comprehension process, but only a means to an end, the end being to maximize the relevance of any information being processed. (pp. 141–42)

Let's imagine an instruction program in a school or academic library setting. The students may presume that there are high costs to paying attention and learning how to think about information in ways that can result in cognitive, intellectual, and academic success. If we were to take cost assessment as a simplistic explanation of behavior, we might be inclined to reduce the presumptive cost entailed in the instruction program. Would this be an appropriate educational response? It could be argued that the program could be more effective if students are willing to accept lower costs in time and effort. But is the outcome such that students will actually enhance their success as defined above? In other words, how low can costs become and still enable a program to be of value? Without a doubt, the costs to students can be so high that little or no learning takes place. In part, effectiveness is a matter for pedagogy; that is, the teaching strategies must be designed with costs in mind. Syllabus construction, content, assignments, and teaching methods can be used to reduce costs, even while retaining a demanding program. Pedagogy should be combined with a clear communication of the short- and long-term benefits of the instruction program. For example, one inclusion at the outset of a course or a classroom experience could be emphasis on the probability that what is learned now can save time and effort later.

For the most part, relevance theory does not address any knowledge-or truth-based claims inherent in relevance judgments. In this way, relevance has a decidedly utilitarian property; a document is relevant if it is "useful" to an information seeker. The utilitarian point of view is problematic in a couple of ways. For one thing, there are some internal challenges. "Useful" may not only be affirmative (in agreement with one's already held representations regarding the topic), but may also be negational (refuting one's representations). There may also be some external challenges. Two information sources may espouse diametrically opposed opinions on the topic; what, then, constitutes the utility of the source? In order to address this dilemma, we have to examine an early stage of information seeking. What does an information seeker want as an outcome of the process? This returns us to the idea of context and its application to LIS thought. Let us suppose two variant desired outcomes. Person A wants to fulfill a task; let's say that this task is the retrieval of data on higher education expenditures to be used in a politician's campaign speech. Person B wants to find out if a claim is true; let us say that Person B wants to assess some data on higher education expenditures that has been reported in a particular source. Person B's aim is to write a paper for a professional journal.

Let's extend this example a bit further. Person A comes across a piece at the American Enterprise Institute Web site. It is a reprint of a July 18, 2004, article by Richard Vedder that appeared in the *Los Angeles Times*. Vedder, a distinguished professor of economics at Miami University, in criticizing the rates of tuition increases at U.S. colleges and universities writes, "In 1960, total spending by colleges and universities was equal to 1 percent of the gross domestic product; today it equals 3 percent" (www.aei.org/news/newsID.20941/news_detail.asp). Person A decides these data will fit well into the politician's speech; the piece is relevant in that context. Person B comes across the very same piece at the same Web site. Person B has examined other data about higher education expenditures; for example, Person B is aware that the total U.S. population rose about 57 percent from 1960 to 2000, while the population of students at U.S. colleges and universities rose by about 500 percent during that period. Knowing those figures, the interpretation of Vedder's statement can be very different from that of Person A. To both individuals, Vedder's piece is judged as relevant, but for very different reasons, and those reasons depend upon the desired outcome of the information search. It is obvious that "relevance" is a large and complex matter, and this realization is integral to information retrieval, to which we will now return.

BACK TO LIS

In early LIS work information retrieval was assumed to be an objective act and relevance was taken to be a measurable object that inhered in the document. Later work recognized the assessment and evaluation of documents by the information seeker to determine relevance as part of a complex information seeking process. Some recent work acknowledged the dynamic situational contexts in which possible relevance judgments arise and in which information seeking takes place. Tom Wilson has, over several years, worked through a progressively deepening understanding of the dynamics of information behavior. He (1997) suggested a model intended to illustrate some of the major factors that interact in the process of a person working with information. Although he did not cite Sperber and Wilson, he began his model with a context-based information need (p. 47). The example he used in applying the model was a person needing health information, but the model has more general applicability. This is a very important segment of the model that may be forgotten in both information retrieval work and in information mediation services. The intervening variables he identified include psychological, demographic, role-related and interpersonal, environmental, and source characteristics. All of these variables are part of the context in which people identify information needs, personalize those needs, and go about trying to satisfy them. Suppose an older person is looking for some information about health care. Not to stereotype such an individual, but this person may place implicit trust in what a physician says and may distrust anything or anyone that offers a contrasting view. Further, this individual may not be aware of, or have confidence in, electronically available information on the topic. The intervening variables will affect how the person receives, processes, and uses information.

There could be an almost unimaginable variety of examples that could be examined according to Wilson's model, and it is essential that we comprehend the potential variety. The reasons for the failings of the objectivist paradigm rest mainly in the extreme variability of human factors, plus the number of factors that influence human action. If we take Wilson's intervening variables, we realize how such variables can be manifest in a vast number of ways, and then try to account for the possible permutations among variables, we quickly understand the difficulty of arriving at a predictable probabilistic solution. David Ellis (1996) put his finger on the heart of this problem:

> The goal of attempting to retrieve all and only those documents which are relevant to the searcher becomes not so much a theoretical ideal, unattainable in practice, as an unsustainable construct.... While it is feasible to describe or analyze changes in knowledge in response to new information

qualitatively, to attempt to do the same quantitatively seems to have no tenable theoretical or practical foundation and represents a similar unsustainable research goal. (pp. 33–34)

In short, as Wilson and Ellis demonstrate clearly, the emphasis needs to be on *human* information behavior. This statement may sound like a truism in librarianship, but the challenge to understanding human information behavior for us as librarians is formidable and requires serious consideration.

There is one shortcoming in Wilson's model that some have tried to correct. In addressing information-seeking behavior in particular he distinguished between a passive and an active search. Our discussion thus far has effectively focused on active searching (for many reasons), and we have seen how complex that focus can be. The *human* side of the complexity of active searching is summed up by Bryce Allen (1997):

Personal and social factors constrain individual or group behavior. It is clear from the above discussion that how people behave at any point in their lives is constrained by their individual knowledge levels, abilities, and personal styles. At the same time, behavior is constrained by situational influences. An individual might be able to behave in a certain manner, but will be constrained by the realities of the situation to avoid such behavior. Similarly, a situation might permit several courses of action, but a specific individual might lack the knowledge or abilities necessary to complete one or more of those possible course of action. (p. 119)

Wilson's intention in referring to passive searching can be inferred, but his language is unclear; "passive search" seems to be a contradiction in terms. The inference one might draw is that, while much of the time we actively and intentionally seek information relating to an articulated topic, there are times when we come across information and only then become aware that the information fits an unarticulated need. While "passive search" is an unsatisfactory term, it is an important concept. The need may be unarticulated but it may be genuine. Also, it is not unconscious (or else it might never be satisfied). Such a phenomenon is not easy to define or study, but some people have tackled it, with results we should be aware of.

One important assessment of "passive searching" has been offered by Sanda Erdelez. She suggested the linguistic improvement "information encountering" to capture the apprehension of information through a process we might refer to as "also-conscious." The term can mean that someone actively searching for information on a specific topic can also be conscious of information related to other topics that are not the present target of attention. As she has pointed out, work in science and technology is rife with encountering, as evidenced by the number of discoveries happened upon in the course of engaging in something quite different from the eventual discovery. She has also pointed out that people in several disciplines have been aware that something other then determined and directed information searching can take place. Erdelez (1997) has written,

> The complex nature of human information behavior is only partially explained by the frameworks that emphasize active, specific, and direct searching for information. Information seeking is a crucial method of acquiring information, however, people also find information when they are not seeking any, or are not involved in looking for the particular information that they happen to find. For example, library research for a term paper, a conversation heard on the subway, or an article left at the copy machine may provide unexpected but useful information that was not sought. Such memorable experiences of accidental discovery of useful or interesting information are in this paper called information encountering. (p. 412)

Because information encountering *can* take place does not mean that it always *does* take place. It is dependent on the kinds of variables Wilson identified; there are psychological and demographic differences among individuals, there are environmental factors that may help or hinder encountering, and in addition to this list, there are system-related factors that can affect the possibility and kind of encountering.

Allen Foster and Nigel Ford (2003) have built upon Erdelez's work and have studied the phenomenon of serendipity in information retrieval. They have written,

> In the context of information seeking, "serendipity" is something of a paradoxical concept. While being perceived as valuable, it is at the same time elusive, unpredictable and—at least at first sight—not subject to either the understanding or the resultant control that would enable it to be "used" as a conscious information-seeking strategy. Possibly for this reason serendipity does not figure prominently in current models of information seeking or behaviour. (p. 321)

Browsing, which has been recognized in LIS as a valuable means of finding useful and interesting information, plays a role in serendipity. In their research, Foster and Ford (2003) found that serendipity can be helpful in the development of new ideas by the people finding the information. They summed up their findings:

- Serendipity was widely experienced among inter-disciplinary researchers.
- Serendipity may relate to the impact of new information on the research process (whether or not the information was encountered by chance).
- Serendipity may also relate to the chance encountering of information (whether or not this information had an unexpected impact on the research).

- Certain attitudes and strategic decisions were perceived to be effective in exploiting serendipity when it occurred.
- Perceptions of the extent to which serendipity could be induced were mixed. While it was felt that some element of control could be exercised to attract "chance encounters," there was a perception that such encounters may really be manifestations of the hidden, but logical, influences of information gatekeepers—inherent in, for example, library classification schemes. (pp. 336–37)

How can libraries enhance the possibility of serendipity? The physical space of the library might, itself, be the object of some inquiry; members of the library's community could help identify relatively simple alterations that could make some differences. Direct services for the public may also be revisited.

MEDIATION IN LIBRARIES

Any kind of mediation service in a library or other information agency is closely related to the information retrieval concerns mentioned above. Someone who approaches a librarian or information specialist may have a question or a need, and may want assistance finding an answer. People's reasons for asking questions can vary considerably but one quite consistent feature of the questioning is an imperfect understanding of information sources and their structures. Of course we have already delved into the matter of reference services, but the reiteration of one point is vital. Libraries and other formal information systems are not entirely self-evident, nor can they be. The possibilities, both of information seeking and of content that may be accessible are far too great and too varied for a simple and transparent structure to be created. Also, building on the earlier discussion of reference services in libraries, we can focus on some specific aspects related to retrieval.

Librarians and other practicing information specialists learned some time ago that the mediation process is complex and not necessarily straightforward. It is not that information seekers are deliberately hiding their real questions (although in some sensitive areas they may not be entirely forthcoming), but there are cognitive, linguistic, and other challenges that can make forming a question difficult. As we have just seen, the process of becoming informed is a continuously iterative one. It does not have an easily discernible beginning and end. In fact, we could say that becoming informed, as is true of learning, is always *in medias res*—we are always in the middle of the process. For the purpose here we can limit ourselves to a couple of considerations. We can take for granted that the preceding elements also apply to mediation, so we will not address further such aspects as cognition, with one exception. Some work suggests that librarians, faced with hypothetical questions, tend to think first of resources rather than responding in ways that could help information seekers encounter information more readily and consciously.

The first consideration, touched on above, is the cultural and social element. People seek information from a standpoint. The standpoint, as we can probably see most clearly, contributes to the framing of the question. For example, a person whose present job is threatened may seek information relating to developing skills of a certain type. A person who has concerns about retirement may look for information about investments and financial management. These are fairly obvious examples, but there can be subtlety to cultural and social situations. For one thing, as Elfreda Chatman (2000) has pointed out, social and cultural situations can have embedded norms of behavior and ways of thinking that has been enforced for generations. Further, the worlds of people can be quite small; a prison population is an example of people living in a small world. Chatman emphasizes a few points that are very instructive for us. First, the cultural and social situation of a person, and the norms that go along with that situation, are intersubjective. It is a life lived with others, which is how social norms develop and become accepted. Also, while recognizing individuality, a typology of situations and their may be identified, allowing outsiders (like us) to comprehend the impact of norms on information seeking and use more readily. Chatman (2000) enumerates five propositions that sum up her idea of normative behavior:

PROPOSITION 1

Social norms are standards with which members of a social world comply in order to exhibit desirable expressions of public behaviour.

PROPOSITION 2

Members choose compliance because it allows for a way by which to affirm what is normative for this context at this time.

PROPOSITION 3

World-view is shaped by the normative values that influence how members think about the ways of the world. It is a collective, taken-for-granted attitude that sensitizes members to be responsive to certain events and to ignore others.

PROPOSITION 4

Everyday reality contains a belief that members of a social world do retain attention or interest sufficient enough to influence behaviour. The process of placing persons in ideal categories of lesser or greater quality can be thought of as social typification.

PROPOSITION 5

Human information behaviour is a construct in which to approach every-day reality and its effect on actions to gain or avoid the possession of information. The choice to decide the appropriate course of action is driven by what members' beliefs are necessary to support a normative way of life. (pp. 13–14)

In all geographic locations there will be groups that share normative behavior; understanding of such cultural and social situations can enhance mediation service effectiveness.

A second consideration also concerns the situation of the information seeker, but the situation is not tied to cultural and social norms. The situation is limited, for the most part, to students at all levels (although it can be manifest in the workplace). In particular, this consideration addresses a predicament that students can find themselves in. While much of the information seeking is self-generated (that is, the individual identifies a question or concern and then seeks information related to it), some seeking is the result of another person's initiation. For instance, a teacher may tell a class to look up information on a particular topic. The query by the student is grounded in a certain kind of semantic and psychological complexity. Melissa Gross has examined this phenomenon of the "imposed query," as she has dubbed, in great detail. There are undeniable and considerable challenges to mediation services as a result of the impetus for information seeking coming from someone other than the seeker. There is certainly a common-sense element to the challenge; if someone else initiates the process there can be either a disconnect regarding the meaning of the query or a distancing of the seeker from the query (or both). Gross (1999) has suggested a number of implications of the imposed query for mediation services:

Identify the question by type. Is it self-generated or imposed? If imposed, is it school related . . . ?
  Develop an awareness of beliefs and stereotypes of self and others. . . .
  Develop a professional stance of contextual empathy. . . .
  Recognize the importance of context to all questions. . . .
  Recognize that with imposed queries, right answers are probabilistic. . . .
  Recognize that with imposed queries you may never get true feedback. . . .
  Be cautious about evaluations of reference service that don't take imposed queries into account. (p. 59)

These implications are essential, and mediation services must take them into account to be effective.

We will continue to explore some of the ways we can think about information (as something that can be sought and retrieved, as some that helps define culture, and other ways) in coming chapters, but Jesse Shera deserves a bit of attention here. Over half a century ago he began articulating a new vision for the study of information and libraries. He termed this new vision "social epistemology." Margaret Egan and Shera (1952) sought to initiate a new discipline based on "the study of those processes by which society as a whole seeks to achieve a perceptive or understanding relation to the whole environment—physical, psychological, and intellectual" (p. 132). Later in his career Shera (1972) attempted to clarify his conception of social epistemology. He said it should be "a study of the ways in which society as a whole achieves a perceptive relation to its total environment. It should lift the study of intellectual life from that of a scrutiny of the individual to an inquiry into the means by which a society, nation, or culture achieves understanding of the totality of stimuli which act upon it" (p. 112). As he defined it, social epistemology was probably misnamed; the application is more akin to sociology than to epistemology. His focus seems to have been on information as process, as the process by which the graphic record can be shared among people so as to enable the development of knowledge.

After Shera coined the phrase, philosophers discovered social epistemology. While there are some definite differences between his idea and theirs, there are also a number of points in common. Since this idea has importance for the study of information, some attention to their thoughts is appropriate here. Integral to an examination of informing is a focus on the social interrelationships that can lead to sharing information. The philosophers I will mention here share one element of social epistemology that is not present in Shera's writings. They claim that the path to knowledge, the process through which people come to know things, is normative. This means that there are ways to assess the direction people take as they seek information, and there are ways to evaluate what they find after they have retrieved it. Alvin Goldman (2002) advocates a normative approach to social epistemology based on some specific goals:

> The four conceptions presented in this section would each invite social epistemology to evaluate some designated social-epistemic practices in terms of their tendencies to promote or inhibit a distinctive goal or value. In other words, each would adopt some consequentialist foundation for normativity. The four goals or values are (A) true belief, (B) consensus, (C) rationality, and (D) cognitive democracy. (p. 199)

To these he adds a fifth goal—the justification of testimony-based belief. We should ask whether testimony is itself a source of justification or whether it depends on other sources or evidence. In either case, there genuinely is a social element to the processes leading to knowledge. Accepting testimony as a source of justification usually relies on *whose* testimony one is listening to. As the example above relating to higher education expenditures illustrates, the acceptance or rejection of testimony is complicated. If acceptance relies on other sources, there will be a similarly complicated social act of weighing the backgrounds, authority, and affiliations of those offering testimony.

Steve Fuller (1988) addresses the production side of information and the process of knowledge. "A producer 'has knowledge' if enough of his fellow producers either devote their resources to following up his research (even for purposes of refutation) or cite his research as background material for their own. The producer continues to 'have knowledge' only as long as these investments by his fellows pay off for them" (p. 30). Another way of looking at Fuller's suggestion from the standpoint of information may be to say that someone is capable of informing others only as long as others pay attention; if no one pays attention, there is no effective process of informing. Philip Kitcher (1994) sums up the social element of transmitting information that may lead to knowledge very succinctly:

> The main social epistemological project consists in the investigation of the reliability of various types of social processes. Once we have recognized that individuals form beliefs by relying on information supplied by others, there are serious issues about the conditions that should be met if the community is to form a consensus on a particular issue—questions about the division of opinion and of cognitive effort within the community, and issues about the proper attribution of authority. (p. 114)

In light of what Kitcher says, we must be alert to opportunities for the study of information sources and the authority of those sources. As he says, people will likely form beliefs on the basis of what they read and hear, so we should ask about the social processes that contribute to such belief formation.

Social epistemology is still epistemology; it is a way of exploring how we can and do know things. Goldman, more than anyone else, stresses the knowledge element. Social processes and relationships (through some kind of formal communicative action) facilitate beliefs that can be evaluated by reliable means aimed at what Goldman calls veritism. We have a truth-appraising capacity that is enhanced through social connections. Goldman and others differ from Shera in that they hold to the more or less traditional epistemological stance—knowledge is a belief held by an individual, and that belief can be justified and true and it is not accidental. Information, in the physicalist/objectivist sense detailed above, has very little relation to knowledge. Informing and becoming informed, on the other hand, are vital to knowledge. Reading, seeing, and listening are all essential (that is, they form a kind of empirical and cognitive whole) to the development of justified, true, non-accidental beliefs. Libraries are integral social components of informing and becoming informed by being a place where the ideas of others are collected and organized, and where services can assist people in finding the various ideas as they are expressed formally. Optimally, libraries can also provide social space where people can question ideas, exchange propositions, and engage in critique. In the field of philosophy Richard Cherwitz and James Hikins (1986) have made a claim that is very similar to the presumption that information equals knowledge. In substitution for information they focus on rhetoric. Where they fall short (and where anyone who would argue that information equals knowledge falls short) is in not recognizing and admitting that rhetoric (and information) is epistemically neutral. Rhetoric can address any number of topics, but with the express purpose of persuasion. Rhetoric is not, by nature, dialogic; neither is physical information. Neither rhetoric nor information-as-thing has anything explicitly to do with truth or justification. Information does equal knowledge (see Budd, 2001).

This chapter has been something of a gateway to the next few chapters. In order to grasp fully the complex examination of information seeking information finding, information retrieval, information use, relevance, meaning, and several other aspects of human information behavior, we needed to cover these essential points. Buckland's distinctions are very important to the understanding of how information may be conceived. Information agencies, in some ways at least, must consider information as thing; there are materials to collect and manage, access to databases that have to be paid for, and use of items that have to be facilitated. Information agencies should remember that information as thing is usually a means to an end. Enter Buckland's other two categories. These agencies exist to do more than collect and store; there are processes of retrieval and use and objectives of learning, becoming informed, and knowing.

The study of information in many ways mirrors the concerns of libraries and librarians. Items can be studied as things, but usually as a means to the processes of dissemination, exchange, system design, use, etc. A key to the study of information, that we can see as applicable to the foregoing, is the observation of Geoffrey Nunberg (1996); information is "a term that incorporates assumptions of nobility and transferability in its meaning, so that it seems foregone that content will be preserved intact when its material and social supports are stripped away. But considering how much work we ask the word 'information' to do, we don't spend time thinking critically about what it means" (p. 107). Of course it is our task to undertake just this critical thinking; one might even say this task is foundational to the field. Critical thinking and action carry some concomitant responsibilities. Perhaps foremost among the responsibilities is action that is ethically sound. Questions relating to what is right, what is good, and what is moral face us every day of our professional lives. Informing and educating certainly have ethical ramifications. The next chapter will address the ethical challenges that are inherent in librarianship.

CHAPTER 4

What's the Right Thing to Do?

THIS TOPIC DESERVES AN entire book, but we'll touch on some of the most important aspects of ethics as they relate to librarianship. As is evident from the preceding chapters, the profession and its numerous organizations of praxis are confronted with decision points. Many of the decisions entail weighing alternatives that carry ethical import. While the first three chapters presented some contexts within which we operate, this chapter offers an examination of the moral and ethical aspects of our professional lives. Every profession includes ethical imperatives and ethical questions. To repeat a point that Gardner and Shulman (2005) make, the judgments of professionals must be faced with integrity and must be accompanied by acknowledgment of the consequences of actions (pp. 14–15). Toward that end, professions frequently formulate codes of ethics, and the main focus of the codes is usually the relationships between professionals and their clienteles (or communities). Given the complexities of human action, the relationships include innumerable possibilities for interaction and the possibilities may include responsibilities, ethics, or assumptions regarding what is good. Of course the professions don't invent ethics from whole cloth; moral and ethical philosophy has a history many centuries long.

In recent years the topic of ethics has been of considerable popular interest; to a great extent the interest has been fueled by scientific and technological developments that carry questions we can't ignore. If medical advances can prolong our lives, does it automatically follow that our lives *should* be prolonged? If technology enables detailed tracking of people's movements, purchases, and associations, does that mean the data collection is inherently benevolent? Instances are ripe for ethical examination: the USA PATRIOT Act is justified on the grounds of national security while it simultaneously raises questions about personal security. Claims that the act is not intrusive because there's no evidence that it's been widely used misses the point entirely; the existence of any legislation that permits scrutiny of purchases and library transactions presents a concern that is legitimate. Very recently the destruction wrought by Hurricane Katrina has led legislators to contemplate exceptions to the Posse Comitatus Act of 1878 (which strictly limits the use of federal troops from acting in a law enforcement capacity). Revision or repeal of the act would have ramifications that extend beyond security during disasters.

Laws that should be based in justice and fairness make little room for the kinds of impositions that are passed and contemplated today. The Terri Schiavo case poignantly illustrates both what medical science and law can accomplish and the human costs of what they cannot accomplish. In our personal lives we're faced with choices that carry moral and ethical import, and the choices we make may affect more than just ourselves. More to the point here, as professionals we're faced with ethical choices that have an impact on us *as* professionals. Further, the choices we make have an impact on librarianship, our organizations, and our communities. In part, what we need to be cognizant of is professional ethics—the right and moral action we take as librarians. Of course it isn't possible to separate entirely professional ethics from personal ethics, which makes answering the questions, "What's the right thing to do?" all the more difficult.

BACKGROUND

The starting point here is a quick review of ethics in general, so that we have a shared background. It is a big field with a long history. In classical philosophy ethics tended to focus on what it means for a person to live a good life. The good life, for philosophers in ancient times, was not merely a comfortable and satisfying life; it was linked to characteristics and qualities that were valued at the time. The good life was grounded in virtues, especially in the virtues that would lead to human excellence. For the Greeks, excellence was connected to human nature and human action. One could be a *good* physician, a *good* soldier, or a *good* ruler. The virtues were those qualities and abilities that enabled people to do something well. A person who was not manually adept, physically strong, persuasive, etc. did not possess the valued virtues. Virtues, in short, were defined by who one was more than by what one did (although someone who possessed physical strength, wisdom, or other virtues was obligated to use those qualities well in order to live a good life). Over time, especially in the Christian West, the tables turned. Virtues began to be defined by action rather than by attribute. Thomas Aquinas drew from Aristotle to redefine the good life; a virtuous person acts honestly, prudently, responsibly, and so on. Additionally, there is an introduction of duty in this later conception of virtue. The defining points center on how we act socially, how we behave among other people. Recently virtue ethics, as a type of philosophical ethics, has taken a back seat to other conceptions of ethics. (For more on virtue ethics, see Richard Taylor, 2002.)

There are two very important stances from more recent time regarding ethics that we can focus on here. The first is expressed by Immanuel Kant (1724–1804), who formulated a principal norm for all ethics, the categorical imperative, which "would be that which represented an action as necessary of itself without reference to another end, i.e., as objectively necessary" (1988, p. 42). The idea of the categorical imperative is essential to Kant's program; it encapsulates his position that some ethical questions stand apart from the consequences of action. Some imperatives—hypothetical imperatives in Kant's terminology—are means to ends and are subordinate to those ends. Categorical imperatives are subordinate to nothing; they are ends in themselves and, furthermore, are grounded in reason. It is this last point, already noted above, that is most frequently the focus of criticism; philosophers since Kant have taken issue with ethics and morality being rooted solely in reason. Related to the categorical imperative is a particular matter in Kant's program that has been criticized by many. While it can be demonstrated that Kant did not follow a blindly deontological path (that is, he did not believe that a principle should be followed if it not based in some rational end), he did at times incorporate deontological elements into his ethics. Some ethical principles, according to Kant, hold rational precedence over values or notions of good. The most frequently mentioned example of deontological principle is his writing on lying. He (1996) states that "a human being's duty to himself as a moral being *only* . . . consists in what is *formal* in the consistency of the maxims of his will with the *dignity* of humanity in his person. . . . The vices contrary to this duty are *lying, avarice,* and *false humility*" (p. 175; emphasis in original). There is one, and only one, condition that Kant applies: telling a lie is not the same as not telling the truth. In other words, there are reasons why an individual does not tell the whole truth (for example, reveal all inner thoughts) all the time. However, there is, for Kant, no moral justification for telling a lie, for intentionally stating or omitting something in order to deceive.

The counterexample some critics have given creates the scenario wherein a killer asks an individual where a third person is at that moment. The individual knows where the third person is and, so, is obliged to tell the killer. To lie in such an instance, for Kant, would jeopardize the individual's entire ethical existence and would necessitate some casuistry on the part of the individual (presuming to know the killer's thoughts and soul). Roger Sullivan (1989) suggests some ways Kant might counter the criticism.

> He could have offered at least five different objections to any such "reconstruction." First, he could have argued that we seldom, if ever, find ourselves in a situation in which we are *not* confronted by evil, both in ourselves and in others. Living in an ethical state of nature is not an extraordinary situation but, rather, our *normal* moral condition, and we often can act rightly only at considerable consequential cost. Second, another person's immorality clearly does not provide a *moral* justification for our emulating his or her unethical standards. . . . Third . . . any argument based on any "necessity" but moral necessity inevitably starts us on the slippery slope toward the complete abandonment of morality. Fourth, moral necessity is defined

by a purely formal—not a consequential—norm. And finally, all moral laws must be genuine universals. So integral is this last claim to Kant's thought that its rejection amounts to rejecting most of his analysis of both morality and politics. (p. 176)

Sullivan then says that Kant's position is untenable, that there are consequences no matter what stance one takes, and that the consequences of leading a killer to a victim is indefensible. The example is an extreme one, but it does not necessarily indicate a serious problem with Kant's ethical thought. In this example the individual is confronted with two conflicting duties—the duty to tell the truth and the duty to see that no harm comes to the third party. It would be irresponsibly naive to think that the initial duty not to lie presents a stopping point. No person in her or his right mind would imagine the individual telling the killer where the third person is and then merrily walking away with a clear conscience. As is mentioned above, Kant did state that ethical and moral judgment cannot be learned solely from experience. Such judgments result from free choice, and freedom is a regulative, rational concept; it is a product of practical reason. Practical reasoning is demanding and precludes the kind of naiveté just discussed.

The second stance is represented by a contemporary of Kant's—Jeremy Bentham (1748–1832)—and one of Bentham's successor—John Stuart Mill (1806–1873). Bentham, in a sense, simplified the moral life and moral choices of humans. While Kant was skeptical of relying too heavily on the consequences of actions (since consequences are, in effect, extra-rational), Bentham embraced a consequentialist stance. At the beginning of his 1781 book, *Principles of Morals and Legislation,* he wrote, "Nature has placed mankind under the governance of two sovereign masters, *pain* and *pleasure*. It is for them alone to point out what we ought to do, as well as to determine what we shall do" (Bentham, 1988, p. 1; emphasis in original). Bentham also said that "utility" does not have the same connection, for most people, with pleasure and pain as the word "happiness" does. Using the word "happiness" is a later concession by Bentham (the first footnote in later editions of his book, recommending "happiness" as a substitute for the word "utility" was added in 1822). Kant's program, grounded as it is in reason, is indeed metaphysical. Bentham's program, on the other hand, is empirical and phenomenalist ("Pain and pleasure are produced in men's minds by the action of certain causes" [Bentham, 1988, p. 43]). In other words, Bentham's ethics is firmly rooted in the physical, natural world.

Bentham's work represents an effort to infuse psychology into the examination of human action. The gist of his thought is evident early in his book as he defines his utilitarian stance: "By the principle of utility is meant that principle which approves or disapproves of every action whatsoever, according to the tendency which it appears to have to augment or diminish the happiness of the party whose interest is in question: or what is the same in other words, to promote or to oppose that happiness" (Bentham, 1988, p. 2). Some of the difficulties with his program are also evident early on: "The community of a fictitious *body*, composed of the individual persons who are considered as constituting as it were its *members*. The interest of the community then is, what?—the sum of the interests of the several members who compose it" (Bentham, 1988, p. 3; emphasis in original). What happens when the happiness of individuals is at odds, especially given that community is no more than the many individuals? Even if one concedes that "community" can be a problematic concept, the interests of individuals and those of groups are not identical. The interests of the members may not simply be additive; they may be subtractive as well. Stephen Holmes and Cass Sunstein (1998) refute Bentham's argument effectively: "It is perfectly plausible to distinguish between performances and forebearances. . . . Because American law recognizes wrongful omissions as well as wrongful commissions, the distinction between rights to require action and rights to prohibit action is useful and important" (pp. 50–51). If one person's interests hold that he desires the property of someone else, he can't simply seize it. The questions are answered in the negative by Bentham (1988) insofar as he admits to pleasure grounded in power (thus differentiating between and among community members), which he defines as the ability of an individual to bend others to his will (p. 35).

The thought of John Stuart Mill is more likely to be associated, in most people's minds today, with utilitarianism than that of Jeremy Bentham. Mill was a more subtle, as well as a more able, thinker than Bentham. To begin with, Mill (1972a) was better able to articulate a general and more inclusive conception of utility: "the happiness which forms the utilitarian standard of what is right in conduct, is not the agent's own happiness, but that of all concerned" (p. 17). One consistency with Mill and Bentham, though, is the assertion that happiness (utility) is not limited to the embodiment, demonstration, or practice of virtue. "Utilitarians are quite aware that there are other desirable possessions and qualities besides virtue, and are perfectly willing to allow to all of them their full worth. They are also aware that a right action does not necessarily indicate a virtuous character, and that actions which are blamable, often proceed from qualities entitled to praise" (Mill, 1972a, p. 21). This is not to say that virtue is ignored or that it is not valued in this program, but that it is not at the center. While Mill speaks of individuals' agency, he (and utilitarians of many stripes) focuses his attention on actions and their consequences, rather than on the kind of internal assessment of happiness that Aristotle and Plato conceived of. Bentham, and Mill much more so, incorporate the political philosophy of liberalism into their ethical positions. Liberalism here is confined more to the kinds of individual freedoms that should be essential elements of societies. In Chapter 5 we'll explore the political in greater depth, but, as we can see, the ethical and the political are, and should be, closely related.

The practical side of ethics arises again. As MacIntyre (1984) emphasizes, the political and the moral do not have separate histories (or presents, for that matter). Theorizing and believing are both political and moral actions. "Every action is the bearer and expression of more or less theory-laden beliefs and concepts; every piece of theorizing and every expression of belief is a political and moral action" (p. 61). MacIntyre's point is extremely important; history is integral to any understanding of ethics and moral philosophy. History, as is ethics, is human and social; it is an essential component to any understanding of our places in society. The challenge is to create an institutional ethos that achieves a very explicit set of goals. In order to achieve the goals, some principles of rights and obligations have to be recognized and upheld. The easiest of these rights and obligations to accept, and the least controversial, are those grounded in law. Individuals must not be harassed, physically attacked, etc. These fundamental principles are referred to by John Rawls (2001) as a system of social cooperation:

> The central organizing idea of social cooperation has at least three essential features:
>
> (a) Social cooperation is distinct from merely socially coordinated activity. ... Rather, social cooperation is guided by publicly recognized rules and procedures which those cooperating accept as appropriate to regulate their conduct.
> (b) The idea of cooperation includes the idea of fair terms of cooperation: these are terms each participant may reasonably accept, and should accept, provided that everyone else likewise accepts them. ...
> (c) The idea of cooperation also includes the idea of each participant's rational advantage, or good. The idea of rational advantage specifies what it is that those engaged in cooperation are seeking to advance from the standpoint of their own good. (p. 6)

Less simple are those rights and obligations that are based in fairness and justice. Rawls (2001) reduces these rights to two:

> (a) Each person has the same indefeasible claim to a fully adequate scheme of equal basic liberties for all; and (b) Social and economic inequalities are to satisfy two conditions: first, they are to be attached to offices and positions open to all under conditions of fair equality of opportunity; and second, they are to be to the greatest benefit to the least-advantaged members of society. (p. 42)

At this point we will leave Rawls's idea of rights and the implications for positions leaning toward rights or toward welfare, but we will return to it in more detailed discussions of individual rights and institutional responsibilities.

ETHICS AND LIBRARIANSHIP

If we take the question of this chapter seriously (what's the right thing to do?), then we have to take a close look at the ethical side of our professional lives. As is true with ethics in general, there is a prodigious literature on professional ethics. Much of that literature addresses the kinds of specific concerns that crop up in fields such as medicine, law, and engineering. Librarianship, though, has its own aims and its own responsibilities to its communities. Professionals have to be cognizant of practical (or applied) ethics; that is, translating the theories of ethics into action. Action, to make any sense at all, should be rational. Reason isn't oblivious to emotion and sentiment, but when it comes to ethical action, reason can help us to sort through emotional and non-emotional factors and point us to an ethical choice. Reason is vital in our profession (and in all professions) because we live daily with uncertainty. If we were able to know precisely what the variables would be in a given circumstance, we could devise a formula to address the problem. Ethical action, as human action, doesn't give us the luxury of certainty, or even definable probability.

Now this won't be a surprise: reason is frequently an area of dispute among philosophers, cognitive scientists, psychologists, and others. After all, why should reason be any different from knowledge, ethics, information, and democracy? There is a powerful strain of thought that is still alive today and that stresses reason's concern with means rather than with ends. Nobel laureate Herbert Simon (1983) has written, "We see that reason is wholly instrumental. It cannot tell us where to go; at best it can tell us how to get there. It is a gun for hire that can be employed in the service of any goals we have, good or bad" (pp. 7–8). There is, of course, no doubt that there is such a thing as instrumental reason. Our daily lives are crowded with applications of instrumental reason. We contemplate the best alternative route to get to a destination if there is a traffic jam; we think about optimal processes for acquiring materials in our libraries. These examples, however, do not exhaust the scope and depth of practical reason; we do think about ends rationally. Simon's conception of reason is unnecessarily and insupportably narrow. We do derive and devise intentions for doing things; in other words, we pre-meditate and the pre-meditation is at the heart of cataloging and classification, mediation services, and the physical arrangement of the building. John Searle (2001) describes the pre-meditation succinctly: "I have a set of beliefs and desires, and by engaging in reasoning on these beliefs and desires, I arrive at an intention. Such intentions that are formed prior to an action I call prior intentions" (p. 44). To take his idea even further for our professional purposes, our rational criteria of assessment of what we do and why and how we do it are *constitutive* of our prior intentions (Searle, 2001, p. 107). The beliefs that shape our prior intentions are themselves shaped by practical reason.

In employing practical reason as professionals we are, in some very real ways, authoring our actions. We are writing the script by which we will both perform an act and justify the performance of the act. Ideally, the order of this authority is reversed; we justify, then we perform. I want to emphasize this professional judgment. In our daily lives it is quite common that we do something and then rationalize what we do. Rationalization is *not* justification and it is *not* rationality; it is an a posteriori excuse we use so that we *appear* to have employed reasoning. Librarians do reason when they formulate policies for action within their organizations. The policies are intended to reflect the nature and needs of the community within a structure of informing. At times the reasoning is very simple; it would be irrational to have an advanced work on plasma physics in an elementary school library. At other times the reasoning must be complex and careful; when we talk about intellectual freedom the complexity of reasoning will become clear. If we accept that we are the authors of our actions we are admitting two things: (1) we as professionals have the right to exercise reason in the formation of policy and in the decisions we make, and (2) we as professionals have the responsibility to employ reason in order to attain the Aristotelian ideal of *phronesis* (practical wisdom) and to act according to that virtue.

Right is easily the more difficult of the two admissions. Unlike other professions, such as medicine or law, we are not (by and large) licensed or certified by any party. There is no formal mechanism of enforcement to ensure that we act with diligence, competence, and in the public's interests. Our educational processes (as we saw in Chapter 2) are inadequate to assure the public that we have the intention or the capability to work in their interest. In short, there is no de jure system that extends a right to us as librarians. I would argue, however, that for most of us (all who are working in publicly funded organizations as well as many who aren't) there is a de facto right that is associated with the position of professional librarian. A requirement that a professional hold a master's degree from an ALA-accredited program is intended to be assurance that the individual be prepared in accordance with the Standards for Accreditation's edicts. The recognition of a professional position, with requirements and expectations specific to the job, is further indication of a right to perform as a professional. Third, ALA has articulated a code of professional ethics that all librarians should adhere to. These three factors can be used to support a claim to a right.

With the above as some background let me now offer a counterargument—librarians have no right, de jure or de facto, as professionals. As has been mentioned, professional education and training is a confused muddle, rationalized by program administrators and faculty on no sound basis at all, other than a notion that professionals should have some narrow technical skills. Of course this is an intentional overstatement; it doesn't apply to all accredited programs. However, there are programs that have minimal requirements of students plus instruction in required areas by adjuncts rather than the regular, full-time faculty. Also, I am speaking here of educational preparation for the profession of librarianship, not for information technology, systems design, or anything else. The educational requirements should be a matter for discussion, but that discussion (and by that I mean open and honest views expressed by all of those designing and those most directly affected by formal educational programs), but that discussion must be reserved for venues at which dialogue is possible. No one can, at the present time, assume that every graduate of an accredited master's program is competent in the areas specified in the Standards for Accreditation. Without demonstrable assurance that graduates *are* prepared, no right can be extended.

Continuing with the counterargument, while ALA has approved a Code of Ethics, the Code itself leaves one with questions and concerns. For example, the Code states, "Ethical dilemmas occur when values are in conflict." This is by no means necessarily the case. For one thing, "value" is not a particularly useful word unless it is used in conjunction with "for whom." A value is held by someone or some group for a reason. "Wealth" might be a value for one person while "poverty" is a value for someone else. The two words do not directly assert particular actions; one needn't attain wealth by immoral, illegal, or unjust means. This is no petty quibble; the Code gives the mistaken impression that values are the grounds for any conflict that might occur. Concentration on two of the principles in the Code can illustrate some of the problems that can arise. The second principle states, "We uphold the principles of intellectual freedom." The inference is that *the* principles of intellectual freedom are universally known and accepted and it only remains that they be applied. As we will see later in this chapter, there is debate within librarianship about what, in fact, the principles of intellectual freedom are.

Whether one holds to the argument or the counter-argument, the Code of Ethics raises some questions that we should consider. The first principle in the Code states that we are to provide accurate and unbiased responses to queries. The intent of the "unbiased" part is fairly clear; we should not impose upon the requestor our own political, religious, or social beliefs since they might conflict with the requestor's beliefs. But what if the requestor is not seeking accurate information? Is this an ethical conflict? One answer may be that it would be presumptuous to claim that we know why someone requests information. The requestor may actually want to refute inaccurate information. This is certainly a reasonable answer, but it may not cover all dilemmas. The "accurate" part of the principle may also open doors to some problems. If someone requests information about a refuted idea, an accurate response would be to provide the information requested. Is that response completely accurate, or partially accurate? Is there some responsibility to inform the requestor that the idea has been challenged or refuted? Is accuracy "nothing but the truth" or is it "the whole truth?" Again, these are not quibbles. Perhaps most important, the questions lead to a major professional concern—whether it is our responsibility to foster truth and attempt to impart it, or to adopt a relativist stance and give community members what they "want."

The latter stance has a following among some public librarians. On the face of it, the position is not controversial; if communities express (by whatever means) the desire to have some kinds of materials, it is legitimate to be sensitive to those desires. In fact, one might even say that this constitutes a form of accurate service. Where the stance falls short is in explicitly catering to a particular minority of the community. If, for example, circulation data drive decisions about selection and acquisition, the self-perpetuating system of collection building holds sway. It is difficult to assess why some people do find what they want in the library and why others don't, but the Code does call for equitable service and equitable access. We can, and should, consider what constitutes "equity," but we can probably agree quite readily that it encompasses the socioeconomic, cultural, and linguistic diversity of a community, and may not be reflected in past circulation activity. If a faculty member at a four-year liberal arts college has a serious interest in the particulars of one region of Incan-ruled territory at some time in the past, does equity require that this individual's interest be supported materially through acquisition of, and access to, materials? Other things being equal, the usual response would be that catering to one individual's interest could detract from the library's ability to serve the entire college well, and thus be inequitable. (There could, of course, be circumstances where an individual's work could benefit the college and so be supported.)

What is perhaps a less straightforward element of the Code is commitment to providing accurate responses to requests. Librarians should not knowingly provide false response, but assurances of accuracy get more complicated. With some requests accuracy is elusive; the appropriate response by a librarian may be to offer data and information and to guide the patron to the means to a critical interpretation. In some instances there may be conflicting data; all sources should be provided to the requestor, with sources made explicit. The very word "accuracy" suggests that there is a normative aspect to mediation services. I do believe that there is a normative aspect; there are standards of seeking and retrieving, evaluating, reasoning, etc. that must be applied. Furthermore, accuracy suggests something objective (in a weak sense of the word); the librarian is not merely concerned with persuading a requestor to accept a particular response. Providing accurate responses requires sincere, critical, and rigorous application of reason and ethics. An important implication of such a realization is that a librarian must engage in reflection so that the distinction between persuasion and truth are understood as clearly as possible. There is also a professional responsibility, not only to seek truth, but simultaneously to seek what J. J. C. Smart (1984) calls "warranted assertibility" (pp. 95–96). Someone might say something that happens to be true, but that person has no grounds, no warrant, to say it. So the accurate response ideally is true and warranted.

I can imagine disagreement with what I've just said. It might sound rigid and prescriptive. Well, to a considerable extent it is. What is the alternative? A first step in a dispute would be to deny normativity and objectivity. I would have to respond that without norms we're lost. In the absence of standards for evaluation we can't even use the word "accuracy" legitimately; there would be nothing against which to judge a response. The corollary to my reply is that if someone does say that there can be some responses that can be judged inaccurate then there are some that can be deemed (according to some standards that apply both ways) accurate. Let me respond to another possible objection: I'll admit that accuracy and inaccuracy are not entirely binary options. A response could be partially accurate; it could even be mostly accurate. Another way of thinking of this kind of claim is that a response may have a number of warrants, a number of elements that are indeed accurate, but may include one claim that is inaccurate. Someone might describe an elephant fully and completely, except that the person concludes that all elephants are red. That last unwarranted claim doesn't negate what went before it (even though it could raise doubt in the hearer's mind about everything the person said about the elephant). This is a rather absurd example, but it's easy to imagine responses to involved, multifaceted questions that are almost entirely accurate, but one or two details can't be confirmed by sources at hand. It would be reasonable to conclude that the responding librarian has fulfilled the spirit, if not an extremely strict interpretation of the letter, of the Code.

One thing that the Code doesn't address satisfactorily is what it means to be a professional. Professionalism is a way of being and doesn't hold to normal working hours. As librarians we present ourselves to the public in all that we do; we represent the profession. This seems to be a responsibility that some of our number take far too lightly. In some individual's personal blogs the profession and other professionals are treated with derision and scorn. One blog provides ample evidence of what I'm talking about. Annoyed Librarian (annoyedlibrarian.blogspot.com) writes about the recent changes that the program of the University at Buffalo experienced: "I'm sure the library school faculty aren't very happy about the return to the School of Education. They probably liked being separate since 'Education' faculty are in general the biggest intellectual joke on any university campus." As egregious as this statement is, the blogger crosses the line and asserts what may be considered misconduct:

> The Annoyed Librarian once published a peer-reviewed library literature article analyzing the results of an online survey about a pilot service in her

library; however, she forgot to publicize the survey. Solution: she took the survey herself 247 times in all sorts of different moods and states of intoxication (to insure fairness and balance), and then analyzed the results. Result: Another line on the vita! (The sad thing is, you won't really be able to tell if I'm kidding you).

This blogger, in public proclamations, expresses contempt for librarianship. It seems incumbent upon the profession to develop some extensions to the Code of Ethics that describes professional behavior. Another ethical lapse by this blogger, and others, is the irresponsibility of not identifying herself. Technology enables anonymity; professionalism requires transparency.

The position I'm espousing here implies some demands on librarianship. It is incumbent upon professionals to be reflective, to examine the nature and the purpose of the profession and how to act as a professional. It is imperative that judgment be an essential action of librarians and that judgment not be reduced to a technical exercise. That is, accuracy based in truth is no mere search of a source or a database to locate what exists; it is an epistemic decision. In order to fulfill the criteria of judgment that is warranted epistemically, empirically, rationally, and ethically, the librarian must strive to enhance her knowledge base, critical acumen, understanding of evidence and warrant, and awareness of ethical responsibilities. These demands are only implicit in the Code of Ethics. Education for librarianship, including continuing education and the actions of professional associations, has to focus programs around the foregoing criteria to be taken seriously as education for a profession. This realization brings us back to the characteristics that Gardner and Shulman enumerate. This is how professions earn trust; prestige, money, and status are pale ancillary concomitants. If librarianship is to hold any values dear, the trust of our communities must be high among them. As we will see with intellectual freedom, trust can be a necessary burden for us.

The responsibilities of any information professional are considerable. ALA's Code of Ethics captures some of the responsibilities, but as we've just seen, doesn't get them all. As professionals, librarians must live up to the demands of integrity (especially, given the nature of the work, intellectual integrity). This is quite an ethical requirement; it imposes upon us all, not only that we act in specific ways, but that we do so for particular reasons. Michael Lynch (2004) details the extent of the demand:

> First, people who run around loudly defending whatever view they happen to land on, whether or not they've bothered to examine whether it is true, lack intellectual integrity. . . . Second, a person with intellectual integrity is someone who is willing to pursue the truth. . . . Third, a person of intellectual integrity stands for what she thinks is true precisely because she thinks it is true. . . . Fourth, intellectual integrity also requires being open to the truth just because it is the truth. (pp. 131–33)

Lynch and Simon Blackburn emphatically disagree with the position of Richard Rorty. Rorty's ideas about truth and knowledge may be attractive to many in our profession, but they constitute a siren song that is far more dangerous than anything Odysseus listened to. Typical of his position, Rorty (1990) says that "we understand knowledge best when we understand the social justification of belief, and thus have no need to view it as accuracy of representation. . . . Justification becomes a 'social phenomenon' rather than a transaction between a 'knowing subject' and 'reality'" (p. 9). If Rorty is correct, then Blackburn (2005) is also correct that any rational conception of authority is lost (p. 148). Further, anything in ALA's Code that even hints at accuracy would have to be abandoned. Rorty echoes Protagoras, whose tag line was that man is the measure of all things. We need to take our cue from Socrates, who successfully refuted Protagoras's followers in *Theaetetus.*

To wrap up this section, the foregoing depends on an enveloping principle. In order for us to act as responsible, ethical professionals, we must understand as completely as possible the relationship between ourselves and our institutions on the one hand, and ourselves and our communities on the other. The relationships are not merely service or the provision of goods; they are complex interweavings of self and other. Following Kant's edict that we always treat others as ends in themselves and never as means to our own ends, the relationship we have with communities is based in clear recognition of community members as other selves.

ETHICS AND OUR ENVIRONMENTS

Overwhelmingly libraries are parts of larger parent organizations, which may reside in the public or the private sectors. It would be easy to defer responsibility for ethical action to those parent organizations, but that would entail abdicating a professional ethos that we should adhere to. In a perfect world librarians would be on the same ethical page as administrators, boards, principals, etc. We don't live in a perfect world, though. Political expediency, injudicious appropriation and use of funds, petty power grabs, and more serious abrogations are not uncommon in schools, colleges and universities, communities, businesses, and the professions. The Kantian edict just mentioned still obtains, but we have to be prepared to understand other selves for what they are. The challenge that we face may extend to the security of our positions. That is indeed an extreme instance; more subtle, but potentially more pervasive pressure could lead to ethical dilemmas, though. Perhaps the most important thing we can realize as professionals working in organizations is that we can and must accept responsibility for our actions and decisions, but that we can't force others to make the decisions we would make.

We *can* try to shape decisions and action through influence and argument, and we must respond to what others say and do.

With that said, let's admit that we live in a world that is shaped by politics, and that the politics affects almost every aspect of our lives. When you hear the word "politics" do you think often think of "ethics?" If the answer is no, this reflects on the failure of politics to form the most elemental issues in the most appropriate terms. The politics of our nation has a particular foundation that has shaped the development, not only of American government, but also of American society. By the eighteenth century, when it was becoming apparent that the colonies needed a unified governance structure, the tenor of the time influenced the people who were most intimately involved in setting the course of our state. The political thought of John Locke was especially attractive to some of the framers of our government. Locke, partly following and partly creating a liberal tradition, set some things before others as good (in the sense that the state should accept responsibility to protect them). Practical ideas of liberty, autonomy, property, and others were paramount. It certainly isn't that these ideas are bad (far from it); they are, however, limited. The stage was set early on in the United States for the primacy of private goods—those things, including property but also extending to education and opportunity, that could be possessed by individuals. Missing is the idea of the collective. I do use the word "collective" advisedly here, and I'm following Richard Bagnall's (2002) distinction between collective and common.

In practice there has been some effort in our nation to defend the idea of the collective. To some extent public education and public libraries have been bastions of the collective good. But only to a certain extent. The concept common rather than collective has actually been much more prominent in our history. By this I mean that official concern has been more for the "American people" than for American peoples. The treatment of American Indians and slaves is stark testimony to the active ignorance of anything resembling plurality. It also betrays the mere rhetorical acknowledgment of liberty and autonomy. The very linguistic structure of "melting pot" signifies assimilation, the diffusing of difference, and the paradox of destroying individuals in the name of the individual. The founding of the United States took the world further than anything else in history toward a democracy; the tragedy is that the democratic promise has diminished by an odd combination—the perversion of liberalism into neoliberalism, and the reversion of politics grounded in Locke to the politics grounded in Thomas Hobbes. Our field would benefit from an extensive study of the influence of politics on our organizational lives, but there is neither the time nor the space to meet that need here. What we can say is that the influence has a dramatic effect on the development and present state of libraries as organizations and their ethical relationships with their parents.

In some ways the political-ethical shortcomings are very clear; we see them repeatedly in news accounts. A recent piece in *Library Journal* (2005) stated, "Facing a 20 percent budget reduction and increasing costs, the Buffalo & Erie County Public Library (B&ECPL), NY, will close some 20 of 52 branches in 2006 and lay off more than 100 people in a desperate effort to maintain a level of service" (p. 16). The last part of that sentence is both mystifying and disturbing. The reduction of staff and the closing of branches is intended to "maintain a level of service." Service cannot possibly be maintained in the face of such cutbacks. The article further indicated that the library's bond request, which was part of a larger county funding issue, was not approved because other elements of the expenditure package were deemed inappropriate. It is not unusual for the funding of a number of governmental agencies or departments to be lumped together; sometimes the strategy presumes that less popular components will be funded on the coattails of more popular ones. Sometimes the strategy works; sometimes it doesn't. This customary political action is antithetical to the best interests of the public. Whether bad programs are funded along with good ones or good programs are not funded because of bad ones, the result is an ethical failure. Did the people of Buffalo and Erie County know the fiscal machinations that were taking place? Did they comprehend the costs of gamesmanship?

Public libraries in many locations may share experiences with Buffalo and Erie County. College and university libraries face somewhat different dilemmas. The similarity of public and academic libraries lies in the parents. The actions of the higher levels dictate what is, and is not, possible for libraries. Public colleges and universities have seen declining state support for a number of years. The percentage of total institutional revenue coming from state appropriations has dropped precipitously. Tuition, as a percentage of revenues, has increased over time as a means to provide for institutional operating expenses. In recent years universities have taken quite drastic measures, such as closing or scaling back the operations of university presses, outsourcing some operations, deferring repairs or improvements to the physical plant, and others. These actions do result in short-term savings, but they have long-term costs that are not simply monetary. Scott Seaman (2005) has observed that "Higher education is now seen as a private gain rather than a public good to be financed by state governments" (p. 306). Seaman identified the single most important and deleterious aspect of American society today for librarians and all they seek to accomplish.

We could point to some apparent reasons for the dilemma (I'm tempted to use the word "tragedy") of public funding, not just for libraries, but for the public good. People's antipathy for taxes is fueled by reports of pork barrel spending (a few billion dollars spent on weaponry and equipment the Pentagon doesn't even want, bridges to nowhere, etc.) and waste by governments at all levels. The skepticism is not misplaced, but these examples are symptomatic of the much larger problem that Seaman spoke of, and which we will address at the end of this chapter. At a glance the problem seems straightforward—public money is misused by officials who are not sufficiently accountable. So when putative accountability solutions are presented, the answer appears to be at hand. Enter what is being dubbed the "65 cent solution," a movement (embraced so far by a few states) intended to mandate that 65 percent of each public K–12 education dollar be spent in the classroom. Embedded in this solution is the implied assurance that if funds are shifted internally, no new taxes would be needed. The ethical challenge presented by this solution lies in the facile and uncritical promise that educational ills can be solved by a formula. In truth, money nominally devoted to classroom instruction can be misspent as easily as any other money. Further, money that is categorized as part of the "other" 35 percent may contribute substantively to pupils' education. Case in point: the salaries of librarians and counselors are not included as part of classroom spending, although athletics is. In short, this solution to a problem of trust is an untrustworthy imposition of an arbitrary number.

The tie that binds libraries is an increasingly explicit tension that accountability helps create. The tension is legitimate and inevitable. Institutions such as libraries, schools, and others function in a public sphere, so the public can and should monitor the extent to which they achieve their goals. A problem arises when the idea and the realization of the goals become distorted. As stated above, I'll conclude this chapter with an examination of the political-ethical side of the dilemma, but for now I'll stick with the matter of trust. Ideally, accountability and trust should be closely related. Unfortunately, a species of false accountability has insinuated itself into American culture and politics. Onora O'Neill (2002) puts it best in her brilliant little book: "The new accountability culture aims at ever more perfect administrative control of institutional and personal life" (p. 46). In other words, it is incumbent upon us to ask in what ways we should be accountable, and to whom. A publicly supported library should be accountable to its communities to provide for—in the most complete way possible—learning, informing, reading, and public discourse. These responsibilities include honesty, integrity (harkening back to Lynch), and truthfulness. O'Neill (2002) points out that there is a perversion of accountability: "Underlying this ostensible aim of accountability to the public the real requirements are for accountability to regulators, to departments of government, to funders, to legal standards. The new forms of accountability impose forms of central control—quite often indeed a range of different and mutually inconsistent forms of central control" (p. 53).

Trust works in many directions. How can we as professionals trust the administrators of our parent organizations if they embrace the perverse accountability? Can we trust one another if we willingly impose false accountability upon ourselves? The trust we place in administrations, boards, and legislatures translates into the resources we receive to fulfill our goals and objectives. The aforementioned examples illustrate that too often the choice we face is between the rock of reduced resources or the hard place of compromised principles. Awareness of the choice can contribute to a conversation among professionals that addresses the fundamental ethical challenge head on.

LIBRARIES AND THE PRODUCTION OF COMMUNICATIVE CONTENT

So far I've mentioned communicative content in a fairly generic sense. According to this sense it means anything that is formally communicated using some medium. As such the assumption is that communicative content is, more or less, equal—all of it is important, so particular communities should have as much possible access to as much communicative content of interest. "Of interest" signifies a realization that no single library can or should aim at providing access to the universe of content, but each library should look to a limited, defined subset. The subset is usually identified by topic: an elementary school library looks first to the curriculum and to support the learning and success of the pupils and teachers; a law library aims to offer access to statutory content, judicial decisions, commentary, and other materials needed by attorneys. A question that comes up from time to time relates to another definition of subset—the economics, politics, and intentional elements of the creation and production of the content. These elements have ethical import, both in themselves and as they influence the work of the profession. In other words, what is said, how it is said, and how what is said gets communicated all include substantive implications for the goals of librarianship.

There is a critical literature that focuses on the economic and political elements of communicative content. Only the briefest summary is needed here; the works are extensive in their analysis. Robert McChesney (1999, 2004) has examined media ownership and its impact on society. He detailed the consolidation of all media—broadcast, print, online—in the hands of very few companies. Of interest to our field, Thomson owns major resources in the areas of law, science, and learning in general. Also, Bertelsmann owns some major publishers and has a powerful worldwide presence. As a result of the consolidation there are just a handful of companies that own almost all radio stations; not many more own most of the nation's newspapers; very few that own the publishers have the majority of market share; and a small number of conglomerates own broadcast and cable networks. None of this is news, perhaps, but the impact of ownership in the hands of the few can be immense. Ben Bagdikian has followed media ownership for a number of years. The most recent edition of his book (2004) includes new chapters that address the political side of the issue. In that edition Bagdikian wrote, "Five global-dimension firms, operating with many of the characteristics of a cartel, own most of the newspapers, magazines, book publishers, motion picture studios, and radio and television stations in the United States" (p. 3). With such consolidation the companies that own so much can wield enormous power and influence.

That power and influence carry ethical implications for us as librarians. A goal that we all share is the ability and commitment to provide our communities with the information (communicative content) that they want and need. Are we in danger of failing to achieve that goal, not because of weakness of will, but because it is extremely difficult to inform our communities? We rely, to a considerable extent, on the market to produce books, magazine, images, and sounds that we can select for the informing of people. In a free market our reliance might not be misplaced, but a free media market doesn't exist. As we've seen, a handful of companies control what is published, filmed, recorded, etc. For example, Clear Channel owns in the neighborhood of 1,200 radio stations in the United States. In the interests of efficiency, Clear Channel wants to standardize what is broadcast on all of those stations. In the interests of ideology, Clear Channel is a primary outlet for political commentary on the right. That political voice not only can, but must, be disseminated. However, if a company as pervasive in its coverage as Clear Channel does not air voices from the center and the left, the polity is endangered. Principles of free speech mean little when an economic power can silence dissenters. Discourse requires multiple speakers; monologue does very little to advance the efficacy of democracy. I realize that these statements sound like absolutes; let me hasten to add that if there is anything approaching the absolute in the current predicament, it is wrought by those in control. For this reason McChesney and others refer to an impoverished democracy.

A free market, it appears, is only as free as the checks, balances, policies, and laws enable. If law and policy is altered so as to allow more concentrated ownership of radio and television stations, broadcast and cable networks, newspapers, magazines, and book publishers, then freedom is redefined. If there is now law to prohibit a rich company from taking over a smaller one, even when that smaller one doesn't want to be purchased, there is no fairness of competition. Choice is inevitably limited; our selection decisions in libraries are shaped by what *can* be selected. Prefacing a set of concerns Cass Sunstein (2001) wrote, "There is a large difference between consumers and citizens" (p. 167). A "give 'em what they want" attitude in public library collection management, for instance, may result in a conflation of consumer and citizen, where the latter's place in a democracy is defined by the former's activities. Sunstein's (2001) three concerns can serve as a guide to all publicly supported libraries:

1. The need to promote exposure to materials, topics, and positions that people would not have chosen in advance, or at least enough exposure to produce a degree of understanding and curiosity;

2. The value of a range of common experiences; and
3. The need for exposure to substantive questions of policy and principle, combined with a range of positions on such questions. (p. 167)

Absent a serious move to address Sunstein's concerns we're faced with another conflation—public and private. What may pass as public media (not in
the sense of state owned, but in the public interest) is little more than pervasive penetration. "Public," then, is illusory, and private interests, agendas, and
ideology (writ large) prevail. To reiterate a statement from above, the conclusion to this chapter will attempt to locate the political transformation of history (including the history we're constructing at this time). At the heart of
the ethical challenge, from the perspective of librarianship, is one of fulfilling
purpose. Community-based purpose entails at least some sort of publicity.
Publicity here refers to making information (communicative content) public, fulfilling a transparent function that enables not just discourse (which
necessitates a kind of presence of the participants), but also other open communicative actions. Libraries (that is, publicly supported libraries) are vital to
a public structure intended to separate from the state and so serve as a site
for potential criticism and dissent. The criticism and dissent is not on the
part of librarians (necessarily) and the intention of collections and access is
not directly to foment criticism and dissent. The intention is to be an open
public resource that allows people to *be* citizens. Libraries are vital to what
John Thompson (1995) has called "regulated pluralism" (pp. 240–42). Libraries
are institutions that are charged with presenting the kinds of options Sunstein
has spoken of. Librarians have the ethical responsibility to provide access to
communicative content that resists state control and market homogenization.
We are the antidote to the forces Thompson (1995) has identified:

> Left to itself, the market does not necessarily cultivate diversity and plural-
> ism in the sphere of communication. Like other domains of industry, the
> media industries are driven primarily by the logic of profitability and capi-
> tal accumulation, and there is no necessary correlation between the logic of
> profitability and the cultivation of diversity. (p. 240)

What we as librarians must do is treat communicative content as informing
potential, as the possibilities that people can use within their lives. Information
is no mere commodity and information exchange is not a capital transaction.
We also have to realize that the market does not share this view.

THE QUESTION OF TECHNOLOGY

The challenges presented by communication media are also reflected in
the profession's uses of, and attitudes toward, technology in general. Some
previous ethical thought, for the most part, assumed a neutral relationship
between us and our creations. Martin Heidegger (1977), perhaps more than

anyone else, demolished that assumption by demonstrating very clearly that technology is *both* a human creation (thus a means to an end) *and* a force that shapes human action and thinking. The most forceful and articulate recent challenge to the old assumptions has been Hans Jonas (1984). Jonas has stated that "technology, apart from its objective works, assumes ethical significance by the central place it now occupies in human purpose" (p. 9), which leads him to conclude, "If the realm of making has invaded the space of essential action, then morality must invade the realm of making, from which it has formerly stayed aloof, and must do so in the form of public policy" (p. 9). It may be impossible to overstate the importance of Jonas's conclusion. A profession that uses technology as a tool in its work (and this includes most, if not all, professions) must see the effects of technology on praxis and the *telos* (purpose) of the profession in its adoption and use of technology. If, as we've seen in previous chapters, media inform (give shape to) messages, then we can't deny that technology could inform purpose. Technology doesn't merely automate (that is, allow us to do the same things more efficiently); it can reshape and present possibilities not heretofore recognized.

The technologies we employ, as Hans Jonas has shown, are also third-party interventions that affect professional ethical action. It may be that our applications of technology illustrate most clearly a distinction between "good" and "value." This distinction may appear to be a philosophical nicety, but it is vital to ethical considerations in any profession. It is necessary to decide what is good—that is, we must consider seriously what may have some objective status, what may be independent of us. It is also necessary for us to decide what has value—that is, what can be used by us to realize some of the ethical goals and objectives we establish. In other words, what has value necessarily is connected to some questions, such as "for whom," "at what times," and "in what amounts." Technology, in following the above reasoning, is not good in itself, but it does have value. Electronic sources of information, for example, do not have a universal intrinsic good, but they can enable us to retrieve useful information for some people in a timely manner (thus demonstrating value). Another way to look at the good-value distinction is that good has an ontological quality; its very being embodies the good (e.g., having personal integrity is good). Value, on the other hand, is realized through application; there is a pragmatic quality attached to it (providing timely access to requested information has value). Jonas (1984) succinctly expressed the relationship of good and value through responsibility: "The concept of responsibility implies that of an ought—first of an ought-to-be of something, then of an ought-to-do of someone in response to the first" (p. 130). "Value" can thus be conceived as an important concept to practical ethics.

Jonas's directive is an effort to solve what has been a persistent debate in philosophy for many years—reconciling "ought" with "is." The debate sometimes uses the terms "fact" and "value" to express what is a dichotomy for some philosophers. Dating at least back to David Hume (1711–1776) there has been an admonition that we cannot infer "ought" from "is." Technology presents possible transformations in action and in policy; for example, it does allow organizations (including libraries) to track the specific items an individual purchases, checks out, possibly even looks at. To restate this, technology presents an "is," a capability. That "is" can be independent of "ought"; the possibility is not itself good, right, or moral of necessity. Another way of looking at Hume's stricture is that what we value is not necessarily (i.e., there is no causal link) what constitutes a fact. The claim makes sense; we see every day, for instance, that traffic laws we all agree are best for public safety are not always followed. Jonas's point is that while ought cannot cause is, each individual can try to bring about "is" from "ought." Another way of looking at the seeming dichotomy is to realize that every school of ethical thought contains—implicitly or explicitly—responsibility. At the very least, it is incumbent upon each of us to hold principles and to be true to those principles. By virtue of responsibility, value is a very important part of ethics. As Hilary Putnam (2002) has written, "it is much easier to say, 'that's a value judgment.' Meaning, 'that's just a matter of subjective preference,' than to do what Socrates tried to teach us: to examine who we are and what our deepest convictions are and hold those convictions up to the searching test of reflective examination" (p. 44). I do want to emphasize Hume's call for understanding the distinction between "is" and "ought." The distinction carries responsibility for all practicing professionals; our attention certainly must be on what is, but we must also aim toward what should be.

Some of the principal challenges that technology presents include some related to the social, the epistemic, and the political. One thread runs through the three elements of challenge—over the last several years there has been a discourse, represented in numerous publications, that has intentionally attempted to transform popular consciousness of the social, the epistemic, and the political. With regard to the social the standard line is gloom and doom: schools are failing students and society; higher education is inefficient and ponderous; and libraries are quaint relics of a past that has all but disappeared. Among the answers to the dilemmas is technology. Learning can be enhanced; information can more readily be accumulated and accessed. The moderate adherents of these kinds of solutions recognize that technology is a part of a much more sweeping solution, but it is still integral to the solution. Such a voice is also evident in our professional discourse; we've seen this practice earlier in the rhetoric of professional education, but it is present throughout the professional literature, conference presentations, organizational meetings, and elsewhere. For instance, Paul Gandel (Chief Information Officer at Syracuse University) (2005) has written, "From the perspective of information-seekers, collections are now Web sites, created by individuals, publishers, and commercial aggregators" (p. 10). What Gandel doesn't address is *why* individuals, publishers, and commercial aggregators build Web sites the way they do, what they include, and what they exclude. The epistemic (knowledge-based) element is likewise changed through discourse. So "knowledge work," "knowledge products," and "knowledge industries" can gain legitimacy in popular parlance. The traditional library may be on the outside looking in unless it too can change so as to facilitate productivity or the creation of profitable knowledge (please note that this warning is intended to be ironic).

There is a more general sense under which the narrow ideas of productivity and capital fall—useful knowledge. Useful knowledge has been a component of the mission of Western public libraries for many years; libraries are to offer people a means to advancement and prosperity. In the present age, though, that mission has been forgotten, not by librarians, but by some creators of current discourse who see different, technological, means to advancement and prosperity. The political presents the most complex challenge of all (so complex that an entire chapter will be devoted to the matter, and especially to libraries and democracy). In fact, the very concept of libraries supporting individuals' advancement and prosperity is a political one, and one that deserves attention. There are claims that technology, the Internet in particular, exerts a democratizing force, since people can be more vocal in an open discursive space. On the other hand, network technology also fosters techno-libertarianism, which is "a pervasive *weltanschauung*, ranging from the classic eighteenth-century liberal philosophy of that-which-governs-best-governs-least love of laissez-faire free-market economics to social Darwinism, anarcho-capitalism, and beyond" (Borsook, 2000, p. 3). A pessimistic political outlook could even lead to the following conclusion: "In so far as we can speculate about its future, then, there is reason to think that the Internet is more likely to increase social fragmentation than it is to promote social consensus. Indeed, there is some reason to take seriously a seemingly more alarming contention— that the Internet will lead to moral anarchy" (Graham, 1999, p. 83).

Yet another distinction needs to be introduced here. While we can (and must) examine technology in light of its possible uses, technology does not include inherent ethical norms. As Graham (1999) argues, the Internet is transformative; it can reshape communicative and social relations. Further, it has the potential uses that could not have been imagined before its existence. The transformative force, however, is just that—potential. It remains for people to seize upon the potential and to create uses, applications, and alterations in human action. The communicative power of the Internet is constantly being explored; the communicative content is still bound by what people believe and say. The communicative content is, as it has been within the context of any medium, of ethical concern. Authority, for example, is not automatically attached to any source simply by virtue of the means by which expression is made. Truth is not evident in the volume or pervasiveness of a voice. Knowledge doesn't emerge because of the existence of statements, claims, or opinions that are unencumbered by traditional communication media or processes. It must also be noted that in a genuinely free communicative environment authority, truth, and knowledge may have a better chance of being realized. (This is an idea propounded by Mill, as we'll see shortly.) We come back to the fundamental distinction between is and ought, and the responsibility that accompanies our professional uses of technologies like the Internet and the communicative content it makes available.

Where does ethics reside in this terrain? The flip answer would be "everywhere." We have to realize that technologies can be (and frequently are) used in unanticipated ways for unanticipated reasons. Still, these uses and reasons are human responses to possibilities that the technologies suggest. Norbert Wiener (1954) was one of the first coming from a technical background to envision an ethics of technology, especially computing. There are two compelling conceptions of technology that have dominated (and limited) our talking and thinking about the challenge (see Feenberg, 1991). The instrumental approach holds that technology is nothing more than a product of our own ingenuity and is used according to purposes and values that are developed by and within society. The substantive approach is based in the concern that technology itself acts upon us and has consequences (intended by us or not) for us. Obviously these two approaches are at odds, but each tends to stifle conversation by effectively constraining our own human agency. In the former instance discourse ignores technology by relegating it to the position of mute servant. In the latter instance discourse imparts a volition to technology that overwhelms our own will. Both obscure what is required for meaningful lives and for becoming informed. What's missing in both is the importance of experience—what it brings to the design, as well as to the use, of technologies. Our experience includes what we do, but also why we do it. It is the cumulative and evolutionary sum of the purposes, actions, thoughts, intentions, desires, and relationships of each of us. The kind of libertarianism Borsook warned us against is, in part, a refutation of experience as a shared phenomenon. Librarians, as innovative adopters of technologies, can find themselves (perhaps reluctantly) as preservers not just of artifacts, but of experience. The ethical need is for a democratic and rational interpositioning between the instrumental and the substantive that accentuates the necessary role for praxis in designing and using *techn*. The point of informing, in such a library as would be populated by librarian/preservers, is a juxtaposition of technology and experience, and neither should be omitted.

INTELLECTUAL FREEDOM

What does it mean to be intellectually free? As is the case with technology, intellectual freedom has instrumental and substantive elements. On the instrumental side, access may be taken to equal freedom; as long as there is unfettered (defined broadly) access each individual is able to use information in any way he or she chooses. On the substantive side freedom is problematic in practice; unfettered access can lead to the corruption of those who are not fully prepared for such freedom. In an extremely simplified sense, librarians are instrumentalists and challengers to accessibility are substantivists. It would be nice if I could now say that there is a large middle ground occupied by the vast majority of people. It's not that there isn't a middle ground, it's just that too few people pay attention to it. Robert Wengert (2001) observes that "library professionals will not take a stand on ethical matters beyond the insistence that patrons should have equal and open access to whatever sources they desire" (p. 497). He is speaking from outside the profession, but the Library Bill of Rights and much commentary on it corroborate his observation. His comment suggests that a deeper ethical response is required; the counter-question is: Are the official statements by ALA not sufficient to convey the ethical position of the position? I have addressed intellectual freedom elsewhere (Budd, 2006), but some points should be revisited here.

Discussion of intellectual freedom in our profession cannot ignore the Library Bill of Rights (LBR). A brief history of the document appears in the *Intellectual Freedom Manual* (1996), and a much more complete background is provided by Louise Robbins (1996). The first iteration was approved by the ALA Council in 1939. The present wording of the Library Bill of Rights is as follows.

LIBRARY BILL OF RIGHTS

The American Library Association affirms that all libraries are forums for information and ideas, and that the following basic policies should guide their services.

I. Books and other library resources should be provided for the interest, information, and enlightenment of all people of the community the library serves. Materials should not be excluded because of the origin, background, or views of those contributing to their creation.

II. Libraries should provide materials and information presenting all points of view on current and historical issues. Materials should not be proscribed or removed because of partisan or doctrinal disapproval.

III. Libraries should challenge censorship in the fulfillment of their responsibility to provide information and enlightenment.

IV. Libraries should cooperate with all persons and groups concerned with resisting abridgment of free expression and free access to ideas.

V. A person's right to use a library should not be denied or abridged because of origin, age, background, or views.

VI. Libraries which make exhibit spaces and meeting rooms available to the public they serve should make such facilities available on an equitable basis, regardless of the beliefs or affiliations of individuals or groups requesting their use.

Adopted June 18, 1948.
Amended February 2, 1961, and January 23, 1980,
inclusion of "age" reaffirmed January 23, 1996,
by the ALA Council.

The intention of the LBR is to be normative and regulative, although it does not carry the power of law. The LBR is primarily an expression of negative rights, as is the First Amendment. The aim of each is to ensure that there aren't incursions on people's abilities to speak, assemble, read, etc. In law and in practice the articulation of negative freedoms is necessary as a means to detail what cannot be imposed. It is also intended, as the *Intellectual Freedom Manual* indicates, to be unambiguous, although it is acknowledged that questions do arise. It seeks to achieve the goal by presenting a set of negative rights, rights intended to prevent incursions into people's abilities to speak, read, view, etc. Of all the practical and theoretical concerns in our profession intellectual freedom poses the thorniest problems.

It's difficult to imagine anyone who doesn't applaud the intention behind the Library Bill of Rights. An open political state requires that ideas be put into circulation, be discussed by all interested parties, and be assessed in a free public sphere. Anything less threatens the survival of a democracy (at least a deliberative democracy). Formal expressions about government, social theory, human behavior, art, literature, the environment—indeed, all "serious" topics—can only be evaluated if they are shared. A question that has always lurked in the shadows of the ethics of intellectual freedom is the possibility of an expression of positive freedoms. Thomas Jefferson said that some rights are inalienable (life, liberty, the pursuit of happiness). Could intellectual freedom possibly be considered a natural right? Is intellectual freedom fundamental to the three rights Jefferson spoke of? A natural right is, by definition, good; it is an essential part of our being. In a book review Gordon Moran (2004) writes, "By now, many persons regard the Firth Amendment and its provision for free speech as a statement of a natural, inalienable right" (p. 91). While the assumption of free speech as a natural right is taken as a given, the assumption itself should be questioned. One of our profession's principles is involved, and we should be as clear as possible on its meaning. Some philosophers have attempted to elucidate the idea of natural right. There is the claim that any natural right must be examined along with a corresponding universal obligation. That is, whatever is deemed to be a natural right—life, for example—carries an obligation that everyone must always and everywhere follow (such as not to interfere with another person's right to live).

If Wainwright's claim is followed, the right to free speech carries its own universal obligation. It would be the responsibility of each person to guard one another's right to expression, regardless of the expression, its intention, and its effects. Speech, in law, politics, the economy, and daily life, is constrained. How might we reconcile free speech as a natural right and the everyday constraints on speech? Oliver Wendell Holmes himself placed constraints on speech, at least when public safety is concerned. The speech of some (primarily the powerful) can silence the voices of others. It is argued that there should be no limits to people's ability to pay to speak, especially on political subjects. However, the more money one has, the freer that person's speech is. If speech has a price, only those who can pay are able to speak. If we examine the inequities according to nature, then it may seem obvious that those with greater resources can put those resources to use to the detriment of the weaker and poorer. In short, nothing in nature ensures any person's ability to speak freely. Raymond Geuss (2001) asserts, "the notion of a natural right is from the start no more than a moralising conception about what would be desirable without any concrete specification of an enforcing agency" (p. 142). The First Amendment's existence is evidence that an enforcing agency does ensure the right to free speech. The freedom of speech and expression is, in fact, regulated by the state, and this fact should actually make us more sanguine about the freedom. The state views it as sufficiently important to protect; nothing is taken for granted in that no one assumes that free speech will occur naturally. Moving forward from the position that free speech is not a natural right, justification of free speech relies on rational, even dialectical, argument.

Tony Doyle (2001) advocates for a utilitarian grounding for intellectual freedom, following John Stuart Mill's suggestion that open exchange of ideas is essential to stimulate discussion and to foster clear and critical thinking. The key point to Doyle's argument is that it is only through open exchange that benefits to society can be achieved, even if there are some costs to this freedom. Doyle writes, "The utilitarian will concede that some things would be better left unexpressed, unpublished, unseen, and unread. The trouble is, we cannot know beforehand precisely which set of ideas or images, if published, would do more harm than good" (p. 69). If one wanted to put something of a negative spin on Doyle's statement one might say that in order for potential good to be realized, potential (perhaps even real) harm must be allowed. As Don Fallis and Kay Mathiesen (2001) counter, there may be instances where the potential harm is knowable and immediate; a utilitarian argument insufficiently accounts for the volition, emotion, and psychology of human agency (p. 438). Their assessment of a utilitarian position is correct; there still remains, though, the difficulty of knowing a priori what will be harmful, to whom, to what extent, in what circumstances.

Martin Frické, Kay Mathiesen, and Don Fallis (2000) argue for a different basis for intellectual freedom—social contract theory that draws from John Rawls's idea of rights. They claim that passages of the Library Bill of Rights are so absolutist that they don't allow for any negotiation among community members as to the relative costs and benefits of intellectual freedom. In a sense, the negotiation does take place in practice through the selection of materials for inclusion in libraries' collections. Robert Hauptman (2002) admits to such negotiation: "No library can acquire and none, except perhaps a national library, would want to own all publications and media formats in all disciplinary areas. Both sexually explicit magazines as well as scholarly disquisitions on topology would be out of place in a children's collection" (p. 21). Suppose, though, that librarian selectors determine that some sexually explicit content does have a place in a particular public library. The Library Bill of Rights (Article V) states that access is not to be proscribed because of age. Librarians may select some materials with a segment of the community in mind, but according to the Library Bill of Rights, the materials are to be accessible by the entire community. In this admittedly narrow interpretation of the document Hauptman's acknowledgment that selection may be specific to some groups doesn't hold in environments like public libraries.

It is here that Mill's position, not on utilitarianism but on liberty, is vital to a discussion of intellectual freedom. While "utility" is a hopelessly problematic measure of good (since utility can only be examined contextually and not universally), "liberty" is essential to any conception of intellectual freedom. Liberty has both moral and political import. Mill (and many others) takes considerable care to discern the difference between liberty and license. The latter is egoistic, includes no concern at all for damage or harm to others, and interferes with the liberty of others. The right to speak freely, for Mill, is constitutive of a free society, and speech that may result in some kinds of harm may be permitted (see Jacobson, 2000). Mill does say that the only official governmental interference with speech is based in harm, but harm is a limited constraint (Mill, 1972b, p. 78). Speech is primarily self-regarding. That is, Mill contends that it is an expression of one's own thoughts and opinions that others are free to ignore. Further, the speech of others is also self-regarding in its reception in that the hearer considers what is said, ideally, on its merits and accepts or rejects it according to the hearer's thoughts and opinions (or revisions of them as a result of what is said). The self-regarding element is extremely important to Mill, but it, too, has its problems. While individuals have, not just the ability, but the responsibility to reflect upon and evaluate what they say and what is said to them, communication doesn't end there. In fact, Mill's argument would be strengthened if he didn't place such importance on the self-regarding character of speech. Mill states his position:

> The real advantage which truth has consists in this, that when an opinion is true, it may be extinguished once, twice, or many times, but in the course of ages there will generally be found persons to rediscover it, until some one of its reappearances falls on a time when from favorable circumstances

it escapes persecution until it has made such head as to withstand all subsequent attempts to suppress it. (Mill, 1972b, p. 97)

Truth may well have an advantage when it is assessed empirically and logically, but ideology can get in the way of the assessment. "Speech" is not a thing in itself; it has varied purposes, depending on who's speaking, to whom, about what. Speech is not indifferently objective; it is the product of subjective voices and has a rhetorical character. If one person wants to persuade another of something, that first person may speak the truth if it will help with persuasion, but he may lie if that will work. Acceptance, belief, even consensus have nothing inherently to do with truth. More important, ideology is not merely persuasion; it is masking, hiding, dissimulating, rationalizing, and legitimating (see Eagleton, 1991). These are the kinds of intentional actions that can extinguish truth, and ideology is most successful when it's very difficult to recognize it as ideology. One of the more common uses of ideological discourse is dominance. If a faction is able to win the minds—and the discourse—of others, it becomes easier to subvert previously held beliefs and insinuate new ones. What is librarianship's response to ideological discourse? Does it/should it have a response? In defining the nature of ideology István Mészáros writes,

> In Western capitalist societies liberal/conservative ideological discourse dominates the assessment of all values to such an extent that very often we do not have the slightest suspicion that we are made to accept, quite unquestioningly, a particular set of values to which one could oppose a well founded alternative outlook, together with the commitments more or less implicit in it. (1999, p. 3)

The neutrality of official stances on free expression doesn't distinguish ideology from truth; the presumption is that this is the purview of the reader. For now we can focus on the ethical aspect of the presumption. To the extent that it holds, we don't have a problem; self-regarding individuals can discern the differences, subtle and overt. To the extent that it doesn't hold, we may be faced with an ethical dilemma.

The resolution of the dilemma rests on the acknowledged mission of the library. A university library will probably include ideological writings of many stripes and will co-locate them with non-ideological works. Telling the difference is an integral part of the educational process and fits with the purpose of such a library. If the mission of a public library is to include writings that are ideological and non-ideological without judgment of the works, then all will be taken as equal. No labeling, no exclusion, no removal of works can be justified by the mission. If the stated mission of a public library is to educate, enlighten, and provide a forum for informed discussion, then what action should be taken? Ideological discourse may drown out reasoned alternatives; if it does the utilitarian conceit falls apart even further. The ethical question revolves around what constitutes the "best" service to communities. The values of the Cincinnati (Ohio) Public Library include "Excellence": "The Library values excellence, individually and collectively. We offer quality service to all customers by displaying a positive attitude, valuing the diversity of people and perspective, and expecting integrity and competence in our personal and professional actions. We strive to earn the trust and confidence of all customers" (www.cincinnatilibrary.org/info/mission.asp). The statement refers to people as "customers," which is itself an ideological construction. Nowhere is "excellence" or "quality" defined. The value of "Open Access," does provide more of a purpose-driven statement of Being: "We are committed to connecting our customers to the ideas, information, and materials they wish to explore in a friendly, nonjudgmental manner." Borders book stores embrace "Discovery as a value: Borders celebrates the universal desire to explore and find personal enrichment and knowledge. We connect the act of exploration to the moment of discovery in a way that feels serendipitous, like a stroke of good fortune." The two statements seem interchangeable. Is the ethos of the public library the same as that of a retailer? More to the point: How intellectually free is this kind of public library, and how socially responsible is it?

We can return to Hauptman (2002) to investigate components of the dilemma further. He says that censorship "prescribes an *a priori* limitation on specific materials based on specious reasoning, religious or ideological persuasion, or emotional reaction" (p. 21). This statement characterizes all censorship in two ways: (1) it is always limiting texts, images, etc. before the fact, that is, before people have a chance to read or view them; and (2) the reasoning for the action is always groundless. The statement is accurate when applied to many efforts at censorship, but not all. If the position of a censor or challenger is (effectively), "I disagree with this material, so no one should see it," then there are no grounds for acceding to a demand for removal of an item. If the position is, "This material promotes action (hate, crime, or something else that is readily recognized as being in opposition to civil behavior) that is abhorrent, so I ask for a reconsideration of its presence in the collection," then the reasoning is not inherently specious. This is not to say that the library should remove the item in question simply on the grounds of the complaint, but the library's response should be in keeping with the nature of the complaint. Also, Hauptman's characterization is, prima facie, ideological in the same sense that censors' reasoning is. A simplistic reading of his characterization may suggest a denigration of individuals and groups because of their beliefs. A fuller reading would recognize that efforts to eliminate items from a library's collection are restrictive, but that the opinions, based on beliefs, of people (if one accepts the absolutism of the Library Bill of Rights) are as legitimately held as those of anyone else. There seems to be a need for some deeper inquiry into intellectual freedom.

While it doesn't carry the force of law, the Library Bill of Rights opens the door to a critical consideration of just what rights are. Let's assume, for the time being, that publicly supported libraries are forums in which free speech is to be honored. Do libraries and librarians have the right to "say" anything they want through collections, access to content, and services? Hauptman (2002) writes, "We are free to articulate anything we imagine. Sometimes free speech can cause others terrible harm, emotionally, psychologically, and physically. Thus, the well-meaning have passed laws, instituted regulations, and found in court decisions, all of which proscribe speech. *All* of these are unconstitutional" (p. 18; emphasis in original). In other words, the text of the First Amendment to the U.S. Constitution is to be taken more broadly than it is written; the *right* to free speech cannot be abridged in any way for any reason at any time. But what exactly does "abridge" mean? How is that word to be interpreted in actual instances, especially when someone is indeed claiming to have been harmed in some way by speech? Moreover, what counts as "speech?"

Later in his book Hauptman (2002) states that research misconduct could lead to serious, even dangerous, consequences, and that librarians should attempt to preserve the ethical integrity of the graphic record, but are enjoined against doing so by ALA Guidelines (pp. 97–98). Should librarians ignore those guidelines and label the fruits of misconduct? Research misconduct of all types violates trust; what is presumed to be the product of diligent inquiry is not. If a biomedical paper is retracted, the National Library of Medicine labels it as such in Medline. Should documented instances of plagiarism be so noted in libraries' catalogs? Perhaps the most salient point would be to initiate discussions among professionals about these matters and ask openly if some alert to readers and library users should be undertaken. In other words, what is librarianship's responsibility with regard to the public trust (see Altman and Hernon, 1997)? I agree that scientific and research misconduct can be a serious problem; if the misconduct is discovered in the process or peer and editorial review the work should not be published. But what distinguishes scientific fraud that makes its way into the literature from other potentially harmful speech? Why does Hauptman see one speech as constitutionally protected but not the other? In one instance free speech appears to be a natural right; in another instance it's not. Few rights are absolute; the same considerations that defend the right to speak also defend the rights of those who may be affected by what is spoken; this is why laws against slander and libel exist.

As part of historical awareness, many legal scholars emphasize that the First Amendment definitely applies to political speech. Of course that just leads to the problem of defining political speech. Cass Sunstein (1995) has said that speech is political "when it is both intended and received as a contribution to public deliberation about some issue" (p. 130). He was careful to add that "some issue" need not relate solely, strictly, or even partly about government; the issues spoken about can be broadly social. In other words (following James Madison), anything that can be deliberated deserves the highest protection in law. Ronald Dworkin (1996) raises a more complicated point regarding the First Amendment. Recall that in the last chapter the concept of constitutive points in reason arose. Dworkin makes a similar assessment of speech. Speech—and our freedom to engage in it—is *constitutive* of a just political society (pp. 200–213). It is a part of the essence of our society and the government *for* the people. This is a sweeping conception of speech, but one that our profession should be able to embrace. Free speech, as constitutive of society, assumes that morally responsible people are capable of and willing to make up their own minds based on what content can be available to them. This is a liberal viewpoint, in the nineteenth-century sense of placing some authority in people and not in a government that must protect people. It is a particular stance on rights.

Within librarianship there is concern regarding the balance of rights. Many libraries have established acceptable use policies as a means to respond to their communities. A number of policies specifically address the viewing of pornography in the library. The concern of libraries and librarians is understandable, but how are these policies reconciled with the LBR? Gordon Baldwin (1996), an attorney and faculty member at the University of Wisconsin–Madison Law School, points out that law does condemn censorship, but it also offers support for teachers and other public-sector professionals to support societal values. It is clear that ethical uncertainty exists, so we should ask if there is some way to clarify our situation. If the concept of free speech is in fact constitutive of a just political society, then we may have a framework according to which the complexity can be examined. Dworkin was careful to say that morally responsible people should be able to make up their minds; a step on the way to clarification is to ponder what "morally responsible" means. The Library Bill of Rights (Article V) suggests that all people, regardless of age or other conditions, are de facto morally responsible. This is a problematic suggestion. Children at certain physical and emotional levels of development may not be capable of appreciating some sexually explicit, overtly violent, or morally ambiguous content. They are treated, de jure, as different from adults. Mill (1972b) recognizes the difference between adults and children: "this doctrine [of liberty] is meant to apply only to human beings in the maturity of their faculties. We are not speaking of children, or of young persons below the age which the law may fix as that of manhood or womanhood" (p. 78). Before Mill, Locke (1988 [1690]) argued that parents' responsibility to their children don't end until the children reach the age of majority; until then one of their primary responsibilities is for the children's educations. Children have not attained full capabilities of reason, according to Locke (p. 311, ¶ 66).

In the limited space here I'll suggest that the bounded responsibility approach actually combines (1) and (2). In particular, I believe this approach is a strong moral response to the dilemma we face. Moral responsibility, first of all, is multifarious. It exists in and with each of us as part of our identities, but it also exists in and with us as we relate to one another. Our ethical being, with regard to intellectual freedom as to all other things, demands a phenomenological imperative (which also has political implications). I've described phenomenology in a previous work (Budd, 2001); the vital tenets include realization that our thoughts and actions are intentional (directed *at* something), concentration of the essences of human existence, and understanding of the connections between self and other (and this last is the most important for the current discussion). Here I differ with Mill; a self-regarding stance is not altogether adequate. Speech is intentional; someone says something to someone. Free speech is unencumbered in its intentionality. Speech is also a manifestation of the relationship between self and other. Speech, of course, can be truthful or not. In either event there is still a relationship between self and other and there is still a responsibility. Truth or falsehood, the speech is still intentional and still affects both self and other. True or false, speech has a speaker and, as Emmanuel Levinas (1969) pointed out, the speaker is, at least to some extent, present in the speech. Further, in a genuine sense, speech (especially free speech as constitutive of a democracy) is dialogic. As each of us reads, hears, or sees, each of us responds in some way to the speech—agreeing, disagreeing, wondering, questioning, or even ignoring. The absence of free speech is also constitutive, but of a repressive, mistrustful state that is capable of enabling only monologue and univocality.

With phenomenology as a background, the moral responsibility that attends speech is evident. For one thing, speech manifests the intentionality that is part of our Being. Morally responsible adults (and we have little choice but to presume that adults who are not in some way diminished have the capacity for moral responsibility) structure their speech intentionally in a free environment. Likewise, morally responsible adults are able to exercise their intentionality as readers, listeners, and viewers in a free environment. It is in precisely these ways that free speech is constitutive of a just political society. That is, intentional free speech has a constitutive quality to the extent that it is exercised. As a case in point, ideological speech (speech intended to shape belief and action along very particular lines, frequently for the purpose of power consolidation) abounds in a free environment. On the other hand, there is, at the very least, competing ideological speech and, at the best, explicit disputations with ideology plus a freedom to weigh the alternative manifestations of speech. Some laws, most notoriously the USA PATRIOT Act, impose univocality by suppressing speech and preventing openness through ideological tactics. There is no need to delve into the restrictive portions of the act, but one item is worth noting. Recently, the Library Connection of Windsor, Connecticut, was allowed to identify itself as a recipient of an FBI demand for library records ("Librarians Win," 2006, sec. B, p. 1). According to the article, about 30,000 such letters are issued by the FBI each year. Former U.S. Attorney General John Ashcroft repeatedly denied that the library-related section of the act was used until, in 2005, he admitted that it was used in one case. The reality of 30,000 letters points to the intrusiveness of the federal government into the activities of people. The phenomenological imperative has the additional advantage of avoiding the reification of "the people" (or in library parlance, "the user") and infusing appreciation of the identity, the "I," of "people" and "users."

The bounded component of bounded responsibility embraces the phenomenological development of each person. Every individual grows in her or his comprehension of the essences of Being, conception and application of intentionality, and rich understanding of the relationship of self and other as defining Being. In the course of phenomenological development, responsibility is partial and incomplete. The cognitive, intellectual, and emotional ability to speak with complete intentionality and to weigh speech in like manner is required for full moral responsibility. These notes here are prolegomena; the idea of bounded responsibility needs further investigation. Specifically, we need to know more about the development of individuals with regard to these phenomenological elements. While Kohlberg suggests some developmental stages, his theory has come under fire from several quarters. An approximation of the time of life when people do reach full moral responsibility in this phenomenological sense could help us better understand the applied concept of intellectual freedom. The understanding can have two components: (1) the ways that individuals begin to grasp the complexities of Being, especially the relationship between self and other (the self-regarding and other-regarding phenomena described by Mill), and (2) the ways we can foster this development in young people, with the end being the enhanced ability to exercise intellectual freedom.

It is the potential of speech to alter people's thinking and action that is the primary reason for its protection. Political speech held a special place for the authors of the founding documents of this nation. No one's voice should be suppressed because she dissents or because he says unpopular things. Speech as challenge is essential for liberty; the complacent majority that Mill speaks of is kept complacent by the control of speech; therefore, it is necessary for free speech to be the bastion of moral action. There is another side to free speech, though, and the other side also has a decidedly moral component. In the case of *Gertz v. Robert Welch, Inc.* (418 U.S. 323, 1974) the court ruled, "Under the First Amendment there is no such thing as a false idea. However pernicious an opinion may seem, we depend for its correction not on the conscience of judges and juries but on the competition of other ideas." This statement is fundamentally agnostic; it trusts no one to decide upon the merit of any speech. The arbiter is a market in which all speech circulates freely and equally. The LBR appears to be consistent with the court ruling. There is no gauge—linguistic, political, or moral—that can ensure that the offending speech doesn't have a positive side. Judith Butler (1997) writes, "The name one is called both subordinates and enables. . . . The word that wounds becomes an instrument of resistance in the redeployment that destroys the prior territory of its operation" (p. 163). Butler's ideal of speech is that of a force for dissent, even in the face of insult. Suppose, though, that the speech is not merely an insult, but calls for an uprising of people driven to kill members of a certain group. Is that empowering speech? Butler's naiveté denies that "excitable speech" can be "incitable speech" that can put people's lives in danger. Herein lies a problem: a wound becoming an instrument of resistance relies on everyone adopting the very same understanding of what language is and what it does. Transforming the inflammatory into the impotent is a laudable goal; is it an achievable one? And at what cost? I bring these issues up so that they can become a part of our discourse. Can it be, as Delgado and Stefancic (1997) urge us to consider, "Sometimes defending Nazis is simply defending Nazis" (p. 162)?

In asking questions about the LBR almost no one intends its abolition. An ethics of professional praxis cries for the guidance that the LBR seeks to give. The questions focus on specific—particular needs, phrasing that offers clarity, inclusion and exclusion of terms. In keeping with a need for guidance, Doyle and Frické and colleagues provide an invaluable start to a discourse that is essential. In order for a guide to intellectual freedom to make sense there must be a philosophical foundation. Deontological (Hauptman, 2002), utilitarian (Doyle, 2001, 2002), social contract (Frické, Mathiesen, and Fallis, 2000), and other stances must be on the table as we continuously consider rights, access, selection, and other vital professional matters. It is clear from the codes offered by ALA and the American Society of Information Science and Technology (ASIS&T) that there are some differences; in fact, there are potential contradictions. According to ASIS&T, the first professional responsibility is that professionals act by "not knowingly making false statements or providing erroneous or misleading information" (www.asis.org). The introduction of concern for truth and accuracy is yet another matter that should be integral to our ongoing discussions about intellectual freedom. Can an ethics of truth and accuracy be reconciled with a mission of customer service? Bounded responsibility indicates that truth is elusive, but falsehood may be discernible. Identifying community members as customers, however, may render truth irrelevant if service is defined by giving people what they ask for. The bounds of responsibility don't eliminate responsibility. A naive reading of the LBR could result in a totalization of any idea of license. All thoughts, works, and expressions have equal legitimacy. Instances of scientific misconduct instruct us that some expressions may be harmful. Within a framework of liberty, our professional discourse must also make room for responsibility. Libraries as just institutions are enemies of ideology. Therefore, intellectual freedom is not a natural right, but a means to an end. Moving from ethics to politics (and commingling the two), we can learn from Onora O'Neill's (2002) warning about a free press; it "is not an unconditional good. Press freedom is good because and insofar as it helps the public to explore and test opinions and to judge for themselves *whom* and *what* to believe and trust" (p. 95; emphasis in original).

As was mentioned in an earlier chapter, selection of information resources for inclusion in a library's collection or access mechanisms is usually done prior to full awareness of the content of the information carriers. Our deliberations should also address the following question: Should consideration relative to intellectual freedom include our ability to examine information content acquired by our libraries? That is, should our responsibility be most effectively fulfilled by a capacity to know what is in every information container? Elements of practicality, as well as idealism, should accompany any answer to the question. Many of the profession's official documents detail action that should be prevalent in libraries. The recommended actions may not be followed in some libraries in part because of expediency. "Expediency" is a word that may carry some baggage, but it isn't intended here to have pejorative connotations. For example, in public libraries that have publicly accessible computers and Internet connections, what one person is viewing may impose upon another person; a conflict results that must be handled by librarians. Openness of access may exacerbate the conflict, leading to considerable amounts of librarians' time spent on monitoring and conflict resolution. Principle and practice butt heads in such instances. So we need to ask ourselves, can principle and practice be reconciled so that an agreed-upon and workable definition of intellectual freedom can be devised? In actuality, the approaches that have dominated in librarianship have been based in two kinds of negative freedom. The first kind is evident in the Library Bill of Rights; people should be free from restrictions on their ability to read, view, inquire, etc. The second kind is evident in such practices as acceptable use policies; people should be free from the imposition of unwanted ideas, images, sounds, etc. Are the two positions irreconcilable? Can a library support the tenets of the Library Bill of Rights and still ensure that individuals are not confronted with anything that is not wanted? The task left to librarians is either to choose the first or the second kind of freedom, or to re-envision the freedom that guides our own action and our assumption about our communities.

The re-envisioned freedom hearkens back to the German model of higher education. The underlying principle of this freedom is what we can call bounded responsibility. As is the case with the German model, the operative assumption is that people are responsible; the addition here is the recognition that responsibility increases with age and cognitive/emotional/phenomenological development. In an elementary school library the assumption of responsibility is limited by the emotional, cognitive, and intellectual states of the pupils.

These pupils are not likely to be cognitively prepared for the complex arguments of, say, the phenomenological philosopher Edmund Husserl, to be intellectually prepared for the intricacies of string theory, or to be emotionally prepared for sexually explicit images. The actions of the librarians, then, are bounded by the responsibilities that the pupils are capable of.

Ethics and moral philosophy, as depicted here, are definitely not mere academic curiosities. Ethics and moral responsibility strike at the heart of librarianship; our daily actions are defined ethically. It's also clear that ethical and moral action is affected by the world outside the profession, perhaps especially the political world. Free speech, if it is indeed to be constitutive of a just political society, has to be examined within the context of politics generally. We've seen some of the ethical-political connections that are, perhaps, inevitable when it comes to the foundations of our profession. The next chapter will attempt to expand upon the political. Chapter 5 will focus on the politics, in particular the requirements of democracy, that have a deep and abiding impact on all that we've dealt with to this point. One of the topics that be addressed in the next chapter is the political reconciliation of intellectual freedom and social responsibility.

CHAPTER 5

In a Democracy . . .

OVER HALF A CENTURY AGO Sidney Ditzion (1947) published his extended essay, *Arsenals of a Democratic Culture*. The title itself is worth some attention. Ditzion's book is a product of the sociological tradition of its time; he sought causation for the establishment of public libraries and saw a narrowly defined "science" as fundamentally contributory to libraries' development. The "democratic culture" part doesn't raise many eyebrows; rhetoric about the democratizing power of public libraries had something of a history even by the mid-twentieth century. That "democratic culture" element is important, though, and it conjures up many thoughts about the political state in which we live and how we, as librarians, fit into it. "Arsenals" evokes something particular—libraries armed against an assault on the very essence of the United States. We have to remember that Ditzion's book was written in the early days of the Cold War, when democracy was perceived to be under attack. Also, the word "democracy" had some different connotations more than a half century ago. This recognition of the difference is no enlightening revelation. "Democracy" has meant many things to many people over time. While the Greeks are credited with establishing the first democracy, it was unlike eighteenth-century England, nineteenth-century France, or twenty-first-century United States. So the title of this chapter is a bit misleading; it's no simple matter either to describe libraries in the U.S. political environment today or to prescribe what libraries should be like. I'll proceed on the assumption that an understanding of today's politics and what libraries and librarianship mean at this time and in this place is needed. One reason for the need is that politics and ethics, as discussed in the last chapter, are closely related. For example, we can, and should, consider both what is morally good and what is politically good. Concerns such as those that surround freedom of information, intellectual freedom, and censorship illustrate the connection well.

When you hear the word "politics," do you usually associate it with ethics? Almost all politics entails the creation of an ethos. Even Machiavelli designed an ethos in describing the world of the Prince and prescribing strategic and tactical means for achieving goals. A mindset of ruling that holds that the ruler can employ what might otherwise be deemed immoral means still has particular ends in sight. The good relates to those ends, and means that may include lies, disinformation, silencing some people, and even waging war as ways to achieve the good. Of course this is by no means the only possible political ethos. Others include adherence to natural law, optimization (sometimes maximization) of individual liberty, equality, representative governance, and populism. All of the exercises of politics have desired ends. Here we can make an explicit link to the foregoing chapters. Libraries of all types exist within clearly delineated political environments. The political world customarily defines funding, personnel management, and many aspects of operation. The environments themselves exist within a larger political environment of regulation, taxation, human relations, legal constraints, etc. For example, a library in a public university must accept budgetary regulations and flows, hiring practices, status and rank within the university structure, and numerous other things. The university, in turn, operates as part of some systematic arrangement of like institutions, may be overseen by a governing board, receive appropriations from a legislature, and so on. Ignorance of the structures leads not only to some operational difficulties, but also to missed opportunities and potential liability. Furthermore, there are political decisions that guide internal policy and practice of the library. In order to address the complexity of politics, this chapter will not follow a linear path. (We'll begin with some of the clearest and most common ways that the political permeates our professional lives. Following that, we'll back up to examine the historical/social nature of politics in the United States as it affects us and our organizations.)

A Start

In order to understand today's politics we need to be aware of the complex, sometimes conflicting, ideas and forces of the past. The understanding includes the effects of the ideas and forces on one another and the reactions to the contests. It isn't as though people arrived in America and immediately intuited consensual opinions on how government should be structured and should work, and what people's responsibilities and freedoms consist in. Grade school history may lead us to think that there is a chronological line that signifies progress, as it may be defined in some particular ways. The definitions include (from the rather parochial U.S. point of view) security, prosperity, technical enhancement, freedom, equality, and democracy. There have been numerous undeniable changes over time, and there has been discernible progress. That said, the changes, and even progress, have had their costs. Our collective memory has, at times, served us well in preserving some of the ideals that were articulated as the United States was formed; our collective amnesia has led to problems as we've forgotten the circumstances in which the ideals were devised. Our libraries are products of political actions, tensions, and compromises. The environments of our careers are fraught with the challenges that typify the political state of today and its genealogy.

The founders of our nation were, by and large, learned men, and some of them were well versed in classical and modern political thought. The classical element (for convenience here) can be reduced to the conflicting ideas of Plato and Aristotle. Of course both have been enormously influential—and rightly so—but their thoughts on democracy were not in concert. While "democracy" and "politics" held different meanings in antiquity, the words of Plato and Aristotle certainly remain important today. Plato was no fan of democracy. In giving voice to many, according to him, democracy not only includes disagreement, it fosters it. For Plato, as expressed his views in *The Republic*, democracy has no basis in commonly held values. In vilifying the indulgences of democracy, Plato (1973) had Socrates say, "Much of [a man's] time is spent in politics, where he leaps to his feet and says and does whatever comes into his head. Or if he comes to admire the military, then that is the way he goes. Or if it's businessmen, then that way. There is no controlling order or necessity in his life" (p. 274, §561d). Order, governance, and justice, for Plato, would only be possible within a system ruled by philosopher-kings, who can know and understand what is good and right. Plato's arguments are not simple or entirely consistent. For example, he does place justice at or near the top of concerns for the city. On the other hand, Plato does *not* articulate a political process, a way to achieve any goals of justice; the absence of process can open the door to totalitarian influences that don't care about systemic political process. Also, Plato argues that women may possess all of the attributes and abilities that suit them for governance. He held that revolutionary idea even though he also held many of the misogynistic prejudices of the age.

Plato did admit that the task of the philosopher-king is to create harmony and community, but Aristotle was much more prone both to trust the citizen in the exercise of government and to impose responsibilities on citizens in that exercise. He made this clear in *The Politics*. In Book 3, Chapter 1 (1984) he wrote, "The citizen in an unqualified sense is defined by no other thing so much as by sharing in decision and office" (p. 87). The civic responsibility of participation is adopted in our form of governance today. It is not just the citizen, though, that captured Aristotle's attention. In Book 3, Chapter 6 (1984) he said, "It is evident, then, that those regimes that look to the common advantage are correct regimes according to what is unqualifiedly just, while those which look only to the advantage of the rulers are errant, and are all deviations from the correct regimes; for they involve mastery, but the city is a partnership of free persons" (p. 95). In short, citizen and state are to coexist and be partners in all aspects of civic life. Coexistence sometimes results in disorder; Plato valued order, but Aristotle insisted on personal autonomy. The good life is an individual choice based in reason. His politics is steeped in process.

While Plato and Aristotle have not been ignored, there is something of a British tradition that has shaped political life in the United States—and it's a mixed tradition. It's only a bit of an overstatement to say that the

Enlightenment shaped the politics of today. The only challenge is to figure out when the Enlightenment began, what it meant, and who can be included in it. The Enlightenment, and modernism generally, have been criticized in recent years as being too intellectually rigid, being unwilling to acknowledge uncertainty, reducing knowledge to method, creating grand narratives, and being prescriptive with respect to most walks of life. To an extent Enlightenment thought, as articulated by some eighteenth-century figures, warrants some criticism. What is not warranted is the wholesale rejection of the modernist program (which began with the immediate precursors to the Enlightenment moral, scientific, and political philosophers. Late sixteenth- and seventeenth-century thinkers paved the way for a different kind of exploration of the natural and social worlds. That some of these individuals conflated the natural and the social may be seen as a particular and problematic path of inquiry; that some individuals continue the conflation can be seen as perpetuating a specific error. Neither the philosophy nor the politics of the eighteenth century can be characterized as wholly subject to the error, though. Historical investigation reveals that the emergence of social and political liberalism has origins in Enlightenment thought. This liberalism has influenced many of the documents founding our nation, and the evolution of documents that guide our profession.

The Library Bill of Rights can be read more as a naively libertarian than a liberal document, with a standpoint that stems from the fundamental position, "that all speech stands on the same ground and that government has absolutely no business censoring speech merely because some people, or some officials, are puritanical or offended by it" (Sunstein, 1995, p. 212). This definition expresses a civil libertarian stance, but there are more extreme forms of libertarianism (that are not infrequently invoked when some forms of speech, such as Holocaust denial and other very sensitive and even fact-contrary speech, are in question). The extreme approaches an absolutist claim; *all* speech must be free. So, if there are any limits on speech, on what is the limitation based? That is, if some form of speech (say, child pornography) is proscribed, what is the explicit rationale that leads to the proscription? Some challenges to the extreme libertarian stance argue that among other things, it is non-theoretical. This means that there are no special conceptual foundations needed to allow for individualist transactions of any sort. A person entering a library and reading a book or magazine, viewing images, or listening to sounds should not be subject to official controls imposed by any institution. The library, like the state, has the responsibility to see to it that whatever the person wants, the person can get. John Rawls (1996), however, observes that

> While the libertarian view makes important use of the notion of agreement, it is not a social contract theory at all; for a social contract theory envisages

the original compact as establishing a system of common public law which defines and regulates political authority and applies to everyone as a citizen. Both political authority and citizenship are to be understood through the conception of the social contract itself. By viewing the state as a private association the libertarian doctrine rejects the fundamental ideas of the contract theory, and so quite naturally it has no place for a special theory of justice for the basic structure. (p. 265)

Also, Samuel Nelson (2005) points out that the libertarian positions on free speech fail to present a comprehensive and inclusive conception of political speech (pp. 30–60).

Nelson (2005) also reminds us that genuine free speech absolutists are rare; almost everyone objects to *some* form of speech. Hauptman (2002), as was discussed in the last chapter, warns against scientific misconduct and urges measures to prevent it. Of course concern about scientific misconduct is entirely legitimate; moreover, the concern is part of our professional responsibility. One reason for the importance of this responsibility is the potential for harm, and in this case the burden for demonstrating harm can be relatively high and the product of misconduct would still exceed it. As we saw in the last chapter, we must be concerned about consequences. But how do we gauge the probability the probability of harm stemming from information? A partial answer to the question follows Sunstein (1995), who advocates a plurality of free speech values. In the case of scientific misconduct, the quest for knowledge (which is valued) may be hampered. The recent incident involving Wu Sook Hwang's putative research on stem cells is a case in point. Hwang was found to have fabricated data, but not before the work was published in prominent journals and affected the research of scientists around the world. Integrity in research and scholarship is valued for its own sake; it is assumed to be essential to formal inquiry.

A plurality of free speech values suggests that a libertarian approach falls short of some intellectual freedom goals. The libertarian stance is grounded in (usually unstated) value neutrality. Each individual is responsible for her or his own reading, viewing, and listening (as is stated above). All librarians should question whether neutrality is, in fact, neutral. In the political world of information there are some serious problems that we have to come to grips with. One problem centers on what is *not* available. For example, the current state of information production (publishing, broadcast media, newspapers, etc.) is not entirely inclusive. Ownership of production outlets is so heavily concentrated in a few hands that alternative voices are difficult to locate, much less provide access to. (This phenomenon will be examined in more detail below.) Rather than present an exhaustive treatment of neutrality, I recommend to all librarians Toni Samek's (2001) *Intellectual Freedom and Social Responsibility*. Samek clearly demonstrates that neutrality in the interests of the status quo is *not* politically neutral. The status quo is based on the acquisition and application of power that leads to the production and dissemination of some information and not other information. In a very real way Samek confirms Hume's dictum that one cannot infer "ought" from "is." Further, she draws from numerous sources to show that the premise of libraries as democratic institutions (we can revisit Ditzion) is likewise not politically neutral. The absence of some voices—or their silencing—can be linked to a mistaken notion of neutrality.

Another problem rests with information that *is* available. As we saw in Chapter 4, a professional value is the provision of accurate information to meet information seekers' needs. Such a value is not neutral; it expresses something positive about the profession. This positive expression relates directly to our professional ethos. John-Bauer Graham (2003) states that, "If one feels that the library is bound to provide information that is considered 'true' or 'just' then the answer is yes—they have an agenda and thus they do not exist as neutral institutions. On the other hand, if one feels that the library is only there to store information, (letting its community decide for itself what is right and wrong) it could be said that they do not" (pp. 9–10). The matter of truth arises again in a very practical way here. It's inconceivable that anyone would argue for either process- or aim-neutrality in something like reference services. Through education and experience, we learn a means by which we can locate valid and reliable answers to people's questions (use authoritative sources for data-based queries and multiple and diverse sources for interpretation-based queries, for example). We also learn that it is our responsibility to identify falsehoods and to present them as such, so that an "accurate" response can be provided. These aims require evaluation of what is available. Of course, the bases for evaluation can vary; a professional responsibility is to ensure that evaluation follows honest efforts to assess the truth conditions of claims; the truth (or accuracy) of some claims may be elusive even as falseness may be ascertained ("I don't know what X is, but I know it's not Y"). As Robert Jensen (2004/2005) put it, "The appropriate question isn't 'are you political?' but instead should be 'can you defend the conclusions you reach?'" (p. 31).

AN ILLUSTRATIVE DEBATE

An example might serve us here. Suppose someone comes into the library and says, "I've heard some people say that John Kerry didn't earn the medals he was awarded for his service in Vietnam. Did he lie about what happened?" Granted, this is a particularly difficult question to answer, and might be beyond the ready knowledge of many librarians. The difficulty puts the urgency of the political concern and the importance of professional responsibility in stark relief. One option for the librarian is to seek out materials (in various media) on the topic and present them to the requestor. The librarian might then encourage the individual to read and evaluate the materials. Noel Peattie (Swan and Peattie, 1989) ably articulate support for this kind of response: "we believe that the most effective advocacy of the truth lies in the act of insuring the widest possible access to all the versions thereof—many of which contain no truth at all" (pp. 16–17). He defended his position by invoking civil libertarian ideals set forth by John Stuart Mill and Oliver Wendell Holmes, arguing that access most effectively meets the democratic test. An alternative response might be to present the various opinions and commentaries on Kerry's military service, and point out the merits and demerits of each of the sets of opinions. Note that I didn't say that the librarian should brand one set of opinions as lies and another set as true. One book, *Unfit for Command* (O'Neill, 2004), presents certain accounts of events, and accuses Kerry of distorting his record. Other works demonstrate that the authors of the book and accusers they quote were not present at many of the events they mention. Further, some of these opposing works offer recounts of the events by people who were present. The latter response (or perhaps an even stronger version) is defended by Noel Peattie (Swan and Peattie, 1989): "I hold that truth is primary to freedom on (at least) some occasions: those in which convention has established a truth—however defined—that the rest of us condemn at our peril" (p. 68).

Swan (1989), in responding to Peattie, reemphasizes that he is not only interested in truth, but that truth is vital to our professional lives. An old edition of the *Physician's Desk Reference* may contain information that has been demonstrated erroneous; weeding that item is not really a matter of contention. He goes on, though, to say that truth, in any sort of unequivocal sense, is elusive in many instances. When truth is not determinate, our professional responsibility is to facilitate access that is as open, free, and complete as possible. Swan's civil libertarianism (which is not in danger of devolving into neoliberalism) is a clear contrast to the extreme libertarianism I've spoken of above. The autonomy of the individual is tempered by responsibility that can be readily recognized and distributed. Swan recalls Oliver Wendell Holmes's minority opinion in the case of *Abrams v. United States*. The case was heard by the U.S. Supreme Court; it involved a violation of the Espionage Act of 1918, which was more prohibitive than almost all previous legislation when it came to constraining some speech. Holmes did recognize that even loathsome speech must be protected and, as Robert Post (2000) demonstrates, Holmes's opinion represents "the first judicial expression of a theory of the First Amendment" (p. 2361).

That said, I do have to take issue with Swan's favorable assessment of Justice Holmes's dissent in *Abrams v. United States* that truth is what withstands competition in the marketplace of discourse. Intellectual freedom and free speech aimed at truth depend on the *free* expression of ideas. Holmes—and Swan—presume a marketplace of ideas that is faithful to ideals of logic, argument, empirical examination, and ethical political presentation. There are two problems with this notion: (1) discourse is not entirely free in that some voices come through loud and clear while others are at best a whisper, and (2) the marketplace can succumb to persuasive voices that can garner support from a majority. Furthermore, Holmes is a rather odd hero for an intellectual freedom movement; while he did fall on the side of freedom in *Abrams*, in other opinions he was less willing to allow for unfettered free speech. Holmes was not a liberal, in the sense I'm using it here, and he tended, on the whole, to be quite cynical regarding humankind and society. Mill himself was more wary of any idea of a marketplace. Jill Gordon (1997), in a masterful analysis of Mill's thinking on liberty and the metaphor of the marketplace of ideas, explicates Mill's writings. Not only did Mill not employ the metaphor, the notion of marketplace is antithetical to his prescription for liberty. As Gordon (1997) explains, "It would seem that the marketplace has become the paradigm we value, but this paradigm, I want to suggest, stems from an ideological framework that Mill did not share. . . . Mill placed considerable value on cooperation, a skill that he believed would come to those who were afforded the opportunity to become educated and developed" (p. 245). The perversion of Mill's idea of liberty institutionalizes the marketplace metaphor.

The matter of liberty is no less complex a matter than those we've discussed so far. Complex or not, it is extremely important for librarians to deliberate on what liberty is and what the role of libraries in promoting it might be. Mill doesn't provide that last word on liberty, but he raises issues and makes observations that we must be cognizant of. For one thing, he (1972b) states clearly what the most typical motivation is of those who would curtail liberty (and censorship is ones means of curtailment): "The practical principle which guides them to their opinions on the regulation of human conduct, is the feeling in each person's mind that everybody should be required to act as he, and those with whom he sympathises, would like him to act" (p. 74). He argues instead that "it is the privilege and proper condition of a human being, arrived at the maturity of his faculties, to use and interpret experience in his own way. It is for him to find out what part of recorded experience is properly applicable to his own circumstances and character" (pp. 125–26). Intellectual freedom, then, is necessary (even if it isn't sufficient) for liberty. The minds and wills of people can be free only if they aren't prevented from individual assessment of ideas. This realization doesn't eliminate all unease and concern related to intellectual freedom, though. Mill (1972b) suggests a position upon which we can base the kind of inclusiveness implied by the LBR: "We can never be sure that the opinion we are endeavouring to stifle is a false opinion; and if we were sure, stifling it would be an evil still" (p. 85). But what of the lie? This is a question we'll return to shortly.

The force of persuasion, mentioned above, is reminiscent of what Michel Foucault (1971) calls the "will to truth," or "will to knowledge."

> But this will to truth, like other systems of exclusion, relies on institutional support: it is both reinforced and accompanied by whole strata of practices such as pedagogy—naturally—the book-system, publishing, [and] libraries. . . . But it is probably even more profoundly accompanied by the manner in which knowledge is employed in a society, the way in which it is exploited, divided and, in some ways, attributed. . . . Finally, I believe that this will to knowledge, thus reliant upon institutional support and distribution, tends to exercise a sort of pressure, a power of constraint upon other forms of discourse. (p. 219)

Swan is not ignorant of this phenomenon, but Peattie stresses it more and, perhaps, more effectively. The will to truth suggests that, while absolute truth may not be determinable, falsehood may be. What is our professional responsibility when the latter is the case? The will to truth is reminiscent of Mill's contention that truth may be opposed and suppressed; for Foucault the suppression can come at the hands of the institutions that ostensibly exist to preserve open mechanisms that allow truth to be known. Among other institutions he names education and libraries as adherents of a will to truth.

There is something even more fundamentally problematic about the naive libertarian position on intellectual freedom. While truth may be a concern, there is an inherent egalitarian assumption at work—all information has the same value. After all, someone can find instructive a work with which she or he disagrees, or even finds offensive. However, if truth (or even accuracy) is a value to be espoused, not all information is equal. An example that Swan and Peattie discuss is that of a Holocaust denier. Swan (1989) offers a defense for allowing the individual to speak: "The speaker has a right to speak, not because his brand of racism just may be one of those truths waiting for vindication, but he also has the right to utter untruths that will never be vindicated. The suppression of any idea can be dangerous to the flow of all ideas" (p. 10). A problem with Swan's position is that untruths can thus be promulgated freely, which can thus impinge on freedom. For example, according to the argument it could be said that the fraudulent scientific work on stem cells, mentioned earlier, deserves a place in discourse on the grounds of freedom, even if it could damage further research and perhaps even have deleterious clinical effects. Also, the U.S. government could state anything it chooses, including deliberate lies, and the only test of veracity would be the marketplace. Hateful speech, when it is protected, can do genuine damage: "The harm to hate speech's victims, out on the periphery, by contrast is treated atomistically, as though it were an isolated event, a mere one-time-only affront to feelings" (Delgado and Stefancic, 1997, p. 155). Such speech frequently relies on falsehoods. To repeat, even when determination of truthfulness is in question, the determination of falseness may be possible. In short, reason and its application is an integral component of freedom. In order to choose from among ideas and claims, one must have some evidence for choosing one way, and not another. We should be able to recognize the difference between alternative viewpoints and lies. What we might call procedural equality (selecting and providing access to multiple viewpoints) does not necessarily result in informative equality (gaining justified, supported, or corroborated reasons for accepting some claims). In fact, the former may at times be antithetical to the latter. The freedom of people to speak does not lead automatically to the necessity for libraries to select everything that is said (although it does necessitate providing some access to speech that is requested). In Rawls's (2001) idea of justice as fairness there are conditions that must be satisfied for fairness to be realized; "these condition must situate free and equal persons fairly and must not permit some to have unfair bargaining advantages over others. Further, threats of force and coercion, deception and fraud, and so on must be ruled out" (p. 15). Rawls provides a rational political argument for freedom not being based on a naive notion of equality.

Returning to the will to truth, which does interfere with a free marketplace of ideas, we can delve into its ramifications. If there were a marketplace of ideas in the sense people have ascribed to Mill, then there would be an ethical/political imperative that would deflate the will to truth. If, on the other hand, the marketplace of ideas is as flawed as the marketplace of commodities, then the will to truth can flourish. The marketplace, after all, exists to buy and sell, and the transaction is at the heart of its purpose. The extreme individualism that is possible in the marketplace is criticized by commentators on the Left and Right. The critique from the Left tends to focus on liberalism as conceived in individual autonomy within the context of a struggle against the institutions that perpetuate the will to truth (see Shapiro, 2003c). From the Right the concern is more with the destruction of values, aesthetics, and a particular definition of culture (that is, high culture). Robert Bork (2003) is one spokesman for the critique from the Right:

> The destruction of standards is inherent in radical individualism. . . . Sooner or later censorship is going to have to be considered as popular culture continues plunging to ever more sickening lows. . . . Censorship is a subject that few people want to discuss . . . because the ethos of modern liberalism has made any interference with the individual's self-gratification seem shamefully reactionary. (pp. 140–41)

In an Afterword that expanded on his position Bork wrote, "Pornography, obscenity, gratuitous depictions of carnage, and the grossest forms of vulgarity will not be censored, given today's Supreme Court, but conservative and traditional ideas and attitudes, which are anathema to modern liberals, may well" (pp. 346–47). The passages demonstrate the role that forceful rhetoric plays in discourse. Does Bork actually provide evidence for any sort of liberalism *causing* an erosion of standards? If we do accept that standards of expression have changed, we'll also see that causation is not easy to ascribe. We can, however, see evidence that markets for commodities don't introduce morality or aesthetics as measures of success; transactions and profits gauge effectiveness in markets. In a different vein, Christopher Lasch (1995) observes, "Having been effectively excluded from public debate on the grounds of their incompetence, most Americans no longer have any use for the information inflicted on them in such large amounts ... a reminder that it is debate itself, and debate alone, that gives rise to the desire for usable information" (pp. 11–12). Lasch's statement is a more politically useful one than Bork's because it is not the content of the information that concerns him, it is the treatment of it in civic discourse.

REWIND

In order to understand today's politics we need to be aware of the complex, sometimes conflicting, ideas and forces of the past. The understanding includes the effects of the ideas and forces upon one another and the reactions to the contest. It isn't as though people arrived in America and immediately intuited consensual opinions on how government should be structured and work, and what people's responsibilities and freedoms consist in. Grade school history may lead us to think that there is a chronological line that signifies progress, as it may be defined in some particular ways. The definitions include (from the rather parochial U.S. point of view) security, prosperity, technical enhancement, freedom, democracy, and domination. There have been numerous undeniable changes over time, and there has been discernible progress. That said, the changes, and even progress, have had their costs. Our collective memory has, at times, served us well in preserving some of the ideals that were articulated as the United States was formed; our collective amnesia has led to problems as we've forgotten the circumstances in which those articulations were made. Our libraries are products of political actions, tensions, and compromises. The environments of our careers are fraught with the challenges that typify the political state of today and its genealogy.

The early seventeenth century saw the birth of many ideas that are still discussed today. Among the many aphorisms attributed to him, Francis Bacon was to have said that "knowledge is power." This could be the motto for our profession, but it requires a little explication. Bacon's writings indicate a very strong concern for the outcomes of human action, especially with regard to scientific endeavors. As Jesse Shera (1964) pointed out, Bacon saw scientific experimentation as potentially shedding light or bearing fruit. Both have value but, according to Bacon, it is fruit-bearing science that can transform the human condition. The term "useful knowledge" has been used over the years in conjunction with libraries. People benefit from libraries in that libraries become means of how to *do* things; in particular, people learn things that enable them to improve their lives. This is an idea that is quite deeply ingrained in American politics; the self-reliant individual is a figure to be admired and emulated.

The place of science in the Enlightenment is a fairly persistent theme over the centuries. Thomas Hobbes picks up the notion, particularly in *Leviathan*. In that, and in other books (such as *On the Citizen*), Hobbes develops an extensive system of governance principles. While he (1998 [1642]) posited that "everyone should be equal to everyone" (p. 50), that equality is extra-governmental; it applies to personal life, occupation, etc. Peace (internally and externally) for Hobbes is best achieved by some sort of consensual rule of the many by the few. "A commonwealth, then, (to define it) is one person, whose will, by the agreement of several men, is to be taken as the will of them all; to make use of their strength and resources for the common peace and defence" (Hobbes, 1998 [1642], p. 73). His justification for governance by the few is largely pragmatic; deliberation among many is difficult to accomplish. Pragmatic or not, Hobbes's ideas of government may frighten us today, especially in that our nation's federal government is leaning in Hobbes's direction. He writes in *Leviathan* (1996 [1651]), "The sovereign of the commonwealth, be it an assembly, or one man, is not subject to the civil laws. For having power to make, and repeal laws, he may when he pleaseth, free himself from that subjection, by repealing those laws that trouble him, and making of new" (p. 176). Much of Hobbes's work is relegated to the academic world these days, but, as we'll see, he prescribed a political life that, consciously or not, is alive today.

Much more of an evident political heritage comes from John Locke. Locke echoes some of Hobbes's observations, but he parts from Hobbes on a number of points. One similarity between the two is a realization that effective and just governance is based in the consensual agreement among individuals, and not by the exercise of force by rulers over "the people." The implications of this idea are profound; individuals are neither aggregated nor subjected. The agreement is not made once for all time, but is a continuous and procedural matter. One hallmark of Locke's idea of government is the definition of property (although this is emblematic of a sweeping prominence of the individual). He specifically looked to America (the colonies) to establish a just conception of property. "Just" he defines as necessary and sufficient for the material needs of families, so that no one would experience want. A fairly lengthy quotation from his *Second Treatise on Government* (1988 [1690]) sums up his stance:

> Where there is not something both lasting and scarce, and so valuable to be hoarded up, there Men will not be apt to enlarge their Possessions

of Land, were it never so rich, never so free for them to take. For I ask, What would a Man value Ten Thousand, or an Hundred Thousand Acres of excellent Land, ready cultivated, and well stocked too with Cattle, in the middle of the in-land Parts of America, where he had no hopes of Commerce with other Parts of the World, to draw Money to him by the Sale of the Product? It would not be worth the inclosing, and we should not see him give up again to the wild Common of Nature, whatever was more than would supply the Conveniencies [*sic*] of Life to be had there for him and his Family. (p. 301, § 48)

As the United States was being born there was forceful (frequently armed) resistance to any sort of aristocratic imposition of control or domination. Locke was a hero to many colonists. "By the 1740s, the Junto [the Club of the Leather Aprons, established by Benjamin Franklin (among others)] was both a political club and a reading society, the two being pleated together. Of the first 375 books the Junto members collected—the foundation of North America's first circulating library—more had come from the pen of John Locke than by any other author" (Nash, 2005, p. 96). So prior to the formal establishment of the United States of America there was a tradition of independence and self-determination, a mindset of confronting threats of corralling that independent spirit. That tradition interestingly thrived as founding fathers debated the nature and structure of a democracy that was consciously different from England's. The early and rapid (for the time) expansion of territory effectively enabled the tradition to continue, since firm, centralized government control was very difficult. The tradition as it might be envisioned in the most extreme possible manifestations would naturally conflict with order ruled by law. Even Hobbes maintains that peace is the most rational state of being, though. So, for a number of decades the politics of the United States entailed finding a balance between the tradition of individual independence and laws that protect both individuals and society. There is inevitable tension in trying to reach a balance. For one thing, positive and negative rights have to be reconciled. "Life, liberty, and the pursuit of happiness" may bump directly into the Bill of Rights. Libraries too must consider positive and negative rights, as we'll see. Some of our thorniest problems arise from conflict between positive and negative rights.

So What Do We Call Democracy Today?

Is this the $64,000 question? In many ways it is. "Democracy" has always meant many things and these things have certainly not always been in agreement. There is an underlying idealistic assumption that tends to pervade almost all ideas of democracy—the stances of all people and all groups regarding rights, responsibilities, justice, and fairness are commensurable.

That is, all of the various beliefs and opinions are understandable by all of the participants. You and I may disagree about, say, a specific piece of information (a book, an article, a Web site), but we can comprehend each other's position. From that vantage point we are (ideally) able to discuss the matter. But take the word "information." Do we all mean the same thing when we use it? If we don't, how do we talk about it? The same applies to "democracy." If a politician says something like, "Our democracy requires that we agree with the position of the President," we will wonder how he is defining the word. If by democracy we mean direct citizen participation in government decisions, we do not have a democracy in the United States. A representative system is supposed to reflect governance by the people, but the supposition is problematic (and will not be discussed here). The idealistic assumption is something, however, that we do have to address with regard to libraries and our profession.

Even more fundamentally, we have to think about purposes that may underpin democracy. In the last chapter we saw that intellectual freedom can be argued for on utilitarian or social contract grounds (among other ways). As we work in our daily lives we may be tempted to ignore the arguments as too arcane for practical application. These ideas, though, strike at our reason for being. If we act in certain ways we are, in fact, following particular conceptual, and perhaps even teleological, paths. If we do so blindly, how do we know we're doing right by our communities? How do we know what other options are open to us? What version of democracy are we defining through our actions? And what are the moral ramifications of what we do? Chantal Mouffe (2000) raises these kinds of questions in her examination of what she calls the democratic paradox. If, for example, we were to say that we function within a "liberal democracy," we may find ourselves between competing aims. "On one side we have the liberal tradition constituted by the rule of law, the defence of human rights and the respect of individual liberty; on the other democratic tradition whose main ideas are those of equality, identity between governing and popular sovereignty" (Mouffe, 2000, pp. 2–3). So are individual liberties and equality at odds in some instances? There is a struggle taking place between such forces, and we're in the middle of it. A responsibility of a professional is to confront the kinds of forces that affect the action of the profession.

I mentioned earlier that the Enlightenment was, in many ways, the progenitor of today's politics. In saying this I also mean to illustrate that some of the contests we find ourselves in the midst of date back to the Enlightenment. It was during the seventeenth and eighteenth centuries that political philosophers sought foundations for a rational structure of government. There are, of course, different paths of rationality in government that depend on the goals that government seeks to achieve. Let's say the primary goal of government is order and security. The rational means to the achievement of the goal may be control that is as complete as possible. To that end, all citizens are required to have proper identification, movement of individuals is restricted, communication is monitored and perhaps limited, and force can be used by officials. The means to accomplish the end flow from the end itself. If people are willing to accept control because the desire for order and security is strong, then the processes the government can engage in are warranted. Any conception of democracy, though, balks at the sole objective of control, since it takes discretion and autonomy away from people—individually and collectively. Even if we limit the perspective on government to democracy, we still face, as Mouffe illustrates, serious definitional challenges that lead directly to dilemmas related to the purpose of libraries.

There is no single, universal definition of democracy, and there is no single structure and/or process that can be said to facilitate democracy. Since the time of the Enlightenment theorists have debated rational foundations for democracy. The rationality tends to be broadly based, since there are multiple points of view in any society. As previously observed, controllers would see rationality as functioning optimally if they are able to ensure order and security for all. On the other hand, for those who desire optimal deliberation (in amount and in kind), rationality would lead to opportunity for as many people as possible to participate in deliberation, in as many forums for deliberation as would be needed by participants, and deliberation governed by reasoned argument wherein all who want to may speak. Even within such a structure, rationality would dictate that no one should be forced or coerced into speaking or listening. The role of the library would follow the rationality of the structure in operation. Order and security would tend to devalue dissent within society and within the library; contents and services would be designed to foster optimal order. Deliberation would welcome and encourage dissent (based in reason), so the library would be a potential forum for argumentation, conjecture, and refutation.

The various forms of democracy exist, to some extent and to widely varying degrees, at this time in the United States. There are ideals of democracy; there are pragmatics of democracy; there are limitations to democracy. In short (and to no one's surprise) "democracy" is contested ground. Robert Dahl (1989) briefly outlines the scope of the contest among theorists:

> Critics are roughly of three kinds: those fundamentally opposed to democracy because, like Plato, they believe that while it may be possible it is inherently undesirable; those fundamentally opposed to democracy because, like Robert Michels, they believe that, while it might be desirable if it were possible, in actuality it is inherently impossible; and those sympathetic to democracy and wishing to maintain nonetheless critical of it in some important regard. (p. 2)

In the popular mind the contest is no less heated, but it may be less conscious. What I mean by that is individuals use the word "democracy" freely, without attaching specific reference to it, without intending the word to mean certain institutions, sets of rights or freedoms, an economic system, or a process for making binding decisions (Dahl, 1989, p. 5). The differences may seem too subtle and nuanced for distinctions to be appreciated, so the speaker who uses the word "democracy" may not be entirely sure what he or she means. In the United States, democratic institutions, narrowly defined, are difficult to find; rationalities of control tend to preclude governance by all. One might say that it's a very good thing that most institutions are not internally democratic; little or nothing would get done. Imagine our institutions administered by committees of the whole. I don't mean to be facetious; democracy is problematic in many ways, even if we believe in it whole-heartedly and want it to be the paradigm of social life.

AGGREGATIVE DEMOCRACY

When democracy does operate, it can do so in several ways. These ways of operating are not necessarily entirely discrete; two or more of them may be in place simultaneously. The interaction among them can lead to tension and can heighten the contest. In particular there may be what we can call aggregative democracy. This version is not often openly acknowledged, but it does tend to work whenever there is a well-established central representative government and a large population. In this kind of government universal deliberation is very difficult for reasons of space, time, and other factors. Representatives thus attempt to assimilate the deliberations that can take place with opinion polls and other suggestions of public will (and I use this term loosely; there really is no such thing as unified public will). Based on the assimilations the representatives assume that public opinion leans in particular directions and then make decisions and policies. Shortcomings of aggregative democracy are rather obvious; in the absence of serious and informed deliberations, polls and media reports fail to capture the complexities of public will. Even when representatives are diligent and well intentioned, distortions of opinion can result in mistaken decisions and policies. If representatives are less than diligent or not so well intentioned, the results could actually be contrary to the will of many segments of society. Also inherent in aggregation is the tendency to reduce decision making to a majoritarian illusion. That is, the aim of this version of democracy is to discern what most people want (frequently through indirect means, such as media reports and other anecdotes and analyses), then to work according to the simplified assumptions based on what representatives think (or wish) most people want. The flaws in reporting and analysis of complex matters render these assumptions illusory.

Let me suggest that we have an example of illusory aggregative democracy in our profession. In an earlier chapter I spoke of a public library management form that has been labeled "give 'em what they want." Charles Robinson, who was director of the Baltimore County Public Library (BCPL), has been the most prominent advocate of this idea. No mere notion, the "give 'em what they want" strategy is a political plan to position the library within a defined governmental area such as a city or county. Notice I didn't say "community" because this political plan is not community based. Given the strategy, BCPL used circulation data (primarily) to alter selection activities. Nora Rawlinson (1981), who oversaw collection development, said at the time that one branch manager's "branch began a vigorous weeding program, discarding all items that had not circulated a certain number of times in one year" (p. 2189). Of course public libraries can and should weed their collections, and circulation is one identifier for items to weed; it is the latter part of Rawlinson's statement, and the single criterion she described, that is cause for concern. While continuing to acquire approximately 15,000 items a year, the unique titles selected fell from about 7,000 to about 3,000 after the strategy was put in place. More copies of titles in demand were acquired, thus satisfying a portion of the county's population. Under the umbrella term "user demand," any tacit, much less active, admission of pluralism within the county is notable by its absence. Rawlinson (1981) further said that, "For the rest of the books, quality is a factor. The first consideration must always be whether a book is likely to be of interest to our patrons" (p. 2190). What is more likely, if a book is of interest to some patrons, and that interest is likely to meet a certain circulation threshold, then it may be acquired.

The theme has been picked up by other librarians. Michael Sullivan (2000) applauds the BCPL strategy: "It looked at what people wanted and in what proportion, then selected materials accordingly" (p. 148). BCPL looked at what some individuals who continued to go to the library checked out, then defined that group as "the people." What neither Rawlinson nor Robinson said explicitly was that the Enoch Pratt Free Library in the city of Baltimore is open to everyone and does not mimic the BCPL ideology. So BCPL created an illusion of democratization while inevitably marginalizing some county residents. Commentators, such as Sullivan, fail to own up to the political decision that is nominally aggregative, but may well be undemocratic. The failure to point out the explicit political nature of the strategy is noted by John Dessauer (1980):

> In the last analysis it will be a vision of what a library is or should be that will determine the course of events. If librarians believe the bulk of acquisition funds should be spent on bestsellers, fad books, and other highly ephemeral and possibly mediocre materials, they will be comfortable with a wholly mathematical, circulation-related approach. If they believe the library has a cultural role and mission to play, they will choose a broader base for selection. In either case, any circulation data will not be able to make the decision. Like all statistics, circulation data are merely tools. The judgment will have to be made by librarians. (p. 68)

Deliberative Democracy

Deliberative democracy is spoken about and written about at much greater length than is aggregative democracy. The ideal of deliberation is the focus of a substantial amount of literature (Gutmann and Thompson, Habermas, Benhabib, Bohman, and Cohen, among others). In much of this literature procedure is of primary importance; structures and mechanisms should be in place to permit and encourage reasoned speech and debate. With the structure in place individuals can participate most fully in civil discourse that leads to agreed-upon decisions and policies. Mouffe (2000) observes that deliberation's supporters' "claim is that it is possible, thanks to adequate procedures of deliberation, to reach forms of agreement that would satisfy both rationality (understood as defence of liberal rights) and democratic legitimacy (as represented by popular sovereignty)" (p. 83). The participants in deliberation are to be committed, not just to reason, but to reason-giving— anyone who speaks accepts the responsibility of articulating the reasons for adopting certain positions, for making interests clear (self-interest, minority interests, etc.), and for subjecting the reasoning to the scrutiny of other participants. For Habermas (1993) a discourse ethics guides the political complexities of deliberation. Given the responsibilities just outlines, all participants are equal. Every reasoned argument that is open to the evaluation of everyone should receive equal consideration before a decision is made. Further, every citizen is free to participate in deliberation to the extent that reason-giving is possible. When all of these procedures are in place and are embraced, Bohman (1996) argues, "the best defense of public deliberation is that it is more likely to improve the epistemic quality of the justifications for political decisions" (p. 27). In focusing on procedures, just about all adherents of deliberative democracy agree that institutions must be in place for deliberation to occur and, moreover, that social conditions emphasize the essential governance import of deliberation.

In preparing this chapter I've been struggling to identify deliberative democracy in action within librarianship. There is no denying that reasoned discussion does take place and that some localized decisions are made on the basis of reason-giving and assessment. Established structural procedures to address all policy decisions are not altogether common, though. The existence of such procedures is an empirical matter; we could examine decision making and determine the extent and kind of deliberation that exists. In such an empirical investigation, instances of some individuals gathering to deliberate on issues that arise at a particular time and place do not constitute evidence of deliberative democracy. These ad hoc actions on the parts of some organizational members are not intentionally structural, nor are the procedures for deliberation set out in advance. The absence of deliberation may be more evident to us. Returning to the "Berninghausen debate" for a moment, it seems clear that the claims made were not done so in dialogue where questions could be asked, reasons given, and evaluation engaged in. The debate (such as it was) fell short of Habermas's ideal of discourse ethics. In reality, the discourse, according to Habermas's model, was distorted, and rather than understanding being the aim, success or winning the moment was the goal.

The Swan-Peattie debate, on the other hand, did come closer to a deliberative ideal. The individuals addressed common concerns, constructed arguments based in reason, and demonstrated respect for the need to listen to one another. Persuasion was still a part of the objective, though, and the stances leaned a bit to forensics, in which each sought to sway an audience. Both the success of Swan's and Peattie's arguments and the shortcomings might be measured by discursive practice. The practice shows the pluses and minuses of deliberative democracy. The primary positive outcome was effective use of public space(s) to present reasoned, but differing, arguments relating to an important professional issue. The conference session enabled attendees to hear each side's propositions and conclusions; the publication of the book allowed a broader audience (in space and in time) to do likewise. Deliberation tends to incorporate rhetoric, and the inclusion is not avoidable. If someone believes in a position and constructs an argument that he or she finds convincing, then that person will probably want others to reach the same conclusion. After all, if a weak presentation is offered hearers may not appreciate the strength of the argument. In other words, some non-rational aspects of presentation may be more persuasive than rational ones. Mouffe (2000) strongly urges abandoning rationalism and instead turning to language games, as described by Ludwig Wittgenstein (1958, pp. 60–77).

Mouffe (2000) suggests a replacement for deliberation—agonistic democracy. While antagonism presupposes enemies in combat, agonism presumes adversaries whose ideas are in conflict but whose recognition of rights is constant. Passion and emotions are powerful forces and may overwhelm communicative rationality, so an emphasis on deliberation, says Mouffe, is misplaced. The passionate response may rest in values that are held by individuals; the values could be non-rational. Religious faith, tradition, custom, allegiance to political party may prevail in a contest for people's attention. "One of the shortcomings of the deliberative approach is that, by postulating the availability of a public sphere where power would have been eliminated and where a rational consensus could be realized, this model of democratic politics is unable to acknowledge the dimension of antagonism that the pluralism of values entails and it ineradicable character" (Mouffe, 2000, pp. 98–99). Mouffe's principal point is that a procedural solution is no solution at all, merely a failed attempt at imposing structure where more visceral motives are predominant. The import of emotions and values is great; no theory or practice of politics should ignore it. That said, Mouffe's assessment of deliberative democracy misses the mark on some key points. Deliberation in a public sphere doesn't, and can't, *eliminate* power; it can help exert some control over it where constraints are placed on some in favor of the speech of the disadvantaged. We do see some challenges to constraints, such as the efforts to protect the political speech of those who have the financial resources to pay for it. It is precisely in such instances where procedure must be part of the solution. Mouffe's other error is the assumption that deliberation exists to reach consensus. Consensus, in practice, is seldom achieved on important issues without coercion; deliberation is intended to minimize coercion and allow for reasoned consideration. Acceptance of a decision is not the same as consensus, and acceptance is more likely to occur than is consensus.

There is another version of democracy we should consider here—social democracy. Not just another species of democracy, this version is almost another genus. Its foundations are at least as close to socialism as they are to, say, aggregative democracy. Not to oversimplify (too much), social democracy attempts to stifle the impact of private ownership and, by extension, capitalism. As an attempt at compromise, social democracy aims to optimize public good, not through any purely utilitarian measures, but through a strong public sector that is responsive to both majority and minority needs. Utilitarianism suffers from a number of shortcomings, including a problematic proclivity of people to favor private interest over public welfare (Shapiro, 2003b, pp. 34–35). This despite the utilitarian's stated purpose of maximizing welfare for all. In order to do so, inevitable inequities would have to be resolved in such a way that those at a disadvantage would receive from those with an excess of advantages. A contrary rationality—individual utility maximization—has typified actual behavior. Without a natural tendency to look outward, a state system of social welfare is needed, according to social democracy. Centralization, taxation, and state control of basic services (such as health care and education) typify social democracy. Social democracy is not a (completely) deliberative structure, but it does tend to be largely procedural. If the appropriate system of taxation and distribution is in place, the general welfare is likely to be enhanced. Of course the high levels of taxation that are required for distribution is a burden that the "haves" may resist. Social democracy is at odds with classical liberalism, which privileges individuals. It is also problematic for capitalism, which seeks to control modes of production so as to optimize profit for capitalists.

The customary operation of the public library in the United States approaches the rhetoric of social democracy. Taxation is usually based in property, so those who do represent ownership fund a public good. Those who do not own property can avail themselves of the public library just as freely and to the same extent as those who do. Public libraries, as putative social democratic institutions, do not destroy liberalism and its emphasis on the individual. Instead, the public library adopts a kind of social democratic means of framing its services, collections, etc. so that both deliberative democracy (according to some expressions of the ideal) *and* individual self-sufficiency and prosperity (according to more expressions of the ideal) can thrive. This lesson offered by the public library in general and Baltimore County Public Library (BCPL) in a particular instance is instructive of the multifaceted nature of democracy (and, indeed, any political system). The structure that supports the public library leans toward social democracy, but the operations of many public libraries leans toward classical liberal individualism. In Ian Shapiro's (2003b) words, "There are many variants of democratic theory, but we will see that there important respects in which they all involve giving up on the more ambitious versions of the Enlightenment enterprise—both with respect to replacing political choices with technical ones, and to treating individual rights as prior to, and in need of protection from, politics" (p. 191). In other words, politics and democracy have been transformed over time to address, positively or negatively, the liberal incursions into social life. These theories of democracy are of undeniable interest; let's look now at practices of democracy.

Social democracy is very seldom spoken of in the United States, even though it's an important political movement in much of Western Europe. Social democratic parties have won parliamentary seats and, arguably, social democracy was central to the Prime Ministerial agenda of Tony Blair in Great Britain. The most vocal proponent of social democracy has been Anthony Giddens (1998, 2001). The ascendancy of conservatism, marked by the elections of Ronald Reagan and Margaret Thatcher, accentuated some of the difficulties of social democracy as it had been practiced in earlier years. The social democracy that arose after World War II had little or no response to capitalist-oriented programs that seemed to promise autonomy for individuals and to realize the goals of classical liberalism. Giddens's "Third Way" has been presented as an alternative to old-style social democracy and to neoliberalism (about which I'll say more in the section on "The Problem with Democracy"). One of Giddens's (1998) centerpieces of the Third Way is a reconception of community. "Community," however, is a vague and largely undefined entity in Giddens's program. It appears to operate according to consensus, but there is no clear indication of how to accommodate pluralism that inherently includes contest. For example, if one group of people wants to declare some neighborhoods blighted and to urge exercise of eminent domain to appropriate them for commercial development, and another group urges a form of residential renewal that preserves the neighborhoods as such, the Third Way essentially assumes that consensus can be reached (see Little, 2003).

To an extent the public library today also embraces some aspects of the Third Way. In particular, as public librarians refer to *the* community there is a presumption of homogeneity and the possibility of consensus on what the library can and should offer. I'll hasten to add that many public librarians reject such Third Way thinking, but it still holds a rather prominent place in the discourse on the library.

The Problem of Democracy

Libraries exist to some extent under all political systems, but in democratic ones (even nominal democratic ones) libraries that serve the public tend to be more numerous and better developed, and tend to offer services that reach more people. This is a good thing. But do these libraries succeed because of the realization of democratic ideals or in spite of the political shortcomings of a flawed structure? The answer is "both." We've seen that the structure of taxation provides support for public libraries and, less directly, school libraries and publicly supported academic libraries. The structure supports libraries as vital contributors to public welfare. Most K–12 teachers and school librarians could report in great detail on needs that are not met because of insufficient resources. Even with structures of taxation there are serious problems ingrained in our political systems. Perhaps of special importance are the discrepancies between wealthier districts and poorer ones. Some of the problems are less derived from privileging some interests over others than they are from the magnitude of needs. *All* schools, in whatever districts they serve, could be better supported. Better educated people gain tangible *and* intangible benefits, and the benefits extend to society as a whole. The root of many of the problems, however, do stem from political choices that dictate where funds will be spent and what the government's revenues will be. This isn't the place for a critique of current party politics, but some examination of the overt workings of government is necessary for a full understanding of the political situation of publicly supported libraries.

When each of us pays federal and/or state income taxes, we add a lump sum to government revenues. The funds from income taxes are not earmarked in advance for education, health care, national security, or other items. The revenues are used to fund budgetary items (at least partially). If I, as a taxpayer, would like a greater portion of my taxes to fund education, my desire is effectively meaningless. Through our system of representation I can contact federal or state senators and representatives and urge them to make education a high budgetary priority. To what extent is my voice heeded? If it is a lone voice, representatives may put little stock in it. (After all, if one person in a library's community urges longer weekend hours we may or may not pay a great deal of attention to the request.) If, however, many communicate the same message to representatives there is a greater chance for effecting some changes in funding. (If many community members request longer hours of operation on weekends, library managers are much more likely to seek a way to meet the requests.) What I've just described is a procedure for exercising a voice in the matters of government, not an expression of what is "best" according to any set of norms or preferences. The communication that takes place usually is a kind of vote for or against certain government actions or policies. If many people were to contact representatives to urge a *decrease* in funding for education the representatives would not entirely ignore them. Even if the representatives were not to heed the call for decreases they would be likely to advocate the opposing view through argument and evidence.

In some ways the procedural emphasis mirrors arguments in favor of intellectual freedom as described above. The freedom of speech does not consider the content of the speech a priori; its focus is instead on the procedures that enable speaker autonomy. Social responsibility definitely values free speech, but does take an interest in the sources and content of speech. The usual emphasis for adherents of social responsibility is on expanding speaker autonomy, on ensuring that more voices can be heard. In short, the customary focus is of a positive bent. To the extent that there is expression of a negative element, any constraints on speech should be, in some way, consequentialist. That is, the speech has been shown to be harmful or to have a strong potential for harm. Determination of harm is very difficult, but the law has made provisions for such determination. So reliance by supporters of intellectual freedom is on the library's procedure that is designed for inclusiveness. Reliance by supporters of social responsibility is on the power of free speech and on the need for activism in opening structural procedures to the production and dissemination of ideas. Here we see the debate in a somewhat different light, one that frames the positions according to the fundamentals to which they adhere. Recall that Cass Sunstein argues that while harm should be considered in relation to free speech, it cannot function as the sole determinate of any restriction. I will suggest, along these lines, that the library's procedure is vital to the protection of free speech and the public good, but it is not adequate as the sole grounds. In the next chapter the topic will be the complexities of an information society; for now let it suffice that there are systemic constraints on what information gets formally disseminated. The procedures we have in place do little to confront the constraints as they may skew available fodder for deliberation. Likewise, liberalism (in the sense of the predominance of individualism with as few limitations as possible) is a vital component of democracy, but it is not a sufficient condition for democracy. A commitment to *public* good and *public* welfare must temper liberalism.

There is a challenge inherent in the concept of democracy. This challenge is felt by professionals in institutions like libraries. We professionals live within a political structure and, as citizens, formulate beliefs (ideally steeped in reason while admitting to emotion), opinions, and positions. As citizens we have interests that we act upon and seek to foster. As professionals we work within political institutions, in situations that include the political as part of their being. Are the two roles always in agreement and, if not, to what extent can they function? Is the tension experienced by the librarian different in kind from that experienced by the teacher? Suppose we take "academic freedom" as a metaphor according to which we can investigate the potential contest that the librarian's two roles can create. The idea of academic freedom strikes at concerns regarding both individual and institution. Further, there is a collective consciousness that undergirds academic freedom; it is intended to provide considerable leeway within a professional's functioning, but it is also subject to norms that mirror a procedural approach to democracy. In a sense this metaphor includes both the individual professional's freedom to seek and to communicate, plus the institutional commitment to certain ethical and political dictates creates responsibilities. The professional challenge we face includes the complex dynamic that accompanies academic freedom. The structure supports libraries as vital contributors to public welfare.

On the individual side, freedom is positive; each of us can explore what we choose, and we can investigate to whatever depth we want those matters that interest us. There is another element to this positive freedom, though. Ronald Dworkin (1996) details a corollary set of responsibilities that accompany the freedom:

> The first is the responsibility not to profess what one believes to be false. This duty is protected, in liberal societies, by a right of conscience that forbids forcing people to religious or moral or political declaration against their will. The second is a more positive responsibility of affirmation: it is a duty to speak out for what one believes to be true. According to ethical individualism, we all have that duty as citizens: it is wrong to remain silent when our society must make a collective decision and we believe we have information or opinion it should take into account. (p. 188)

There is an aspect of Dworkin's observation that should be emphasized—the duty to speak what we believe to be true is an antidote to totalitarianism. In other words, it is a democratic duty. It is opposed to conformity and orthodoxy for their own sakes, while it may preserve them on epistemological, and perhaps even axiological, grounds in some instances. That is, orthodoxy is to be subjected to critical scrutiny; only if it stands up to the scrutiny should it be preserved. Academic freedom as a metaphor that we can use awakens us to the active political responsibilities we have, especially to tell the truth. Ours is not a passive service occupation. Recall the hallmarks of professions that Gardner and Shulman enumerate (see Chapter 3). Judgment is one of the elements, and judgment is not exercised passively.

"Academic freedom" in the sense I'm suggesting is by no means limited to educational environments. It does, admittedly, have greater pertinence for librarians working in the public sector. In the private sector this freedom extends only as far as the parent organization operates in public. Obviously, if the library is situated in a corporation which functions in a competitive field, much information will be, and will have to be, proprietary. Even in private sector settings "academic freedom" doesn't have to be completely abrogated. Louis Menand (1996) reminds us that academic freedom and freedom of speech are not exactly the same thing. Academic freedom, as metaphor and as applied in education, extends to the professional activities that take place within self-regulated organizations (pp. 6–7). It has an ethical component that addresses relationships (usually teacher-student, but also librarian-user as I'm suggesting). Regardless of the environment, the work to be done includes the gap between what is and what ought to be (Scott, 1996). The freedom I'm talking about emphasizes the positive—the duties we have to continue our own educations and judgment we apply in the best interests of our communities. It includes the negative as well, though—freedom from coercion and from forced denial of the positive freedoms. Academic freedom is not such a conceptual stretch for us; it speaks to the political nature of our profession along with the realization that the positive freedoms are pointed outward. We exercise the version of academic freedom not merely for our own welfare, but as an essential means of operating within a democracy. That is something we can't lose sight of, especially as traditional academic freedom is seriously threatened by the overt imposition by governments and the deceitful insinuation of efforts such as the "Academic Bill of Rights." The threats are not irrelevant to us in librarianship; the extension of academic freedom I'm arguing for necessarily includes resistance to any efforts aimed at limiting or denying that freedom.

David Horowitz is the principal author of the "Academic Bill of Rights" (see www.studentsforacademicfreedom.org). The document concludes with the stricture that to perform their functions adequately, "academic institutions and professional societies should maintain a posture of organizational neutrality with respect to the substantive disagreements that divide researchers on questions within, or outside, their fields of inquiry." The call for organizational neutrality may seem similar to some intellectual freedom positions. Committee A of the Association of American University Professors (AAUP), however, challenges the whole of the Academic Bill of Rights on the grounds that it actually advocates political judgment of pluralism and neutrality. In short, it questions whether "neutrality" is always neutral (or even if it can be at all). On January 25, 2006, ALA Council adopted a resolution opposing documents like the Academic Bill of Rights as contrary to academic and intellectual freedom (see www.ala.org/ala/oif/statementspols/ifresolutions/academicfreedom.htm). Not fully recognized explicitly, libraries are part of the contested territory. In library collections balance—representation of thought and opinion from multiple viewpoints—is seen as a social good that can foster democratic deliberation. "Balance" can also be used, as is evident from Horowitz's efforts, to prevent critical democratic deliberation. Academic freedom includes the quest for the body of information that will help people know more, as well as the quest for truth.

If interpretations of Mill are correct and the *active* and *critical* marketplace of ideas enables us to test ideas and accept those that withstand challenge and discard those that don't (see Doyle), then we should revisit why we build certain collections (say, those in college and university libraries) as we do. Robert Ivie (2005) provides a very useful summary of one component of academic freedom: "The standards of truth-seeking scholarship, as correlative duties of academic freedom, include gathering evidence thoroughly, recording it accurately, and weighing it carefully, reasoning analytically from the evidence while remaining open to unexpected findings, and communicating the results clearly, honestly, and persuasively with due acknowledgement of academic debts and sources" (p. 75). Alan Charles Kors (2004), on the other hand, writes, "It will not be long—I hope—before almost no one will remember Foucault, Lacan, Derrida, Althusser, Gramsci, or Lukacs," and said that scholars in fields such as "so-called cultural studies . . . have led to works of fatuity and agitprop" (pp. 10–11). Is that list of scholars to be forgotten because they don't agree with Kors? He provided no evidence of the fatuity of some work, nor of the "quality" of other work; he offers only dicta. How would the forgetting of some individuals enhance learning? If someone else were to say that forgetting Leo Strauss, Carl Schmitt, Russell Kirk, Irving Kristol, and David Horowitz should be the rule, would that person's opinion be as legitimate as Kors's? Likewise, could we legitimately take similar positions with regard to library collections? Ivie (2005) reminds us, "Rather than holding the accusations of politically ascendant ideologues to a heavy burden of proof and showing how their claims fall short of meeting that burden, academic are too quick to go on the defensive, to respond as if they must establish their own bona fides and prove that they are not abusing students' academic freedom" (p. 55). Librarians also should avoid defensiveness, but should apply stringent burdens to discourse.

Neoliberalism

Academic freedom admits to pluralism and contest in ways that Third Way social democracy does not. Consensus is not the goal of either intellectual freedom or social responsibility; access to voices so that critical opinions are heard is. Even though it does have merits, social democracy, as well as all of the forms of democracy discussed here, is placed in jeopardy by a political force that goes by the name of neoliberalism. I believe firmly in a form of democracy (that I'll go into in some detail shortly) and the necessity of a vibrant public sphere. I believe that the library (writ large) is vital to the health of a public sphere. I also believe that unchecked capitalism (capital formation without state or civic constraints) does not constitute establishment of free markets and, further, operates for its own, and not for civic or public, good. Neoliberalism is the epitome of a political structure that eschews public good in favor of private interest. While Giddens's (1998) Third Way has some serious problems, he has very clearly seen that neoliberalism is anti-democratic. If *the* market (which is at least as problematic as *the* community) is the regulating force, according what criteria does it regulate, for whom, with what benefits and costs, and to what end? Answers to these questions are not easy to come by from proponents of unrestrained capitalism. There are some answers, though, that can be derived from empirical evidence. The neoliberal faith in (and awarding of power to) markets results in short-term objectives that are limited to the growth of capital. The means of growth have little or nothing to do with the public, primarily because the public (in the senses of the state and the vast majority of people) do not control or own large amounts of capital (although the state can favor capital growth through policy and law).

Perhaps the most insidious aspect of neoliberalism is its destruction of the public sphere and public space. In fact, there is no room for public in neoliberalism. In a world (and I use the word advisedly, because neoliberalism takes advantage of globalization) governed by markets, the only thing that holds value is the exchange. Markets exist to exchange; one party gives up something to another party in order to get something. It's neither a coincidence nor a surprise that Enron, WorldCom, and other companies could create illusions of transactions and, thus, profits within a formal structure in which such activities seem natural. The fallout for the company executives began when both state and market interceded and divested the neoliberal activities of some of their power. Henry Giroux (2004) offered,

> The ascendancy of neoliberal corporate culture into every aspect of American life both consolidates economic power in the hands of the few and aggressively attempts to break the power of unions, decouple people from productivity, subordinate the needs of society to the market, and deem public services and goods an unconscionable luxury. It thrives on a culture of cynicism, insecurity, and despair. (p. 105)

The decoupling, or disruption may be the better word, stems from the disconnect between the economic and the social worlds, or the usurpation of the social world by the economic one (see Touraine, 2001, pp. 17–19). Under the control of the market, what happens to libraries, schools, colleges and universities, and other public institutions?

The short answer is that the public space that is necessary for any realization of democratic participation (as Habermas has repeatedly called for) is missing. Let's examine the library's position within an operational public sphere. Court rulings aside (see below), the public library does function as a public forum in many ways. School and academic libraries function as educational forums.

There is little doubt that many individual libraries could embrace the forum function more fully, but all libraries that serve the public are forums in meaningful ways. "Neoliberalism undermines and dismantles the institutions set up to stabilize the capitalist economy and alleviate capitalist social contradictions" (Li, 2004, p. 23). The social contradictions, the contests, can and should be rendered more transparent by public institutions such as libraries. Here again we have the ethical and functional challenge of narrowing the gap between what is and what should be. Not meaning to belabor a point, the Baltimore County Public Library again represents political betrayal in the guise of market sensitivity. As Charles Robinson has been quoted as saying, "There are two things wrong with librarians. They don't think about where their money comes from so they don't spend enough on books, and they buy the wrong books" (Davis, 1979, p. 26). Robinson, during his time as director of BCPL, was fully engaged in trying to position the library within the dominant political milieu of neoliberalism. This is an activity that John Buschman (2003) decries. I won't summarize his book here, but I will recommend it as extremely important in the discourse on the political nature of libraries. If circulation equals transaction, and the goal is to maximize circulation, then a library's raison d'être is de facto neoliberal. The why and how of library usage and community service fall by the wayside in favor of the what, defined as what "stock" moves off the shelves. Purpose itself is defined by this embrace of markets and abandonment of democracy.

One specific point should be emphasized here. The description of neoliberalism here does not include an indictment of capitalism. Neoliberalism does, however, turn capitalism in a particular direction that downplays production and creation. The predicament is depicted well by Frederic Jameson (1991): "The technology of contemporary society is therefore mesmerizing and fascinating not so much in its own right but because it seems to offer some privileged representational shorthand for grasping a network of power and control even more difficult for our minds and imaginations to grasp: The whole new decentered global network of the third stage of capitalism itself" (pp. 37–38). Jameson further says that we are inside the culture of the market, so it is extremely difficult to escape the snare of transactions. If there is such a thing as late capitalism, in which production (regardless of mode) is secondary to transference of capital itself, then meaning can be altered to fit the culture of the market. Transactions, in order to be maximized, rely on speed. Speed, in turn, relies on the internalization of the market, so that we cease to think of ourselves and what we do as autonomous. Neoliberalism is in reality the destruction of liberalism. The individual—and the individual's volition, choice, and action—is reduced and constrained; the individual, in fact, is meaningless except for providing the monetary element of exchanges. What's worse, *people* are deluded into thinking that they *are* acting on the bases of their own wills. Within (on the inside of) the market choice is illusory, since there is only the choice among limited and not easily distinguishable commodities of what to consume. Many things are thus simplified by force of neoliberal markets; we no longer have to think seriously about meaning (see Agger, 1989; Bewes, 1997, for example).

The foregoing indicates the ways of thinking and being that explain BCPL policy. When meaning is co-opted, language is transformed. "Give 'em what they want" is a useful trope that sounds attractive, but that hides an anti-individualist bent. Neoliberalism operates most effectively through rhetoric. If an idea can be stated in a way that is attractive to a reader or listener, it is more likely to be accepted. Further, if an idea that inherently contains elements that are explicitly damaging to polity, the public good, and the public sphere, it is more likely to be accepted if the rhetoric paints the opposite picture. The rhetoric of neoliberalism relies on insinuating the language of markets and transactions into common usage, so that practices that are not market- and transaction-driven adopt the language as representing truth. As Foucault points out, this will to truth is effective insofar as it can be institutionalized. In a work that is obviously well intentioned, Jeanette Woodward (2005) incorporates the language even though she argues for services, collections, and access aimed at communities:

> Bookstore corporate headquarters assiduously control what they view as the "bookstore experience." Maybe we need to place the same emphasis on the "library experience." When the overall experience of our customers becomes our focus, the picture changes. It doesn't matter what marvelous resources we have if customers don't use them. It doesn't matter how skilled the reference librarian is if customers don't ask reference questions. It doesn't matter that we sincerely want to serve immigrant groups if no one speaks their language. (p. 223)

What Woodward misses is the embeddedness of the culture of markets in our lives. "Customers" make their choices on grounds that are influenced, if not largely determined, by the characteristics of markets that Jameson and others recognize. In a more overt and openly neoliberal piece Gary Deane (2003) betrays an ignorance of the possible intrusiveness of a will to truth and bought fully into a market-based mission for public libraries. He writes,

> Libraries must start looking in different directions and in different places for value, not as directed to do so by what professionals believe but by what customers want. . . . Perhaps library funders should start to ask for more by moving away from the current practice of giving libraries global budgets based on historical spending patterns and program incrementalism. Instead they should begin to fund on the basis of the demonstrated quality and effectiveness of the services that libraries are actually delivering to their customers. (p. 319)

It may be that viewpoints like Deane's belie political naiveté (less than consciously adopting language that has the power to transform thought and action), but it is also possible that the rhetoric his article represents a deliberate and conscious means of altering the political *telos* of the library. The rhetoric can't and shouldn't be dismissed (if it is discussed at all) as *mere* semantics. Semantics, as the examination of meaning in language, seeks to identify the intentions that speakers have in saying what they say and the truth conditions pf statements. Semantics, in short, is a tool that is invaluable to the study of politics.

Far too many librarians find it easy to use the language of consumerism when describing place, collections, access, services, and (most disturbing of all) users. When libraries in all environments are market driven, the purpose— its meaning—is transformed to accommodate practice, and this is a political choice. As Giroux (2004) says,

> As the space of criticism is undercut by the absence of public spheres that encourage the exchange of information, opinion, and criticism, the horizons of a substantive democracy in which the promise of autonomous individuals and an autonomous society disappear against the growing isolation and depoliticization that marks the loss of politically guaranteed public realms. . . . Also rapidly disappearing are those public spaces and unmarketed cultural spaces in which people neither confuse the language of brand names with the language of autonomy and social engagement nor communicate through a commodified discourse incapable of defending vital institutions as a public good. (pp. 128–29)

A few years ago Steve Coffman (1998) suggested (one assumes seriously) that public libraries should operate on the same staffing, pay, and inventory model as a bookstore. The public library, if operated on this model, would forgo all use value as a public space and public good, and reduce itself to a commodity within a world of commodities. The following is not apt to happen in the very near future, but is it unimaginable?

> **Scenario**: Public libraries (not all, but many) eliminate reference services, most (especially adult) programming, and materials that are intentionally selected for their instructive or edifying value. The collections are almost entirely replaced by popular fiction and nonfiction, sounds, images, and technological information access. Retention on shelves is based on a strictly applied exchange-value model—say, 10 circulations per twelve-month period. Study spaces, such as tables, are replaced by cushioned chairs. Policies are altered to state that those who enter the library are customers and the goal is to maximize turnover of stock. A major bookstore chain brings suit against a number of libraries for unfair competition. They admit into evidence comparative photographs of the libraries and their bookstores, plus the libraries' policies. The difference is that the libraries do not charge customers to read books and magazines away from the premises.

If, legally, the public library is not a limited public forum, does the bookstore chain have a chance of winning the suit?

There are critiques of the language of customer and commodity (see Budd, 1997), that cite a number of writers who openly embrace the terms and urge that they become part of the lexicon of librarianship. The problem with language persists today; this rhetoric is powerful. Buschman (2003) articulates the implications of the rhetorical strategy: "The democratic public sphere roles of libraries as disseminators of rational, reasoned, and organized discourse, as a source of verifying or disputing claims, and as a space for the inclusion of alternative views of society and reality have no place in the vision of the library as the instant-satisfaction, fast-food equivalent of information" (pp. 120–21). The rhetoric is one of imbalance; like Buschman, I am not calling for some "pure" library that can be all things to all people. I *am* calling for balance. Libraries that serve publics are not businesses in a market, and the mistake of thinking and acting like they are can do long-lasting damage to any conception of a democratic society. Andrew Levine (2004) puts it best: "The main problem facing our polity, the road blocks that must be removed first, are the factors that allow economic inequalities, objectionable in their own right, to spill over into the political sphere, impeding even distant approximations of that equality of political influence that deliberative democratic theory celebrates" (p. 145).

IT'S THE LAW, BUT IS IT A GOOD IDEA?

The problematic nature of the "give 'em what they want" stance has actually been heightened by recent court rulings that have focused primarily on filtering the Internet. The consequences for library policies are not obvious in light of the decisions, but I believe it isn't much of a reach to discern connections. Professional acclamations of openness, inclusiveness, and (perhaps especially) the need to include minority and dissenting voices offer one outward sign of what a library exists for. Further, library policies aimed at services to entire communities emphasize the purpose of public libraries. In such a context we can read the opinion of Judge Leonie Brinkema in the case of *Mainstream Loudoun v. Board of Trustees of the Loudoun County Library* (24 F. Supp. 2d 552, 1998). Judge Brinkema, basing her opinion on previous court rulings, affirms that the Loudoun County Library is a limited public forum, a space designated by the state to provide people access to the range of ideas. The Loudoun County Library's own policy documents, which are grounded in ALA policies, constitute the public forum function of the library. As limited public fora libraries are able to offer a wide range of resources to communities, within limits of legal constraints (e.g., access to child pornography, being a criminal activity, can be constrained). Advocates of intellectual freedom could perceive affirmation of the beliefs in Judge Brinkema's decision and opinion.

On the other hand, some library practices cast the role of the limited public forum into doubt. The uncertainty, plus a need to reach some resolution, comes to a head as libraries implement the requirements of the Children's Internet Protection Act (CIPA). The U.S. Supreme Court upheld this law in 2003 in a decision based on the review of a case filed in lower courts by ALA, among other bodies. Many librarians have spoken and written in support of the ALA position, arguing that any filtering is opposed to the letter and the spirit of the LBR, and some have further argued that it violates the First Amendment of the U.S. Constitution. The particular case of CIPA throws the aforementioned assumption into a muddle. Perhaps the most problematic aspect of the decision in the case of the *United States v. American Library Association* (the appeal to the U.S. Supreme Court) is the opinion that

> in their roles as providers and selectors of content, libraries are neither traditional nor designated public forums. This makes sense because libraries' acquisition decisions do not present a systematic discernible risk that government will deliberately manipulate the content of public debate, or attempt to distort its outcome, or censor, punish, or selectively deny speech opportunities to disfavored views. (BeVier, 2003, p. 185)

That libraries, especially public libraries, are not public forums is an idea that many librarians find difficult to accept. Other librarians, regardless of their expressly held views on intellectual freedom, who actively propound a give-'em-what-they-want managerial stance effectively deny that their public libraries are public forums. The crux of the problem in our profession is the contradiction between stated positions (such as the Library Bill of Rights) and practices (including not selecting certain kinds of materials that could potentially broaden public discourse). The contradiction is personified by Hauptman, who says that any restriction on speech are unconstitutional (itself an ahistorical claim) while at the same time attempting to silence dissenters by dismissing their reasoning as "specious." The contradiction demonstrates disarray and chaos in the profession's conception of intellectual freedom.

I realize that the foregoing will find disfavor with some colleagues; I can only urge that readers not shoot the messenger. While the description of the contradiction isn't flattering, I will readily agree with Dworkin that free speech is constitutive of a just political society. The liberal tradition of which Mill is part provides a sound and reasoned rationale for insisting that ideas be placed in circulation (utilitarianism aside). One could argue that the shortcoming of our profession is not that it's too liberal, but that it's not liberal enough, at least in some ways. As Sunstein (2003) has written, "Conformists of all kinds suffer, much of the time, from a crippled epistemology. . . . Public forums do not supply a complete corrective. But things are likely to go far better if dissenting views are heard and if people reject those views only after actually hearing them" (p. 109). But if libraries are not public forums, can libraries be corrective in any way? The state of libraries as they may or may not be public forums is in immediate need of critical scrutiny. One particular point can be introduced here to begin the scrutiny. Lillian BeVier (2004) has said that the Supreme Court decision in the CIPA appeal was a doctrinally easy one; in other words, ALA didn't have a leg to stand on. In support of her assertion she wrote that "decisions not to purchase printed material also, and inevitably, 'block'—suppress—a substantial amount of protected speech, and this fact has never been thought sufficient to bring strict scrutiny into play" (p. 187). This opinion screams for a response, but only a logical, legally salient, rational response will have any effect. If, in fact, we agree that BeVier does describe practice (and many legal commentators do not agree with her), then two options await us: (1) our rational response to BeVier demonstrates clearly that the absence of materials in collections is not suppression of speech, or (2) we rethink the essential meaning of intellectual freedom. In addition to philosophical arguments, there are the legal realities of cases that have indeed found libraries to be limited public forums (see Wu, 2004). The Supreme Court's decision and BeVier's analysis are thus directly called into question. In his analysis of the Supreme Court decision, John Gathegi (2005) cogently reminds us that the legislation that provides for connectivity is directly at odds with legislation that would restrict connectivity: "The U.S. Supreme Court seems to have ignored even the usual homage to public libraries as designated forums; it merely focused on what it concluded was the nonforum nature of Internet access" (p. 18).

Moving Ahead

With the background on various forms of democracy and problems that have beset a democratic society, we can wonder where we go from here. It should be clear that the central tenets of democracy should guide the future of libraries. An aggregative form is seriously problematic, since the assumptions of the policy makers can be at odds with the wishes of the people and, in fact, the public interest. Classical liberalism holds invaluable promise; individual rights cannot be sacrificed. Liberalism is a response to censorship and attacks on intellectual and academic freedom; it is an antidote to the tyranny of the majority. Liberalism is also opposed to the kind of powerful sovereignty that Hobbes argued for, and that we see emerging in the United States today (see Levine, 2004, pp. 97–98). Where liberalism creates difficulties, as we've seen, is when the rights of individuals become confused with individual autonomy. A political form based solely in individual autonomy can lead to problems when it comes to resolving disputes and balancing interests. With an emphasis on private property, liberalism has united politics and economics more strongly than ever before. Levine (2004) has pointed out that "liberalism is linked historically and conceptually with capitalism. However, it has long been a matter of controversy whether economic freedoms and civil liberties comprise a seamless web or whether it is possible consistently to support the one, but not the other" (p. 100). His observation is trenchant; neoliberalism broke whatever putatively necessary connection there ever was between economic rights and civil liberties. Moreover, neoliberalism has broken the connection in such a way that the dissatisfaction with the political state of affairs that exists now is poorly articulated and largely unvoiced. The language of markets, transactions, capital, etc. is so embedded in discourse that it's difficult to express alternatives and be understood. Political protest against the reduction of human life to transactions has found difficulty in identifying the source of dissatisfaction and suggesting transformations that would alter the political course.

An aggregative form of democracy, classical liberalism that is carried too far into individual autonomy (at the expense of groups) and neoliberalism damages the polity. As ideas and as political structures they pervert the nature of society, of people associating with one another. They isolate individuals and the isolation has deleterious effects on the public and a public sphere. If a notion of man as the measure of all things is taken to be fully realized in singular form, then deliberation becomes systematically and practically difficult. Any solution to today's dilemma—which is manifest in libraries both in microcosm and as experienced in American society—must address the forces that have historically influenced politics. In part, the solution will reject a historicism that claims there are laws of history that determine who we are and how we act. In short, we have to recognize the human construction of politics that has been shaped to an extent by changes in familial systems of ownership and structures of sovereign governance, alterations to commerce and trade, development in communication, and the introduction of numerous technologies. All of the past contributes to a dynamic transformation of nation states, religious affiliations, individual opportunities, ideas of wealth, relationships between governance and the government, and many other elements of life. Within the historical framework the words of John Dewey (1954 [1927]) are more important than ever: "Regarded as an idea, democracy is not an alternative to other principles of associated life. It is the idea of community life itself" (p. 148).

I want to urge us all to take Dewey's thought very seriously. In some of his most penetratingly perceptive work he identifies certain problems that the public has, the most essential of which is uncovering the best means to select representatives and to define their responsibilities (Dewey, 1954 [1927], p. 77). Dewey's philosophy is based in action; he is identified with pragmatists (such as William James and Charles Sanders Peirce), but his thinking is not to be so conveniently labeled. He was a progressive in the root sense of the word. He saw growth and development in the sciences, in knowledge, in communication, and in human association. That said, he was certainly not a technological uto-pian. His realism was sufficient to see that technology, regardless of creators' intentions, moved ahead at a rate that did not proceed apace with human knowledge and moral consciousness. The technologies, intentionally or not, demand attention, which is in limited stock in individuals and communities. What may suffer, then, is attention paid to the political or public sphere. Thus, he saw the public in eclipse. This is not to say that technology is the demon destroying public life; the reality is much more complex than that, as he (1954 [1927]) says, "In reality, the trouble springs rather from the ideas and absence of ideas in connection with which technological factors operate. Mental and moral beliefs and ideals change more slowly than outward condi-tions" (p. 141). The solution, argues Dewey, is reconstruction rather than revolution; progressive politics and human association require enhanced connections that Habermas detailed.

Communication enhancements are the corollary to a proceduralist idea of democracy. Not only must there be structures (including policies, laws, offices, and regulations), there must also be free and open lines of communi-cation among people so that power, status, and action can be continuously critiqued. In the absence of open communication of a necessarily dialogic sort, it becomes easier for a regime to win the emotional allegiance of people. In particular, allegiance is more readily won if the public, in Dewey's sense, is weak and community is largely nonexistent. The totality of people's atten-tion, emotional connection, and imagination is the result of a delusion that is individual in creation and collective in manifestation (that is, indi-vidual persons are won over by the totalitarian regime) (Dewey, 1989 [1939], pp. 16–17). The public challenge is exacerbated by the reality that passive compliance is easier, requires less work and effort, than active reconstruc-tion. So much more important is communication, given the challenge, and the role of information in shaping communication.

Of course Dewey is not alone in emphasizing the importance of communi-cation. For example, Habermas (1996) has suggested that, "the public sphere distinguishes itself through a *communication structure* that is related to a third feature of communicative action: it refers neither to the *functions* nor to the *contents* of everyday communication but to the *social space* generated in communicative action" (p. 360; emphasis in original). In a recent article Robert Dahl (2005) includes alternative and independent sources of infor-mation among the requirements for large-scale democracy:

> Citizens have a right to seek out alternative and independent sources of information from other citizens, experts, newspapers, magazines, books, telecommunications, and the like. Moreover, alternative sources of infor-mation actually exist that are not under the control of the government or any other single political group attempting to influence public political beliefs and attitudes, and these alternative sources are effectively protected by law. (p. 189)

Moreover, Habermas and Dahl (and others) recognize with Dewey that association is essential to democracy. The primary difference between these thinkers and Dewey is that for Dewey, association and freedom to associate are *constitutive* of democracy. Others admit that association provides a means to education and information exchange, but Dewey held that association is a part of human existence that defines the institutions we create. Association is essential for the existence of the public, which in turn is essential to the existence of community.

These ideas of Dewey (shared to a considerable extent by many others) have ready application to our profession. While preservation is vital, a library that merely preserves is of limited worth (refer to the excellent novel by Walter M. Miller Jr., *A Canticle for Leibowitz*). The record—texts, images, sounds, etc.—is a product of, and a means of, communication. The communication that librarianship should be engaged in is not simply passive presentation, but should be active in giving shape to otherwise inchoate "information." The central question is: What kind of activity is needed and how do we bring it about? As we've seen, there are some shortcomings to the major theories of democracy. Liberalism in some form is necessary so as to recognize individual rights and freedoms, but it cannot address all of the complex social needs of a large society. Social democracy has held some promise, but it has little response to devolution into neoliberalism. For librarianship to thrive in the future, it must find a political vision that simultaneously embraces much of the rhetoric of our profession while forging a progressive path. In short, I'm calling for a radical new liberalism that shares the most positive elements of socialism. This new liberalism can and should be called democracy, but only as long as egalitarianism is the true purpose of democracy.

EGALITARIAN DEMOCRACY

Dewey and Michael Walzer have critiqued latter-day liberalism (the liberalism that grew from that of Bentham, Smith, and Mill). Walzer (2004) goes so far as to say, "I want to argue that with regard to this struggle [against inequality], liberalism in its standard contemporary versions is an inadequate theory and a disabled political practice" (p. xi). His analysis of the shortcomings of contemporary liberal theory may be the most salient that exists today. What makes his critique so effective is his description of the constraints on freedom that are inevitable components of social life. While sociologists like Robert Putnam indicate shifts in the voluntary associations in which people engage today (as opposed to a generation or two ago), Walzer shows that social life is also comprised of involuntary associations, including familial and social (including class), cultural practices (perhaps especially affecting children), and political. Moreover, the more socioeconomically disadvantaged a person is, the more the involuntary associations tend to affect that person's life; escape from the associations may be hypothetically possible, but are practically extremely difficult. The strain of liberalism that values pulling oneself up by one's bootstraps does not, *cannot*, contend with the impact of involuntary association. Not only does involuntary association provide social definition for people, in the extreme it can severely limit choices and opportunities for voluntary association. I'll hasten to add that involuntary association is by no means an inextricable trap, but it is a powerful force that limits what can be called self-fashioning individualism. It should be remembered that involuntary association is still association, and it affects the identities of those within the group. Walzer (2004) recognizes this phenomenon and said, "A one-by-one emancipation won't work when group identity, however it looks from the outside, is valued on the inside—as it commonly is" (p. 39).

The approach that Walzer suggests is the empowerment not just of individuals, but of groups. If we are to achieve an egalitarian future, then we can't simply assume that individuals *qua* individuals have the wherewithal to progress on their own. The mere existence of schools, libraries, jobs, and capital is insufficient and reliance on it can lead to a naive confidence in the classical liberal ideal. If we reread Foucault carefully we can see beginnings of a critique of classical liberalism in which he sees the power that groups can wield against individuals. In short, Foucault (as we've seen) depicts the impact on discourse of control, and the power that institutions hold and exercise. In the extreme the power is totalizing; it encompasses an individual's life and frames the vision and hearing of the individual. Walzer (2004) recognizes such totalizing power and has emphasized the need for the state, in its role of enhancing a civil society. The state's responsibility, according to Walzer, is to balance allowing a natural self-correction brought about by voluntary association with an active encouragement (through resource allocation and adjustment) of organizations that can counter the totalizing effects of those groups that constrain opportunity. Given Foucault's diagnosis and Walzer's proposed remedy, we have our work cut out for us. True, librarianship can't change national politics, but there are numerous reasons to rethink the politics we employ within the profession.

Publicly supported libraries are, willingly or not, agencies of the state. As state agencies one potential purpose these libraries have is to provide a conscious and open locus for living out the dialectic just described. The task is to work through the seeming contradictions of individual freedom and public good. I'm not suggesting that librarians are the ones who should be charged with resolving the tension, but that we must be aware of the nature of the dialectic and that we should—through collections and access to information, services, and place—provide the means by which the tension can be discussed. In achieving these goals our profession needs to discuss the tension intramurally. Primarily through commitment to intellectual freedom, librarianship articulates principles of individual autonomy and volition. Through practices such as outreach, librarianship articulates principles of social democracy, which focuses on groups. In many ways it is possible to achieve both objectives without encountering contradictions. However, the two ideas require different ways of thinking; while an individual may want particular materials, that individual may also be a member of a group that is economically disadvantaged. This person's identity is shaped by both components. Perhaps more realistically, the individual may be a member of that disadvantaged group and may not bother to seek information at all. A passive stance by the library will not bring about empowerment of the group. Is knowledge power? If it is, it is not gained passively.

With our profession, and integrated into the workings of our profession, the complex associations that Dewey and Walzer speak of exist in a nascent form and have for some time. Libraries, while not omitting competition from their being, have cooperated in meaningful ways. Union catalogs and serials lists, interlibrary loans, reciprocal borrowing privileges, and other mechanisms have broadened the scope of patrons' experiences. More recently consortia have systematized cooperation; one intended outcome has been to create as seamless a process of access as possible. I'll propose here that consortia cannot fully realize their potential unless they embrace the radical new liberalism. An explicit goal of egalitarianism *for library users* is essential. That goal refocuses attention away from libraries themselves to the intentional ends of libraries' existence. When libraries begin to consider the costs and benefits on the basis of an individual organization, the shortcomings of classical liberalism are reinforced and means become confused with ends. This is not to say that efficiency flies out the window, but efficiency and effectiveness are assessed with the true end of egalitarian user access in mind. Effectively functioning consortia achieve the democratic socialist ideal of the new liberalism by treating not just individuals, but groups (in the form here of participating institutions and, by extension, their communities) equitably. In order for consortia to achieve the egalitarian goal there must be conscious and deliberate acceptance of the goal *as* political. The acceptance is vital to avoidance of the trap that Dewey (1954 [1927]) warns of: "The belief that thought and its communication are now free simply because legal restrictions which once obtained have been done away with is absurd. Its currency perpetuates the infantile state of social knowledge" (p. 168).

Even more fundamentally, publicly supported libraries must address the dynamics of association that Walzer describes. Librarians have to understand the critiques that Walzer and Dewey offer so that they will be able to define "community" more comprehensively than in the past. If we accept that the tenets of traditional liberalism are limited (as I've argued we should), then the extension of those tenets to communities served by libraries are likewise limited, possibly to the point of omitting some groups. The liberal tendency to presume that negative freedoms (elimination of restrictions on freedom, such as the First Amendment) fails to account for the kinds of restrictions that result from some involuntary associations. For example, the presence of schools and libraries in towns and counties, and corresponding absences of restrictions to free access to these institutions, by no means ensures egalitarian access to learning, ideas, and facilitated participation in democracy. Later in his life Dewey acknowledged, "schools were inextricably tied to prevailing structures of power and therefore extremely difficult to transform into agencies of democratic reform" (Westbrook, 1991, p. 509). Could we assume that libraries are less strongly tied to power structures? The power structures are complex and do not reside in one sector or sphere of life. Governments, private sector entities, and even some groups that claim to be public exert influence over institutions like schools and libraries. These bodies and groups have particular interests and are positioned so as to articulate their interests. Other groups, however, are far less able to articulate their interests. Public institutions are supposed to be cognizant of the voiced *and* the silenced interests.

François Matarasso (2000), speaking of libraries in the United Kingdom, says "that the fundamental goal of the public library is to empower the individual to improve his or her social and economic situation through access to information, education and culture. That, in an unequal world, is an emphatically egalitarian mission, destined to change society" (p. 42). His call for an egalitarian mission is a noble one, but emphasis on the individual and ignoring groups perpetuates some of the shortcomings of classical liberalism. Furthermore, assuming that libraries, through providing information and education, can lead directly to transformation of people's social and economic lots is seriously flawed thinking. Social and economic predicaments are too complicated to have one simple fix, and a radical new liberalism admits to this. My goal in this chapter has certainly not been to undermine liberalism (writ large) and democracy, but to suggest that we begin a quest for a radical re-formation of democracy. The elements of responsibility *and* autonomy can be reconciled if (and perhaps only if) democracy is defined in terms of both society and the individual. Two keys to the realization of a form that can be called democratic socialism are a critical non-indoctrinational education system and a democratically developed (à la Walzer) public library system. Democratic socialism was an idea of Dewey's, but he didn't develop a unified political philosophy of it. There are, though, some necessary components that he did envision: strong civil liberties, decentralization of authority, educational reform, and representative public institutions where dissent and the questioning of power structures can thrive. Of course librarians alone can't bring about large-scale political reform, but we can integrate political action into our organizations. Accomplishing such an objective will require sustained and profession-wide discussion of mission and purpose (in other words, discussion of ends). This will be a gargantuan task; professional discourse tends to focus overwhelmingly on means. Herein lies what may be the most pressing challenge for our profession. As we tackle it we should keep in mind the meaning of Richard Harvey Brown (2005): "Means are considered morally neutral, since they are now viewed as a matter of technique. Since the technicist language is inherently incapable of ethical self-reflection, it eschews substantive moral criticism. Thus, reasoned moral judgment about both means and ends is little by little excluded from the public sphere" (p. 92). The technique he writes about is related to the operational use of "information" today. In the next chapter we'll investigate a particular and powerful manifestation of "information" that has political, ethical, and pragmatic ramifications—the Information Society.

CHAPTER 6

The Information Society

I'LL BEGIN THIS CHAPTER with a series of claims, and then address them all. The claims are developed from the discussions in the preceding chapters and bring the discussion together. Since the claims are closely related, the discussion here will not presume that each stands alone. Instead, it will have to treat the claims as intertwined. The first claim isn't mine, but we need to start with it. Here it is: We now live in an "Information Society" in which communication, information (or rather data available for interpretation and use), and knowledge are essential for both the good life and the successful life. This claim is sweeping, so the following discussion will have to be quite involved. The second claim flows from the first: The Information Society has depended on technological innovation, development, and spread for its dominance. The third: Technology is different from science; it is a different thing with a different ontology. The fourth: The different ontology of technology results in a different epistemology, ethics, economics, and politics. The claims, combined, result in the conclusion that there are particular epistemological, ethical, economic, and political components to the Information Society. In the extreme the combined claims can be said to *create* a new environment, so that the old rules no longer apply. The components have been shaped, so far, by the interests of some individuals and groups for their benefit. The forces are powerful, but they do not absolutely determine the path ahead. These claims can all be challenged; at the outset I'm making no commitment to the support of any of them. In fact, each claim includes a dialectic, so a dialectical approach to them is appropriate. The dialectic will have to include the very word "information."

The term Information Society (IS) isn't made up for convenience here, but is in widespread, and international, usage. In spite of, or perhaps because of, the wide use of the term, it doesn't have a single, agreed-upon meaning. One element of the IS that is more or less pervasive is technology, particularly what Europeans and others call information and communication technology (ICT). I will use this construction because it is explicitly more inclusive than what we in the United States call information technology. Where there is variance in the definition of the Information Society the locus tends to be in how ICT is used and for what purposes. Since ICT is a part of almost all aspects of life (work, leisure, personal), the potential variance in definition is considerable. While there is a clear difference in purpose between, say, a public library and the Walt Disney Company, ICT is vital to both endeavors. Of the numerous issues pertinent to defining the Information Society, two stand out. One is influenced by a push to a global economy grounded in large part in the potential presented by ICT. This definition may employ terms such as globalization, e-commerce, and the like. An issue (volume 19, no. 1, 2003) of the journal *Information Society* includes articles on perspectives relating to electronic commerce in a variety of nations. Much of the discussion of e-commerce includes elements of economic development on a large scale, and much of it hails the Internet as a transformational force enabling commerce and trade. On the other hand, there is a strain of discourse that focuses on the social implications of emerging technology. For example, the 2003 World Summit on the Information Society, held in Geneva, states that the common vision is to build a people-centered, inclusive, and development-oriented Information Society, where everyone can create, access, utilize, and share information and knowledge, enabling individuals, communities, and peoples to achieve their full potential in promoting their sustainable development and improving their quality of life (www.itu.int/wsis).

Of course these two matters can be seen as a continuum. There is no doubt that enhanced economic prosperity has the potential to benefit developing countries as well as wealthier nations. This kind of combination could achieve the ends of both poles of the continuum. It would be folly for the profession of librarianship, or any of the information professions, to ignore the explicit or implicit discussions, policy decisions, impact, or enterprises surrounding any conception of the Information Society. The one thing that holds true regardless of preferred definitions or stances on the continuum is that technological development, past and future—and the impact on social, cultural, political, and economic matters—has changed our lives and the way we live them. Social institutions, including libraries and other information-based organizations, have likewise changed and are challenged to participate actively in the change that is yet to come.

Two Views

Of course there are many more than two conceptions or definitions of the Information Society, but we can focus on two large families of views. One might be categorized as essentially utopian. Technology, as it enables access to information and to communication, has the power to unite and to fulfill any number of metaphysical goals. Some commentators have gone so far as to say that ICT frees us from the bonds of meat, or our physical selves. This view is very popular and there is some truth to many of its claims. Erik Davis (1998) expresses such a hope: "Whatever social, ecological, or spiritual renewal we might hope for in the new century, it will blossom in the context of communicating technologies that already gird the earth with intelligence and virtual light. Prometheus is hell-bent in the cockpit, but Hermes has snuck into Mission Control, and the matrix is ablaze with entangling tongues" (p. 335). This view is very popular and there is some truth to many of its claims. ICT (or, more to the point, the Information Society) is both real and unreal, both proximate and distant. Practically speaking, ICT enables us to stay in touch at times when the need is great. The availability and use of cellular phones have literally saved lives when people have been in dire need. Beyond anything quite so dramatic, families and friends are able to communicate more frequently and, now, to do much more with mobile phones than simply place calls. The Internet is accessible from hand-held devices and can save time locating addresses, finding needed information, etc. Devices in homes save time, enable people to manage their investments, contact local and federal government officials, do business, and much more. Only the most diehard anti-technologist would deny that the Information Society has brought benefits to millions of people.

The utopian outlook extends well beyond connectivity and embraces an ideal of knowledge and its accessibility. Richard Barbrook (2003) suggests that "Information is for sharing not for selling. Knowledge is a gift not a commodity. . . . The media corporations are incapable of reversing this de-commodification of information. . . . This time around, community has trumped commerce" (pp. 91–92). His words seem almost quaintly naive. The concept of information and knowledge as free is of an oddly independent nature. The two exist in space and, because of technology, can exist in all spaces simultaneously. The assumption appears to be that they are there for all people at all times. The implicit responsibility is to use this virtual space of knowledge well and to add to it. The existence of this networked knowledge is, in effect, its own moral imperative. Since the Information Society is comprised of knowledge, it is, by its very nature, good. The sort of wonderment might actually be labeled "hypermodern" for a couple of reasons. An occasionally held Enlightenment ideal of knowledge—more particularly, a new science that can inform a new engineering that, in turn, gives us a new life—is not far removed from an Information Society vision of knowledge. However, the locus of knowledge (if such a word as locus can even be employed) is not *in* or *of* the world or the body; it is an encompassing entity. In ways that extend modernity's conception of knowledge, the locus is at once immanent and transcendent; it is both with us and beyond us. We may situate ourselves within the locus, but we may never occupy that locus as we can occupy space in an office or a home. The Information Society, reduced to the space of knowledge, is metaphysical in every sense of the word (the examination of the physical and the non-physical).

The opposing view also makes a great deal of sense. This conception holds that many of the claims of the other side are overblown. While there are material gains that result from ICT, there are concomitant losses in less tangible areas. Some areas of loss are discretion regarding choice of content (e.g., when one provider of information contains certain sources, such as journals, and does not contain others), limitations on methodologies (using technology in such a way that it dictates how questions might be answered and, in extreme situations, which questions are asked), or invasions into privacy (when the government or even individuals have surveillance devices that can intrude anywhere). It may also be that ICTs impose particular structures on information that affect retrieval and, in some cases, transform the information itself (Borgmann, 1999, pp. 27–29). Some, such as Jacques Ellul (1990), warn that technology can affect human rationality through its social applications. For Ellul (whose position is radical), there is a possibility for the intervention of politicians and economists who think that given the crisis, unemployment, etc., extreme technical development is the only solution, so that willingly or unwillingly we must adapt to it (p. 19). Alvin Gouldner (1976) articulates a difficulty that predates what most would deem the Information Society proper and says, "This sheer increase in the information intensified the problem of information *processing* and, above all, of clarifying the meaning of the information. Acquiring *meaning*, not information, became increasingly problematic" (p. 93; emphasis in original).

It is essential to recognize that the customary counter to utopian vision tends not to be a dystopian one (although that does exist and has its proponents), but a skeptical one. Skepticism questions even more than it argues. The questions asked and the problems identified may be more important and more instructional than a doomsday promise of inevitable dystopianism. For this reason, the possibility of a moral Information Society eschews dystopia, perhaps even more strongly than it does utopia. With the two extremes out of play, some questions can be asked that relate to the three issues mentioned above. As a hypermodern phenomenon (that is, incorporating many of the characteristics of modernity, but at turbo speed and on steroids), does the Information Society avoid, perhaps obliterate, the obstacles thrown up by bureaucracy, thus opening economic potential, social justice, and equilibrium of power relations? Is the Information Society truly transformational—is it trans-capitalist, trans-cultural, trans-disciplinary, trans-ethical? Does information equate to freedom, thus engendering educational and knowledge-sharing growth of a scale and kind heretofore unseen? In trying to respond to such questions, a program aimed at fostering a moral Information Society has to listen to Mark Taylor's (2001) admonition that "Complexity is both a marginal and an emergent phenomenon. Never fixed or secure, the mobile site of complexity is always momentary and the marginal moment of emergence is inevitably complex" (pp. 23–24). Complexity, as we'll see, includes some room for ideology.

It may seem that a discussion of the Information Society is not going to lend itself to immediate practical application in specific organizations. I contend that it has practical implications for us all. In fact, we could say that it could have the most profound practical implications. A friend of mine who has worked in public libraries and who studies them very closely observed that today much of the expressed concern on the parts of directors especially, but not exclusively, is effectively on public management. There is no doubt that in all organizations we need to think seriously about how libraries are managed, but the gist of the observation is that the definition of management is far too narrow. It would be easy to claim that capitalism is at the heart of the dilemma that libraries and information face, but (1) that's far too facile an excuse and (2) it's not entirely true. There are benefits of capital, some of which aid development of social programs and institutions and actually work towards the public good. That said, every facet of life, and especially public life, has a large and complex set of interests. After all, "Capital is not a physical thing but a social relation" (Harvey, 2000, p. 28). The public has its own set of interests that may, at least sometimes, be expressed as advocacy for policies and actions that benefit all people, or at least a clear majority of people. This may also be expressed as public welfare, and may include equitable opportunity to avail oneself of public services and products, and equitable access to information. Other interests may be opposed to the above and may focus on private ownership of property as ascendant, private access to public property, including land, and exclusive rights that may preclude public access to some goods and services. Those interests may also entail the exploitation of resources, including labor, for their own purposes. Obviously there is the potential for conflict between these two sets of interests; one key matter to consider is how the conflict may be resolved—what considerations weigh in decision making; who controls the decision-making process; who benefits and who might be disadvantaged by the outcome; what recourse there may be for appeal or reversal; and in what venues the conflict might play out. All of these considerations have an impact on the concerns we have regarding information, including how we define it, who produces it and how, how it gets disseminates, who puts a price (if not a value) on it and how, who gets to use it and how, and how it gets interpreted.

If a claim that we live in an IS is posited, then definitions and usages of the word "information" must be examined. This isn't a purely academic exercise; the practical purposes of all information-related organizations depend, frequently implicitly, on preferred or imposed usages. By way of background, in our profession of librarianship there are disparate definitions with sometimes radically different implications for practice. For example, there is a strain of information theory that goes back more than half a century to the work, mainly, of Claude Shannon (1949). Shannon's theory is actually one of message transmission and has nothing at all to do with meaning (semantics); his focus is on the fidelity of transmission. In more traditional informational services, such as those that have been in place in libraries, meaning is everything. Even in many strains of information science, where the attention is on retrieval and relevance, there is a necessary interest in meaning. The determination of meaning may be related to those interests just described. According to one set of interests, meaning may be rooted in advancing the aims of capital and the modes of production that support capital. According to another, meaning may be rooted in ideas of the public good.

The root of information—inform—is older than the derivative term. As Albert Borgmann (1999, pp. 9–10) points out, it originally came from a somewhat philosophical exercise—imposing form on a thing so that the mind may, first, apprehend it, and, then, to improve or instruct it. In time, the imposition factor was de-emphasized and the discernment of form was what people were trying to do. Borgmann introduces what people in several disciplines might call "cognitive information." He then focuses on one particular conception of cognitive information that he refers to as constructivism (or may also be called social constructionism; we don't limit the phenomenon to individual cognition). At the heart of such a view is the assertion that knowledge cannot develop simply from the perception of a physical thing for two reasons. He refers to Adelbert Ames, who indicates that many physical things might be perceived in the same way; conversely, one physical thing may be perceived differently by different people (pp. 12–13). The social element enters in the latter conception, because, as a number of people claim, perception is contextual, and that context has social frames of reference. Constructivist cognitive information, then, is realized because of both external and internal causes, with the internal predominating.

Something Borgmann doesn't mention is that there is a counterpoint to the constructivist cognitive information—realist cognitive information. That view is defined by the claims that knowledge does root itself in physical things; that there is a unity of perception of the physical world (or at least a possible unity of perception); that language is genuinely referential (that when we say something about a physical thing our statements actually describe the thing itself); and that this kind of cognitive information leads to progressive knowledge of the physical world. An extreme form of this position holds that the above points are not only fundamental, they are necessary and sufficient, since all there is is a physical world; our impressions of individual perception (and by extension interpretation, understanding, etc.) are indeed physical phenomena.

Mark Poster (1990), in his book *The Mode of Information: Poststructuralism and Social Context*, looks at, for lack of a better expression, ways of informing and being informed. Right away he recognizes that in today's society there are many "modes of information" that, taken together, form a more metaphysical kind of mode of information. He writes, "What is at stake are new language formations that alter significantly the network of social relations, that restructure those relations and the subjects they constitute" (p. 8). The individual modes include all of the print forms that have existed for some time plus many electronic forms that may be either active or passive. In the world of virtual space, he maintains, it is more difficult for people to locate themselves in either time or place; people become decentered and removed from objects that may have surrounded them in previous, print-based ways of communicating. He asks if the electronic modes change speech and writing in some ways. Other commentators, such as Jay David Bolter (1991) and Richard Lanham (1993) answer that question in the affirmative. Lanham goes so far as to say, "The central self is threatened not by a lively social self but the lack of one. Electronic networks permit a genuinely stylized public life, one with formal roles that we can play and that are not isomorphic with our 'real selves'" (p. 219).

In the course of his book Poster makes some observations that, I think, are extremely important for us to consider as we study the nature, purposes, and outcomes of an information society. He asserts that as our forms and means of communicating have changed, so have (1) our conceptions of history (and by this he does not mean simply the account of events of the past, but the way we see our own development, especially in light of how we see our present state), and (2) our ideas of the relationship between self and other (p. 6). Part of the alteration Poster speaks of could be traced to the way the communications are structured insofar as they are configurations of signs that exist in a particular space. Each of these forms of communication uses a particular space to communicate. I don't simply mean physical space that has implications for size and type of audience; I mean cognitive space so that we perceive signs differently with each form. The communication space is both a creation of, and helps to create, relationships among people—social relations. One may conceive of self differently according to the mode of communication. For example, think of yourself in conversation with one other person, then think of yourself e-mailing that same person, then think of yourself contributing to an electronic discussion group, then think of yourself writing for presentation to a large audience. Do you see any changes in the way you see yourself as the space changes? In part, discursive practice changes with each change in social space; you structure your discourse in ways that are particular to each space. A problem, according to Poster, is that, as space has changed and some spaces have more or less replaced others we have created and are victims of a communicative dilemma—the loss of the referent; the representational character of language is becoming lost. A corresponding social loss occurs, which might contribute to a diminishing of meaning.

Taking Poster at his word for now, let's return to "information." If there are multiple definitions and usages of the word, and if it becomes increasingly difficult to discern which usage dominates in a certain communicative space, then what happens to understanding and knowledge? Is there is a single, unified and unifying, definition of information in librarianship? This background may help all of us examine, throughout our careers, the various spheres in which information exists, is defined, and is employed in the context of particular interests.

Another issue relating to the claim that we live in an IS is described by Manuel Castells (1996). He speaks of the space of flows, but information can also be seen as the site of a contest between controllers of information and resisters of that control. Castells (2001) reminds us that technologies (and network technologies are certainly no exception) are socially produced and culturally informed. It would be naïve to think that exercises of power would not have a profound impact on any realization of the Information Society. All three of the issues return any consideration of technology and society to Heidegger's (1977) questioning of technology's effects on *Dasein*, or the being of humankind. The issues we're talking about here carry serious ethical and moral implications and can be seen to constitute points on converging continua. That is, there is fluidity within each issue and also between the issues. Economics, social relationships, and power are conjoined in many complex ways. There is no doubt, for example, that enhanced economic prosperity has the potential to benefit developing countries as well as wealthier nations, thus enabling a global social good. For good *or* ill, economic transformations could effect a reshaping of cultural, social, economic, even national relationships.

Christopher May (2002) takes an admittedly skeptical view of many of the claims associated with the Information Society, but he lists the principal claims thusly:

- that we are experiencing a social revolution;
- that the organization of economic relations has been transformed;
- that political practices and the communities involved are changing;
- and that the state and its authority are in terminal decline. (p. 3)

It would be folly for any of the information professions to ignore the explicit or implicit discussions, policy decisions, impact, or enterprises surrounding any conception of the Information Society. The one thing that holds true regardless of preferred definitions or stances on the continuum is that technological development, past and future, and the impact on social, cultural, political, economic, and moral matters, has changed our lives and the way we live them. Social institutions have likewise changed and are challenged to participate actively in the change that is yet to come. Specifically, the challenge is to concretize technology's promise into accessible education,

enhanced health care, more widespread and participative political deliberation, and improvements in the material well-being of the world's citizens.
Ignoring the challenge could have decidedly deleterious moral consequences.
Poster (2001) presciently points out, "without a concept of culture, the study
of new media incorporates by default the culture of the dominant institutions
in society" (p. 2).

IDEOLOGY AND CONSUMPTION

As we look at various families of usage of information (both as concept
and as thing), we need to be aware that the symbolic use of "information"
(and "society" for that matter) may at times be ideological. As is true of a
number of words and terms in common usage today, original intents were
not exactly what we have in mind. Ideology was supposed to be the scientific
study of ideas, much as sociology was to have been the science of society. In
the twentieth century, the meaning of the word was transformed as engineering and science began to appropriate it, but it still has multiple applications,
and this can be quite confusing for anyone hearing or reading the word. At
times it seems the speaker is really saying that everything that does not agree
with his or her stance is necessarily ideological. At other times, "ideological"
seems to refer to outright lies. At still other times, it may simply refer to any
set of beliefs shared by a group. We can see that if this is going to make any
sense at all to us, we need to look further into the meaning of the word.

As John Thompson (1990) says, and as others attest, one fairly common
usage of "ideology" is neutral. It means only the statements, beliefs, and codes
that a group creates, discovers, and shares. In this way each of us probably
holds a number of ideologies, each depending on the group that we happen
to identify with at a particular time. For example, I may hold to a national
ideology, an educational ideology, a religious ideology, a professional ideology, etc. I should note that this meaning is not useless, especially since expressions of identity can be fruitful tools for investigation. However, using
the word "ideology" in this way waters down its meaning to the point that it
doesn't do us any good in our study of the Information Society. Thompson
employs the non-neutral meaning of the word as a means of investigating
the ways in which domination can be created, exercised, and maintained. He
tells us that his usage omits some possible meanings; for instance, he does
not use it to refer to efforts at countering domination. He also says that in
his conception, truth or falsity, correctness or incorrectness, do not play a
role; it is the intent of the use of language that matters. Intention is indeed
important, but when the intention is to deceive, then truth and falsity do
matter. For evaluation of the use of language, at the very least, a broader conception of ideology is needed.

Some, such as Terry Eagleton (1991), identify more uses of ideology; in fact, he defines and expands upon six:

1. The neutral meaning that simply refers to the production of ideas, beliefs, and values.
2. The ideas and beliefs (true or false) that symbolize the experiences of a specific group or class.
3. The promotion and legitimation of the interests of specific groups or classes in the face of opposing interests.
4. The promotion and legitimation of interests, but limited to a dominant group or class.
5. Legitimation of the power of the dominant group through distortion or dissimulation.
6. Emphasis on false or distorting beliefs, but those arising not from a particular group; rather those that are part of the material structure of society as a whole.

The distinctions Eagleton describes may seem subtle, but they are important. Thompson basically focuses on number 4. I think it would be a mistake not to add number 5, especially given that 4 and 5 are not entirely independent. There are other writers who say that ideological discourse is usually characterized by language that is true in some way or at some level, but false at another. This definition is the character of dissimulation, that even Thompson admits exists.

Eagleton points out that to be effective, ideology has to be plausible in some way, so an outright lie does not usually work as ideology (even though there may be components of claims or statements that are false). Here is another aspect of ideology that is important. Yes, ideology is played out through language, but especially through language as employed discursively; that is, ideology is not a single statement or claim, but a structured discourse that builds upon itself to appear (at least) coherent. Our concern here will be a combination of the processes that are part of the construction of ideological discourse, and the outcomes of those processes. Regarding outcomes, we can recall the words of István Mészáros (1989): "In Western capitalist societies liberal/conservative ideological discourse dominates the assessment of all values to such an extent that very often we do not have the slightest suspicion that we are made to accept, quite unquestioningly, a particular set of values to which one could oppose a well founded alternative outlook, together with the commitments more or less implicit in it" (p. 3).

We can return to Thompson. For one thing, even if we broaden his definition of ideology a little, we should heed his advice that the analysis of ideology requires situating symbolic phenomena within social-historical contexts. The discourse is not divorced from time and place; it exists within that space for particular purposes, frequently related to creating and/or sustaining domination. One of the postmodern reactions against ideology is the denial that there is such a thing as a grand narrative that purports to provide all that we need to know about a phenomenon or even a way of being. The narrative is generally a creation designed to make a point; our perspective should take into account the reasons for the creation and the purpose of the narrative. We should perhaps be reluctant to claim that there are no genuinely meaningful grand narratives.

Ultimately, Thompson says, the study of ideology is interpretive. Some would say that every act of interpretation is itself ideological, because each of us adopts a particular stance or set of stances that politically, economically, or epistemologically are grounded in some form of domination. That is, some people might see ideology everywhere and as defining all relationships. That quickly reduces to meaninglessness; if it is everywhere, it is effectively nowhere. And it means analysis is not possible. Thompson (1990) says, "we must also offer reasons and grounds, evidence and arguments, which, in our view, render the interpretation plausible; and whether the interpretation is plausible, whether the reasons and grounds are convincing, is not a matter for the interpreter alone to judge" (p. 72). If an interpretation is to make sense, not just to ourselves, but to others, it must respond to questions that can be posed of it.

Some particulars of ideology in an IS include consideration of consumption and consumerism (as they relate to legitimation and dominance). First off, capital has changed since Marx's day. As Robert Bocock (1993) points out, Marx could not have foreseen the shape of consumer capitalism that exists today, because he could not have foreseen consumerism as it is today. That is, it would have been very difficult for Marx—or even his contemporaries—to grasp the social, cognitive, emotive, identity, and economic changes wrought by consumption. Workers do still work in order to earn money that enables them to purchase things. The things purchased are not merely needed for survival, though. They transcend, in many ways, anything required for survival so as to become another type of commodity. The removal from the production mode leads in part, Bocock says, to alienation (which Marx said was a characteristic of capitalism). Marx said that workers in the nineteenth century were alienated because there was a kind of self-estrangement. Not only were workers estranged from each other because of competition for the ultimate reward, wages; they became estranged from themselves. The work they were then doing was not related necessarily to their own being, to the sense of self someone might have. Work was a means to an end, the end being the wages paid for the work. Work also became separate from family and even place, as workers migrated to cities because that's where jobs were. Producers and sellers of commodities have latched on to the separation (either knowingly or not). Theodor Adorno (1991) claims that production and distribution entails this separation: "Organizations of convenience in an antagonistic society must necessarily pursue particular ends; they do this at the expense of the interests of other groups" (p. 110).

There is a mechanism of legitimation at work; people perceive need for some commodities, but the need is not tangible or physical; it is psychological and is a product of intentional ideological discourse. The response to the need legitimates both the structure of production and commodification and the aim of reify those psychological states that support the structure. The act of reification, of objectifying the psychological state, rests to a considerable extent on the creation and sustaining of consumer's identities *through* the commodity itself. Bocock (1993) says, "Modern consumption is based upon symbolic systems of meaning, symbols which are linked in with alienated forms of creativity, as in the design of modern consumer goods and the advertisements for them" (p. 49). He further says, "Consumption is more than ever before an experience which is to be located in the head, a matter of brain and mind, rather than seen as the process of simply satisfying biological bodily needs" (p. 51). Tim Kasser (2002) emphasizes consumption in advertising and the effects of distancing and, worse yet, the treatment of people as objects. One may look at the present state of consumerism and the role information plays in this state as a Kantian nightmare. If we accept Kant's moral dictum that people are themselves ends and are not to be used as means, we see the damage done by the commodification of relationships among people in a capitalist Information Society. The study of consumption and production of commodities raises other questions. As we investigate what is produced, how it is marketed, what is said to be a commodity, and what is consumed and how, we have to be wary of a problem that Michel de Certeau (1984) identified some time ago. In observing inquiry, and quantitative inquiry in particular, he saw that in too many instances, "What is being counted is what is used, not the *ways* of using" (p. 35). In quantitative study it is almost imperative that we create, or use existing, taxonomic categories for what is studied. In many cases this is possible and appropriate. In others, it systematically misses the point. This is one of Ellul's characterizations of technique and its shortcoming.

It is possible to call the state of consumption and consumerism symptomatic of a postmodern condition (not the same as advocating postmodernism)—a state of being in a society that results from intentional actions aimed at such strategies as legitimation and dissimulation, and this can be accomplished in part through commodification and feeding consumerism. Jean-François Lyotard (1984) observes that

> The nature of knowledge cannot survive unchanged within the context of general transformation. It can fit into the new channels, and become operational, only if learning is translated into quantities of information. . . . The relationship of suppliers and users of the knowledge they supply and use is now tending, and will increasingly tend, to assume the form already

taken by the relationship of commodity producers and consumers to the commodities they produce and consume—that is, the form of value.... Knowledge ceases to be an end in itself, it loses its "use-value." (pp. 4–5)

In Lyotard's critique it is knowledge that is transformed and commodified. Information (conceived both in broad and in specific ways) can likewise be commodified. A library purchases, licenses, and subscribes to products that are marketed within a systemic cycle of production and consumption. It is important that librarians understand the complex and sometimes ideological nature of the cycle; the alternative is an assumption of a "natural" process tied to the perfect equilibrium of the "marketplace of ideas." As we saw in the last chapter, "marketplace" is a seriously flawed and skewed metaphor.

GLOBAL ECONOMY, CHALLENGES, AND ETHICAL POTENTIAL

The fourth claim is at once the most intuitive and the broadest. It makes sense that if technology carries unique ontological characteristics, it would have its own challenges. We can begin with economics. Even more basic is a realization that David Nye (2006) made: "the human relationship to technology is not a matter of determinism; it is unavoidably bound up with consumption" (p. 66). Let me be clear that this statement does not necessarily mean that every person's search for, or use of, information is reducible to a financial transaction. If the utopian dream were true, people would still be able to "consume" information that they otherwise wouldn't be able to get. This utopia would be the best possible welfare state, in which a fundamental resource like information would be available to all. This utopia doesn't exist. The other meaning of Nye's observation is that technology *is* a commodity that can be consumed. The customary economics applies at the surface level—people who have more money can make greater use of technologies like ICTs. They can purchase computers, pay for connectivity, buy peripheral hardware, own and purchase use plans for cell phones, etc. The inequity is touted in much fiction, even fiction aimed at younger audiences. Eoin Colfer's series of young adult novels featuring Artemis Fowl has the protagonist's wealth and technological know-how as prominent elements. The customary economics is frequently invoked when people speak of the digital divide, and herein lies a limitation of the term "digital divide." The root problem is not just that some people can avail themselves of information available via ICTs. It is that some people comprehend that many elements of a good and successful life are enhanced by becoming informed about important aspects of life (finances, employment, health care, government action, and many other things). Others have little or no grasp of such elements and are unaware either of how to become informed (being able to begin with a question is the first step) or why becoming informed could be beneficial. The genuine and deeper divide hearkens back to the first claim and why it is impossible to say simply that there is, or isn't, an IS. The divide is embedded in educational, social, environmental, economic, political, and epistemological factors. It is impossible to give it a simple label, a brand. Yet consumption—in both of the above senses—is key to the divide.

ECONOMICS AND INFORMATION

Some economic analyses focus on principles of equilibrium and other economic mechanisms, but now we will consider ownership here. More specifically, this topic brings us back to a consideration of the impact of interests on decisions, functions, operations, and outcomes. The very first sentence of Dan Schiller's (1999) book points to the place of interests in any thinking about ownership and control: "The architects of digital capitalism have pursued one major objective: to develop an economy-wide network that can support an ever-growing range of intracorporate and intercorporate business processes" (p. 1). This purpose, according to Schiller, stems from a neoliberal stance. Neoliberalism, in this usage, comes from Victorian England, and is grounded in efforts at eliminating unwanted oversight and regulation. Of course, one difficulty—in this and in other arenas—is figuring out what is unwanted (unwanted by whom, at what time, for what reasons, etc.). Schiller points out, correctly I think, that the very creation (and also the maintenance) of a network on the scale we are talking about here depends inherently on mechanisms of regulation, and that means that there is an inevitable political element to digital capitalism.

That political element becomes clear in the claims made in recent statements by Michael Powell, former chairman of the Federal Communications Commission (FCC). At one point he made the analogy that the digital divide is like a Mercedes divide; there are people who would like to own an expensive car but cannot afford one. Such a statement ignores an essential claim of the Information Society—that everyone is affected in every realm of life by information, and access to information is vital for the most mundane, as well as the loftiest, of activities. Powell has also spearheaded recent FCC moves to expand possible ownership of media outlets by conglomerates, which would enable a few companies to have even larger and more pervasive presences in markets (for example, one company would be able to own more radio stations in a particular market than they have been able to own to date). This FCC move has met both popular and congressional resistance. In the context of a critique of interests and the creation of an Information Society, we should take a closer look at Powell's analogy.

For one thing, the digital divide might also be examined in terms of education. This has decidedly economic facets; schooling costs money. If this is a democratic society, should there be equity in educational opportunity, in educational content? Equity, of course, could be conceived in many different ways. One way to look at equity is in terms of access to higher education. Tuition has been rising in recent years, and financial aid, such as federally funded Pell Grants, has not kept pace with the cost. There could be the eventual possibility that individuals, or even groups of people, are excluded from higher education. The exclusion of people from educational opportunities is in no way akin to the inability to purchase a particular make of automobile. There are transportation alternatives to an expensive car that are effective. There is no legitimate alternative to education; a person who doesn't have access to education will be denied access to many opportunities in life. In other words, without an education, there's no way to get "there." Another way to envision equity is in curricular matters. An educational institution might bend to every demand that certain subjects be taught or that subjects be taught from all points of view. Equity, however conceived, carries implications for information and informing. The recent past has also seen the rise of for-profit higher education. For instance, networking enables institutions like the University of Phoenix to be effectively a global higher education institution.

In the midst of the challenges of the digital divide, there is also the increasing commercialization of networking. This makes perfect sense if we look at what lies at the heart of networks: information sharing. Schiller (1999) points out that the demand for information sharing has been building in three ways: intraorganizationally, interorganizationally (think about the layers of multinational corporations and B2B, but also about libraries and schools), and between corporations and individuals (the core of e-commerce). The essential commercial character of networks now presents something of a paradox for us as examiners of this complexity. There remains a fairly strong drive toward a proprietary stance; witness the fact that many corporations treat scientific information as their own and as a means to a financial end for themselves. However, if the beginnings of networking had been business originated, the proprietary urge might well have stopped growth before it ever occurred. Now businesses realize that the openness and accessibility of networks is what makes growth possible. If we are tempted to question the proprietary urge, look no further than agriculture. With the possibility of patenting genetic material, agri-business companies can hold patents on, and can exercise almost complete control over, the genetics of seeds. These companies have been aggressive worldwide at bring suit against farmers who maintain the customary practice of putting aside some seed from their harvests so that they buy less seed for the next growing year. The companies claim ownership of the seed used for planting; all of the harvest has to go to market. It's rather difficult to imagine an information analogy for the workings of agri-business, but if a company can own the rights to the information that comprises a genetic entity, could a company claim ownership to thoughts and ideas? This seems the stuff of science fiction, but librarianship should be concerned about the lengths to which ownership can go.

It is the potential for ownership of the previously unowned, along with the opening of new markets for commodities that leads the corporate world to espouse neoliberal ideals—freedom of action without unwanted state regulation (a kind of corporate libertarianism). Digital capitalism, directly or indirectly, makes another phenomenon possible—consolidation. Some might call this convergence; the end is a reduction in the number of corporate entities engaged in a particular business. It also results in much larger market shares for the remaining companies. Where in the past it might have been possible for companies to expand their reach across a country or even into other companies, communication difficulties limited such growth so that more companies could establish territories. With enhanced communication that extends to unifying inventory control, ordering, and delivery of products comes the possibility of global expansion. The technical development has been accompanied by (or perhaps has facilitated) loosening of regulation that can allow for the realization of the corporate neoliberal ideal.

We can turn to Marx to help us gain some understanding of the world of digital capitalism; in some important ways, it is an extension of the capitalist program. In particular, we can refer to a couple of Marx's (1976 [1867]) statements: "Commodities come into the world in to form of use-values, or material goods, such as iron, linen, corn, etc. . . . However, they are only commodities because they have a dual nature. . . . Therefore, they only appear as commodities, or have the form of commodities, in so far as they possess a double form, i.e., natural form and value form" (p. 138), and "It is only by being exchanged that the products of labour acquire a socially uniform objectivity as values, which is distinct from their sensuously varied objectivity as articles of utility" (p. 166). In this century, Georg Lukács (1971) provides some very helpful commentary on Marx's idea of commodity: a commodity structure's "basis is that a relation between people takes on the character of a thing and thus acquires a 'phantom objectivity', an autonomy that seems so strictly rational and all-embracing as to conceal every trace of its fundamental nature: the relation between people" (p. 83).

We have dealt briefly about productivity in the age of digital capitalism, and have seen that many economists, including Alan Greenspan, have attributed much of the gain to the rapid and pervasive employment of technology. However, there have been additional social changes that have affected corporate perception of work and the treatment of workers. Christopher May (2002) points out that class, in the sense that Marx meant it (a distinction between capital and labor), has not disappeared in the Information Society. We can close this section with the words of Heather Menzies (1998): "With pay directly hinged to performance—especially as performance-based compensation has become widespread in North America in recent years—workers start to identify with this commoditized expression of their work, and to drive themselves faster and faster" (p. 93).

TECHNOLOGY, DESIGN, ETC.

The second claim holds that technology is not just integral to, but is constitutive of, the IS. This section tackles technology, but not in the technical sense. Instead, the focus here is on the impact of technology upon information and society. In part, this is a continuation of the discussion on economics, since it probably is not possible to separate impact from economics, especially on a global scale. One place to start is with Manuel Castells. His program is a large and broad one; he's trying to understand and describe the totality of the global economy in terms of what he defines as the network society. A basic premise he begins with is that society, if it does not determine technology, can employ technology to either stifle its development (and, by extension, economic development) or accelerate the use of technology to foster economic activity. That is, the kinds of information and communication technologies that are of concern to us are, as he says, extensions of the human mind. For example, weapons technology is not extra-human, nor is entertainment technology, nor is any kind (or usage) of technology.

A major difference today from not very long ago is that the shape of organizations has changed. Castells (1996) admits this in his definitions of organization and network organization: the connections that are made through networking extend the reach of organizations and necessitate (or make possible, depending on your point of view) reaching beyond traditional political and national boundaries. A global economy is a product of networked organizations; it is what happens when organizations can operate in real time on a planetary scale. Part of the connections between and among (and within) organizations allows the diffusion of innovations on a large scale and in rapid fashion by enabling an inherently less proprietary stance on the part of organizations. One might take issue with Castells on that last point, especially in light of the years since the publication of his book in 1996. There seems to have been a reaction to the enabling factor of networking that has led to at least efforts at tighter control on the information that is produced within the organization, and the knowledge that may be possible as a result of the information. His observation does have relevance for librarians, though. Effectiveness of services can doubtless be enhanced through cooperation and the relaxing of a proprietary attitude. Consortia of all types rely on such enhancement and relaxation.

Throughout his book Castells (1996) recognizes and points out the kinds of complexity that is at the heart of the Information Society. He says that he believes that cultures manifest themselves through their institutions, and he identifies three errors that have been made repeatedly in analyses of transitions across time:

1. It assumes homogeneity between the transition from agriculture to industry and that from industry to services, overlooking the ambiguity and internal diversity of the activities included under the label of "services."
2. It does not pay enough attention to the truly revolutionary nature of new information technologies. . . .
3. It forgets the cultural, historical, and institutional diversity of advanced societies, as well as the fact that they are interdependent in a global economy. (p. 228)

Perhaps one of his most useful conclusions is, "the new informational paradigm of work and labor is not a neat model but a messy quilt, woven from the historical interaction between technological change, industrial relations policy, and conflictive social action" (pp. 240–41). Technology changes employment, the kind of work that people do, and the value of that labor. Along with the transformation of kinds of work comes potential transformation of ways of working and the place of work within people's lives. Perhaps not as much as in pre-industrial days, but still true today is the reality that people's identities and selves are connected to their work. Among the transformations is mobility—voluntary and involuntary. Both kinds of mobility lead to a reduced loyalty to employers; a person may leave one employer for better (or at least different) opportunities with another one, and people may be fired or laid off with little or no warning and little or no connection with job performance by an employer. Given such dynamics, we may wonder if librarians have some duty to prepare people for disruption, or at least to help people respond to it.

Any discussion of technology in the context of this book has connections to information. At this point in time it is difficult to isolate consideration of information from technology. As we contemplate the place of philosophy (with particular attention to the possibility of technological determinism), we should think about the transformational quality of technology in many areas, including informing. These sorts of imperatives are addressed by the likes of Frederick Ferré (1995) and Don Ihde (1993) (among others). Ihde observes that in some areas the ethical considerations have centered on calculations of social good, which is the fundamental position of utilitarianism. We should ask, in these cases, who defines "social good," and how it is defined. Ferré opens up the question of justice in the employment of technology; this has implications for applications in particular places (as the technology used may have specific local consequences), and across time. He sums up by saying that decisions both "to do" and "to refrain from doing" become morally significant choices. We could ask what sorts of choices or motivations have been important underlying principles with regard to information technology.

Leo Marx (1994) observes a kind of "technological pessimism" that reflects an attitude of dismay, anxiety, or depression that arises in the face of technological developments. One manifestation of the pessimism may be the hand-wringing that goes along with the "information explosion," especially in the academic sense. Through some means that we lost control over, there has been a growth of information (perhaps seen in a limited way as object) that is unwanted, unneeded, and unintentional. However, the explosion is a result of human use of technology, but for particular ends that may not be congruent with (may even be antithetical to) other ends. This idea is in contrast with utopian or ideological views that stress optimism in the face of new and pervasive technologies. Advertisements for information technology products and services tend to reflect this kind of optimism; technology has the power to break down different kinds of barriers, to create wealth, to enable and empower, to enhance humanness. Or the view of technology may be that it transforms humans into almost a new species—"The Digital Generation." As part of critique of the Information Society we need to explore the extent to which such kinds of presentations (1) reflect what is; (2) reflect what some people would like to be; (3) might be employed as a mechanism of potential control; and (4) actually does serve to help in the effort to control (and, related to that, whose purposes may be served).

IMPACT ON SOCIETY AND CULTURE

It would be irresponsible of us not to pay some attention to education as we consider information in today's society. It is necessary that we to address education because the IS makes a number of claims about education—both about traditional means and modes and emerging ones. This also has practical implications for our profession. The services that are necessary for educational endeavors are grounded in meeting the needs of information seekers, facilitating discovery, building knowledge, and exploring applications of knowledge. The conversation about "information" in elementary and secondary schools is not entirely consistent; in some ways the role of information is lauded as contributing to students' discovery and learning. This praise not infrequently addresses the Internet and the rapid access to "stuff." On the other hand, information is demonized by some in the sense that it obstructs students' construction of knowledge and their creativity. Information is occasionally linked with authority in a hegemonic sense and is criticized as undermining the intellectual growth of youth. It is an open question whether either point describes reality. As is evident, the ideas of education are rooted in foundational philosophies of education. If, for instance, individual discovery is privileged in one philosophy, then information occupies a role that is related, but secondary, to discovery.

In *The Social Life of Information*, John Seeley Brown and Paul Duguid (2000) observe that universities are tending to behave more like businesses—looking at competitors, markets, customers, and productivity. The observation should not be taken uncritically; we should ask some questions relating to it: Is there evidence of universities acting like businesses? Is there any improvement because of such behavior? Are there any problems of this attitude? Information and ICT in these kinds of environments can have the dual roles of a simulacrum of education (that is, pretense of being able to educate, but not really having the ability) and a competitive tool. The particular matter of commodification of education deserves attention. There are some quite large-scale efforts to commercialize at least some higher education endeavors. For example, there are some national, private, online universities, the best known of which is probably the University of Phoenix, which has been around for a few decades, but has grown especially in the last ten years or so. As of July 2006 the University of Phoenix has more than 180,000 students taking courses and thousands of instructors. Most recently they have been expanding the range of degrees offered, as well as their geographic coverage. Courses from the University of Phoenix have employed technology, but they have also created small campus presences in dozens of locations across the country. That an institution with the market share that the University of Phoenix has would increase the "brick" component of its enterprise is by no means trivial. The mix of online and classroom instruction may (if we draw from the University of Phoenix's experience) be *both* effective *and* efficient.

A critic of distance offerings that are aimed at increasing numbers of students and revenues is David Noble. Here is a brief excerpt from one of his (2001) writings:

> One the one side [of a conflict] university administrators and their myriad commercial partners, on the other those who constitute the core relation of education: students and teachers.... It is no accident, then, that the high-tech transformation of higher education is being initiated from the top down, either without any student and faculty involvement in the decision-making or despite it. (p. 31)

We should not take this on its face, but should read it critically. This is only a part of his argument, but we should give this line of thought serious consideration. In a similar vein, Thomas Valovic (2000) argues that "While our libraries are being neglected, the Internet is being lionized as the bold and ineluctable future. Funding for schools and libraries is quietly and without adequate debate or discussion flowing away from books and toward technology" (p. 50). If this is indeed the case, is it necessarily a bad thing? We do have an interest in a debate on funding, given an understandable desire to maintain and develop operations, but are we certain that our motivation is directed to communities served?

Duguid and Brown (2000) point out that two things the university represents are learning to the individual and knowledgeable individuals to society. With regard to both they state, "The extent to which education can serve both students and society with more than they know to ask for depends on the extent to which society can trust educational institutions, their judgments, and the certificates they provide for their students' degrees" (p. 217). There is, they say, sheltering from external micromanagement and close scrutiny. They also claim that innovation tends to come from people with broad interests, but then why are the humanities and arts not more central to universities? There is a distinction they make between undergraduate and graduate education that has some importance for an examination of information and society. Undergraduate education entails learning about and graduate education entails learning to be. Their model for adjustment to the structure now in place includes three fundamental elements: "access to authentic communities of learning, interpretation, exploration, and knowledge creation; resources to help them work with both distal and local communities; and widely accepted representations for learning and work" (p. 232).

There are, of course, other parts of our society that are affected by elements of the Information Society. Again, we have touched on some aspects, such as consumption and consumerism. At this point we can briefly revisit consumption, especially consumption as symbol. Symbolic elements such as consumption depend on some kind of expressiveness, such as enunciation, according to de Certeau, as was demonstrated above. This does indeed recall the now commonplace distinction between language and speech. Enunciation (speech) necessitates a realization of language through specific speech acts. The speaker in some ways makes language his/her own; that is, the speaker must first engage in some decoding before encoding the speech act. A speaker speaks *to* someone. The speech act takes place now (in the present). In a research method such as discourse analysis, everyday speech is frequently examined through these kinds of enunciations, but the analysis is contextual; it is set within a sometimes complex social setting that should account for place, time, and elements that are not present at the time of the speech act, but influence the act (such as politics, music, film, etc.). Consumption as symbol is not merely an act of buying and use; consumption itself has symbolic value. *What* is bought and *how* it is used (perhaps especially how conspicuously it's used) communicates to others. Marketers of consumable goods employ the symbolic value to reach consumers.

We can see that the Information Society is a complex and contested idea. In many ways the time is ripe to shape the conceptions of information and informing in today's world, and we in our profession are ideally positioned to take a leading role both in conceptualizing the possible and in realizing goals of accessibility to meaningful information. The challenge awaits.

FLOWS OF POLITICAL POWER AND MORAL COUNTERPOSITIONS

Following the fourth claim, "Information Society" can be defined in a variety of ways, so the idea (to the extent that it does indeed permeate society) can be reflected in the political sphere and/or it can contribute to shaping the political. Acceptance of ICT as "good" may lead to action on the basis of a unified and universal acceptance of ICT as good. This good, to the extent that it is presumed and that it is embraced by markets and by the state, conveys power to ICT and to the idea of the Information Society. In such circumstances there is no perceived need for deliberation regarding the fundamental premise of ICT as good. Following this, there may or may not be deliberation on implementation of ICT in specific ways for specific purposes. Suppose the following claim is made at high levels in the government: "Of course we know that emerging technologies have the power to enhance people's lives and well being, as well as helping to provide security for our nation and people." A dissenting opinion must first question the surety of the statement before an alternative stance can be articulated. For the question to be taken seriously, an admission of its legitimacy is required, as is a willingness to avoid its incontrovertibility. If such conditions are absent, where, then, is the possibility for deliberation? For example, Francis Fukuyama asserts,

> A society built around information tends to produce more of the two things people value most in a modern democracy: freedom and equality.... Hierarchies of all sorts, whether political or corporate, come under pressure and begin to crumble. Large, rigid bureaucracies, which sought to control everything in their domain through rules, regulations, and coercion, have been undermined by the shift toward a knowledge-based economy, which serves to "empower" individuals by giving them access to information. (Fukuyama, 1999, p. 4)

His dictum seems to allow for no contravening stance; authenticity is rendered difficult if not impossible. Further, there is little empirical evidence that his claim holds water. We have not seen reduction in bureaucracies, and the empowerment he has written of is very limited. There are, of course, blogs that offer readers alternative points of view and even opportunities to participate, but many political blogs are somewhat authoritarian and provide little room for dialogic discourse. Technologies have affected markets, particularly entertainment markets, but it is an open question whether new or expanded markets constitute freedom.

The kinds of consolidation just described have, in general, taken place as a result of, and as a means to advance, the interests of particular corporate and state entities. The consolidation, even though it is grounded in information and technology, is non-deliberative in its exercise of power. All forms of meaningful democracy—and certainly the version explicated at the end of the last chapter—depend on deliberation for vitality and egalitarianism. The absence of deliberation is not, on its face, immoral, but it does lack an essential moral element—fairness. Deliberation can afford some structural checks to the consolidation:

> The general aim of deliberative democracy is to provide the most justifiable conception for dealing with moral disagreement in politics. In pursuing this aim, deliberative democracy serves four related purposes. The first is to promote the legitimacy of collective decisions. . . . The second purpose of deliberation is to encourage public-spirited perspectives on public issues. . . . The third purpose of deliberation is to promote mutually respectful processes of decision-making. . . . Inevitably, citizens and officials make some mistakes when they take collective decisions. The fourth purpose of deliberation is to help correct these mistakes. (Gutmann and Thompson, 2004, pp. 10–12)

While it is implicit, the four purposes rely on people's ability not simply to be informed through the deliberative process, but to communicate ideas, support, and dissent. The most important point that Gutmann and Thompson raise is that the kinds of decisions, plus the nature of deliberation, in a democracy has a moral, as well as an informational, component. In view of the power of the Information Society metaphor, morally sound deliberation includes some fundamental tenets—all claims (positive and negative) about ICT's role in society are open to examination; it is everyone's responsibility to undertake such an examination of claims; collective and individual welfare must be considered; equity and fairness are foremost as goals; and the economic is not separable from the social when information is considered.

The connection between politics and the IS should be made as explicit as possible here; this will require delving once again into democracy. A necessary distinction also must be recognized: democracy exists as a form of rule, a principle of governance, and it also exists as a framework in which decisions are made, citizens participate, symbolism is expressed, etc. (Mouffe, 2000, p. 2). As a form of rule democracy is value-laden; it is either defended as the most efficacious path to liberty, freedom, equality, and opportunity, or it is attacked as hedonistic, disorderly, and irreligious. As a framework, democracy articulates (at least in some conceptions) a prima facie neutrality that permits a debate about values, economics, representations, and rights (or a questioning of a static essentialism regarding these matters). Both of these ideas of democracy are sites of contest. The role of democracy may be aggregative; that is, people's preferences may be taken for granted. An example that has been used here is that the IS is a force for public and social good, therefore it is to be pursued and secured as an embodiment of *Dasein*. The assumption of preferences can result in policy and legislation that rely on markets to locate economic and social equilibrium. Consolidation and conglomeration in the corporate sector are common and are explicitly viewed as an inherent public good (given that mergers are governmentally approved by agencies charged with protecting the public good). In aggregative democracy deliberation is subsumed under the legitimated umbrella of public opinion, which is almost definitionally aggregative. There is a presumption that the aggregate is in fact the majority and, so, democratic action results from assessment of public opinion. An advocate of a kind of aggregative democracy is Richard Posner. He refers to his version as pragmatic, and he borrows from the earlier arguments of Joseph Schumpeter. Posner's pragmatic democracy is grounded, in large part, in economics and he uses analogies for market economics to illustrate his perceived superiority of his stance. He writes, "in political as in economic markets, relatively uninformed 'consumers.' That is, the voters, can and do use information shortcuts to make up for their information deficits, as by inferring a candidate's suitability from the identity of his supporters and opponents" (Posner, 2003, p. 191).

One path to a moral Information Society follows deliberation and counters Posner's version of pragmatism. A unifying principle of deliberative democracy is presented by Gutmann and Thompson, "The underlying assumption is that we should value reaching conclusions through moral reasoning rather than through self-interested bargaining [contra Posner]. Citizens and officials, we assume, can learn how to take each other seriously as moral agents" (Gutmann and Thompson, 2004, p. 80). As has been shown, an impact of technology's use can be to alienate and disembody. Disembodiment alters communication, changes the ways people converse, negotiate, argue, and reach agreement. The fulfillment of moral reasoning includes speech. More specifically, reasoning requires dialogue. Dialogue, in order to an effective discursive strategy, is fundamentally phenomenological. It rests on recognition of the other as a distinct self, with some common experiences and concepts, but also with differences of perception and consciousness. So, a moral IS depends upon dialogic communication that intentionally leads to moral reasoning.

MEDIA AND LIBRARIES

The politics of the IS, as expressed in part through technology, includes the media through which people can be informed. In the utopian vision of the Information Society as it relates to the world's economy and economic problems, there is confidence that ICT has the power of equalization. The technology, and the information that can be shared by means of the technology, can place all players on an equal footing. The underlying assumption is that information is indeed free—free in the sense of the gift economy that Barbrook speaks of and also financially free (or so close to being free that there are no economic barriers). A curious, and unstated, accompanying assumption is that ICT in itself is not bound by economic reality, that it will be treated as a pure public good so that all people can be networked. ICT, however, is part of labor-produced capital and, as such, is subject to controls by the state and/or private interests. The recent U.S. Federal Communications Commission approval of more concentrated private ownership of media outlets (approval that the U.S. Congress refused to endorse) provides ample evidence of the blurring of public-private lines. Robert McChesney (2004) and Ben Bagdikian (2004) demonstrate the many effects of media control in the hands of very few entities on the open dissemination of information. Tessa Morris-Suzuki (1997) warns that "with the rapid globalization of information capitalism, it has become evident that there are also profound implications encourages a process which can be called 'formatting'. To 'scientize creativity', and to turn the resulting science into a salable commodity, it is necessary that knowledge should be presented in certain standardized ways" (p. 69). For example, the research conducted by academic scientists is, at times, supported by funding from corporations. The corporations may want competitive advantages as a result of the research outcomes. Consequently, attention in the academy may be on particular kinds of applied research (leading to marketable products); the research might be influenced by the demands of the funders for marketable products. Heeding such a warning necessitates understanding strong tendencies toward the commodification of information and knowledge.

So much has been written about media ownership that little remains to be said here. A few observations on the political ramifications of the phenomenon will suffice. Following from the discourse of economics and the IS it becomes evident that markets and consumption—as ways of being and not just structures of transactions—shape a different kind of politics. Henry Giroux (2004) has pointed out that the neoliberal reconstruction of politics tends to reorient the needs and wants of individual. Instead of a public sphere, in which the collective good is considered in open forums, the needs and wants are individualized and privatized; solutions can be bought by individuals for their own use. Giroux (2006) said, "Under late capitalism, the spectacle was reforged in the crucible of mass consumption and mass media, producing new modes of communication constitutive of everyday life" (p. 35). The key word here is "constitutive." For the employment of media and information to be instrumental there is an awareness that the use is instrumental; they are intended to accomplish a purpose. When consumption-based communication is constitutive of our lives it pervades our being; it becomes part of who we are, so we are less likely to be conscious of its pervasiveness. The insinuation of the force Giroux noted is not linked to individuals; it can affect the

being of institutions—libraries included. David Allen (2005) has put his finger on the principal implication of the transformation: "Democratic theory
that follows a market model. Such as the theory of Joseph Schumpeter and
more recently social choice theory, builds on economic terms and aggregates
individual decisions. Democracy that functions as a forum is less about individual decisions and more about collective action for a common purpose"
(pp. 37–38).

Libraries reside at the heart of this political tension. As we've seen, the tac-
tic employed by public libraries of emulating bookstores is an abandonment
of any contribution to a vibrant public sphere. Rationalizations based on circulation data, gate counts, and favor with city/county/educational administrations only obscure the abandonment behind a facade of democratic commitment. The rationalization is grounded in the neoliberal market-driven
consumerism. It is a refashioning of the IS that perverts both the mission of
informing (broadly stated) and the aim of serving society. It defines informing according to a tightly constrained set of commodities and presumes that
a narrow profile of resultant library users constitutes society. Additionally,
this political sell-out makes a mockery of the ideals librarians supposedly
hold dear. Again, John Dewey (1954 [1927]) identifies the problem: "But a
belief in intellectual freedom where it does not exist contributes only to com-
placency in virtual enslavement, to sloppiness, superficiality and recourse to
sensations as a substitute for ideas" (p. 168). The academic world has its
version of the sell-out, with both production and consumption implicated.
John Thompson (2005), in a sweeping examination of the present state of
books in the academy, has described the need for universities to award more
doctoral degrees (ensuring both a supply of capital in the form of tuition and
cheap labor in the form of teaching assistants), along with an inflation of the
misplaced notion of publication as a currency contributing to institutions'
prestige. The outcome is the production of potential commodities (books)
that have marginal value in terms of consumption (pp. 174–80). Academic
libraries, as markets and consumers, contribute to the flawed logic of a dys-
functional marketplace where the purposes of teaching, learning, and inquiry
become mere instrumentalities in a large capital, and increasingly private,
sphere.

The preceding sounds like a leftist diatribe. To reiterate an earlier point, the
dilemma can't be blamed solely of capitalism. A particular form of capitalism
(just as there are versions of democracy) that seeks maximum short-term profits may contribute to the production of information (including books, journals, magazines, databases, commercial Web sites, and so on). The question
that remains is whether that production contributes to an Information *Society*.
In other words, are the amounts and kinds of information being produced
conducive to enhancing people's awareness of civic matters, education,
health care, the economy, foreign affairs, as well as recreational possibilities.

Again, here is an opportunity for libraries. If we agree that the function of an Information *Society* is important (and in many ways we have *not* realized that ideal), then publicly supported libraries are the civic institutions that can bring it to fulfillment. This is a goal that has yet to be attained. The ideological influence of the particular form of capitalism just described is one force that stands in the way. The ideology is bound tightly to consumption that affects being and identity; it shapes desires and re-forms needs in ways that operate to this capitalism's benefit. It is the ideology that Bocock (1993) examines thoroughly.

Fulfillment of the social goal of the IS necessarily relies on a different framework than that of consumption's ideology. I want to emphasize the word "framework" here. Any ideology, and certainly the ideology of consumption, succeeds in large part because it shapes people's thinking about a particular matter. In shaping thinking the ideology creates a new or revised structure for receiving the message of the ideology. It *frames* the language and presentation so the people are changed in small, but cumulative, ways. Belief in the framework may be achieved through presentation that connects the ideological target to known goods, thus placing that target (say, consumption) within an existing constellation of beliefs. To combat the ideology and strengthen civic kinds of informing, libraries would be advised not to attack the ideology directly. Instead, libraries can be involved in the creation of a different framework (and this is something that venues such as national conferences can assist with). In an effort to enhance citizen engagement in a broad spectrum of issues the new framework can link informing to genuine outcomes that can include greater educational achievement (real learning), more effective and accessible health care, a safer and cleaner environment, protection of civil liberties, and an inclusive community. The new framework cannot rely on mythic hyperbole to accomplish the goal, but rather adopt a language of attainability. The creation of a framework is definitely not a passive option; it requires, among other things, a theoretical foundation. The last chapter was intended to be a first step toward a theory of civic librarianship. The revised liberalism is essential to the action of creating a civic informational framework.

The rhetoric discussed in the last chapter about "customers" and "give 'em what they want" illustrates the effectiveness of ideological framing. Since customer service is a positive idea in the private sector, then it must be good for the public sector as well. The reduction of services and informing to transactions falls prey to the essentially neoliberal fallacy that David Hawkes (1996) defines: "In the consumer societies of the later twentieth [and twenty-first] century, exchange-value (a purely symbolic form) has become more real, more objective, than use-value (a material phenomenon). Objects are conceived, designed and produced for the purpose of making money by selling them, rather than for reasons of practical utility" (p. 169). A different framework developed by librarians should focus positively on the genuine reason for the services, collections, and access provided for communities by publicly supported libraries. The technology aspect of the IS may facilitate the ideology of neoliberal consumerism. "Digital" and "digitized" become fetishes; that is, these artificial phenomena (in the sense of being human creations) come to dominate the human intent behind their creation and take on lives of their own. Vincent Mosco (2004) suggests that Nicholas Negroponte is an emblematic ideologue when it comes to technology's power over humans. For example, Negroponte (1995) writes, "The change from atoms to bits is irrevocable and unstoppable" (p. 4), and that the digital age "is almost genetic in its nature, in that each generation will become more digital than the preceding one" (p. 231). Negroponte saw the change as utopian; whether one agrees with him or not, his vision is deterministic.

PROCESSES FOR APPLICATION OF THEORY

In the last chapter I drew from John Dewey and Michael Walzer to suggest a different way of looking at liberal democracy. Barely present in that discussion was detailed examination of the contributions of Jürgen Habermas, but his work will feature more prominently here. There are some conceptual deficiencies in Habermas's basic political theory, but his ideas of communicative action and discourse, which he has developed throughout his life, are vital to framing a civic informational society (and how libraries can help bring it about). As a preface to a look at what Habermas has to say, David Allen's (2005) observation sets a tone that is necessary to considering a social IS: "The point [the public's potential to form an active public sphere] is central to my claim that there is a qualitative difference between an informed and an active public. Information does not merely go to citizens, but in a sense it creates a public sphere. An active public collects information, but it also uses that information to participate in public life" (p. 152).

Insofar as librarians have believed that their work and institutions enhance the functioning of, and participation in, democracy, there is an unavoidable ethical element to our profession. We've discussed the ethics of intellectual freedom and social responsibility (among other things); it's time now to examine the ethics of political operation. With the political as the central concern the first task we have is to define the criteria or standards by which we can judge action to be ethical or not. As is the case with intellectual freedom, for example, there are several options open to us. If we follow Kant then we define ethics according to duty, formal structures, and the universality of application. If we lean toward utilitarianism we focus on maximizing happiness while maintaining individual liberties. If we see ourselves as proceduralists we try to create structures and systems that are designed to treat every person as equal according to laws, rules, and regulations. As we've seen before, there are some necessary aspects to these, and other, ethical systems, but each alone is inadequate. If we were to take the requirement of some form of duty, some standard of normativity, some goal of general welfare for all, and some regulatory structure that ensures equitable treatment for all, we'd be on the road to a political ethics which librarianship can take a leading role in creating. Let's add one requirement that Habermas (1990) urges: "As long as moral philosophy concerns itself with clarifying everyday intuitions into which we are socialized, it must be able to adopt, at least virtually, the attitude of someone who participates in the communicative practice of everyday life" (p. 48).

There are two points made by Habermas (1990): (1) ethics is concerned with the mundane, with everything that affects our daily lives, and (2) the social lives we lead are laden with communicative action in that each of us speaks, listens, reads, and watches as a means to live. The latter component is integral to discourse ethics, which not only requires the accounting for the communicative action of us all, it bases moral norms on the approval of all who participate in practical discourse (p. 66). The practical discourse is the effective means for testing, and eventually validating, moral norms. The addition of discourse to the above list of requirements for political ethics necessitates rules for argumentation (if discourse is indeed to have an ethical purpose). In other words, the speaking and listening we do as part of deliberation have to follow standards of logic, civility, claims to truth, and dialogue. The moral norms that are accepted have to be defensible against logical, civil, truth-theoretic, and dialogic opposition and must be accepted by all (explicitly or tacitly) in order to be observed by all. These strictures constitute what Habermas has called the universalization principle. Habermas (1990) sets out a program of regulations according to which discourse ethics can operate:

1. A definition of a universalization principle that function as a rule of argumentation
2. The identification of pragmatic presuppositions of argumentation that are inescapable and have normative content
3. The explicit statement of that normative content (e.g., in the form of discourse rules)
4. Proof that a relation of material implication holds between steps (3) and (1) in connection with the ideas of the justification of norms
Step (2) in the analysis, for which the search for performative contradictions provides a guide, relies upon a maieutic [Socratic method] method that serves
2a. to make the skeptic who presents an objection aware of presuppositions he knows intuitively,
2b. to cast this pretheoretical knowledge in an explicit form that will enable the skeptic to recognize his intuitions in this description,

2c. to corroborate, through counterexamples, the proponent's assertion that there are no alternatives to the presuppositions he has made explicit. (pp. 96–97)

Habermas's program is idealistic, which is simultaneously a problem and an advantage. The problematic element is its reliance on formal argument, adherence to logical reason, and the goal of moral norms. All of these present stringent demands on participants; they don't adequately allow for passion and emotion (see Walzer, 2004). Stepping back from vested interests, ego, and investment is never easy, nor is the embrace of dispute, refutation, and listening. The demands are immense, and human behavior does not usually demonstrate the characteristics on a prolonged and consistent basis. The intensity of the demands and countervailing human behavior mean that we are likely to fall short of the ideal frequently. The advantage of the program also resides largely in the demands. The principles of universalization and discourse ethics are clear, as are the rules Habermas sets out for the procedures. In the preface to his book, *The Inclusion of the Other*, Habermas (1998) explicitly admits to differences among people:

> Equal respect for everyone is not limited to those who are like us; it extends to the person of the other in his or her otherness. . . . Here inclusion does not imply locking members into a community that closes itself off from others. The "inclusion of the other" means rather that the boundaries of the community are open for all, also and most especially for those who are strangers to one another and want to remain strangers. (pp. xxxv–xxxvi)

In some important ways Habermas echoes Walzer's position on the autonomy of groups combined with the necessity for open communication among groups. There may also be intrusion by some groups (primarily nations) into the affairs of others when some force is oppressing those in the group intruded upon. In other words, when the autonomy of one group is threatened, intervention by another group for the purpose of preserving or restoring the first group's autonomy is not only allowed, it may be required.

The stance of Habermas and his agreement with Walzer provides a clear *telos* for librarians. Further, the ideals of universalization, discourse ethics, and the autonomy of groups suggest a reconciliation of intellectual freedom and social responsibility in an IS. The present professional orthodoxy on intellectual freedom is a combination of negative rights and laissez-faire markets. There are, of course, positive elements of the position, but there are shortcomings that came out in the American Library Association ACONDA and ANACONDA efforts. Social responsibility was posited as an activist supplement to intellectual freedom, intended to stimulate opposition to restrictions (frequently systemic) that silence some voices. The neutrality principle tends to flow from the reliance on free markets to create an information equilibrium. To the extent that free markets result in the equilibrium there are few, if any, restrictions on intellectual freedom. The empirical evidence that markets are not completely free (a great deal does *not* get communicated through customary mass media) necessitates the conclusion that we must address disequilibrium. The discourse ethical structure is intended to lead to dialogue that can describe the existence the existence and nature of the disequilibrium, as well as ways to combat it. Within the discourse ethical framework the common ground shared by intellectual freedom and social responsibility can be articulated openly and the difference can be explained reasonably. Moreover, as a continuous process, discourse ethics can lead to resolution of particular instances of disequilibrium (including the groups affected, the causes, and the specifications needed). The Habermas/Walzer solution is, at the same time, a theoretical framework that encompasses a set of philosophical challenges *and* an action-based framework that points to the practical means by which problems can be solved.

Preferring normative, rather than empirical, justifications for deliberation and decision making, Habermas envisions a structure that if applied intentionally, might contribute to a moral Information Society.

> Discourse theory takes elements from both sides [liberal and republican] and integrates these in the concept of an ideal procedure, which establishes a network of pragmatic considerations, compromises, and discourses of self-understanding and of justice, grounds the presumption that reasonable or fair results are obtained insofar as the flow of relevant information and its proper handling have not been obstructed. . . . According to discourse theory, the success of deliberative politics depends not on a collectively acting citizenry but on the institutionalization of the corresponding procedures and conditions of communication, as well as on the interplay of institutionalized deliberative processes with informally developed public opinions. (Habermas, 1996, pp. 296, 298)

The intentionality of the application of discourse ethics relies on freedom, conceived in a particular way when applied to information and ICT. Cass Sunstein captures the essential character of this freedom: "I urge that in a diverse society, such a system [of free expression] requires far more than restraints on government censorship and respect for individual choices. . . . First, people should be exposed to materials that they would not have chosen in advance. . . . Second, many or most citizens should have a range of common experiences" (Sunstein, 2001, pp. 8–9).

This proposed framework responds to a number of commentaries within our profession. Michael Harris, Stan Hannah, and Pamela Harris (1998) valorize the commercial value of information and ICT in claiming, "Librarians appear incapable of acknowledging the extent to which the idea of information as a public good in American society has been discredited or completely abandoned, and the degree to which the idea that information is the key commodity in the post-industrial marketplace has been adopted" (pp. 122–23).

The blanket statement that information as a public good has been abandoned is unsupported and unsupportable. The claim itself is intended to represent truth; simply saying such a thing makes it so. By that logic, saying the opposite should also be taken as true. Making the claim in print privileges it as somehow more than the product of the minds of one set of authors. Harris, Hannah, and Harris are neither alone nor the first to say that libraries should embrace commodified information. Pauline Wilson urged the profession, through ALA, to welcome the commercial standpoint in 1978. Commodification, as a force of privatization, is not necessary by the virtue of the power of those responsible for privatizing it; a moral IS recognizes domination for what it is. At about the same time Wilson was writing F. W. Lancaster (1978) declared emphatically that the paperless society was imminent and libraries as repositories of physical things would fade away. Patricia Wallace (1993) has gone so far as to suggest introduction of fees levied on libraries patrons, even if the fees disadvantage a portion of the population. Within the new age of libraries there should be, at least according to Hannah and Harris (1999), decisions regarding *how* the vision of libraries should change in the next several years (p. 150). Their dictum is *preceded* by any questioning whether the vision of libraries *should* change. It would be a good idea to examine purpose regularly and frequently, but not necessarily with a self-imposed requirement that it be altered.

The ideas just presented represent the antithesis of the argument offered in this book. Numerous assumptions are made by pundits in our field and beyond, but two are the most pernicious: (1) the capital power of ICT is so overwhelming that we have to take its force to be good and right, and (2) the instrumentalities of technologies and markets destroy the complexities of human learning, knowledge seeking, personal and collective growth, decision making, and action in general. A framework that omits all of the human characteristics can build an internally rational, if perverse and impoverished, strategy for organizational and personal motivation. As John Buschman (2003) puts it, "The democratic public sphere roles of librarians as disseminators of rational, reasoned, and organized discourse, as a source of verifying or disputing claims, and as a space for the inclusion of alternative views of society and reality have no place in the vision of the library as the instant-satisfaction, fast-food equivalent of information" (pp. 120–21). The kinds of actions he speaks of are purpose driven; they begin with humans comprehending and formulating a reason and only then proceeding to operations related to that reason. His ideas are also consistent with those of Robert Dahl. The traditional IS, connected very closely to dominant instrumentalities of commodification and consumption, embodies its own purposes, and is blind and deaf to human purposes. It is amoral; it admits to no ethical or moral telos according to which certain tools and systems are used. It is ahistorical; it claims, as Francis Fukuyama (1992) does, that we are at the end of history primarily because it (and Fukuyama) ignores everything that doesn't fit its fixation on the present. It is linear and deterministic; all development has progressed in order to get us to this stage, and our future course is set. (This characteristic may be the most mythic, in that it creates a heroic and timeless drive to an ideal state.) What it is *not* is apolitical; a politico-economic rationality pervades everything that the IS stands for.

The realm in which a moral Information Society must operate is the public sphere. While there may be objections based on privacy and, perhaps, identity, the argument here is that an Information *Society* is necessarily public. It is true that private (in the sense of non-social) uses of information are common and are part of the lives of individuals, but the focus here is on interaction, on the things we do and are part of that make us social. Jodi Dean (2003) distinguishes between the social, cultural, and political on the one hand, and the state and the economy on the other, claiming that they are analytically separate. No doubt there are some distinct concerns pertinent to each domain, but the hypermodern condition has rendered them inseparable. People, at least in the first world and increasingly in the second and third, are not fully and solely economic beings, but are beings of the state. The economy is bolstered by the state and vice versa, and both impinge upon social relations through complex flows of power. To separate the domains is the separate potential resolutions to challenges that do not recognize analytical niceties. Further, such separation serves to perpetuate the taxonomy and categorizations that have been created to legitimate the hypermodern condition. Only a unified response has a chance to suggest a revised taxonomy.

What follows is a beginning, an initial and partial effort, at revising the taxonomy that currently defines the Information Society. The revision can best be seen as a juxtaposition of what tends to be and what is possible.

REVISED TAXONOMY

Information Society	Moral Information Society
Information	
Manifestations	
As thing to be transmitted, used, bought, sold, given, or horded (see Negroponte 1995).	As processes of giving shape to notions and concepts that can be exchanged through discourse.
Society	
Manifestations	
An agglomeration of individuals that can be technologically connected so as to serve the needs of the state or the market.	As a coalition of people who come together of their own volition to understand differences and likenesses.

State

Manifestations

As decentralized republic that allows territorialization and that fears a tyranny of minorities (see Kirk 1993).	As inclusive and free mechanism for the understanding and operationalization of the interests of all citizens (see Habermas 1998).

Politics

Manifestations

As a top-down imposition of will, whether deemed good or not.	As a means to explore social relationships that can help insure justice and fairness (see Rawls 1996).

Democracy

Manifestations

As a presumed aggregation of preferences according to which officials legislate and adjudicate (see Schumpeter 1976).	As deliberative engagement through which majority and minority voices are heard. (see Gutmann and Thompson, 2004).

Organizations

Manifestations

As cooperatives of experts which state aims of functional efficiency while maintaining hierarchical control (see Drucker 1993).	As correctives to the reality-imposing bureaucracies aimed at freeing thought and language (see Hummel 1994).

Reason

Manifestations

As application of considered preferences and choices that are intended to maximize instrumental utility (see Becker 1993).	As imagination and metaphorical activity, systematically applied (see Johnson 1993).

Education

Manifestations

As preparation for entry into the practice of capitalism (see Vedder 2004).	As expansion of the scope and depth of individual and societal potential (see Giroux and Giroux 2004).

Knowledge

Manifestations

As product that can have economic value and that can contribute to corporate productivity (see Nonaka and Takeuchi 1995).	As approximation of truth, arrived at through logical, justificatory, and/or social means.

Capitalism

Manifestations

As putative means of distribution but actual means of consolidation.	As actual means of consolidation but potential means of distribution.

Progress

Manifestations

As economic prosperity brought about by free markets working on a global scale (see Friedman 2002).	As enhanced social and political participation, facilitated by ICT (see Lessig 2004).

Library

Manifestations

As archaic and obsolete warehouse where physical materials are stored.	As place and space where people engage with information and with one another to learn, read, and grow.

This list presents a beginning that can serve a few distinct but interrelated purposes. The first purpose is to challenge what appears to be a received view of the Information Society, formulated on behalf of some specific interests that may not necessarily have people's well-being in mind. The claims illustrate the received view, but that orthodox view is insufficiently critical in its understanding of all aspects of the IS. The claims, by themselves, only point to a few tentative acknowledgments of an existing state of affairs. A more complete understanding is, I hope, offered in the discussion of each claim. The revised taxonomy offers a different way of speaking and thinking about some core concepts. Another purpose of the taxonomy is to suggest some alternative discursive starting points so as to counter aggregative tendencies that may be evident in current flows of power. Yet another purpose is to emphasize the moral element inherent in all human action. Consideration of ethical and moral good is ubiquitous; even its absence from discourse is a moral stance. One additional purpose is to illustrate some grounds of contest in which ICT plays a prominent role. All of the purposes are intended to remind us of the importance of what Habermas (1987) calls the lifeworld. The lifeworld includes all the presuppositions (see his criteria above) needed for meaningful communications. He (1987) says, "the lifeworld is constitutive for mutual understanding *as such*, whereas the formal world-concepts constitute a reference system for that *about which* mutual understanding is possible: speakers and hearers come to an understanding from out of their common lifeworld about something in the objective, social, or subjective worlds" (p. 126).

ICT may have the potential to enhance deliberation, but only if information can become organized and ordered, and remain essentially free (as

Sunstein details). These are all responsibilities of librarianship. Prevailing neoliberal discourse is limiting; discourse about deliberative democracy can include the roles of information and ICT as a way to bring conversation to practical applicability. Given that some powerful interests are vested in the former, considerable effort and attention is required to bring about the latter. The danger of not engaging in a discursive contest is predicted by Alain Touraine (2001): "We are in fact witnessing the very opposite of [an integrated social-economic model]: a growing divorce between the economic system (and especially the financially economy) and the social whole to which it should belong" (p. 18). Such a divorce could result in an ascendant role for one (perhaps the economic system) and a subservient role for the other (society and democracy). Whether discursive practice follows or leads to action is less important than its influence on action once it has begun. Since libraries are sites for discursive practice, it is there that the practice and its corresponding action relating to deliberation can begin. Any theory, normative or empirical, of the Information Society needs to account for the goals, purposes, and uses of information and ICT. Theory of librarianship must include theory of the IS; in fact librarianship is the ideal place for an encompassing ethical and political theory to be developed. A revised taxonomy that addresses economic matters, social relationships, and flows of power in ways that contrast to dominant ideologies is a step toward theorizing a moral Information Society.

Why does the taxonomy matter to librarianship? There are two principal reasons for providing the list. On the one hand, it is important that we realize the extent to which existing rhetoric has become institutionalized. The IS is seen to be inseparable from technology. Global information policy has technology as the centerpiece, and to an extent it is completely right and proper that the construction and extension of ICT networks connect people in meaningful ways. Even with more extensive connectivity there are deeply embedded cultural patterns of communication that may be either impervious to technological fixes or destroyed by forces external to the culture. In either case there is a cost; we may choose that the benefits of an IS outweigh those costs, but we cannot ignore them. The traditional IS also imposes particular kinds of literacy globally. Other forms of literacy, including the reading of natural signs, are not valued; there are costs to the uniformity of literacy as well. In ethical-political terms some costs are too high. The moral IS taxonomy suggests alternatives to the orthodoxy while not denying the efficacy of capitalism or democracy. Instead, the list (along with the conclusion of Chapter 5) provides a means to put ideals of librarianship into practice. In the traditional IS people are subservient or mere means to the consolidation of capital and political power. In short, the ends of the traditional IS are largely hidden; means are the substance of the discourse. The emphasis on connectivity and classical liberal individualism are at odds; instead of Dewey's Great Community being created, individual competition is fostered.

The revised taxonomy places people at the center and ensures that community formation and the kind of democracy suggested in the last chapter are explicit ends.

Librarianship, insofar as it is intended to foster democracy, is not in a position to leave the orthodoxy unchallenged. An ethical stance toward communities demands action on the parts of professionals. The kind of action that can make a difference should be part of the consciousness of professionals and education for the profession. Any forecasts that diminish the role of libraries in the informational future are—consciously or not—deliberately denying the possibility of a moral IS. The deliberate denial may include a neutral, if not a beneficent, intention, but adherence to a clear and overt structure that privileges some interests and disadvantages others widens the gap between interests (again, the "digital divide" does not capture the extent or the import of the gap). Given the official professional statements that exist (and ignoring the internal inconsistencies for now) librarianship as a profession is clearly committed to enhancing people's ability to thrive in a complex informational world. The discourse in our profession that speaks of customers and of focusing services on some segments of populations is advancing the traditional IS at the expense of the moral IS. The achievement of the profession's goals, though, depends on opposition to any potential determinism based on those interests that have substantially shaped the IS to date. In other words, librarianship in the public interest must be self-aware and reflexive so that the public interest is best served.

CHAPTER 7

Optimistic Synthesis

SO FAR WE'VE DISCUSSED some different ways of looking at our past, present, and future. There are some definite and serious concerns that our profession should address immediately, but there's ample room for optimism. Professional discourses in many areas have a tendency to dwell on some less than positive matters; some amount of attention to the negative is necessary and useful. We all have take care not to fall into a utopian trap. Critical scrutiny of concerns, though, must ultimately lead to potential solutions to problems, creative innovation, and refocusing on services to communities. In this chapter I'll attempt to articulate a theoretical position for the future. Ideally this will build on the educational, ethical, and political proposals of the preceding chapters. One of the features of those proposals is that they don't constitute restoration; that is, they don't aim at bringing us back to some golden age that may exist only in imperfect memories. In fact, our foundational future requires that we think differently than we have and that we question our previous practices and ideas. Following David Papineau (2002), I'm suggesting that we overcome a conservatism (not in the party-political sense) that preserves past action and thought as inherently good and useful. Some of the past must be retained, but only on the grounds that it is tested in an open context and is not taken to be "common sense."

Earlier we saw that previously undirected (some might say misdirected) educational programs must be centered on the essential goals of the profession, that a more encompassing ethical program should inform our lives as professionals and our relations with communities, that a radical democratic socialism presents an alternative to existing political systems, and that a moral information society can be realized. Restructuring can extend also to libraries as places. The idea of library as place may strike some as the latest in a line of faddish trends, but it does have a history in this country. Early public libraries, such as the Boston Public Library, were built according to monumental designs of the day. The buildings were designed to represent ideals of literature, useful knowledge, and traditions of learning. Generations of public and academic library buildings followed the representational intent, incorporating (customarily) neoclassical exterior design elements and interior spaces that elicit reverence for the place and everything in it.

The designs and buildings have not been without some critics; the monumental architecture might be seen as elitist and exclusionary. On the other

hand, emulating the monumental intention of churches might be interpreted as inclusive and even as a compulsory symbol of a civilized society. If
the monumental structures are interpreted today as representative of a certain social class by some, that doesn't necessarily signify a unitary interpretation shared by everyone.

In the late nineteenth and early twentieth centuries, Andrew Carnegie purposely limited the design choices for the libraries he funded. The exteriors
and interiors were quite simple and, in general, were built so that the librarian would be able to see everyone in the building. Abigail Van Slyck (1995)
depicts a common design (p. 33). The sightlines provide a more or less sweeping view of the floor. That design could be analyzed in terms of the panopticon proposed by Jeremy Bentham and critiqued by Michel Foucault (see
www.tformaro.com/thesis/panpic.html). The panopticon was Bentham's design for a prison in which a central guard station would provide a view of all
cell blocks radiating out from that center. For Foucault the panopticon signified the paradigm of control; the movements of all prisoners could be
monitored in minute detail. It's likely that some librarians used the Carnegie
design as a control mechanism, but it's even more likely that the design allowed for optimum service—not only could the librarian see everyone, everyone could see the librarian and that central point of service. The middle of the
twentieth century was something of a design malaise, with the means of the
daily work taking place in the building being mistaken for the end of users'
access to materials and services. We do have to remember, though, that designs of libraries more than a century ago weren't all intentional monuments
to the word, and that not all libraries of the not-so-distant past were sterile
and industrial.

American Libraries celebrates new architectural achievements each year.
While the recognition is not an assumption that the library as place is thriv-
ing, it does suggest that some communities and campuses are concerned
about the physical spaces in which people interact with words, images,
sounds, and one another. All evidence points to increasing use of electronically available information, not surprisingly. The amount that's accessible is
formidable, and people's ability to get *some* useful information is much
greater than it was last year. The construction of new buildings and the enhancement of access are not necessarily incompatible, even though some
within and without librarianship may think they are. On college and university
campuses the construction of information commons has resulted in dramatic
increases in gate counts, even when the total square footage of the building is
unchanged. The difference tends to include space configurations that allow
people to work as they choose—in groups, in comfortable privacy, and with
technological connectivity to gain access to the library's online resources.
There is the added advantage of the ready assistance of librarians when questions arise. A stated reason for the change is frequently the enhancement of

student success. Public library construction tends to follow these same user-centered configurations. Space, in short, tends to be designed with people in mind. The interactions of people with one another, and of people with resources. Libraries can be not only useful, but also usable.

The foregoing sounds like a paean to architecture; it is, in fact, acknowledgment of some genuine successes in our profession. It may be that the new constructions and renovations are not always unqualified successes. Space is one ingredient of a complex recipe. It is, as communities and campuses are discovering, a vital ingredient, but not the only one.

Virtual Libraries

Almost all existing libraries might be called digital libraries (provided the definition of a digital library is a rather relaxed one). A substantial portion of the content that libraries provide to their communities is in a digital format. Much of it, in fact, is born digital. That is, it's created, reviewed, edited, and disseminated in some digital form. Even works that are printed on paper and distributed formally (for example, as parts of subscriptions) have lives as digital entities. The dissemination of images and sounds is amenable to digital life. A public library patron can "check out" an audio book, download it to a personal computer or to a device such as an MP3 player. That person can listen to the recording of the book while walking, jogging, traveling, etc. A service that has been a mainstay of a public library for some time becomes more useful to communities. With support from several sources, including state libraries, collections are also being digitized. A couple of examples from the state of Missouri illustrate some benefits of digital projects. Project Whistlestop is a multiyear program to digitize many items in the Truman Presidential Library. It's recently been incorporated into the Truman Presidential Museum, and it provides invaluable research and educational resources. Virtually Missouri, the result of the Missouri Digitization Planning Project, aggregates the projects of numerous libraries across the state so that centralized access can be provided. It's a rich resource with contributions from all types of libraries.

"Visitors" to public, academic, school, and many special libraries search for, and retrieve, a wealth of content from any number of locations. This, too, is beginning to sound like an unmitigated celebration. As professionals we have found over time, though, that new capabilities bring challenges. Technological innovations aren't free; emerging technologies may be embraced by some and rejected by some; access to content may not be equal on the parts of all community members. The challenges illuminate what has been said in preceding chapters. For one thing, the history of libraries is not unitary and monolithic. Libraries have had multifarious purposes and have been built and supported by various individuals, groups, and states. Development, growth, and usefulness have had ups and downs due to changing religious, political, territorial, and cultural factors. It was no accident that the Bosnia's National Library in Sarajevo was fire-bombed. That library housed the cultural record of a people; much of what was lost was unique and irreplaceable. During World War I some American librarians willingly and actively purged collections of German and German-language works. In the 1950s colleges and universities were very sensitive to all expressions of support for communism. These object lessons should teach us that articulations of professional ideals amount to little if action doesn't follow them.

Virtuality is now a considerable boon to libraries' usefulness and vitality in communities. When I was in the tenth grade in 1968, I was assigned to write a term paper on Millard Fillmore (by a teacher who delighted in giving me that particular assignment). Neither the school nor the local public library had anything more than encyclopedia entries on Fillmore. The State Library did have some books, and they shipped them to my home. A tenth grader with a similar assignment today would almost certainly have ready, local access to a sufficient amount of background information to complete the assignment successfully. Students, readers, and inquirers can benefit from the services of all types of libraries because of the embracing of emerging technologies and creative thought given to their integration into what libraries can do. Many leaders in librarianship have looked first to the potential benefits to communities and then have made innovative uses of technologies, specifically to reach people in meaningful ways. Lest we take these developments for granted, we should continually remind ourselves (individually and collectively) of the ideas that have sprung from librarians' minds and that are put into action every day in libraries.

The assessment, both of accomplishments and potential, should not be made uncritically, though. To take just one example of a technology that can affect libraries, let's look at electronic books (e-books). After garnering a lot of attention in the late 1990s, e-books have been hovering on the periphery of the awareness of readers and librarians. Perhaps their potential is still unrealized; perhaps their potential is limited. James Gall (2005) set out to dispel five myths surrounding e-books, including cost, competition with printed books, and longevity. In actuality the myths collectively constitute a straw man. Librarians with any experience are well aware of pricing issues, the utility of some information in e-book formats, and the digital life of the word. Gall sets up opponents—the traditional bibliophile and the modern (perhaps it should be postmodern) technologist—but these two species are very rare. Students and scholars are more likely to praise than damn digital representations of manuscripts and unique records (even while acknowledging the limitations of such representations). Early adopters of technologies may grant that there are advantages to reading documents on paper if they extend beyond a certain length. Gall's article is another example of attention to "what" without inquiry into "how." The existence of titles that are available digitally, and increases in their numbers, are indicators of volume. How are the e-books being used? Are people purchasing them or checking them out and reading them in their entireties on computers or devices? Texts are being disseminated and received onto any of a number of hand-held devices; the growth of such reading is still an open question. Gall mentions a 2002 survey (Henke, 2003) of 263 attendees at a "New York City is Book Country" event. Respondents indicated receptivity to e-books, but the report of the results raises some red flags. The following passage appears in the "Discussion" section: "Are people who had read an article on eBooks more likely to have read an eBook on their computer or more likely to have purchased an eBook than those who had not read an article on eBooks?" (p. 17). The question isn't answered; only a vague and self-contradictory choice is made. It's evident that one shouldn't put much stock in this survey. What's needed is an examination of people's uses of e-books.

COMMUNITIES

The first six chapters of this book propose that there is a *telos* of librarianship. The purpose, as is true of almost all professions, is outwardly directed. Our profession is not post-industrial in the sense Daniel Bell defines the term. If anything, it's non-industrial. The tools and technologies change constantly, but the purpose—at least the roots of the purpose—endures. The discussion of librarianship as profession here represents an effort to make the telos explicit, and to connect education to that purpose. The set of characteristics of professions that Gardner and Shulman articulate is one of the most succinct and clear statements of the external vision of librarianship and all professions. What can sometimes afflict libraries as organizations (and this isn't unique to libraries) is a form of dualism. This dualism is not the mind-body dichotomy that's usually attributed to Descartes, but tends to be a libraries-as-means/libraries-as-ends dualism. The libraries-as-means component entails the outward focus of serving communities by being loci of learning opportunities, useful information, recreation, exploration, and interaction. Libraries-as-means is an epistemological position wherein purpose may be defined as vision that takes in everything in the environment. It attempts to remove anything that can obstruct vision and to translate the vision into action that is responsive to the environment.

Libraries-as-ends is a different epistemological position. It, too, can be defined as vision, but vision that is faced with a mirror. Sight can't penetrate beyond the mirror, so the reflection is what is seen. The environment may not be beyond the librarians' awareness, but it's not within the lines of sight. A library operating from this position may use the reflection to adjust the organization's internal structure, work flow, image, or political situation, but

all from the limited perspective of the mirror. This position is essentially egoistic. I'm not suggesting that egoism is entirely bad or undesirable, but it's
inadequate. Dualism separates the two positions and a symptom of the condition is an inability to connect the positions. Rejection of Cartesian dualism
manifests itself in the idea that mind and body are one. So the physical and
the mental are inextricably connected. This idea is referred to as monism. I
want to suggest that we reject the library-related dualism and try to envision
a monistic teleological state—a unified purpose centered on communities. A
library, within this conception, is a means and an end. The egoistic element
of libraries-as-end is necessary for survival; it's the grounding for attracting
qualified staff, garnering financial support, ensuring visibility, and becoming
an essential community place. Library-as-means provides the basis for the
definition of objectives, the development of collections and information access, the design of services, and the construction of space. The two positions
should be viewed as parts of a whole; the organizational existence of a library
can be illustrated as a helix. A helix describes the continuous referencing of
one position by another, as well as the forward movement of the organization. (When I speak of "library" here, that name is intended to refer, not to
the building, but to the collective of individuals who are responsible for the
organization's operations, facilities, resources, and purpose.)

An unintended dualism (unintended because its reception, rather than the
original idea, can perpetuate separate and distinct perceptions) is apparent
in a popular notion, first articulated by Douglas Zweizig (1973) and resur-
rected by Wayne Wiegand (2003, 2005). Zweizig maintained that the research
in our field has tended to examine the user in the life of the library, and inquiry may be more fruitful if it were to shift to the library in the life of the
user. The recognition of these two epistemological positions (and, like the
dualities described above, these are usually less than conscious, but still intentional) is a helpful development in our understanding of purpose. So I'll
admit that Zweizig's observation itself is not dualist, but its use over the years
has come to fit the metaphor of dualism. In general, Zweizig's call that has
been quoted frequently has sometimes denoted a choice, rather than a dualism. If his intent is followed, it should more properly be seen as an expression
of monism. Wiegand (2005) use the library-in-the-life-of-the-user frame to
investigate libraries as cultural agencies, but he wouldn't be able to do this
were it not for the user in the life of the library. The library can affect people,
but people simultaneously affect libraries. Neither should be ignored because
both determine the library's identity and purpose.

AN EXAMPLE

There is a particular example that may illustrate what I mean by the dualist tendency that can be countered by a monist epistemology. This is by no

means the only possible example, but I hope it can clarify this important condition of purpose. For several decades academic libraries have offered instruction programs aimed at enabling (primarily) undergraduate students to wade through the swamp of information resources. When indexing and abstracting tools were in print, librarians employed a variety of instructional strategies, and becoming competent with one source didn't necessarily mean one was competent with them all. And these resources differed from the library's catalog. It's almost as though secondary sources collectively threw down a gauntlet and challenged information seekers to decode their secrets. Instruction efforts began, more often than not, to help students with the decoding. The name "bibliographic instruction" was not really inappropriate, since students were taught about the structures of content in books. Another name, "library instruction," has also been applied, on the reasoning that it's the entirety of the library and its contents that needs to be decoded. More recently "information literacy" is the name applied to programs. That name has engendered some controversy; we won't divert into that controversy here. What is said about instruction programs at this time illustrates some of the conceptual and practical challenges that dualism presents.

First, I want to be clear. I don't argue that all librarians embrace a dualist epistemology; in fact, many offer counter-arguments to dualism (although not explicitly). The counter-arguments need to be emphasized as models for a resolution to the challenge. But first, the standards for information literacy approved by the Association of College and Research Libraries (ACRL) embody the tension that a dualist epistemology can include. In many ways the standards hearken back to discussion from an earlier chapter. The encompassing assumption that permeates the standards and many existing courses is that information is a thing. Beginning with the premise that a first task for students is the determination of their information need presupposes that: (1) there is such a *thing* as an "information need"; (2) undergraduate students are able to identify it; and (3) it can be satisfied through a process. Once the need is identified, a process of retrieval is to be applied. Later, individuals are to incorporate the retrieved and evaluated information into their knowledge bases. The inference from these standards probably isn't deliberate, but it holds that a knowledge base exists (which is accurate, as far as it goes) and newly found information is plugged into it as though the knowledge base were is a physical instrument, a vessel, that can be added to. Lori Arp and Beth Woodard (2002) quote Bonnie Gratch-Lindauer (2002), who says, "probably the most direct contribution the library makes to achieving institutional goals is its role in developing clear student learning objectives for information literacy skills; assessing the progress and achievement . . . and showing how outcomes are used to improve student learning" (p. 19). Arp and Woodard state that Gratch-Lindauer's proclamation is a way to achieve the instructional and institutional end of accreditation. That end, however, is instrumental and material; it is not necessarily related to student learning.

Diane Mittermeyer (2005) reports the results of a survey of Canadian students. The students were asked questions about the use of thesauri, correct terminology, and OR and AND operators. The survey purports to measure levels of information literacy, but it, too, is instrumental in its approach. These kinds of mechanics are necessary, but they are definitely not sufficient. Imagine trying to teach someone to read by introducing only grammar. The student may grasp some things like tense, mood, and subject-verb agreement, but a missing element is semantics (meaning). What do words mean? How do we make sense of outcomes? How do we appreciate a narrative? How do we make connections among texts? What do we do when words have more than one meaning? The ability to interpret relies on more than an awareness of grammatical construction. Likewise, learning entails more than the retrieval of information-carrying things. James Elmborg (2006) diagnoses the problem: "By objectifying and decontextualizing phenomena in the search for broad structural patterns, information literacy researchers have separated students from social and economic contexts, thereby detaching them from school, teacher, and society in an effort to isolate variables to create more pure 'scientific' studies" (p. 194). Elmborg and John Doherty and Kevin Ketchner (2005) draw from Paolo Freire's critique of a capitalist-inspired banking metaphor of knowledge growth. People do not acquire a currency—bits of information—and put it aside in a safe place for future use. Doherty and Ketchner (2005) correctly observe that resistance to the banking metaphor requires acceptance of the authority of the learner as a shaper both of questioning and of integration into a knowledge base (p. 8). The suggestions of Elmborg and of Doherty and Ketchner can't be overemphasized. They begin at a point prior to the ACRL standards, temporally and epistemologically.

The ACRL standards represent the kind of dualism I'm speaking of. The ultimate purpose of integrated learning is separated from the action that is to take place in the library and is sometimes disconnected from the students' experiences at the college or university. The language used in the two environments illustrates the dualism. For instance, in a Western civilization survey course the instructor speaks of events, people, times, the connections among them, and the flow (smooth or disruptive) over time and place. The components of the course are not spoken of as "information." The narrative is not presented as a means to dissect bits. The goal of this course, and other courses students take, is an understanding of something that is dynamic. Understanding is the end, and some would argue that it's accomplished by apprehending complex narratives. Instructional programs in libraries may not have a goal the broader understanding that's grounded in content and dynamics. For example, a performance indicator attached to ACRL Standard One is, "The information literate student defines and articulates the need for information." The library exists to assist people on their paths to understanding, not merely to help people navigate through a building, a catalog, or a database as an end in itself. The navigation, to reiterate, is necessary, but not sufficient. If it's not explicitly linked to learning, reading, and exploring, it may not be integrated into a library user's experience and action. In other words, the action is intended to lead to learning, but the path could be explained more completely. The "library in the life of the user" and "the user in the life of the library" are parts of one whole. Christine Pawley (2003) expresses the whole well: "we need to recognize that information 'access' is not just about information consumerism but also about individuals and groups of people actively shaping their world as knowledge producers in a way that renders the consumer-producer dichotomy irrelevant" (p. 448).

The dualism has real and rhetorical components, and one influences the other. If we believe that there is a separation—that user and library are distinct, though interacting—we find ways to speak about the distinction. While I'm sure it's not entirely intended, the user-in-the-life-of-the-library and library-in-the-life-of-the-user frames connote the distinction. Likewise, the instrumentality of information literacy instruction separates the library and what librarians do from the full educational experience of students. These things are perceived as distinct from one another in some way, and are spoken of as distinct. The rhetoric could also come first, though. This need not occur, and some accreditation standards do place learning outcomes first. "Customer service" could be a useful metaphor, as long as it is clearly and openly recognized *as* a metaphor. That is, it could communicate the importance of the clientele that professionals serve if it is clear that the clientele aren't literally customers. Just as the reality can lead to the rhetorical, so can the reverse be the case. When we speak in particular ways we begin to perceive *that speech* as representing reality. Action in libraries, then, can take the form of selling to consumers rather than serving communities. The language enforces the dualism; if someone who avails himself or herself of a library's services is a customer, then he or she is a means to an end for the library. After all, someone who makes a purchase at a store is a means to revenue, and more sales at a certain margin are means to profit. The dualism becomes the antithesis of librarianship—it abandons those characteristics that define a profession. My emphasis on this point here and earlier in the book is a measure of the importance we should ascribe to the cornerstones of professionalism and the future of librarianship. It might be said that the foregoing is oversimplified. There is no doubt that the services offered in libraries are complicated, but the customer metaphor itself distorts the complexity of the services and the relationship between library/librarian and community.

SPACE AND PLACE

At this time there are abundant virtual resources that can help people become informed about, for example, legal and health matters. It's not unusual for a Web site on, say, estate planning to urge viewers to use the site as a way to frame questions that can be asked of an attorney or a financial planner. The producers of these kinds of sites understand the complexity of the work they're dealing with and that the secondary information of the Web site is background for a conversation with a professional. There's something behind the recommendation to talk with a professional that librarians should explore. Professions, by and large, are built upon expertise that is gleaned from years of study and practice. Their homes are the complicated foundations, structures, and interrelations of physical or textual arcanities. Professionals, and not just health care professionals, engage in diagnosis and remedy in doing things that their clientele don't have the expertise to do for themselves. The intensely complex work of diagnosis and remedy is best effectuated through genuine interaction. This is not to say that technological mediation has no place; in fact, technologies are broadening the scope of most traditional professions. For the most part, though, the work of professionals takes place in a physical place shared with clients. In such places professionals can question people, prompting them to think of things that might not have occurred to them otherwise. It is a space for dialogue, for speaking *and* listening. Some physicians complain that the present state of commercial health care—a state that prices transactions as a means to revenue—precludes listening to patients' descriptions, not just of the surface of maladies, but of a host of physical sensations that can guide the physician's diagnosis.

Space can be perverted in the same ways that thoughts, emotions, and speech can be. While it may be a fine distinction, let me suggest that "space" is not the same as "place." Space is impersonal as a designator of physical existence. When we hear the word "space" we may think of emptiness; it isn't a location. Place, on the other hand, is occupy-able and occupied. It is where life happens. The virtual world is a world of space, not of place. The physician, the attorney, and the psychiatrist practice in places where clients can see them and be seen by them (even though some exchanges are technologically mediated). Here, too, our language indicates the layered meaning of our actions; we say, "I'm going to *see* the doctor." There's more than linguistic structural difference between this and, "I'm going to get a haircut." There's been something of a revival of the notion of library as place recently. The library is a place to *be* and to be *with* others. Wayne Wiegand urges librarians to study phenomena of reading; one possibility is to investigate the act of reading *in* a library. Does the place make a difference? What happens when a student studies *in* a library? The very name "commons" in an academic library denotes a shared place, a place where one is joined with others in a particular action. Does a commons, then, alter the psychology of study and learning? Does the place prompt a change in one's cognitive state?

I've referred to Michel Foucault in past chapters. One more idea of his is pertinent here. In writing about language he (1977) says:

> The visionary experience arises from the black and white surface of printed signs, from the closed and dusty volume that opens with a flight of forgotten words; fantasies are carefully deployed in the hushed library, with its columns of books, with its titles aligned on shelves to form a tight enclosure, but within confines that also liberate impossible worlds. The imaginary now resides between the book and the lamp. The fantastic is no longer a property of the heart, nor is it found among the incongruities of nature; it evolves from the accuracy of knowledge, and its treasures lie dormant in documents.... The imaginary is not formed in opposition to reality as its denial or compensation; it grows among signs, from book to book, in the interstice of repetitions and commentaries; it is born and takes shape in the interval between books. It is a phenomenon of the library. (pp. 90–91)

In this extraordinarily eloquent passage he captures both the human action of perceiving and transforming something into knowledge *and* a place where the perception and transformation can occur. Between the page and the lamp is the person—the reader, the learner, the seeker. It's not the medium of print on paper that's the essential point here; it's the proximity of the person to the word/image/sound. The one shortcoming of Foucault's idea is that it doesn't capture the place between persons. A genuine exchange between and among people is also a place of learning, informing, and knowing. Add to the human interchange an array of texts (very broadly envisioned) and there is a complex topology of learning, informing, and knowing (as well as questioning, arguing, and deliberating) created. While the library is not the only place where this can be created, it is *the* prototypical public place. I'm not limiting the concept of library to the public library here, but I am adjusting the definition of "public." The public library is certainly a place where all community members can avail themselves of such a place. The college or university library, the school library, and many special libraries function as such a place for *their* publics.

With Foucault in mind, librarianship will have to reflexively address the phenomenon being referred to as "Library 2.0." Somewhat related to the rhetoric of Web 2.0, Library 2.0 is rooted in emerging technologies that enable communication, sharing, access to content, and more. One feature that some note relating to Web 2.0 is an enhanced social capability; the tools that people can use to build what is sometimes called "collective intelligence." In a review of some tools, Laura Gordon-Murnane (2006) says, "Web 2.0 tools harness the collective intelligence of the Web, and, by tapping into that intelligence, make the service better and more powerful" (p. 29). (For more on Web 2.0 see http://www.snipurl.com/ictw.) As might be expected, there is little formal analysis of Library 2.0; this is a recent tag that is being applied to a perception of a desired future for libraries and the services they offer, and the "collective intelligence" idea is applied here as well. Ken Chad and Paul Miller (2005) of Talis.com offer their view of what Library 2.0 is.

> With Library 2.0, libraries move beyond the notion of 'libraries without walls', in which they offered a destination web site that attempted to reproduce the total library experience online. Instead, relevant aspects of that library experience should be reproduced wherever and whenever the user requires them, without any need to visit a separate web site for the library.

The vision that Chad and Miller articulate is impressive and must be taken seriously. Beyond their viewpoint, though, there may be many other conceptions of what Library 2.0 can be, how it can be realized, and what the implications for the physical library—and the profession—may be.

Library as place doesn't simply appear out of the ether. It is an intentional creation resulting from human action. Librarians make the place; they take space and shape it, imbue it with texts, add their professional expertise, and open it to people. Couched in this way, we can see that every library is a remarkable place. It's a place fraught with potential, with possibilities for achieving what Foucault envisions, and more. It's a place where the spatial opportunity is fulfilled, squandered, and everything in between. While there are some newly constructed libraries that don't build a place where people can read, learn, and explore, others are creating designs that enable people to interact, use technologies, read in solitude, etc. The most effective library buildings are especially inviting to children and teens. Traditional programming, such as storytelling, is augmented by teen film clubs, gaming groups, and other opportunities. Academic library commons include flexible and accommodating spaces that can be used in a variety of ways, including advising and tutoring. The examples abound; people do make use of the places that are designed and built *for* them.

THE POLITICS OF PLACE

It isn't accidental that libraries tend to be casualties of revolutions, wars, and insurgencies. One reason is that some want to destroy what is housed in libraries—cultural records, explorations in languages, or the imaginings of peoples. Physical destruction is an obvious political action and forces target libraries for material and symbolic reasons. Less obvious are the kinds of limitations, constraints, and rhetorical damage that some inflict upon libraries and librarians. We've seen that libraries are political and that they can act as sites of contests. I'd like to focus on one expression as a way to draw some of the political concerns together. Phil Giangarra of Medway, Massachusetts, is quoted in *American Libraries* ("Thus Said . . . ," 2006) as saying, "My opinion is, no one dies if the library closes. We have to look at parts of the budget that reflect people's ability to live—not to enjoy life, but to live" (p. 29). On one level the statement captures a political reality that many counties and municipalities face. In straitened economic times difficult choices have to be made; fire and police protection can't be compromised. No one would deny that county and city leaders must ensure public safety first.

The statement expresses more than a concern for people's safety, though. Without imparting a motive to Giangarra, a reader of his words may interpret them as stating a political position. If there is a genuine fiscal crisis, then something may have to be sacrificed in the short term. Most counties and municipalities are not experiencing such severe financial straits, so elimination of agencies and services is not usually necessary (even if reductions may be). It appears, in the extreme case, to be that there is a "safety" problem that can be solved with more police and fire fighters. There is no hint (at least not in the brief quotation) that there is a larger social challenge that may manifest itself in actions that require public safety measures. If a place that represents and brings life to learning, reading, and exploration (such as a library), and if that place is not open to people, then the social challenges will not be addressed fully. The political stance that is implicit in Giangarra's statement is that people neither need nor deserve a good life. The elements that are vital for ethical and political strength (following Aristotle) are wrested from people through a paternalistic edict that purports to have the people's welfare at heart. The single statement by Giangarra is not a momentous event, but it may be an articulation of the political will of a number of city and county officials. People need to *be* somewhere (in the full phenomenological sense); if *places* are excluded, where will they *be*? The probability is high that the places that attract people—by choice or by default—do not serve the polity.

The claim by Giangarra, the opinion of some Supreme Court justices, and other expressions by people in authority may appear innocuous, but they lead to insidious actions based on political positions I critiqued earlier. Underlying these expressions is the radical individualism of classical liberalism. It is not an egalitarian liberalism; those people who have the wherewithal don't need (or don't want) public places where the possibility of social exchange can take place. Giangarra apparently values public safety but doesn't value an informed public. The Supreme Court values proscription of pornography, but doesn't value public deliberation. If a public place, like a public library, isn't a public forum, the authorities can exercise a very sweeping kind of restriction. What is in the place, who can enter the place, what can happen in the place are subject to potential controls. The foregoing may sound like radical and impossible political positions, but public library branch closings and the Supreme Court decision follow from the recent history of the United States. John Dewey's call for a more socialist democracy not only hasn't been heard, a very different set of beliefs, policies, and actions has arisen. What governs today not only isn't democratic, it isn't republican. Until the Supreme Court decision the public library had been presumed—popularly and legally—to be a public forum. The magnitude of the shift (if future legal challenges are made) can't be overstated. The place that is the library is in serious jeopardy.

There is a possible interpretation of the Supreme Court decision and the opinion that asserts public libraries are not public forums. That some of the justices are to the right on the political spectrum shouldn't be a matter of dispute. Some may hail the situation and some may damn it; the reaction isn't germane to the interpretation. History, especially from the nineteenth century on, suggests that rule from the right tends to exhibit some particular characteristics. By way of background, at the heart of a public forum is the necessity of popular sovereignty—people deciding their own presents and futures. If democracy is to have meaning (except aggregative democracy, which is actually a faux democracy) people have to have the wherewithal to contemplate and deliberate those things that affect their lives, and they must have some vehicle for expression. In one sense deliberation and expression are pathways to reform and progress; they are actually bottom-up pathways. From the Boston Brahmins to the contemporary Supreme Court, the pathway (sometimes to destinations unknown) is top-down. There is a small and fundamentally closed group that sees itself as the adjudicator of the good life for people. A Platonic version of the group may think itself manifest as benevolent guides, whose authority is intended to provide a safe and prosperous dominion. In the extreme right version of the group the intention is not so much safety *for* people as safety *from* people, and prosperity is reserved for those who can become members of the group. The latter version, as John Lukacs (2005) explains with clarity and insight, is pessimistic with regard to human nature. Stemming from the authoritarianism of Hobbes, the objective of the latter group is control, and control is most effectively exercised by perverting classical liberalism. The intense individualism that characterizes that liberalism is altered so that cooperation and deliberation become both epistemologically and ontologically difficult.

In achieving the perversion of liberalism the steps to isolation become simpler. Put it this way: if people can begin to distrust openness and some political, aesthetic, and cultural expressions, the exclusion of the distasteful ideas follows an equally perverse rationality. The Supreme Court opinion (admittedly articulated by only some justices) is part and parcel of a pessimistic authoritarianism that can bring about, not only the USA PATRIOT Act, espionage without warrant, selective adoption of enacted legislation, and secret decisions, but also popular support for such actions. Moreover, these actions can be taken—and accepted—in the name of freedom. While not, in the Supreme Court opinion, a public forum, public libraries can still claim to, and be seen to, be bastions of free speech (that is, politically pluralistic speech). In the absence of deliberation, freedom of thought may be in shorter supply. We'll see in a moment that "social epistemology" is a powerful force for knowledge growth, but it depends on the "social" element.

Social epistemology is an optimistic side of the challenge that Lukacs (2005) identifies:

> people do not *have* ideas but *choose* them. This is a difficult subject, for at least two reasons. One is philosophical (more precisely: epistemological): there is an overlap between ideas, faiths, and beliefs. . . . The other difficulty is that we must consider how the older, nearly perennial difference between what people believe and what they think and say has now become even more complicated because of a democratic and populist phenomenon: the difference between what people think they believe and what they really believe. (p. 235)

While I don't agree that the problem of belief is connected to democracy, Lukacs's diagnosis has merit. Permit me to insert a religious metaphor here—we have to have a conception of sin in order to comprehend that we've been sinned against. The Supreme Court, then, can be seen within a tradition of authoritarian denial of positive freedom, perpetrated in an effort to control.

One way to look at the politics of place is to examine what makes a difference in people's lives. The question was posed earlier. Giangarra frames the issue in terms of security versus luxuries and this may persuade people to accept cuts to funding for libraries, schools, museums, etc. That is, some things that are deemed by authorities as non-essential are less vital than some services and actions that emphasize control. There are alternatives to this framing, though. For example, we could say that the enhancement of schools, colleges, libraries, and other cultural institutions could enable people to live good lives (again, in the Aristotelian sense) and to contemplate the meaning of local, national, and global events. A populace that's better educated, better informed, and better equipped to deliberate on public matters may be less prone to overreact to events and less vulnerable to rhetoric aimed at fear and prejudice. Public places, including schools, colleges, and libraries, can be the sites of critical assessment of political claims and can help the United States build a genuine social democracy. The reframing of the issue alters perspective. A kind of political Heisenberg Principle is in operation; consideration of a state of affairs from one point of view suggests a particular response. A different point of view suggests a different response. Real social democracy relies on the evaluation of multiple perspectives through informed deliberation. Further, the evaluation depends on public places where the perspectives are accessible and can be discussed. The absence of public places lessens the potential for deliberation. Closing public places like libraries may not be universally and intentionally directed at a unified point of view, but the motivation for the closing is itself a point for deliberation. Decisions regarding libraries as places, including the decisions we make professionally, are inescapably political. Librarianship has a responsibility to take the decisions seriously.

Place and Knowledge

The politics of place is important, but it's not the only issue we should consider. If we accept that libraries are places of reading, learning, and exploration, then they are places where knowledge is created. This occurs in multiple ways. An individual may read and find a different or new way of thinking about some important aspects of life. The presentation of what is read is compared to and weighed against what the reader knows prior to finding the text. The transformation may take the form of an enlightenment stemming from the experiences of a character in a work of fiction. Mark Haddan's novel, *The Curious Case of the Dog in the Night-Time*, can illuminate the modes of perception experienced by a person with autism. The knowledge gained by the reader is genuine. A different kind of text can present an argument relating to a historical event or a scientific theory. A reader can examine the elements of the argument to determine whether the premises have sound logical and/or empirical bases. The reader can then evaluate the conclusions that follow from the premises. Further, the argument in one text can be compared with alternative or differing arguments in other texts. While it may not be necessary for the reader to be physically present in the library, the place of the library makes the experiences of the reader possible, a place that is open to the public and that collects, organizes, and makes available a range of texts that hold the promise Foucault envisions. Unlike the experience of hearing a single speaker address a group one is in, reading multiple texts embodies an intentional act. The choice of texts, the content and reading of the texts, and the action of interpretation and evaluation are anything but passive. Since the growth of knowledge is not passive, the accessibility of multiple texts is a necessary condition for knowledge growth.

Is the accessibility of texts *sufficient* for knowledge growth? The short answer is no. I've (Budd, 2002a, 2002b) studied Jesse Shera's ideas of the place and the event of the library as they contribute to knowledge on a collective, rather than an individual, scale. Shera (1970) saw social epistemology as the culmination of librarianship's quest for an intellectual foundation. Specifically, Shera hoped that social epistemology would provide a link between theory and practice. Margaret Egan and Shera defined social epistemology in 1952 as, "the study of those processes by which society *as a whole* seeks to achieve a perceptive or understanding relation to the total environment—physical, psychological, and intellectual" (p. 132; emphasis in original). While Shera wrote profusely about social epistemology throughout his career, he really didn't arrive at a coherent theory that could be applied within our profession. He did provide some clues, though, to potential shifts in our practices. For example, he (1970) critiqued the systems of classification (both Dewey and Library of Congress). He observed that earlier structures of classification developed by Linnaeus and Darwin (that influenced Dewey and Library of Congress systems) were morphological, primarily because they were basing the structure on the physical attributes of organisms. For Shera, the classification, first of texts and then putatively of knowledge, is insufficiently grounded in normative epistemic language. Shera (1968) also spoke of mediation services in libraries within a social epistemology context. The exchange between a questioner and a librarian has social and knowledge-based elements. There is a process of negotiation through language that, ideally, leads to greater knowledge of the query by the librarian and greater knowledge growth on the part of the questioner through the recognition by the librarian.

Philosophers have appropriated the concept of social epistemology and have redefined it in some very useful ways that librarianship can adopt. Social epistemology can be much broader than Shera conceived, and it can help us better understand the role of librarianship in the complex social environment. Alvin Goldman is the most articulate proponent of social epistemology and his use of the term connotes an active process of communicating, evaluating, and deciding. Goldman (1999) describes the social aspect of social epistemology, and we can see that librarianship fits into the social phenomena: "An enormous portion of our truth seeking, however, is either directly or indirectly social. It is directly social when one verbally requests information from others, or consults written texts" (p. 4). While the social element is a formidable and essential *process*, it is a means to an end. The use of testimony, evidence, opinion, and belief is tempered by an evaluation of what is said, written, and believed. The real aim people have (or, speaking normatively, should have) is justified true belief. "Knowledge partly consists of belief, and belief is always local or situated because it is always the belief of a particular knower or group of knowers who live at particulars points in time. But knowledge also partly consists of truth, and when a fully determinate proposition is true, it is true for all time, not just at particular times or places" (Goldman, 1999, p. 21). Had John Stuart Mill taken his ideas on liberty, especially as liberty assists knowledge growth, further, he might have found himself in agreement with Goldman. Philip Kitcher (1994) hits the nail on the head in describing the broader normative purpose of social epistemology:

> The main social epistemological project consists in the investigation of the reliability of various types of social processes. Once we have recognized that individuals form beliefs by relying on information supplied by others, there are serious issues about the conditions that should be met if the community is to form a consensus on a particular issue—questions about the division of opinion and of cognitive effort within the community, and issues about the proper attribution of authority. (p. 114)

Let's assume a premise, based on what philosophers say about social epistemology. Being social, the achievements of social epistemology result from human action. The library provides a place for the human action necessary for social epistemology. Here the type of library is less relevant. Public, academic, and school libraries are places where the social exchange is possible. The place, by its nature and through its symbolic representation, can enable civil discourse and deliberation in ways that other places may not. The premise, just stated, relies on some claims I made in earlier chapters—principally that librarianship must be concerned with truth. It's not enough that we provide what *some* people want or what fits into the comfort zone of some in the community. It's not the library's goal to offend people, although some people might be offended by texts available in the library. The offense is an unfortunate and unintended outcome of the effort to provide a place where alternative, and sometimes conflicting, texts may be encountered. The nature of the library could be such that the encounter can be private or social. One of the values of social epistemology, according to Goldman (2002) is, "cognitive democracy" (p. 199). He mentions Jürgen Habermas in particular (suggesting another connection between social epistemology and the discussion of previous chapters). Habermas's thought can be assessed according to the goal Goldman mentions of evaluating social practices and their contributions to true beliefs. Habermas adds another dimension to the goal—ethics as it relates to *how* we assess social practices, and, especially, how we build ways to speak with one another about meaningful objects. In many of his writings Habermas urges that we adopt a discourse ethics as a means of discussing important matters. This framework is to enable everyone who wants to speak to have a voice, to emphasize the importance of listening (in the way Mill says can allow for open debate), and to compel everyone involved to follow rules of argumentation so that the logical and empirical merits of what is said can be evaluated. As such, this is a constrained freedom; certain conditions must be met for inclusion in deliberation.

It's clear that Habermas's discourse ethical framework relies on social interaction and on the kinds of justification that Goldman requires. Libraries are public—in the somewhat narrow sense that there are communities, albeit potentially limited, that have free access to the place and its contents—so they can meet the social element of social epistemology and discourse ethics. Further, many libraries are public *places* in that they allow groups to meet, offer programming for targeted audiences, and may open the place as limited public forums. On the other hand, many libraries don't embrace the norms of social epistemology and discourse ethics. Habermas (1998) defines norms: "A norm is valid when the foreseeable consequences and the side effects of its general observance for the interests and value-orientations of *each individual* could be *jointly* accepted by *all* concerned without coercion" (p. 42; emphasis in original). This definition, and Goldman's insistence on the veritistic element, seems quite stringent. Let's look a little more closely at them, though. Undeniably, Goldman and Habermas propose a process through which particular goals may be achieved. The process is regulated by logic, evidence, and ethics, and there should be no objections to such regulations, fairly applied (especially given the necessary openness of social epistemology and discourse ethics). One question that should be part of our professional conversation is: Should social epistemology and discourse ethics inform our practice? If we limit the parameters of the conversation to certain environment, such as schools and higher education, the answer may be *a bit* simpler. This is not an easy question to answer, in part because there could be corollary questions related to putting the framework into practice.

As might be apparent from the first six chapters, the question just asked represents a struggle. I can't (and won't) offer an answer here; perhaps I can contribute something to begin the conversation. As we've pondered the ethics and politics of librarianship, there have been some recurrent and ongoing problems. Intellectual freedom and social responsibility, for example, are extremely important to our profession, but, as we've seen, there's definite tension between them. Neither addresses social epistemology head on—perhaps on purpose—but there's evidence of a nascent belief in a discourse ethical mode of communication. Political disputes about libraries (what they are, their functions, their responsibilities, etc.) likewise avoid social epistemology. Ideology may enter the politics, so veritistic judgments can become difficult. If ideology prevails, the norms of discourse ethics are at risk as well. I lean toward supporting the infusion of social epistemology and discourse ethics into our professional consciousness. Our Code of Ethics only hints at their inclusion, but the importance of testimony, evidence, analysis, and so on can't be denied and could be more explicit. As places of learning, reading, informing, and exploring, libraries could be said to have a responsibility to, at the very least, acknowledge veritism as a possible ideal. Social epistemology and discourse ethics could even be considered for inclusion as professional values. I'll emphasize *ideal*, because, in practice, it's very difficult to apply the goal of veritism to the entirety of libraries' contents and access. I'll further propose that to the extent that we take the notion of library as place seriously, we have no alternative but to employ discourse ethics as an ideal framework. Inasmuch as all libraries serve some civic purpose (even corporate libraries), the norms inherent in discourse ethics are necessary.

DIALECTICAL CHALLENGE

This chapter has raised several questions and has argued that we inaugurate a more active professional discourse to respond to them. As the chapter title implies, there is cause to be optimistic. What still faces us is the way(s) to shape our discourse so that we can synthesize issues en route to some possible resolution. We're faced with a problem, though; the questions and the practices that accompany librarianship are characterized by poles (and not always just two poles), similarities and differences among alternatives, and even some contradictions. We have to find a way, first, to understand the complex relationships among collections, services, communities, publishing, access, and professional responsibilities. It's only by seeking such understanding that we can then begin to respond to questions and challenges. The approach I'm urging here is dialectical. To help us proceed I'll provide a brief background on a few of the conceptions of dialectic, suggest a preferred means of investigation, and apply that means illustratively.

As is true of a number of important words and terms, dialectic has several definitions, ranging from generic to specific. Hegel's use of the word is among the most specific. For him, dialectic involves the tension between a thesis and its antithesis, temporarily resolved through synthesis. Synthesis, then, becomes a new thesis, and the process begins again. A famous example of Hegelian dialect is:

Thesis – Being → *Antithesis* – Nothingness → *Synthesis* – Becoming.

As could be anticipated, "becoming" is itself problematic and subject to the proposition of its antithesis. The serious work of philosophy (and we have to remember that, for Hegel and his contemporaries, philosophy was not an arcane and ethereal exercise; it was a means to understanding ourselves, our world, and ourselves in the world) has had to address dialectic. While Hegelian dialectic is useful as one way to envision the kind of challenge that just doesn't go away, it may be *too* specific for us. The aim of synthesizing is particularly useful, but it's not as straightforward and logical a process as Hegel would like it to be. For one thing, it's difficult to construct theses and antitheses that are unitary or absolute (such as nothingness). Theses that are meaningful to us in librarianship, for example, can be multifarious. Even "being" is not so simple that it means one thing only, and so an antithesis can't be easily construed. One thing that tends to unite all definitions of dialectic is its anti-positivistic character. Those things that can (perhaps must) be interpreted or represented in our field are such ideas as mission, service, collection, community, etc. These can't be reduced to objects, since they embody, or are imbued with, intentionality. They are products of, and are answerable to, consciousness. Synthesis, or any other kind of possible resolution that comes from a dialectical process, is likewise conscious and intentional.

The most generic definition for dialectic is the process of resolving contradictions. This definition goes too far in the opposite direction from Hegel. A more workable, if somewhat abstruse, definition is: "dialectic has come to signify any more or less intricate process of conceptual or social (and sometimes even natural) conflict, interconnection and change, in which the generation, interpenetration and clash of oppositions, leading to their transcendence in a fuller or more adequate mode of thought or form of life (or being) plays a role" (Bhaskar, 1993, p. 2). It's important that Bhaskar includes the social in dialectical examination. One of Marx's developments that he based on Hegel is his recognition of conscious social forces that contribute to dialectic. Exchange value, wealth, and capitalism are social concepts and actions. "Capitalism" is as much an ethical-epistemological frame as it is a political-economic one. For Marx, the political-economic framework that's employed within capitalism silences and hides the ethical-epistemological one, and it is taken to be *the* way of knowing the world. Further, unless the ethical-epistemological framework is consciously placed in opposition to the political-economic one, through discourse, the political-ethical framework subsumes everything else. In other words, some exercises of power avoid dialectic assiduously; if everyone accepts the one framework, then there is no contradiction in the narrow sense of the word—there is no speaking against. In the absence of contradiction, according to Marx and Georg Lukács, there is reification. Speaking of the structure of commodities (but his analysis is expansive in analytical power), Lukács (1971) says, "Its basis is that a relation between people takes on the character of a thing and thus acquires a 'phantom objectivity', an autonomy that seems so strictly rational and all-embracing as to conceal every trace of its fundamental nature: the relation between people" (p. 83).

Dialectic, as I'm employing it here, is itself optimistic. Inherent in the process is the assumption that conflicting, competing, or contradictory ideas can be described in sufficient detail that we can talk about them in depth. Further, there is the assumption that we can contemplate resolution. The dialectical approach I'll emphasize here is borrowed from Roslyn Wallach Bologh. She (1979) expounds on the theory behind what she calls dialectical phenomenology:

> Instead of assuming that an object's meaning or sense is inherent or given with the object, phenomenology claims that we can know the meaning or sense of an object only in its relation to a knowing subject. The meaning is grounded or internal to the relation of subject and object. It is not internal to the subject. This approach is by its nature dialectical. (p. 2)

She applies this theory specifically to Marx, but it's a potentially rich analytical mechanism for any instance where there is a temptation to objectify something. In her examination, capitalism separates subject from object; for example, labor is objectified to the point that it is only a production value. The commodities produced through labor have exchange value; workers are not treated as subjects.

Dialectical phenomenology may still seem hopelessly abstract at this point, so let's revisit something that's been discussed earlier. The notion of information-as-thing has attained a positivistic power to some extent in librarianship, but to a greater extent in information science. "Information" is an analyzable entity; an atomistic measurement of information's properties can be conducted. Texts, images, and sounds become objects to manage, store, retrieve, and quantify—bit by bit. This is not a new tendency; for many years the statistics gathered by the Association of Research Libraries have included the counting of volumes held, volumes added, subscriptions, and other discrete bits of data as a way to rank libraries. The inescapable presumption is that more is better, and "better" is tacitly accepted as fostering and supporting inquiry and learning. In other words, Harvard is better able to engender research and student success because of the size of its libraries. Of course very few people in our profession would fall prey to such a naked fallacy, but the fixation on numbers as representing something more than is counted persists. The amount of "stuff" is not a particularly useful measure if we ignore the relationship between inquirers and students on the one hand, and the veracity, intelligence, and thoughtfulness of what is said and demonstrated within the physical items on the other hand. The relationship is the locus of the dialectic. Suppose a university library retains a dozen copies of an old introductory Spanish grammar text in order to maintain its collection size. The number of copies of that title may have no relation to the mission of the university or the action of the faculty and students. If we examine the dynamics of people searching for meaningful content in a physical environment that is occupied by objects of limited connection to the search for meaningful content, we can see that there is a contradiction that should be resolved.

Education for librarianship is certainly ripe for the application of dialectical phenomenology. There is, at present, the duality of education and the profession. In some important ways education, as it's sometimes related to librarianship now, is analogous to capitalism. The framework that is currently quite powerful in education includes an emphasis on exchange value (the "currency" of a degree) at the expense of use value (acculturation and integration into the profession). The mode of production in education takes insufficient notice of the labor (as the action of subjects/librarians), and education tends to objectify labor (devalues it as intentional ethical-epistemological action). In at least some discourse in education, information is commodified; it's the "thing" that can be linked to academic or institutional prestige, external funding, and less "professional" academic departments. For example, an excerpt from the Web site of the School of Information at the University of Michigan reads,

> As you specialize in librarianship, you will become familiar with LIS in general and other research, theories, and approaches, and will learn the values and practices of library and information science. You will develop knowledge of information representation and organization, information

architecture, content and collections, and information needs and uses. Moreover, you will gain a thorough grounding in information technology skills.

Our graduates have the knowledge they need to increase access to information in a variety of library and information environments and beyond. With the knowledge and skills gained at SI, LIS graduates become a part of the new librarianship that leads the field as it continues to anticipate and respond to future challenges. (www.si.umich.edu/msi/lis.htm)

There's a strain in education's discourse that denies contradictions and, in some ways that should cause concern, admits to no dialectic. In a survey designed to gauge the credence that master's programs' deans and directors place in ALA's Standards for Accreditation, Michael Mounce (2005) reports some cautionary results. Only twenty-five deans or directors of ALA-accredited programs in the United States responded, but the responses are troubling from the standpoint of dialectical phenomenology. When asked to assess the overall influence of the Standards on their programs, six of the twenty-five deans and directors said the Standards have very little, or no, influence. It appears that this is a matter for the application of dialectical phenomenology. The examination should include what is presently being said and done about accreditation by educators and professionals. This analysis can assist in identifying particular instances of contradiction that can be resolved. The phenomenological aspect is necessary for a resolution that based on anti-positivistic inter-subjective relationships. We could say that the Standards, as norms, fall short of Habermas's definition. His definition, however, assumes rational, ethical, non-ideological foundations. The absence of any of those criteria can be a source of contradiction. Rather than reject the Standards as norms, the dialectical-phenomenological approach requires close examination of the discourse to assess whether the criteria are met. Again, the characteristics identified by Gardner and Shulman provide an example of attempted dialectical resolution.

Following Marx, who said that the purpose of philosophy is to change the world, the emphasis should be on the analysis of the roots of any contradiction. The tension that we see between education for librarianship and the profession of librarianship can't be ignored or wished away; the tension is real. Attempts to dispel the tension by claiming that the other side simply doesn't understand is an analytical failure. Bologh (1979) stresses that the aim of analysis is not to provide a concrete solution; that is, the goal is to engender an understanding of the dynamic nature of relationships, rather than to objectify or reify an "answer." Unfortunately, the discourse on education today does reify positions. To some educators the answer rests on technical manipulation of information as thing or commodity. To some professionals the answer rests on technical application of some rules of organization or mediation. Of course these are not the only positions, but they do represent the heart of the contradiction. One common trait the two positions share is an embeddedness in the immanent to the point of ignorance of the transcendent (among other things). That is, the focus of attention is one the concrete actions that typify practice (especially those that begin and end with the human agent), while ignoring the reasons for the actions and their desired outcomes. The most dangerous position of both educators and professionals are characterized by what Lukács (1971) refers to as reality constructed by these groups. Each side builds a set of "laws" so that the positions are almost natural phenomena and can't possibly be disputed. In actuality, the laws are ideological and represent preferences instead of potential relationships. If, for example, some educators eschew the purpose (including the ethics and the politics) of librarianship in favor of advancement in their home institutions and success in attracting external funding, then their preferences are couched in terms of serving the "real" purpose of the profession (see the above statement of the University of Michigan's program). Statement of the substitute purpose is articulated monologically; the piece by John L. King (referred to earlier)—delivered as a speech at an ALISE Annual Conference—was a lecture that didn't openly invite dialogue. Similar examples could be culled from writings and speeches by professionals on what educational programs "ought" to teach.

Dialectical phenomenology poses a different form of communication on the predicament of education for the profession. Mounce (2005) reports one comment by a respondent to his survey: "in most cases we do not make decisions about what we will do because of the standards [for accreditation]." In other words, the Standards do not communicate meaningful guidelines for that particular program and its faculty. At the time of this writing there is some talk of revising the Standards for Accreditation. The revision of the Standards can be an opportunity for dialectical phenomenology as a method for deliberation. The Standards themselves can be defined as interstitial and occupying ground between the immanent and the transcendent. Through dialogic communication, aimed at understanding the relation of self and other, a path to knowledge can be blazed. The dialogue must be analytic; it must explore the complexities of the relationship, as well as of each position. The dialogue is explicitly directed at the contradiction so that dialectical phenomenology can be applied. Through dialogue the relational aspect of dialectical phenomenology is realized. Mikhail Bakhtin (1986) wisely observes, "Actual contextual meaning inheres not in one (single) meaning, but only in two meanings that meet and accompany one another" (p. 146). Paolo Freire (2000 [1970]) adds that dialogue is broken if either party lacks humility (p. 90). A dialectical means of revising the Standards would have to begin with the core purpose of the profession; it is with that beginning that contradictions between education and the profession can be resolved.

THE PROFESSION'S FUTURE

It would be hubris to think one *knows* what the future of librarianship will be and folly to try to predict it. But it would be irresponsible not to envision a preferred future. Also, if that preferred future is not an option, then there's no point in continuing in the profession. The task, then, is to imagine a future that's both good (again, in the Aristotelian sense, but also following Aquinas, Kant, Ricoeur, Rawls, and others) and attainable. In other words, our duty is to seek the good and the right for librarianship. This is a tall order. The political can't be ignored, but we have to be careful not to revert to an expedient realpolitik. Pragmatism certainly isn't evil, but some strains of it jeopardize an ethical outlook on which the future can be based. As we've seen, Richard Rorty's convenient dismissal of any sort of metaphysical truth is an easy pathway, but it leads to a dead end. To put this in the context of librarianship, we can look at Susan Hill's (2005) attempt at reconciling faith and the profession. The job of reconciliation is an important one for a great many librarians, but the pathway Rorty suggests won't result in a meaning-ful reconciliation. Hill states that intellectual freedom and a balanced collec-tion are essential goals, but she concludes her piece by saying that the majority rules. Freedom and balance are, to hearken back to Mill once again, necessary to counteract the numerical advantage of the majority. The contradiction Hill articulates is another event which makes dialectical phenomenology necessary. At the same time, the contradiction also illustrates the need for a particular kind of pragmatism. William James is proponent of the kind of pragmatism I'm suggesting is needed; he may be overly enthusiastic in favor of empiricism and overly harsh in his criticism of rationalism, but his cri-tique of absolutes has merit. James doesn't address politics quite thoroughly enough, though.

John Dewey is generally categorized as a pragmatist, but his pragmatism is imbued with a strong sense of social responsibility, political progressivism, and moral commitment. Dewey's work demonstrates the importance of the public face of philosophy, the need for those exercising authority and re-sponsibility to recognize that it has been an adaptive process, subject to mul-tiple, sometimes conflicting, forces. "The democratic convergence, moreover, was not the result of distinctly political forces and agencies. Much less is de-mocracy the product *of* democracy, of some inherent nisus, or immanent idea" (Dewey, 1954 [1927], p. 84; emphasis in original). In fact, it's Dewey's pragmatism that presents a component of librarianship's preferred future. The majoritarian politics inherent in "give 'em what they want," including Susan Hill's confusion of majority rule with balance, are emblematic of the kind of monism that Dewey and James decry. (This monism is different from the sort I argued for earlier. Their target is an ignorance of pluralism, which embodies acceptance of skepticism regarding purpose, causes, an absolute, dogma, and so on [see James, 1981 [1907], pp. 61–76].) An absolute rarely admits to dialectic, since there are *no* contradictions. It also negates phenomenology, since authority and control rest in the one (person or group).

The pragmatism of Dewey includes a particular notion that can help us envision a preferred future. In rejecting absolutes and singular causes Dewey (2004 [1920]) identifies a logical flaw that tends to infect even what he calls "organic" alternatives that see individuals and society as correlative. The tendency, when discussing grand social topics, is to define *the* individual and *the* state or *the* society. Conflicts and opportunities, however, are usually specific, not general, so any conception holding that the individual and society are two components of one unity includes an inability to reconcile conflicts. As we've seen here, "library" doesn't represent one single institution, and "politics" is extremely varied. We should heed Dewey's (2004 [1948]) words: "Just as 'individual' is not one thing, but is a blanket term for the immense variety of specific reactions, habits, dispositions and powers of human nature that are evoked, and confirmed under the influences of associated life, so with the term 'social.' Society is one word, but infinitely many things" (p. 115). One warning should be added to Dewey's observation, though. While individuals are just that, and society has many forms and compositions (existing simultaneously), we still need to avoid the radical individualist trap of classical liberalism. The egalitarian liberalism of Walzer, within the social democratic politics of Dewey (not Giddens), points us to a worldview that can enable us to accomplish our professional goals. A preferred future is not accidental; it is a conscious and intentional and attainable state. Without such preceding vision, we would have no idea how to get from here to there.

Should this be a venue for pondering a preferred future for librarianship? My answer, with caution, is yes. I'll emphasize that the attention here, in keeping with the theme of this book, will be primarily on librarianship, not on libraries (although the former has definite implications for the latter). There are a few indicators that could spur conversation on the future. For example, following Dewey (and many others), we, collectively, can continue to discuss what intellectual freedom means. That is, our profession can open communication to consider how absolute intellectual freedom can be, how specific it should be, and how it relates to social responsibility. There are many reasons to have these conversations, not the least of which is a continuous shift in moral politics in this country. It's not that librarianship should pander to prevailing moral attitudes (that would be irresponsible), but librarianship should assess prevailing moral attitudes—how they manifest themselves, what arguments underlie them, what political proscriptions they might insist upon. By moral attitudes I don't mean only views regarding sexuality, but ideas of "right" and "good" generally. This broad canvas is largely untouched in our professional discourse. We must remember that the characteristics of professions that Gardner and Shulman identify have moral underpinnings. Service to clientele, judgment, and education are moral undertakings, so we must consider seriously what moral principles will guide our actions. Perhaps especially we should take the moral principles to the realm of responsibilities. While I do take issue with Dewey on the grounds that general moral and ethical principles are not only possible, but necessary, I readily agree with him that our actions stem from specific instances. A rather lengthy passage from *Reconstruction in Philosophy* (2004 [1948]) clarifies my agreement:

> It surprisingly turns out that the primary significance of the unique and morally ultimate character of the concrete situation is to transfer the weight and burden of morality to intelligence. It does not destroy responsibility; it only locates it. A moral situation is one in which judgment and choice are required antecedently to overt action. The practical meaning of the situation—that is to say the action needed to satisfy it—is not self-evident. It has to be searched for. There are conflicting desires and alternative apparent goods. What is needed is to find the right course of action, the right good. Hence, inquiry is exacted: observation of the detailed makeup of the situation; analysis into its diverse factors; clarification of what is obscure; discounting of the more insistent and vivid traits; tracing the consequences of the various modes of action that suggest themselves; regarding the decision reached as hypothetical and tentative until the anticipated or supposed consequences which led to its adoption have been squared with actual consequences. (p. 94)

Take the apparent official stance on intellectual freedom, to further this example. Anything that is said should not be excluded from specific libraries on the basis of point of view or certain other reasons. To extend this point, everything said may possibly be essential for inclusion in *some* libraries. Professional judgment may dictate that a close look be taken at some expressions, however. Alisdair MacIntyre (2006) offers and admittedly unlikely case where a professor in the humanities attempts to revive the phlogiston theory and denounces Priestly and Lavoisier. Should anyone, including librarians, pay any attention to this professor? Suppose, though, that a biology professor states that the Holocaust is a fiction—it never happened. Is this a different kind of expression? Now let's take a couple of real instances. Not long after September 11, 2001, Ward Churchill, on the faculty of the University of Colorado at Boulder, said that the victims of the World Trade Center destruction were "little Eichmanns," tacitly complicit in immoral behavior. The remarks were unquestionably insensitive, and Churchill was attacked by politicians and others for making the statements. Some called for his dismissal from the university. We won't get into his freedom to say what he said, but should some library collection include it? More recently, former U.S. Secretary of Defense Donald Rumsfeld gave a speech in which he compared dissenters to the conflict in Iraq to those who tried to appease Hitler. Is there a difference between Rumsfeld's statement and Churchill's? Should both be tolerated? Should neither? In other words, what is our professional responsibility toward speech that may be overtly political, but inflammatory? If we do choose to take a cue from Dewey, then we should look at the full contexts of the utterances, recall the general principles according to which we work, and exercise judgment that is particular.

Let's turn to more (seemingly) mundane matters that require professional judgment. One strikes at the heart of the public library. We won't rehash demand-based collection and services or business models as ideals for public libraries. Instead, our professional conversation can pay attention to educational roles. To an extent, at least rhetorical inclusion of education still occurs (see the Hartford [MD] County Public Library mission statement, "Library Mission Statements," 2004, p. 31). We can ask, in all seriousness, how the support of learning translates into acquisition, access, and services in public libraries. Bill Crowley (2005) explicitly urges a return to the centrality of education in public library missions. One of his justifications for this call is the place of education within the profession of librarianship. It could be argued that professional and institutional purpose should cast a wider net, but there are many reasons why education should be a component of purpose. Throughout this book I've used "learning" and "exploration" as frequent and essential reasons why many people visit libraries. I intentionally have not used the word "schooling" because the other two reasons are less instrumental. Further, the connection has been made here between those individual reasons for using libraries and the political necessity for those forums as integral as integral to a true social democracy. Douglas Raber (1997) demonstrates clearly that in the middle of the twentieth century a massive study, the Public Library Inquiry, voiced the position that public libraries are *the* locations for assurance of democratic ideals. As he says, the Inquiry argued that public libraries are remedies to threats to democracy (p. 147). To the detriment of our profession, the Inquiry is all but lost to time. The Public Library Inquiry shouldn't be taken as *the answer*, but the issues it framed are still with us.

Another, different, challenge faces academic libraries. Since college and university libraries exist within colleges and universities, they are profoundly influenced by the missions, objectives, tactics, and ideologies of their parents. Some of the influence is relatively subtle: "Throughout the centuries, the intellectual focal point of the university has been its library, its collection of written works preserving the knowledge of civilization. Today such knowledge exists in many forms—as text, graphics, sound, algorithms, and virtual reality simulations—and it exists almost literally in the ether" (Duderstadt, 2000, p. 222). According to Duderstadt, knowledge is something that exists within things; unaware of, or disagreeing with, Foucault, he misses the point that the library is a *place* where people encounter ideas. Of more immediate impact is the release of a report commissioned by U.S. Secretary of Education

Margaret Spellings (Commission on the Future of Higher Education, 2006). The Spellings Report castigates higher education; if the report's recommendations are followed, academic libraries will inevitably be affected. For example, one recommendation, putatively relating to the purpose of higher education institutions, emphasizes cost containment, accelerating the accreditation of programs and institutions, and increasing productivity. Since the recommendation includes nothing about the public's responsibility to support higher education, one can infer that the accomplishments are to be made with no additional resources (or, at least, more money from public sources). The members of the commission issuing the report seem immune to irony; a stated aim is greater accessibility to higher education, but sources of funding are not mentioned. Also, the pace of publishing and disseminating scholarship hasn't slowed, and public ownership of the results of research and inquiry, especially those results that stem from public funding, is still ignored. Academic librarianship (as a species of librarianship) has the duty to study the amount of scholarly information produced, the use of the information, and its price. The Spellings Report is very like other recent federal initiatives—instrumental standards that inadequately address outcomes, fiscal accountability akin to that of a manufacturing company, and economic outcomes for graduates that obscure any mention of learning or intellectual growth. Dictates from without—and the Spellings Report is one example—have to be part of professional discourse.

School libraries' predicament is similar to that of academic libraries. State and federal assessment mandates cloud concerns about students' learning and development. Easily quantifiable and instrumental mechanisms abound, and the continued existence of schools and their libraries is jeopardized by the deterministic measures. The plight of school librarians is complicated by widespread ignorance of the essential contributions of the libraries to student learning. With less-than-adequate funding (and that description may be kind), the choices made by school administrators and boards may effectively eliminate libraries from the learning equation. Policies such as No Child Left Behind employ particular rhetorical devices to accomplish political and ideological ends. Proposals, such as the Sixty-Five Cent Solution, are no less ideological; rallies for support of the proposal state that this is a way to ensure that money goes to the classroom, not the bureaucracy. What is less clearly stated is that athletics are classified as "classroom," while librarians (as well as school counselors) fall into the bureaucracy category. Librarians, as professionals, *must* comprehend the rhetoric and its cognitive and emotive impact on people. If professional disagree with the substance of these kinds of policies and proposals, we must also understand the terms in which these ideas are couched.

What has gone before in this book is an extended argument for good, right, and justice, with and for others (see Ricoeur, 1992, pp. 169–202), within our profession and our institutions. To repeat, a primary purpose here is to provoke conversation—a phenomenological process of speaking *and* listening. The future of librarianship rests upon an objective that I hope we can agree upon in its fullest expression. Alisdair MacIntyre (2006) supplies the simple articulation of the objective: "*Phronesis* is the virtue of those who know how to do what is good, indeed what is best, in particular situations and who are disposed by their character traits to do it" (p. 28). Aristotle first proposed phronesis as a goal; he knew the achievement of it was nowhere as simple as the expression. Still in all, phron sis is a professional virtue we can cultivate. Our professional future is, in the spirit of dialectic, bound to the reconciliation of discontents. Classical liberalism includes the seeds of discontent if we try to adopt it as a sweeping social-political philosophy—emblematic of absolute freedom, absolute tolerance, and absolute individualism. These are, admittedly, characteristics of a certain type of liberalism, but this type is the professional paradigm today. Both the political right and the political left (and I confess to affiliating myself with the latter) are less than pleased with this paradigm. Our discontent extends to the economic as well. Consumerism and commodification are, to an extent, necessary to the availability of some goods. Reconciliation of the public good with consumable goods is therefore necessary. The "public good" *is* multifarious; it cannot be reduced to consumables. We have our work cut out for us; the only inescapable reality is that we must get down to work.

References

Abbott, Andrew. 2001. *Chaos of Disciplines*. Chicago: University of Chicago Press.

Adorno, Theodor. 1991. *The Culture Industry*. London: Routledge.

Agger, Ben. 1989. *Fast Capitalism: A Critical Theory of Significance*. Urbana: University of Illinois Press.

ALA. 1999. *Congress on Professional Education: Focus on Education for the First Professional Degree*. Available online at www.ala.org/ala/hrdrbucket/1stcongressonpro/1stcongresssteeringcommittee.htm.

Allen, B. L. 1991. "Cognitive Research in Information Science: Implications for Design." *Annual Review of Information Science and Technology*, 26: 3–38.

Allen, Bryce L. 1997. "Information Needs: A Person-in-Situation Approach." In *Information Seeking in Context: Proceedings of an International Conference on Research in Information Needs, Seeking and Use in Different Contexts*, eds. Perrti Vakkari, Reijo Savalainen, and B. Dervin. London: Taylor Graham, pp. 111–22.

Allen, David S. 2005. *Democracy, Inc.: The Press and Law in the Corporate Rationalization of the Public Sphere*. Urbana: University of Illinois Press.

Alm, David. 2004. "Atomism about Value." *Australasian Journal of Philosophy*, 82 (June): 312–31.

Altman, Ellen and Peter Hernon, eds. 1997. *Research Misconduct: Issues, Implications, and Strategies*. Greenwich, CT: Ablex.

Aristotle. 1984. *The Politics*, trans. Carnes Lord. Chicago: University of Chicago Press.

Arp, Lori and Beth S. Woodard. 2002. "Recent Trends in Information Literacy and Instruction." *Reference & User Services Quarterly* 42 (Winter): 124–32.

Bagdikian, Ben H. 2004. *The New Media Monopoly*, rev. ed. Boston: Beacon Press.

Bagnall, Richard G. 2002. "The Contingent University: An Ethical Critique." *Educational Philosophy and Theory*, 34, no. 1: 77–90.

Bakhtin, M. M. 1986. *Speech Genres and Other Late Essays*. Austin: University of Texas Press.

Bakhtin, M. M. 1993. *Toward a Philosophy of the Act*, trans. Vadim Liapunov. Austin: University of Texas Press.

Baldwin, Gordon B. 1996. "The Library Bill of Rights—A Critique." *Library Trends*, 45 (Summer): 7–27.

Barbrook, Richard. 2003. "Giving Is Receiving." *Digital Creativity* 14, no 2: 91–94.

Becker, Gary S. 1993. *Human Capital*, 3rd ed. Chicago: University of Chicago Press.

Belkin, N. J., R. N. Oddy, and H. M. Brooks. 1982. "ASK for Information Retrieval: Part I. Background and Theory." *Journal of Documentation*, 38 (June): 61-71.

Bentham, Jeremy. 1988 [1781]. *The Principles of Morals and Legislation.* Amherst, NY: Prometheus Books.

Berry, John N. III. 2004. "Don't Dis the LIS 'Crisis.'" *Library Journal,* 129 (October 1): 10.

Berry, John N. III. 2000. "Dumbed-Down Core Values." *Library Journal,* 125 (May 1): 6.

BeVier, Lillian R. 2003. "*United States v. American Library Association*: Whither First Amendment Doctrine." *Supreme Court Review:* 163–95.

Bewes, Timothy. 1997. *Cynicism and Postmodernity.* London: Verso.

Bewes, Timothy. 2002. *Reification, or the Anxiety of Late Capitalism.* London: Verso.

Bhaskar, Roy. 1993. *Dialectic: The Pulse of Freedom.* London: Verso.

Blackburn, Simon. 2001. *Being Good: A Short Introduction to Ethics.* Oxford: Oxford University Press.

Blackburn, Simon. 2005. *Truth: A Guide.* Oxford: Oxford University Press.

Bocock, Robert. 1993. *Consumption.* London: Routledge.

Bohman, James. 1991. *New Philosophy of Social Science.* Cambridge, MA: MIT Press.

Bohman, James. 1996. *Public Deliberation: Pluralism, Complexity, and Democracy.* Cambridge, MA: MIT Press.

Bologh, Roslyn Wallach. 1979. *Dialectical Phenomenology: Marx's Method.* London: Routledge and Kegan Paul.

Bolter, Jay David. 1991. *Writing Space: The Computer, Hypertext, and the History of Writing.* Hillsdale, NJ: Lawrence Erlbaum.

Bookstein, Abraham. 1979. "Explanations of Bibliometric Laws." *Collection Management,* 3 (Summer/Fall): 151–62.

Borgmann, Albert. 1999. *Holding on to Reality: The Nature of Information at the Turn of the Millennium.* Chicago: University of Chicago Press.

Bork, Robert H. 2003. *Slouching towards Gomorrah: Modern Liberalism and American Decline.* New York: ReganBooks.

Borsook, Paulina. 2000. *Cyberselfish: A Critical Romp through the Terribly Libertarian Culture of High-Tech.* New York: Public Affairs.

Bourdieu, Pierre. 1998. *Acts of Resistance: Against the Tyranny of the Market,* trans. Richard Nice. New York: New Press.

Braudel, Fernand. 1982. *The Wheels of Commerce.* Berkeley and Los Angeles: University of California Press.

Brown, John Seely and Paul Duguid. 2000. *The Social Life of Information.* Boston: Harvard Business School Press.

Brown, Richard D. 1989. *Knowledge Is Power: The Diffusion of Information in Early America, 1700–1865.* New York: Oxford University Press.

Brown, Richard Harvey. 2005. *Culture, Capitalism, and Democracy in the New America.* New Haven, CT: Yale University Press.

Buckland, Michael. 1991. *Information and Information Systems.* New York: Praeger.

Buckland, Michael. 1996. "The 'Liberal Arts' of Library and Information Science and the Research University Environment." In *Second International Conference on Conceptions of Library and Information Science: Integration in Perspective,* eds. P. Ingwersen and N. O. Pors. Copenhagen: Royal School of Librarianship.

Budd, John M. 1997. "A Critique of Customer and Commodity." *College & Research Libraries,* 58 (July): 310–21.

Budd, John M. 2002a. "Jesse Shera, Social Epistemology and Praxis." *Social Epistemology,* 16 (January): 93–98.

Budd, John M. 2002b. "Jesse Shera, Sociologist of Knowledge?" *Library Quarterly,* 72 (October): 423–40.

Budd, John M. 2001. *Knowledge and Knowing in Library and Information Science: A Philosophical Framework.* Lanham, MD: Scarecrow Press.

Budd, John M. 1992. *The Library and Its Users: The Communication Process.* Westport, CT: Greenwood Press.

Budd, John M. 2006. "Toward a Practical and Normative Ethics for Librarianship."*Library Quarterly,* 76 (July): 251-69.

Budd, John M. and Corrie Christensen. 2003. "Social Sciences Literature and Electronic Information." *Portal: Libraries and the Academy,* 3 (October): 643–51.

"Buffalo System to Close 20 Libraries." 2005. *Library Journal,* 130 (September 1): 16–17.

Bush, Vannevar. 1945. "As We May Think." *Atlantic Monthly,* 176 (July): 101–108.

Buschman, John E. 2003. *Dismantling the Public Sphere.* Westport: Libraries Unlimited.

Butler, Judith. 1997. *Excitable Speech: A Politics of the Performative.* London: Routledge.

Butler, Pierce. 1961 [1933]. *An Introduction to Library Science.* Chicago: University of Chicago Press.

Cahill, Thomas. 1996. *How the Irish Saved Civilization.* New York: Anchor.

Campbell, Jeremy. 1982. *Grammatical Man: Information, Entropy, Language, and Life.* New York: Simon and Schuster.

Canfora, Luciano. 1990. *The Vanished Library: A Wonder of the Ancient World,* trans. Martin Ryle. Berkeley: University of California Press.

Cantor, Norman F. 1993. *The Civilization of the Middle Ages,* rev. ed. New York: HarperCollins.

Carruthers, Mary. 1990. *The Book of Memory: A Study of Memory in Medieval Culture.* Cambridge: Cambridge University Press.

Casson, Lionel. 2001. *Libraries in the Ancient World.* New Haven, CT: Yale University Press.

Castells, Manuel. 2001. *The Internet Galaxy: Reflections on the Internet, Business, and Society.* Oxford: Oxford University Press.

Castells, Manuel. 1996. *The Rise of the Network Society.* Cambridge: Blackwell.

Chad, Ken and Paul Miller. 2005. *Do Libraries Matter: The Rise of Library 2.0.* Available online at www.talis.com/downloads/white_papers/DoLibrariesMatter.pdf.

Chandler, Daniel. 2002. *Semiotics: The Basics.* London: Routledge.

Chang, Briankle G. 1996. *Deconstructing Communication: Representation, Subject, and Economies of Exchange.* Minneapolis: University of Minnesota Press.

Chappell, Warren. 1970. *A Short History of the Printed Word.* Boston: Nonpariel.

Chatman, Elfreda. 2000. "Framing Social Life in Theory and Research." *New Review of Information Behaviour Research,* 1: 3–17.

Cherry, Colin. 1978. *On Human Communication: A Review, a Survey, and a Criticism,* 3rd ed. Cambridge, MA: MIT Press.

Cherwitz, Richard A. and James W. Hikins. 1986. *Communication and Knowledge: An Investigation in Rhetorical Epistemology.* Columbia: University of South Carolina Press.

Clement, Richard W. 2003. *Books on the Frontier.* Washington, DC: Library of Congress.

Coffman, Steve. 1998. "What if You Ran Your Library Like a Bookstore?" *American Libraries,* 29 (March): 40–46.

Colish, Marcia L. 1997. *Medieval Foundations of the Western Intellectual Tradition, 400–1400.* New Haven, CT: Yale University Press.

258   *References*

Commission on the Future of Higher Education. 2006. *A Test of Leadership: Charting the Future of U.S. Higher Education*. Available online at www.ed.gov/about/bdscomm/ list/hiedfuture/reports/pre-pub-report.pdf.

Cooper, William S. 1971. "A Definition of Relevance for Information Retrieval." *Information Storage and Retrieval*, 7: 19–37.

Crowley, Bill. 2005. "Save Professionalism." *Library Journal*, 130 (September 1): 46–48.

Cunliffe, Anne L. 2003. "Intersubjective Voices: The Role of the 'Theorist.'" *Administrative Theory & Praxis* 25, no. 4: 481–98.

Dahl, Robert A. 1989. *Democracy and Its Critics*. New Haven, CT: Yale University Press.

Dahl, Robert A. 2005. "What Political Institutions Does Large-Scale Democracy Require?" *Political Science Quarterly*, 120 (Summer): 187–97.

Dance, Frank E. X., ed. 1967. *Human Communication Theory: Original Essays*. New York: Holt, Rinehart, and Winston.

Darnton, Robert. 1990. *The Kiss of Lamourette: Reflections on Cultural History*. New York: Norton.

Davis, Erik. 1998. *Techgnosis: Myth, Magic + Mysticism in the Age of Information*. New York: Harmony Books.

Davis, Kenneth C. 1979. "Selling of the Library: Baltimore County System Challenges Assumptions about Library's Role." *Publishers Weekly*, 216 (September 3): 26–28.

Dean, Jodi. 2003. "Why the Net is not a Public Sphere." *Constellations*, 10 (March): 95–112.

Deane, Gary. 2003. "Bridging the Gap: Getting Pat Professional Values to Customer Value in the Public Library." *Public Libraries*, 42 (September/October): 315–19.

De Certeau, Michel. 1984. *The Practice of Everyday Life*. Berkeley: University of California Press.

De Gramont, Patrick. 1990. *Language and the Distortion of Meaning*. New York: New York University Press.

Delgado, Richard and Jean Stefancic. 1997. *Must We Defend Nazis? Hate Speech, Pornography, and the New First Amendment*. New York: New York University Press.

Dervin, Brenda. 1983. "Information as a User Construct: The Relevance of Perceived Information Needs to Synthesis and Interpretation." In *Knowledge Structure and Use: Implications for Synthesis and Interpretation*, eds. S. A. Ward and L. J. Reed. Philadelphia: Temple University Press, pp. 155–83.

Dervin, Brenda. 1977. "Useful Theory for Librarianship: Communication, Not Information." *Drexel Library Quarterly*, 13, no. 3: 16–32.

Dessauer, John. 1980. "Are Libraries Failing Patrons?" *Publishers Weekly*, 217 (January 18): 67–68.

Dewey, John. 1916. *Democracy and Education*. New York: Macmillan.

Dewey, John. 1989 [1939]. *Freedom and Culture*. Buffalo, NY: Prometheus Books.

Dewey, John. 2000 [1935]. *Liberalism and Social Action*. Amherst, NY: Prometheus Books.

Dewey, John. 1954 [1927]. *The Public and Its Problems*. Athens, OH: Swallow Press/Ohio University Press.

Dewey, John. 2004 [1920]. *Reconstruction in Philosophy*. Mineola, NY: Dover.

Ditzion, Sidney H. 1947. *Arsenals of a Democratic Culture*. Chicago: ALA.

Doherty, John J. and Kevin Ketchner. 2005. "Empowering the Intentional Learner: A Critical Theory for Information Literacy Instruction." *Library Philosophy and Practice*, 8 (Fall): 1–10.

Doumani, Beshara, ed. 2006. *Academic Freedom after September 11.* Brooklyn: Zone Books.

Doyle, Tony C. 2002. "A Critical Discussion of 'The Ethical Presuppositions behind the Library Bill of Rights.'" *Library Quarterly*, 72 (July): 275–93.

Doyle, Tony C. 2001. "A Utilitarian Case for Intellectual Freedom." *Library Quarterly*, 71 (January): 44–71.

Drucker, Peter F. 1993. *Post-Capitalist Society.* New York: Harper and Row.

Duderstadt, James J. 2000. *A University for the 21st Century.* Ann Arbor: University of Michigan Press.

Dworkin, Ronald. 1996. *Freedom's Law: The Moral Reading of the American Constitution.* Cambridge, MA: Harvard University Press.

Eagleton, Terry. 1991. *Ideology: An Introduction.* London: Verso.

Eco, Umberto. 1984. *Semiotics and the Philosophy of Language.* Bloomington: Indiana University Press.

Eco, Umberto. 1976. *A Theory of Semiotics.* Bloomington: Indiana University Press.

Egan, Margaret E. and Jesse H. Shera. 1952. "Foundations of a Theory of Bibliography." *Library Quarterly* 44 (July): 125–37.

Ehrman, Bart D. 2005. *Misquoting Jesus: The Story Behind Who Changed the Bible and Why.* San Francisco: Harper.

Eisenstein, Elizabeth L. 1983. *The Printing Revolution in Early Modern Europe.* Cambridge: Cambridge University Press.

Ellis, David. "The Dilemma of Measurement in Information Retrieval Research." *Journal of the American Society for Information Science*, 47 (January): 23–36.

Ellul, Jacques. 1990. *The Technological Bluff.* Grand Rapids, MI: Eerdmans.

Elmborg, James. 2006. "Critical Information Literacy: Implications for Instructional Practice." *Journal of Academic Librarianship*, 32 (March): 192–99.

Epstein, Richard A. 2003. *Skepticism and Freedom: A Modern Case for Classical Liberalism.* Chicago: University of Chicago Press.

Erdelez, Sanda. 1997. "Information Encountering: A Conceptual Framework for Accidental Information Discovery." In *Information Seeking in Context: Proceedings of an International Conference on Research in Information Needs, Seeking, and Use in Different Contexts*, eds. Perrti Vakkari, Reijo Savolainen, and B. Dervin. London: Taylor Graham.

Fairclough, Norman. 1989. *Language and Power.* London: Longman.

Fallis, Don and Kay Mathiesen. 2001. "Response to Doyle." *Library Quarterly*, 71 (July): 437–38.

Febvre, Lucien and Henri-Jean Martin. 1976. *The Coming of the Book: The Impact of Printing, 1450–1800.* London: Verso.

Feenberg, Andrew. 1991. *Critical Theory of Technology.* Oxford: Oxford University Press.

Ferré, Frederick. 1995. *Philosophy of Technology.* Athens: University of Georgia Press.

Festenstein, Matthew. 2001. "Inquiry as Critique: On the Legacy of Deweyan Pragmatism for Political Theory." *Political Studies*, 49: 730–48.

Foster, Allen and Nigel Ford. 2003. "Serendipity and Information Seeking: An Empirical Study." *Journal of Documentation* 59, no. 3: 321–40.

Foucault, Michel. 1971. *The Archaeology of Knowledge and the Discourse on Language*, trans. A. M. Sheridan Smith. New York: Vintage Books.

Foucault, Michel. 1977. *Language, Counter-Memory, Practice: Selected Essays and Interviews*, ed. Donald F. Bouchard. Ithaca, NY: Cornell University Press.

Foucault, Michel. 1970. *The Order of Things: An Archaeology of the Human Sciences*. New York: Vintage Books.

Franklin, Benjamin. 1964. *The Autobiography of Benjamin Franklin*, 2nd ed., eds. Leonard W. Labaree, Ralph L. Ketcham, Helen C. Boatfield, and Helene H. Fineman. New Haven, CT: Yale University Press.

Freire, Paolo. 2000 [1970]. *Pedagogy of the Oppressed*, trans. Myra Bergman Ramos. New York: Continuum.

Frické, Martin, Kay Mathiesen, and Don Fallis. 2000. "The Ethical Presuppositions behind the Library Bill of Rights." *Library Quarterly* 70 (October): 468-91.

Friedman, Milton. 2002. *Capitalism and Freedom*, 40th anniversary ed. Chicago: University of Chicago Press.

Frohmann. Bernd. 2004. *Deflating Information: From Science Studies to Documentation*. Toronto: University of Toronto Press.

Fukuyama, Francis. 1992. *The End of History and the Last Man*. New York: Avon Books.

Fukuyama, Francis. 1999. *The Great Disruption: Human Nature and the Reconstitution of Social Order*. New York: Touchstone.

Fuller, Steve. 1988. *Social Epistemology*. Bloomington: Indiana University Press.

Gadamer, Hans-Georg. 1989. *Truth and Method*, 2nd rev. ed., trans. Joel Weinsheimer and Donald D. Marshall. New York: Crossroad.

Gaddis, John Lewis. 2002. *The Landscape of History: How Historians Map the Past*. Oxford: Oxford University Press.

Gall, James E. 2005. "Dispelling Five Myths about E-Books." *Information Technology and Libraries*, 24 (March): 25-31.

Gandel, Paul B. 2005. "Libraries: Standing at the Wrong Platform, Waiting for the Wrong Train?" *Educause Review*, 40 (November/December): 10-11.

Gardner, Howard and Lee S. Shulman. 2005. "The Professions in America Today." *Dædalus*, 134 (Summer): 13-18.

Gathegi, John N. 2005. "The Public Library as a Public Forum: (De)evolution of a Legal Doctrine." *Library Quarterly*, 75 (January): 1-19.

Geuss, Raymond. 2001. *History and Illusion in Politics*. Cambridge: Cambridge University Press.

Geuss, Raymond. 2005. *Outside Ethics*. Princeton, NJ: Princeton University Press.

Geuss, Raymond. 2001. *Public Goods, Private Goods*. Princeton, NJ: Princeton University Press.

Giddens, Anthony. 1998. *The Third Way: The Renewal of Social Democracy*. Cambridge: Polity.

Giddens, Anthony. 2001. *The Third Way and Its Critics*. Cambridge, MA: Polity.

Giroux, Henry A. 2004. *The Terror of Neoliberalism: Authoritarianism and the Eclipse of Democracy*. Boulder, CO: Paradigm Publishers.

Giroux, Henry A. and Susan Searls Giroux. 2004. *Take Back Higher Education*. New York: Palgrave Macmillan.

Goldman, Alvin I. 1999. *Knowledge in a Social World*. Oxford: Clarendon Press.

Goldman, Alvin. I. 2002 *Pathways to Knowledge: Private and Public*. Oxford: Oxford University Press.

Gordon-Murnane, Laura. 2006. "Social Bookmarking, Folksonomies, and Web 2.0 Tools." *Searcher*, 14 (June): 26–38.

Gorman, Michael. 1998. *Our Singular Strengths: Meditations for Librarians*. Chicago: ALA.

Gorman, Michael. 2004. "What Ails Library Education." *Journal of Academic Librarianship*, 30 (March): 99–101.

Gouldner, Alvin W. 1976. *The Dialectic of Ideology and Technology*. New York: Oxford University Press.

Gordon, Jill. 1997. "John Stuart Mill and the 'Marketplace of Ideas.'" *Social Theory and Practice*, 23 (Summer): 235–49.

Graham, Gordon. 1999. *The Internet: A Philosophical Inquiry*. London: Routledge.

Graham, John-Bauer. 2003. "Now's Not the Time to Be Neutral: The Myth and Reality of the Library as a Neutral Entity." *Alabama Librarian*, 53, no. 1: 9–11.

Gratch-Lindauer, Bonnie. 2002. "Comparing Regional Accreditation Standards: Outcomes Assessment and Other Trends." *Journal of Academic Librarianship*, 28 (January–March): 14–25.

Grendler, Paul F. 2002. *The Universities of the Italian Renaissance*. Baltimore: Johns Hopkins University Press.

Gross, Melissa. 1999. "Imposed versus Self-Generated Questions." *Reference & User Services Quarterly*, 39 (Fall): 53–61.

Gutmann, Amy and Dennis Thompson. 2004. *Why Deliberative Democracy?* Princeton, NJ: Princeton University Press.

Haack, Susan. 1993. *Evidence and Inquiry: Towards Reconstruction in Epistemology*. Oxford: Blackwell.

Habermas, Jürgen. 1996. *Between Facts and Norms: Contributions to a Discourse Theory of Law and Democracy*, trans. William Rehg. Cambridge, MA: MIT Press.

Habermas, Jürgen. 1998. *The Inclusion of the Other: Studies in Political Theory*, eds. Ciaran Cronin and Pablo De Grieff. Cambridge, MA: MIT Press.

Habermas, Jürgen. 1993. *Justification and Application: Remarks on Discourse Ethics*, trans. Ciaran P. Cronin. Cambridge, MA: MIT Press.

Habermas, Jürgen. 1990. *Moral Consciousness and Communicative Action*, trans. Christian Lenhardt and Shierry Weber Nicholsen. Cambridge, MA: MIT Press.

Habermas, Jürgen. 1987. *Theory of Communicative Action*, trans. Thomas McCarthy. Boston: Beacon Press.

Hale, John. 1994. *The Civilization of Europe in the Renaissance*. New York: Atheneum.

Hamlin, Arthur T. 1981. *The University Library in the United States: Its Origins and Development*. Philadelphia: University of Pennsylvania Press.

Hannah, Stan A. and Michael H. Harris. 1999. *Inventing the Future: Information Services for a New Millennium*. Stamford, CT: Ablex.

Hannay, Alistair. 2005. *On the Public*. London: Routledge.

Harris, Michael H. 1984. *History of Libraries in the Western World*, compact textbook ed. Metuchen, NJ: Scarecrow.

Harris, Michael H., Stan Hannah, and Pamela C. Harris. 1998. *Into the Future*. Greenwich, CT: Ablex.

Harter, Stephen P. 1992. "Psychological Relevance and Information Science." *Journal of the American Society for Information Science*, 43 (October): 602–15.

Harvey, David. 2000. *Spaces of Hope*. Berkeley: University of California Press.

Haskins, Charles Homer. 1957. *The Rise of the Universities*. Ithaca, NY: Cornell University Press.

Hauptman, Robert. 2002. *Ethics and Librarianship*. Jefferson, NC: McFarland.

Hawkes, David. 1996. *Ideology*. London: Routledge.

Haycock, Ken. 2005. "Education for Librarianship: Intersecting Perspectives from the Academy and from the Field." *Feliciter*, 51: 18–22.

Heidegger, Martin. 1977. *The Question Concerning Technology and Other Essays*. New York: Harper and Row.

Helmick, Catherine and Keith Swigger. 2006. "Core Competencies of Library Practitioners." *Public Libraries*, 45 (March/April): 54–69.

Henke, Harold. 2003. "Consumer Survey on E-Books." Available online at www .openebook.org.

Herlihy, David. 1997. *The Black Death and the Transformation of the West*. Cambridge, MA: Harvard University Press.

Hill, Susan N. 2005. "A View from the Right." *American Libraries*, 36 (January): 46.

Hjørland, Birger. 1997. *Information Seeking and Subject Representation*. Westport, CT: Greenwood Press.

Hjørland, Birger. 2002. "Principia Informatica: Foundational Theory of Information and Principles of Information Services." In *Emerging Frameworks and Methods: Proceedings of the Fourth International Conference on Conference on Concepts of Library and Information Science*, eds. Harry Bruce, Raya Fidel, Peter Ingwersen, and Pertti Vakkari. Westport, CT: Greenwood Press, pp. 109–21.

Hjørland, Birger. 1998. "Theory and Metatheory of Information Science: A New Interpretation." *Journal of Documentation*, 54, no. 5: 606–21.

Hobbes, Thomas. 1996 [1651]. *Leviathan*, ed. J. C. A. Gaskin. Oxford: Oxford University Press.

Hobbes, Thomas. 1998 [1642]. *On the Citizen*, ed. and trans. Richard Tuck and Michael Silverthorne. Cambridge: Cambridge University Press.

Hodge, Robert and Gunther Kress. 1988. *Social Semiotics*. Ithaca, NY: Cornell University Press.

Holmes, Stephen and Cass R. Sunstein. 1995. *The Cost of Rights: Why Liberty Depends on Taxes*. New York: Norton.

Houghton, Bernard. 1975. *Scientific Periodicals: Their Historical Development, Characteristics and Control*. Hamden, CT: Linnet Books.

Hummel, Ralph P. 1994. *The Bureaucratic Experience*, 4th ed. New York: St. Martin's.

Ihde, Don. 1993. *Philosophy of Technology: An Introduction*. New York: Paragon House.

Ingwersen, Peter. 2002. "Cognitive Perspectives of Document Retrieval." In *Emerging Frameworks and Methods: Proceedings of the Fourth International Conference on Conference on Concepts of Library and Information Science*, eds. Harry Bruce, Raya Fidel, Peter Ingwersen, and Pertti Vakkari. Westport, CT: Greenwood Press, pp. 285–300.

Ingwersen, Peter and Martha E. Williams. 2001. "Cognitive Information Retrieval." *Annual Review of Information Science and Technology*, 34: 3–52.

Intellectual Freedom Manual, 5th ed. 1996. Chicago: ALA.

Irwin, Raymond. 1958. *The Origins of the English Library*. Westport, CT: Greenwood.

Ivie, Robert L. 2005. "A Presumption of Academic Freedom." *Review of Education, Pedagogy, and Cultural Studies*, 27: 53–85.

Jackson, Sidney L. 1974. *Libraries and Librarianship in the West: A Brief History*. New York: McGraw-Hill.

Jacobson, Daniel. 2000. "Mill on Liberty, Speech, and the Free Society." *Philosophy and Public Affairs*, 29, no. 3: 276–309.

James, William. 1981 [1907]. *Pragmatism*. Indianapolis: Hackett.

Jameson, Fredric. 1991. *Postmodernism: Or, the Cultural Logic of Late Capitalism*. Durham, NC: Duke University Press.

Janes, Joseph. 2004. "Andrew Carnegie, Seattle, and the Internet." *American Libraries* 35 (February): 54.

Jardine, Lisa. 1999. *Ingenious Pursuits: Building the Scientific Revolution*. New York: Doubleday.

Jensen, Robert. 2004/2005. "The Myth of the Neutral Professional." *Progressive Librarian*, 24 (Winter): 28–34.

Johns, Adrian. 1998. *The Nature of the Book: Print and Knowledge in the Making*. Chicago: University of Chicago Press.

Johnson, David Martel. 2003. *How History Made the Mind: The Cultural Origins of Objective Thinking*. Chicago: Open Court.

Johnson, Mark. 1993. *Moral Imagination: Implications of Cognitive Science for Ethics*. Chicago: University of Chicago Press.

Johnston, John. 1998. *Information Multiplicity: American Fiction in the Age of Media Saturation*. Baltimore, MD: Johns Hopkins University Press.

Jonas, Hans. 1984. *The Imperative of Responsibility: In Search of an Ethics for the Technological Age*. Chicago: University of Chicago Press.

Kant, Immanuel. 1988. *Fundamental Principles of the Metaphysics of Morals*, trans. T. K. Abbott. Amherst, NY: Prometheus Books.

Kant, Immanuel. 1996. *The Metaphysics of Morals*, ed. and trans. Mary Gregor. Cambridge: Cambridge University Press.

Kasser, Tim. 2002. *The High Price of Materialism*. Cambridge, MA: MIT Press.

Kelly, John. 2005. *The Great Mortality: An Intimate History of the Black Death, the Most Devastating Plague of All Time*. New York: HarperCollins.

Kelly, Thomas. 1977. *History of Public Libraries in Great Britain, 1845–1975*. London: Library Association.

King, John Leslie. 2005. "Stepping Up: Shaping the Future of the Field." Available online at www.so.umich.edu/~jlking/ALISE/talk.doc.

Kirk, Russell. 1993. *The Politics of Prudence*. Wilmington, DE: Intercollegiate Studies Institute.

Kitcher, Philip. 1994. "Contrasting Conceptions of Social Epistemology." In *Socializing Epistemology: The Social Dimensions of Knowledge*, ed. Frederick F. Schmitt. Lanham, MD: Rowman and Littlefield, pp. 111–34.

Klapp, Orrin. 1982. "Meaning Lag in the Information Society." *Journal of Communication*, 32 (Spring): 56–66.

Koenig, Michael. 2000. "Knowledge Management." In *Librarianship and Information Work Worldwide 2000*, eds. Maurice Line, Graham Mackenzie, and Paul Sturges. London: Bowker-Saur, pp. 193–221.

Kors, Alan Charles. 2004. "Where Is History?" *Academic Questions* (Summer): 10–14.

Kranich, Nancy, ed. 2001. *Libraries and Democracy: The Cornerstones of Liberty*. Chicago: ALA.

Krass, Peter. 2002. *Carnegie*. Hoboken, NJ: Wiley.

Kuhlthau, Carol C. 1999. "Accommodating the User's Information Search Process: Challenges for Information Retrieval Systems Designers." *Bulletin of the American Society for Information Science*, 25 (February–March): 12–16.

Kuhlthau, Carol C. 1993. "A Principle of Uncertainty for Information Seeking." *Journal of Documentation*, 39 (December): 339–55.

Lakoff, George. 1987. *Women, Fire, and Dangerous Things: What Categories Reveal about the Mind*. Chicago: University of Chicago Press.

Lancaster, F. W. 1978. *Toward Paperless Information Systems*. New York: Academic Press.

Lanham, Richard A. 1993. *The Electronic Word: Democracy, Technology, and the Arts*. Chicago: University of Chicago Press.

Lasch, Christopher. 1995. *The Revolt of the Elites and the Betrayal of Democracy*. New York: Norton.

Laugher, Charles T. 1973. *Thomas Bray's Grand Design: Libraries of the Church of England in America, 1695–1785*. Chicago: ALA.

Lause, Mark. 1991. *Some Degree of Power: From Hired Hand to Union Craftsman in the Pre-Industrial American Printing Trades, 1778–1815*. Fayetteville: University of Arkansas Press.

Le Goff, Jacques. 1993. *Intellectuals in the Middle Ages*. Cambridge, MA: Blackwell.

Lehuu, Isabelle. 2000. *Carnival on the Page: Popular Print Media in Antebellum America*. Chapel Hill: University of North Carolina Press.

Lessig, Lawrence. 2004. *Free Culture*. New York: Penguin.

Levinas, Emmanuel. 1969. *Totality and Infinity: An Essay on Exteriority*, trans. Alphonso Lingis. Pittsburgh: Duquesne University Press.

Levine, Andrew. 2004. *The American Ideology: A Critique*. New York: Routledge.

Li, Minqi. 2004. "After Neoliberalism: Empire, Social Democracy, or Socialism?" *Monthly Review*, 55 (January): 21–36.

"Libraries Win as U.S. Relents on Secrecy Law." 2006. *New York Times* (April 13): B1, B6.

"Library Mission Statements." 2004. *Public Library Quarterly*, 23, no. 2: 31–32.

Little, Adrian. 2003. "Community and Radical Democracy." *Journal of Political Ideologies*, 7: 369–82.

Locke, John. 1988 [1690]. *Two Treatises on Government*, ed. Peter Laslett. Cambridge: Cambridge University Press.

Locke, John. 2003 [1689]. *Two Treatises on Government and a Letter Concerning Toleration*, ed. Ian Shapiro. New Haven, CT: Yale University Press.

Lukács, Georg. 1971. *History and Class Consciousness: Studies in Marxist Dialectics*, trans. Rodney Livingstone. Cambridge, MA: MIT Press.

Lukacs, John. 2005. *Democracy and Populism: Fear and Hatred*. New Haven, CT: Yale University Press.

Lynch, Michael P. 2004. *True to Life: Why Truth Matters*. Cambridge, MA: MIT Press.

Lyotard, Jean-François. 1984. *The Postmodern Condition: A Report on Knowledge*, trans. Geoff Bennington and Brian Massumi. Minneapolis: University of Minnesota Press.

MacIntyre, Alisdair. 1984. *After Virtue*, 2nd ed. Notre Dame, IN: University of Notre Dame Press.

MacIntyre, Alisdair. 2006. *Ethics and Politics: Selected Essays, Volume 2*. Cambridge: Cambridge University Press.

Magendanz, Douglas. 2003. "Conflict and Complexity in Value Theory." *Journal of Value Inquiry*, 37, no. 4: 443–53.

Man, John. 2002. *Gutenberg: How One Man Remade the World with Words*. New York: Wiley.

Markey, Karen. 2004. "Current Educational Trends in the Information and Library Science Curriculum." *Journal of Education for Library and Information Science*, 45 (Fall): 317–39.

Martin, Henri-Jean. 1994. *The History and Power of Writing*. Chicago: University of Chicago Press.

Marx, Karl. 1976 [1867]. *Capital, Volume 1*, trans. Ben Fowkes. London: Penguin.

Marx, Leo. 1994. "The Idea of 'Technology' and Postmodern Pessimism." In *Does Technology Drive History? The Dilemma of Technological Determinism*, eds. Merritt Rowe Smith and Leo Marx. Cambridge, MA: MIT Press.

Matarasso, François. 2000. "The Meaning of Leadership in a Cultural Democracy: Rethinking Public Library Values." *Logos*, 11, no. 1: 38–44.

May, Christopher. 2002. *The Information Society: A Skeptical View*. Cambridge: Polity.

McChesney, Robert W. 2004. *The Problem of the Media: U.S. Communication Politics in the 21st Century*. New York: Monthly Review Press.

McChesney, Robert W. 1999. *Rich Media, Poor Democracy: Communication Politics in Dubious Times*. Urbana: University of Illinois Press.

McKenzie, Pamela J. 2003. "Justifying Cognitive Authority Decisions: Discursive Strategies of Information Seekers." *Library Quarterly*, 73 (July): 261–88.

McKitterick, David. 2003. *Print, Manuscript and the Search for Order, 1450–1830*. Cambridge: Cambridge University Press.

Menand, Louis. 1996. "The Limits of Academic Freedom." In *The Future of Academic Freedom*, ed. Louis Menand. Chicago: University of Chicago Press, pp. 3–20.

Menocal, María Rosa. 2002. *Ornament of the World: How Muslims, Jews, and Christians Created a Culture of Tolerance in Medieval Spain*. Boston: Little, Brown.

Menzies, Heather. 1998. "Challenging Capitalism in Cyberspace: The Information Highway, the Postindustrial Economy, and People." In *Capitalism and the Information Age*, eds. Robert W. McChesney, Ellen Meiksins Wood, and John Bellamy Foster. New York: Monthly Review Press, pp. 87–98.

Mészáros, István. 1989. *The Power of Ideology*. New York: New York University Press.

Miksa, Francis L. 1998. *The DDC, the Universe of Knowledge, and the Post-Modern Library*. Albany, NY: Forest Press.

Mill, John Stuart. 1989. *On Liberty, with The Subjection of Women and Chapters on Socialism*, ed. Stefan Collini. Cambridge: Cambridge University Press.

Mill, John Stuart. 1972a. *On Liberty and Other Writings*, ed. Stefan Collini. Cambridge: Cambridge University Press.

Mill, John Stuart. 1972b. *Utilitarianism, On Liberty, Considerations on Representative Government*, ed. H. B. Acton. London: Everyman's Library.

Milton, John. 1957. "Areopagitica." In *Complete Poems and Major Prose*, ed. Merritt T. Hughes. Indianapolis: Odyssey Press, pp. 716–49.

Mittermeyer, Diane. 2005. "Incoming First Year Undergraduate Students: How Information Literate Are They?" *Education for Information*, 23: 203–32.

Mizzaro, Stefan. 1997. "Relevance: The Whole History." *Journal of the American Society for Information Science*, 48 (September): 810–32.

Moran, Gordon. 2004. "Free Speech: 'The People's Darling Privilege.'" *Journal of Information Ethics*, 13 (Spring): 91–93.

Morris-Suzuki, Tessa. 1997. "Capitalism in the Computer Age." In *Cutting Edge: Technology, Information, Capitalism and Social Revolution*, eds. Jim Davis, Thomas Hirschl, and Michael Stack. London: Verso, pp. 57–71.

Mosco, Vincent. 2004. *The Digital Sublime: Myth, Power, and Cyberspace*. Cambridge, MA: MIT Press.

Mouffe, Chantal. 2000. *The Democratic Paradox*. London: Verso.

Mouffe, Chantal. 2005. *On the Political*. London: Routledge.

Mounce, Michael E. 2005. "The Effects of ALA Accreditation Standards on Library Education Programs Accredited by the American Library Association." *LIBRES*, 15 (March).

Nash, Gary B. 2005. *The Unknown American Revolution: The Unruly Birth of Democracy and the Struggle to Create America*. New York: Viking.

Negroponte, Nicholas. 1995. *Being Digital*. New York: Knopf.

Nelson, Samuel P. 2005. *Beyond the First Amendment: The Politics of Free Speech and Pluralism*. Baltimore, MD: Johns Hopkins University Press.

Nietzsche, Friedrich. 1967 [1887]. *On the Genealogy of Morals*, trans. Walter Kaufman and R. J. Hollingdale, and *Ecce Homo*, trans. Walter Kaufman. New York: Vintage Books.

Nilsen, Kirsti and Lynne (E. F.) McKechnie. 2002. "Behind Closed Doors: An Exploratory Study of the Perceptions of Librarians and the Hidden Intellectual Work of Collection Development in Canadian Public Libraries." *Library Quarterly*, 72 (July): 294–325.

Noble, David. 2001. *Digital Diploma Mills: The Automation of Higher Education*. New York: Monthly Review Press.

Nonaka, Ikujiro and Hirotaka Takeuchi. 1995. *The Knowledge-Creating Company*. New York: Oxford University Press.

Nunberg, Geoffrey. 1996. "Farewell to the Information Age." In *The Future of the Book*. Berkeley: University of California Press, pp. 103–33.

Nye, David E. 2006. *Technology Matters: Questions to Live with*. Cambridge, MA: MIT Press.

Olson, Hope. 2001. "Sameness and Difference: A Cultural Foundation of Classification." *Library Resources & Technical Services*, 45, no. 3: 115–22.

Olson, Jonas. 2004. "Intrinsicalism and Conditionalism about Final Value." *Ethical Theory and Moral Practice*, 7, no. 1: 31–52.

O'Neill, John E. 2004. *Unfit for Command: Swift Boat Veterans Speak out Against John Kerry*. Washington, DC: Regnery.

O'Neill, Onora. 2002. *A Question of Trust*. Cambridge: Cambridge University Press.

Ong, Walter J. 1982. *Orality and Literacy: The Technologizing of the Word*. London: Routledge.

Papineau, David. 2002. *Thinking about Consciousness*. Oxford: Clarendon Press.

Pawley, Christine. 2003. "Information Literacy: A Contradictory Coupling." *Library Quarterly*, 73 (October): 422–52.

Peperzak, Adriaan T. 2004. *Elements of Ethics*. Stanford, CA: Stanford University Press.

Plato. 1973. *The Republic and Other Works*, trans. B. Jowett. New York: Anchor Books.

Posner, Richard A. 2003. *Law, Pragmatism, and Democracy*. Cambridge, MA: Harvard University Press.

Post, Robert. 2000. "Reconciling Theory and Doctrine in First Amendment Jurisprudence." *California Law Review*, 88: 2355-74.

Poster, Mark. 1990. *The Mode of Information: Poststructuralism and Social Context*. Chicago: University of Chicago Press.

Poster, Mark. 2001. *What's the Matter with the Internet*. Minneapolis: University of Minnesota Press.

Putnam, Hilary. 2002. *The Collapse of the Fact/Value Dichotomy and Other Essays*. Cambridge, MA: Harvard University Press.

Raber, Douglas. 1997. *Librarianship and Legitimacy: The Ideology of the Public Library Inquiry*. Westport, CT: Greenwood Press.

Raber, Douglas. 2003. *The Problem of Information: An Introduction to Information Science*. Lanham, MD: Scarecrow Press.

Raber, Douglas and John M. Budd. 2003. "Information as Sign: Semiotics and Information Science." *Journal of Documentation*, 59, no. 5: 507-22.

Ranganathan, S. R. 1952. *Library Book Selection*. Delhi: Indian Library Association.

Rawlinson, Nora. 1981. "Give 'Em What They Want." *Library Journal*, 106 (November 15): 2188-90.

Rawls, John. 2001. *Justice as Fairness: A Restatement*. Cambridge, MA: Belknap Press of Harvard University Press.

Rawls, John. 1996. *Political Liberalism*. New York: Columbia University Press.

Readings, Bill. 1996. *The University in Ruins*. Cambridge, MA: Harvard University Press.

Ricoeur, Paul. 1992. *Oneself as Another*, trans. Kathleen Blamey. Chicago: University of Chicago Press.

Robbins, Louise S. 1996. *Censorship and the American Library: The American Library Association's Response to Threats to Intellectual Freedom, 1939–1969*. Westport, CT: Greenwood Press.

Robinson, Charles. 1989. "Can We Save the Public's Library?" *Library Journal*, 114 (September 1): 147-52.

Rorty, Richard. 1990. *Objectivity, Relativism, and Truth: Philosophical Papers*. Cambridge: Cambridge University Press.

Rorty, Richard. 1979. *Philosophy and the Mirror of Nature*. Princeton, NJ: Princeton University Press.

Rublack, Ulinka. 2005. *Reformation Europe*. Cambridge: Cambridge University Press.

Saenger, Paul. 1997. *Space Between Words: The Origins of Silent Reading*. Stanford, CA: Stanford University Press.

Sager, Don. 2001. "The Search for Librarianship's Core Values." *Public Libraries*, 40 (May/June): 149-53.

Samek, Toni. 2001. *Intellectual Freedom and Social Responsibility in American Librarianship, 1967–1974*. Jefferson, NC: McFarland.

Sayer, Andrew. 1992. *Method in Social Science: A Realist Approach*. London: Routledge.

Schamber, Linda, Michael B. Eisenberg, and Michael S. Nilan. 1990. "A Re-Examination of Relevance: Toward a Dynamic, Situational Definition." *Information Processing and Management*, 26, no. 6: 755-76.

Schiller, Dan. 1999. *Digital Capitalism: Networking the Global Market System*. Cambridge, MA: MIT Press.

Schlesinger, Andrew. 2005. *Veritas: Harvard College and the American Experience.* Chicago: Ivan R. Dee.

Schmitt, Carl. 1996. *The Concept of the Political,* trans. George Schwab. Chicago: University of Chicago Press.

Schön, Donald A. 1983. *The Reflective Practitioner: How Professionals Think in Action.* New York: Basic Books.

Schramm, Wilbur L. 1954. *The Process and Effects of Mass Communication.* Urbana: University of Illinois Press.

Schumpeter, Joseph A. 1976. *Capitalism, Socialism and Democracy.* New York: Harper and Row.

Schutz, Alfred. 1967. *The Phenomenology of the Social World,* trans. George Walsh and Frederick Lehnert. Evanston, IL: Northwestern University Press.

Scott, Joan W. 1996. "Academic Freedom as an Ethical Practice." In *The Future of Academic Freedom,* ed. Louis Menand. Chicago: University of Chicago Press, pp. 163-80.

Seaman, Scott. 2005. "Another Great Dissolution? The Privatization of Public Universities and the Academic Library." *Journal of Academic Librarianship,* 31 (July): 305-309.

Searle, John R. 2001. *Rationality in Action.* Cambridge, MA: MIT Press.

Severin, Werner J. and James W. Tankard. 1979. *Communication Theories: Origins, Methods, Uses.* New York: Hastings House.

Shannon, Claude E. 1949. *The Mathematical Theory of Communication.* Urbana: University of Illinois Press.

Shaping the Future: ASERL's Competencies for Research Librarians. Atlanta, GA: Association of Southeastern Research Libraries.

Shapiro, Ian. 2003a. "John Locke's Democratic Theory." In John Locke, *Two Treatises on Government and a Letter Concerning Toleration,* ed. Ian Shapiro, pp. 308-40. New Haven, CT: Yale University Press.

Shapiro, Ian. 2003b. *The Moral Foundations of Politics.* New Haven, CT: Yale University Press.

Shapiro, Ian. 2003c. *The State of Democratic Theory.* Princeton, NJ: Princeton University Press.

Shera, Jesse H. 1964. "Darwin, Bacon, and Research in Librarianship." *Library Trends,* 3 (July): 141-49.

Shera, Jesse H. 1968. "An Epistemological Foundation for Library Science." In *The Foundations of Access to Knowledge: A Symposium,* ed. Edward B. Montgomery. Syracuse: Syracuse University Press.

Shera, Jesse H. 1972. *The Foundations of Education for Librarianship.* New York: Becker & Hayes.

Shera, Jesse H. 1949. *Foundations of the Public Library: The Origins of the Public Library Movement in New England, 1629–1855.* Chicago: University of Chicago Press.

Shera, Jesse H. 1976. *Introduction to Library Science: Basic Elements of Library Service.* Littleton, CO: Libraries Unlimited.

Shera, Jesse H. 1970. *Sociological Foundations of Librarianship.* Bombay: Asian Publishing House.

Shiflett, Orvin Lee. 1981. *Origins of American Academic Librarianship.* Norwood, NJ: Ablex.

Shores, Louis. 1966. *Origins of the American College Library, 1638–1800.* Hamden, CT: Shoe String Press.

Simon, Herbert. 1983. *Reason in Human Affairs*. Stanford, CA: Stanford University Press.

Smart, J. J. C. 1984. *Ethics, Persuasion and Truth*. London: Routledge and Kegan Paul.

Smith, Mickey. 1988. "A Model of Human Communication." *IEEE Communications Magazine*, 26 (February): 5–14.

Sperber, Dan and Deirdre Wilson. 1986. *Relevance: Communication and Cognition*. Cambridge, MA: Harvard University Press.

Stieg, Margaret F. 1992. *Change and Challenge in Library and Information Science Education*. Chicago: ALA.

Sullivan, Michael. 2000. "Giving Them What They Want in Small Public Libraries." *Public Libraries*, 39 (May/June): 148–55.

Sullivan, Roger J. 1989. *Immanuel Kant's Moral Theory*. Cambridge: Cambridge University Press.

Sunstein, Cass R. 1995. *Democracy and the Problem of Free Speech*. New York: Basic Books.

Sunstein, Cass R. 2001. *Republic.com*. Princeton, NJ: Princeton University Press.

Sunstein, Cass R. 2003. *Why Societies Need Dissent*. Cambridge, MA: Harvard University Press.

Svenonius, Elaine. 2000. *The Intellectual Foundation of Information Organization*. Cambridge, MA: MIT Press.

Swan, John and Noel Peattie. 1989. *The Freedom to Lie: A Debate about Democracy*. Jefferson, NC: McFarland.

Tanis, Martin and Tom Postmes. 2003 "Social Cues and Impression Formation in CMC." *Journal of Communication* 53 (December): 676–93.

Taylor, Mark C. 2001. *The Moment of Complexity: Emerging Network Culture*. Chicago: University of Chicago Press.

Taylor, Richard. 2002. *Virtue Ethics*. Amherst, NY: Prometheus Books.

Taylor, Robert S. 1968. "Question-Negotiation and Information Seeking in Libraries." *College & Research Libraries*, 29 (May): 178–94.

Tebbel, John. 1987. *Between Covers: The Rise and Transformation of Book Publishing in America*. New York: Oxford University Press.

Thompson, John B. 2005. *Books in the Digital Age*. Cambridge: Polity.

Thompson, John B. 1990. *Ideology and Modern Culture*. Stanford, CA: Stanford University Press.

Thompson, John B. 1995. *The Media and Modernity: A Social Theory of the Media*. Stanford, CA: Stanford University Press.

"Thus Said. . . . How the World Sees Us." 2006. *American Libraries*, 37 (August): 29.

Tocqueville, Alexis de. 1945 [1835]. *Democracy in America*, ed. Phillips Bradley. New York: Vintage Books.

Touraine, Alain. 2001. *Beyond Neoliberalism*, trans. David Macey. Cambridge: Polity Press.

Trible, Paul. 2005. "Colleges Must Get Used to Collaborating with Congress." *Chronicle of Higher Education*, 51 (July 15): B16.

Valovic, Thomas. 2000. *Digital Mythologies: The Hidden Complexities of the Internet*. New Brunswick, NJ: Rutgers University Press.

Van Slyck, Abby. 1995. *Free to All: Carnegie Libraries and American Culture, 1890–1920*. Chicago: University of Chicago Press.

Vedder, Richard Kent. 2004. *Going Broke by Degree: Why College Costs too Much*. Washington, DC: American Enterprise Press.

Von Dran, Raymond. 2004. "Putting the 'I' in IT Education." *Educause Review*, 39 (March/April): 8–9.

Wallace, Patricia M. 1993. "How Do Patrons Search the Online Catalog When No One's Looking?" *RQ*, 33 (Winter): 239–52.

Walzer, Michael. 2004. *Politics and Passion: Toward a More Egalitarian Liberalism*. New Haven, CT: Yale University Press.

Walzer, Michael. 1983. *Spheres of Justice: A Defense of Pluralism and Equality*. New York: Basic Books.

Weaver, Warren. 1949. "The Mathematics of Communication." *Scientific American*, 181 (July): 11–15.

Wengert, Robert. 2001. "Some Ethical Aspects of Being an Information Professional." *Library Trends*, 49 (Winter): 486–509.

Westbrook, Robert B. 1991. *John Dewey and American Democracy*. Ithaca: Cornell University Press.

White, Howard D. and Katherine W. McCain. 1998. "Visualizing a Discipline: An Author Co-Citation Analysis of Information Science, 1972–1995." *Journal of the American Society for Information Science* 49 (April 1): 327–55.

Wiegand, Wayne A. 1994. "Catalog of 'A.L.A.' Library (1893): Origins of a Genre." In *For the Good of the Order: Essays in Honor of Edward G. Holley*, eds. Delmus E. Williams, John M. Budd, Robert S. Martin, Barbara Moran, and Fred Roper. Greenwich, CT: JAI Press, pp. 237–54.

Wiegand, Wayne A. 2005. "Critiquing the Curriculum." *American Libraries*, 36 (January): 58–61.

Wiegand, Wayne A. 1986. *The Politics of an Emerging Profession: The American Library Association, 1876–1917*. Westport, CT: Greenwood Press.

Wiegand, Wayne A. 2003. "To Reposition a Research Agenda: What American Studies Can Teach the LIS Community about the Library in the Life of the User." *Library Quarterly*, 73 (October): 369–82.

Wiener, Norbert. 1954. *The Human Use of Human Beings: Cybernetics and Society*. New York: Discus Books.

Williams, Bernard. 2001. "From Freedom to Liberty: The Construction of a Political Value." *Philosophy and Public Affairs*, 30, no. 1: 3–26.

Williams, Julie Hedgepeth. 1999. *The Significance of the Printed Word in Early America: Colonists' Thoughts on the Role of the Press*. Westport, CT: Greenwood Press.

Williamson, Charles C. 1971. *The Williamson Reports of 1921 and 1923*. Metuchen, NJ: Scarecrow.

Wilson, Tom. 1999. "Exploring Models of Information Behaviour: The 'Uncertainty' Project." *Information Processing and Management*, 35, no. 6: 839–50.

Wilson, Tom D. 1997. "Information Behaviour: An Interdisciplinary Perspective." *Information Processing and Management*, 33, no. 4: 551–72.

Wittgenstein, Ludwig. 1958. *Philosophical Investigations*, 3rd ed., trans. G. E. M. Anscombe. Englewood Cliffs, NJ: Prentice Hall.

Wittgenstein, Ludwig. 1990 [1922]. *Tractatus Logico-Philosophicus*, trans. C. K. Ogden. London: Routledge.

Woodward, Jeanette. 2005. *Creating the Customer-Driven Library: Building on the Bookstore Model*. Chicago: ALA.

Wroth, Lawrence C. 1964. *The Colonial Printer*. Charlottesville: University Press of Virginia.

Wu, Felix. 2004. *"United States v. American Library Association*: The Children's Internet Protection Act, Library Filtering, and Institutional Roles." *Berkeley Technology Law Journal*, 19: 555–83.

Zweizig, Douglas. 1973. Predicting Amount of Library Use: An Empirical Study of the Role of the Public Library in the Life of the Adult Public. Dissertation, Syracuse University.

Index

About the Author

JOHN M. BUDD is Professor and Associate Director of the School of Information Science and Learning Technologies at the University of Missouri–Columbia. His 2001 book, *Knowledge and Knowing in Library and Information Science: A Philosophical Framework*, was awarded the 2002 Highsmith Library Literature Award.